The Voice of Prophecy

EDWIN ARDENER

The Voice of Prophecy

and other essays

EDITED BY MALCOLM CHAPMAN

BASIL BLACKWELL

Basil Blackwell Ltd
108 Cowley Road, Oxford, OX4 1JF, UK

Basil Blackwell Inc.
432 Park Avenue South, Suite 1503
New York, NY 10016, USA

British Library Cataloguing in Publication Data
Ardener, Edwin, *1927–1987*
    The voice of prophecy and other essays.
    1. Social anthropology
    I. Title II. Chapman, Malcolm
    306

    ISBN 0–631–16304–2
    ISBN 0–631–16686–6 (Pbk)

Library of Congress Cataloging in Publication Data
Ardener, Edwin.
The voice of prophecy and other essays/Edwin Ardener; edited by
Malcolm Chapman.
    p. cm.
    Bibliography: p.
    Includes index.
    ISBN 0–631–16304–2
    ISBN 0–631–16686–6 (pbk.)
    1. Anthropological linguistics. 2. Ethnology. I. Chapman,
Malcolm (Malcolm Kenneth) II. Title.
P35.A73 1989
408.9—dc19   88–8015
                                               CIP

Typeset in 10 on 11 pt Baskerville
by Graphicraft Typesetters Ltd Hong Kong
Printed in Great Britain by
T.J. Press Ltd, Padstow, Cornwall

Contents

Introduction

Edwin Ardener, whose major recent papers are gathered here, died unexpectedly while this volume was in preparation. The volume was never intended to signify that a totality of work had been achieved, with a beginning and an end. On the contrary, this was no more than a rough tidying-up exercise, a bundle bound up with string – it would allow the past to be carried lightly, and put no obstacle in the way of all the work that the future might hold.

Ardener's death, however, has changed matters. This volume has become, in spite of itself, biographical in a rather keen sense. It seems, therefore, appropriate to accept this part, and to sketch in, however briefly, some details of his life and work. It is also perhaps worth suggesting, at the very beginning, that the greater implications of his work are many, and still largely unexploited. The reader will of course form his, or her, own opinion on this matter. In order to suggest, however, that Ardener's papers constitute a work which can profitably be kept open, I have asked two anthropologists who were close to him to contribute a final chapter. Professor Kirsten Hastrup and Dr Maryon McDonald, writing at the end of the volume, open it out, as Ardener would have wished, to 'work in progress . . .'

Edwin William Ardener was born on 21 September 1927. His adolescence was spent in wartime England, after which, in October 1945, he went to the London School of Economics (LSE). He had early interests in language, archaeology and Egyptology, which led him to Malinowski's former department, where he read anthropology, with psychology as a supporting subject. He attended the seminars over which Malinowski's shadow still loomed, then being run by Raymond Firth, and came into contact with other senior figures in the subject, including Darryl Forde. Audrey Richards was, perhaps, the teacher who most influenced him at this time, although Major Edmund Leach taught the young Ardener a course in 'material culture', and Phyllis Kaberry was also an important figure. Ardener was, beginning in 1945 at the age of eighteen, one of the very youngest of the post-war recruits to the anthropological profession, and he became the first from the LSE to take final examinations in anthropology since 1938. Much of his later work might be seen as an intellectual rendering of this demographic singularity – an attempt to work out a relationship between the orthodoxies of older social anthropology, the contemporary post-war situation in Africa, and developments coming in to social anthropology since the 1960s.

After graduating in 1948, he went to Nigeria in May 1949, thus beginning a lifelong involvement with West Africa. He spent thirty months in Nigeria, among the Ibo of Mba-Ise, which gave rise to his first ethnographic writing, *A Socio-Economic Survey of Mba-Ise*. Several other reports and publications came from this fieldwork, and material from this period was regularly drawn upon in later works (see 1954a, 1954b, 1959b, 1972a).

In 1952 he became a research fellow (later senior research fellow) of the West African (later Nigerian) Institute of Social and Economic Research (WA/NISER), and went to Cameroon, where he spent most of the next eleven years. He carried out extensive fieldwork, statistical and linguistic studies, in village and in plantation, particularly among the Bakweri, but also among the Esu and more generally, and lengthy reports from this work were submitted, through the NISER, to the government of the Southern (later West) Cameroons. A large body of published ethnographic writing came out of this long stay in Cameroon (for the complete bibliography, see appendix): the major works for which Ardener was solely responsible were *Coastal Bantu of the Cameroons* (1956), 'Social and Demographic Problems of the Southern Cameroons Plantation Area' (in Southall (ed.) 1961), and *Divorce and Fertility* (1962a). Much of Ardener's work was assisted by his wife Shirley: in particular, a collaborative study of the social and economic effects of the plantation system in what was then the Southern Cameroons, which resulted in the volume co-authored by the Ardeners and W. A. Warmington, *Plantation and Village in the Cameroons* (1960).

In the Cameroons, the Ardeners were involved in many projects, often in connection with the concerns of its people and their government and administration. Together they were personally responsible, with official encouragement and backing, for setting up the Buea (West Cameroon) state, later provincial, archives. The difficulties faced in this enterprise are described by the historian Martin Njeuma, who speaks of the modern archives as 'living testimony to Ardener's story of success' (Njeuma 1987: 1964). The achievement has also been described by another Cameroonian scholar, Simon Epale, who speaks of the Ardeners as:

this couple who painstakingly gathered bits and pieces of weatherbeaten German and English files from the moth-infested attic of the old German-built secretariat in Buea and set up the present provincial archives in Buea, which today is crowded with young Cameroonians either preparing for higher degrees at overseas or Yaounde Universities, or trying to develop the history of their country in order to rediscover their cultural heritage and build up new values that are in keeping with the present realities of their country . . . the country owed the Ardeners a great debt for bequeathing to it this storehouse of information about its past (Epale 1985: xviii).

Ardener became not only Adviser on Archives to the West Cameroonian government, but also Adviser on Antiquities, roles he played both for their intrinsic worth, and for the sustained fieldwork opportunities that they afforded him at all levels of Cameroon society. He encouraged scholarship and discussion among Cameroonian students, running an occasional seminar series in his home in Buea. As Njeuma puts it, in an obituary in *West Africa*, 'at a time when no one thought of it, he directed his efforts to encourage local intellectuals to take up research as a profession' (Njeuma 1987: 1964). Ardener also established and edited a small series of government publications on the Cameroons, two of which he wrote (see, for example, Chilver and Kaberry 1967; Ardener, S. 1968; Ardener, E. 1965a). He produced many shorter pieces of ethnographic and political analysis and comment, particularly for the journals *Nigeria* and *West Africa*. Of these earlier short pieces, 'The "Kamerun" Idea' (1958), and 'The Political History of Cameroon' (1962) have been of particular influence. The importance of the Ardeners' work for Cameroonian life and scholarship is recognized by all reference works on the subject. Le Vine and Nye, in reviewing West Cameroonian historical and political literature, say that 'pride of place must go . . . to the indefatigable Ardeners' (Le Vine and Nye 1974: 142), and continue, 'needless to say, all scholars of the Cameroons have relied heavily on their efforts' (ibid.: 143). The judgement is echoed in other works (see, for example, Delancey and Schraeder 1986: 17, 69, 76). Njeuma says:

history will remember Ardener as one of the very few English men who fully integrated himself among Cameroonians with a sense of humanity, free from racial or class bigotry . . . by encouraging many graduates to do research at a time when this was not popular and was not a gateway to high status and influence, especially by organizing a National Archives with provision for public use, Ardener deserves to be called one of the fathers of modern scientific studies in Cameroon (Njeuma 1987: 1965).

Later works added to this impressive body of historical, political and linguistic work, among them 'The Nature of the Reunification of Cameroon' (in Hazelwood (ed.) 1967), 'Documentary and Linguistic Evidence for the Rise of the Trading Polities between Rio del Rey and Cameroon 1500–1650' (in Lewis, I. M. (ed.) 1968), 'Kingdom on Mount Cameroon: Documents for the History of Buea, 1844–1898' (forthcoming in *Facing Mount Cameroon*; see below), and 'Witchcraft, Economics, and the Continuity of belief' (in Douglas (ed.) 1970b).

During the early 1960s, the constitutional rearrangements that brought about 'the re-unification of Cameroon' (see Ardener, E. 1967a) took Ardener's area of principal fieldwork interest out of Nigeria; the Nigerian Institute of Social and Economic Research, of which Ardener had long been a fellow, temporarily closed down, and Nigerian funding for research in Cameroon also stopped. The year 1963 saw Ardener in Oxford, as an Oppenheimer student, experiencing one of those awkward gaps in fieldwork research-funding which were then, and are once again, so typical a feature of the anthropological scene. It was at this delicate moment that E. E. Evans-Pritchard, Professor of Social Anthropology in Oxford from 1946 to 1970, invited Ardener to take up a post as university lecturer in social anthropology. Ardener accepted this, on condition that he be allowed time for a further nine-month visit to the Cameroons. After this, he took up the position at Oxford, which he held until his death. He returned to Cameroon, however, every summer (with the exception of 1967) for the three months of the long vacation, until his last visit in 1969. During this last visit the West Cameroon Archive building, which he had been instrumental in establishing, organizing, designing and staffing, was officially opened.

The yearly commute between Oxford and Cameroon, between 1963 and 1969, meant that the Ardeners spent the winter in Oxford and the rainy season in Cameroon, and so saw much less of the sun than might have been desirable. Ardener was able, however, by means of these yearly visits, to maintain most of the appearances of a continued presence in Cameroon. As he pointed out, and as anyone who makes regular return visits to a well-established fieldwork location will appreciate, if you are away for nine months, and then return, most people do not know, and have no reason to suppose, that you have been in another country for the best part of the year. They will simply suppose that, for one reason or another, it has been a few months since they last saw you, and will take up where they left off. This is of great use in continuing fieldwork, and one can say with truth that Ardener's fieldwork in West Africa, in Nigeria and then in Cameroon, spanned the best part of twenty years.

Having been appointed to his lectureship in 1963, Ardener retained his membership of Queen Elizabeth House, and became a senior common room member of St Antony's College. In 1969 he became a supernumerary fellow of St John's College, and his life was subsequently centred round Oxford, although he maintained close contact, socially and intellectually, with Cameroon.

Ardener's close contact with Evans-Pritchard in Oxford was a fruitful one, and acknowledgement of it is extensively made in chapter 1. The literary, historical, philosophical and more generally humane, aspects of Evans-Pritchard's work, coupled as they were with great achievements in fieldwork and in ethnographic writing, were particularly attractive, in the context of the problems that Ardener himself came to deal with.

In Oxford and England, as once in Cameroon, Ardener became closely involved in the organizational as well as the intellectual aspects of his work. He fought the corner for social anthropology, both in the university and in the country, recognizing that if the interests of the profession were not looked after by those involved in it, they would be looked after by no one. The tasks were not always pleasant or rewarding, and Oxford anthropology in the 1970s went through an acutely difficult period. Nevertheless, in various capacities in the Oxford Institute of Social Anthropology (including a long period as chairman), in the ASA (the Association of Social Anthropologists of Britain and the Commonwealth, of which he was chairman for four years), on committees of the SSRC (Social Science Research Council), on the executive committee of ALSISS (the Association of Learned Societies in the Social Sciences), and in connection with the Human Sciences degree in Oxford, he brought insight, wit and commitment to the professional life and interests of social anthropology.

On top of normal teaching activities, Ardener became closely involved with the attempt to establish, in Oxford, a joint honours school which would bring together various biological and social aspects of the study of humanity. This was a long, often tedious, and sometimes controversial business, but it was rewarded in 1970 with the first intake of students to the 'Human Sciences' honours school. It was largely through Ardener's efforts in committee that social anthropology had a prominent place in this school, and so became, for the first time, a subject that could be studied seriously at undergraduate level in Oxford; this may well prove to have been of lasting significance for the continued prosperity of social anthropology at Oxford. The Human Sciences connection is important, providing as it did an institutional expression of the contact that Ardener maintained with the more observational and statistical disciplines – with demography, ethology, and so on. Some of the chapters below (in particular chapters 3, 6, 7 and 11, part 1) are the direct result of problems arising from this meeting of disciplines, in the context of the Human Sciences degree course. It is important to stress Ardener's sustained interest in, and contact with, the resolutely positivist and empirical aspects of the 'human sciences', since such preoccupations may not be self-evident to those who knew him primarily as an expert on 'linguistics'.

In 1972, Ardener published a paper called 'Belief and the Problem of Women' (see below, chapter 4), which became, over the following years, the crystal upon which a formidable body of work and endeavour in 'women's studies' was to grow. His original expression of problems concerning 'muted groups', and the differential bounding of groups of men and women, have proved to be of enduring value, and he continued to be associated with the lively intellectual effort that his work had, in part at least, provoked. It is perhaps worth noting that this work was never, either in principle or in practice, exclusively about 'women', for the 'problem' to which he drew attention was a general one (and cf. Hardman 1973; Maguire 1974; Chapman 1978, for other applications). He was a founding member of the Oxford University Women's Studies Committee, on which he remained until his death. He encouraged the establishment of the 'Centre for Cross-Cultural Research on Women', at Queen Elizabeth House, Oxford, with which his wife and several of his one-time students have been particularly associated. From these Oxford endeavours a long list of publications has come forth (see, for a few examples among many: Ardener, S. (ed.) 1975a; 1978; Macdonald, Holden and Ardener (eds)

1987), continuing evidence of the 'intellectual stamina' of 'the local style of women's studies' (cf. Ardener, E. 1980: x).

Ardener's graduate students tended in the first place, as was natural, to seek research locations in Africa. A shift of interest back to Europe and Britain was pending in social anthropology, however, and Ardener encouraged this from early days. The study of linguistics, not only in Europe but throughout the world, has long been influenced by what has always been, and will doubtless remain, the best documented domain – that of the 'Indo-European' languages. Ardener had extensive exposure to the scholarly study of these languages. In the British context, early linguistic work is inevitably tied to problems concerning ethnicity, population movement, historical sources and so on, and he brought an anthropologically trained mind to this area. His thirst for languages was such that he had, in the Cameroons, while the tropical rain beat down, begun a serious study of modern Welsh, learning initially from a native-speaking Welshman and local District Officer, Cledwyn Hughes (for a Welsh language account of the surprising phenomenon of an English Welsh-speaker in the Mountain Hotel, Buea, Southern Cameroon, see *Y Faner* 15 November 1985: 13). Early British and English histories were never far from Ardener's mind, even in the West African context. He edited and annotated an important early linguistic work on West African languages, J. Clarke's *Specimens of Dialects* (1848, see Ardener, E. 1972c) and, searching for an image to contrast Clarke with a contemporary, S. Koelle (see 1854), he produced 'Koelle is Bede where Clarke is Nennius' (Ardener, E. 1972c: 19). It was only a short step from this to modern ethnographic study of British and European ethnic and linguistic groups, and this he increasingly encouraged.

Several of Ardener's students had turned to the problems posed by minority languages in the European context, and Scottish Gaelic had attracted particular attention. Ardener applied himself to the phonetics of the varieties of Scottish Gaelic with the same enthusiasm and rigour that he had brought to earlier studies of the languages of West Africa. He had begun a comparative study of the Gaelic dialects, in a characteristic attempt to map linguistic and social variation on to one another. In the last few years of his life, he had begun making regular summer trips to the Outer Hebrides, the last stronghold of spoken Gaelic. These trips he made with his wife Shirley, and they had begun to seem, although much more modest, rather like those earlier yearly trips to the Cameroons. The fruits of this work were still, for the most part, in the future, although the experience of Hebridean life is delightfully rendered in one of the last papers in this volume – 'Remote Areas' (below, chapter 14).

The Cameroonian example served Ardener as a model for the relationship between 'history' and 'ethnicity', which he pursued in several papers (see 1958; 1967a; below, chapters 3 and 7). Throughout the last decade of his life he convened a weekly seminar with the title 'History and Ethnicity' (for some of the period in collaboration with Michael Hurst). This led, fairly directly, to the 1987 ASA conference with the same title, a selection of papers from which is in press (see Chapman, McDonald and Tonkin (eds),

1989). Other publications arising from the preoccupations of these seminars are imminent, and many more will doubtless appear.

Every year, at Oxford, Ardener gave a series of lectures on problems associated with the theoretical meeting of social anthropology and linguistics, society and language. In these lectures, and in his other activities, he became involved in the attempt, widespread perhaps, but particularly vigorous at Oxford, to assimilate structuralism to the British anthropological tradition, and to advance further once that assimilation had been made. The lectures, changing and developing from the first delivery in 1963 to the last in 1987, are only inadequately represented in the published papers. They were taxing, stimulating and often extremely funny. Besides these lectures, Ardener was involved in a range of seminars, classes and introductory lectures, particularly involving the Human Sciences degree. His introductions to anthropological linguistics, and to problems presented by language, staged for Human Scientists, but sometimes attracting a much wider audience, were masterpieces, both in content and delivery. These, similarly, are poorly represented in the published papers (although see chapter 1 on Saussure and chapter 11 on Whorf). This is a pity, for Ardener's verbal deliveries, formal and informal, in conversation, tutorial, lecture, seminar and conference, were often his most brilliant and characteristic contributions. He had a rare and remarkable capacity to turn thought in unexpected and exciting directions, and the results were often profound, unsettling and hilarious, all at once. It is a minor tragedy that financial retrenchment in academia in recent years, coupled with the *amour-propre* of the disciplines, denied him the large audience that he merited. The groups of students who had his lectures on their lists (undergraduate human scientists and graduate social anthropologists), were, in recent years, held down in size through various problems of funding. The natural audience was, therefore, when Ardener was at the height of his powers, diminishing or static. And those who did not have his lectures on their lists did not, of course, come. Social anthropology is a little out of town, in fact and in metaphor. Ardener was, of course, concerned about the decline in academic funding and morale in recent years, but he was not, in a sense, surprised by it. As he remarked himself, 'there is of course no inherent justice in demographic patterns' (Ardener, E. and Ardener, S. 1965: 307), and the age structure of the academic community in Britain has demonstrated the acute truth of this over the last twenty years. Ardener was not of the charmed generation that flooded into the universities as very young academics in the 1960s and 1970s, and he had not its illusions to lose.

One area of neglect of Ardener's work is, however, particularly noteworthy. The relationships between language, thought and reality, philosophical issues as they are, were discussed in Ardener's presentations in a serious and novel way that should, I think, have commanded the attention of Oxford philosophy. The absence of such attention (except on the part of a handful of individuals) is partly to be explained by the often intellectually restrictive structures imposed by the categorization of the disciplines. It is also, however, evidence of a characteristic and rather general feature of

academic philosophy – happy to raid anthropology for ethnographic examples torn out of context, but rather blind to the sophisticated blend of
conceptual finesse and empirical command that social anthropology can
bring to 'philosophical' discussion. Social anthropology's philosophy is of
the world, one might say, not of the seminar room. Rare it was, at any rate,
that one of the great army of Oxford undergraduate philosophers found
their way to Ardener's lectures. If he had been lecturing in Paris they
would, I think, have been fighting for seats (for what that is worth).

Ardener never sought publication avidly, and took much more pleasure
in students' publications than in his own. Many of those that knew him
will, perhaps, feel that his written work did not capture the essence of their
relationship to him, or the essence of what he communicated to them; much
of his work remained in lecture notes, and in the memory of those who had
listened to him. He was wryly aware that people might one day try to 'do a
Saussure' on him, and this has indeed begun to happen (see the appendix
for forthcoming works). He was also, however, aware that posthumous
concern creates not a reality, but a simulacrum of it (see 1987a: 44). He
would certainly have agreed that he could, and perhaps should, have
written a great deal more. Most of his publications since 1971 are contained
in this volume, and the result in pounds and ounces is not particularly
impressive. This relatively slight physical aspect is not, however, a reliable
measure of intellectual weight. He did not repeat himself, or labour a point.
His apparently relaxed style conceals a tense economy of expression and of
argument. He could make a terse article do where others might produce
a book and say less; make one phrase serve where others might require
laboured paragraphs.

Some found Ardener's conversation and story-telling baffling, and sometimes they were. It is true that he did not give away the key to a good story
until the very last line, and took pleasure in the suspense (sometimes of
several hours' duration!). And some have complained of obscurity in his
writing. This is a difficult point to deal with briefly. It might be said,
however, that while there doubtless *are* obscurities, as in all truly original
writing (and I discuss below some of the difficulties of expression which
attended the intellectual enterprise on which Ardener was engaged), it
would be imprudent to be too ready to identify these. I know, from the
experience of myself and others, that many of what one might take at first
sight for obscurities, turn out to be failures of one's own understanding
rather than of Ardener's expression.

Ardener was closely associated with the origin (in 1970), and continued
production, of the *Journal of the Anthropological Society of Oxford*, known in
Oxford as 'JASO' [dʒasou]. This journal began as a means of allowing
graduate students to cut their intellectual and literary teeth. It has grown,
over the years, into one of the front ranking anthropological journals in the
English-speaking world. In a short article in the tenth year of its publication, Ardener looked back upon these ten years, saying of JASO that it
had, in its early years, an 'urgent provisionality' (Ardener, E. 1980: xiii).
Something of the same might be said of his own work, which he was

continually revising, in response to developments in his thought, and in response to commentary from his students. He would probably, in relation to himself, have rejected the adjective 'urgent', as being rather too magniloquent for the often rather leisurely process by which his papers drifted from hand to hand in unpredictable directions, and re-appeared, cited, summarized, plagiarized, or misunderstood, in the works and conversations of others. He would certainly have been happy, however, to have his work thought of as 'provisional'. He often said, in typical vein, that the only way in which works of this provisional nature could acceptably assume published form, was as posthumous works. So much so, indeed, that he sometimes spoke of this volume, before his death, and without any anticipation of that sad event, as a 'posthumous' work. At the time of his death, publication of these papers was imminent – the contract with the publishers was ready to be signed, the papers had been collected and collated by the present editor, the introduction was waiting to be written. It would be wrong, of course, to think of Ardener's premature departure from the scene at this stage as an act of autobiographical finesse. I think he would, however, be happy to have it remembered as such. Circumstance delivered the joke, and he was not one to refuse such a gift.

THIS VOLUME

This volume contains most of the major papers produced in their final form by Edwin Ardener since 1971. There are one or two important absences (see below), and no minor pieces (reviews and so forth) have been included. Neither has any effort been made to bring in any of the variety of unfinished works, which exist in partial and note form. In the foregoing biographical account, it has been noted that Ardener's African fieldwork involvement, and the ethnographic writing arising from this, were remarkably and unusually complete, and that this work is held in the highest esteem by Africanists. This should be remembered in reading this collection, for the papers that follow are not, in any simple sense, ethnographic writings. Indeed, most of these works were commonly perceived to be highly 'theoretical', an adjective frequently used to mean the very opposite of 'ethnographic' or 'descriptive'. This dichotomy, 'theoretical/descriptive', like many others forming the fabric of comfortable debate in the human sciences, is largely dissolved through Ardener's treatment, and this will be discussed at greater length below. For the moment, however, it is enough to stress that there is no sudden discontinuity in Ardener's work, between the specifically African works published before 1970, and the more general anthropological papers gathered in this volume. The close interlinking of anthropological concerns with linguistics, history and demography, so characteristic of the later work, is already fully present in the earlier papers. The meeting of empirical and definitional problems is there from the first.

There is no obviously privileged starting point, therefore. Readers familiar with Ardener's recent work may find the omission of 'Witchcraft, Economics and the Continuity of Belief' particularly notable, and a word of explanation is necessary. This paper was given to an ASA conference in 1968, and published in 1970 in the volume *Witchcraft Confessions and Accusations* (ASA 9), edited by Mary Douglas. It was commonly perceived as being the theoretical precursor of some of the papers presented here, introducing the idea of the 'template', a temporary theoretical and figurative device which Ardener developed, and renamed, in later formulations. The decision to omit this paper was based on two considerations. Firstly, the paper fits naturally into a sequence of studies of the Cameroons, and is to be published as part of such a sequence, in a volume edited by Shirley Ardener. This will also contain the substantial and previously unpublished manuscript of 'Kingdom on Mount Cameroon' (the title of the volume will be *Facing Mount Cameroon – Studies in the History of the Cameroon Coast 1500– 1970*). Pressure on space in *Facing Mount Cameroon* was less intense than in this volume, and so it was decided that 'Witchcraft, Economics and the Continuity of Belief' should go there rather than here. The continued availability of this paper is, therefore, assured, and readers should note its importance as an immediate precursor of the papers presented here.

The second reason for leaving out this paper applies also to three other important omissions – a need to keep the length and cost of this book within reasonable limits. The three papers to which I refer particularly are: 'A Directory Study of Social Anthropologists' (1965, with S. Ardener); 'Social Anthropology and the Historicity of Historical Linguistics' (1971); and 'Evidences of Creation' (1987 conference paper, in press) (the location of these papers can be found in the appendix). The decision to omit these papers and not others may seem arbitrary or misguided. The 1965 paper, co-authored with his wife, remained a favourite of Ardener's throughout, and invites omission only because it is slightly outside the obvious theoretical range of the other papers. The 1971 paper is often perceived as an exercise in technical linguistics, and as such, as Ardener well knew, risks seeming unappealing to the general reader, although it has an immediate relevance to the theoretical concerns of the rest of this volume. The 1987 conference paper was Ardener's last major contribution, and is forthcoming in the volume *History and Ethnicity* – ASA Monographs 27 (see Chapman, McDonald, and Tonkin (eds) 1989). It will, therefore, be readily available at the same time as *The Voice of Prophecy*. All three of these omitted papers are of the highest quality, and these excuses (for that is all they are) for leaving them out are clearly not good ones. All ideally would have found a place. The same also goes for several shorter pieces, among which particular mention might be made of Ardener's note on 'Edward Sapir (1884– 1939' (1987; see the appendix).

The reason this volume begins with two 1971 papers is, therefore, largely to do with length. A variety of earlier papers could profitably have been included. The two 1971 contributions presented here are significant, however, in that both were directly addressed to the entire British anthropological population, through its two major institutions, the Association of Social Anthropologists (ASA), and the Royal Anthropological Institute (RAI). The 1969 conference of the ASA, convened by Ardener, has come to be recognized as a landmark in modern British anthropology (see, for example, Parkin 1982: v). The introduction to the ensuing ASA monograph, written by Ardener, is itself a major work, in which linguistics and social anthropology, as they then were, were brought face to face. The 1971 paper 'The New Anthropology and its Critics' continued the same concerns in something rather like polemic form. This paper was first given as the Malinowski lecture at the London School of Economics, and was greeted with a rather characteristic and dramatic mixture of excitement, speculation and doubt. It was subsequently published in *Man*, the journal of the RAI. The novelty of the 'New Anthropology' was not something that Ardener claimed for himself, of course, for any such novelty was already 'largely over', and full and explicit acknowledgement is made of sources and inspiration. There was, however, a claim for a break between one period and another, whose implications had not been fully appreciated by the greater anthropological community in which this break had occurred. Hence the polemical tone, and the sometimes hostile reception. The theoretical concerns were by no means all new, but this paper focused them in a particularly challenging way. Beginning this volume with the two 1971 publications is, then, appropriate. It is, however, in another way, no more than expedient, and readers should bear in mind the work that went before.

Shirley Ardener and I have both tried, at different times and in different ways during Ardener's lifetime, to devise some sort of thematic grouping of the following papers (into, say, papers concerned with 'population and ethnicity', papers concerned with 'language' and so on). All such groupings, however, lacked conviction, and this for reasons which are fundamental to Ardener's thought and style. All of his papers reach out to the others, in ways that conventional themes, topics and titles simply cannot accommodate (and I return to this point below). The papers in this book are therefore presented more or less according to the date of their composition. Details of where each paper was first delivered, and first published, can be found in the appendix. Two of the pieces are previously unpublished, chapter 9, 'The Voice of Prophecy', and 'Total Translation', the third part of chapter 11, 'Comprehending Others'. ('Comprehending Others' is thus presented here for the first time in full.) Both chapter 9 and chapter 11 were, in Ardener's own opinion, vitally important parts of his work, and as such it is entirely typical that they should have remained unpublished, in whole or in part.

Having said that thematic grouping does not do justice to the following papers, some suggestion of the inter-relationship of the following papers may be useful.

Chapter 1 stands, in many respects, alone. It is a major summary of past and present trends, with many pointers to the future. Written as a commentary on a conference which took place in 1969, as an introduction to a diverse collection published in 1971, as a summary of relationships between two sophisticated disciplines from the late nineteenth century to 1971 and as a polemical and predictive intervention in a difficult and controversial area, one which divided the anthropological community of the time, it is not surprising that it is a piece which is firmly tied to its context. In the early stages of the preparation of this book, Ardener was considering rewriting this chapter, and much early momentum was lost, broken upon the problem of how this might be achieved. We had solved the problem by deciding to leave it out altogether, and let Ardener provide some substitute for it in his introduction. Now that he will not write the introduction, however, inclusion of chapter 1 becomes vital, since so much work refers back to it. In the year or so before Ardener's death, I had attempted several editings of the piece, in order to fit it for inclusion in this work, and the changes that I have presumed to make (and see the editor's preface to chapter 1) are those that met with at least some approval. Readers should bear in mind, however, the provenance and context of this piece.

Chapter 2, 'The New Anthropology and its Critics', might be said to be the first of the main series of theoretical papers, which is continued in chapter 5 ('Some Outstanding Problems in the Analysis of Events'), chapter 9 ('The Voice of Prophecy – Further Problems in the Analysis of Events'), and chapter 11 ('Comprehending Others'). Three pieces with clear affinities to one another are those that concern 'the problem of women' – chapters 4, 8 and 12. Chapter 8, indeed, takes the form of an extended commentary on chapter 4, and the two were published together in 1975.

Beyond these few comments, one can do little without going into detail that is rendered otiose by the volume itself. Chapters 3 and 7 might be said to concern 'population and ethnicity'; chapter 6 and the first part of chapter 11 to derive from the problematic meeting of anthropology and animal behaviour. One could go on, but only at risk of producing a pale imitation of the papers themselves – their inter-relationships, at a level well above conventional thematization, are manifold, and the reader can be left to discover these. The reference section at the end of the volume contains all the works cited in the various papers (including this introduction). I have also added, as an appendix, a complete list of Ardener's publications.

There has been a need for a collection of Ardener's papers for some years, for it was clear that, at a local level at least, demand for them far exceeded supply. Some of the papers gathered here, before, if ever, they were published, had a long history of informal circulation, in typewritten form, photocopied and re-photocopied, and passed around from one student to another. Those that existed in published form were often difficult to find, either because the books in which they appeared were out of print, were not commonly accessible, or were simply rather expensive. It was, in consequence, very difficult to assemble, at the same time and in the same place, a complete run of the papers that have been gathered together here. Ardener's attitude to the publication of his work was, as we have seen, rather equivocal, and he often preferred to give his papers to conferences, to circulate them in typewritten form, and to let them develop over the years. He was also anxious that his work should be circulated, locally, at the least possible cost to those, often classically 'impoverished' students, who wished to read them. This sometimes lent a feeling of conspiratorial informality to the propagation of his works, which was both a relish and a frustration, according to whether or not you were able to get what you wanted. This volume will, by contrast, be a rather sober reality. All the words will be legible, and all the references made in full. As I was putting the final touches to this introduction, in a village in a remote part of West Cumbria, an entirely unexpected and unheralded visitor knocked on my window, having made a long detour on a longer journey, to ask if I had a spare copy of 'the Munro lecture', published below as chapter 9. The publication of this volume will, in some small sense, be the end of an era.

I discussed the title of this book with Ardener at some length. Two possibilities were seriously considered, *Comprehending Others* and *The Voice of Prophecy*. I leaned towards the latter, on grounds of euphony and interest. Ardener, however, had serious reservations about it, and inclined towards the safer *Comprehending Others*. This was not because he preferred it, exactly, but because, he said, 'If I call it *The Voice of Prophecy*, they'll think I mean me'. In the end, Shirley Ardener and I have decided that *The Voice of Prophecy* is the better title, and it is perhaps necessary to point out, for those that might have been inclined to wonder, that the prophet in question is not E. W. Ardener.

THE INTELLECTUAL CONTRIBUTION

There is, however, perhaps more to be had out of the notion of prophecy than an unwanted joke. In a situation of theoretical and conceptual innovation, statements from within a novel structure of understanding are always likely to be perceived, at worst, as laughably meaningless, and, at best, as oracular – an oracle spiced, perhaps, with the exciting hint of fulfilment. It is no exaggeration to say that Ardener's writings and oral deliveries were often received in this way, even by those essentially sympathetic to his enterprise. There is nothing dramatic about this, for it is a common response to original thinking. Ardener draws attention, in chapter 1, to the problems faced by Lévi-Strauss in trying to express an intuitive insight in a conceptual language ill-suited to it, and the same problems might be said to have faced Ardener himself. In chapter 9 (1975) he says 'Lévi-Strauss should appear banal, not merely "outmoded"' (see below, p. 154), and this was not a criticism of Lévi-Strauss. For it was the very success of some, at least, of the innovations made by Lévi-Strauss that *should*, at least, have made the original pronouncements seem banal. As Ardener notes, a prophet is incomprehensible before the prophetic fulfilment (should any occur), and commonplace afterwards. The 'voice of prophecy' was not Ardener's own, but the argument concerning prophecy and world-structure can indeed be applied to his own work and to its reception, as Kirsten Hastrup shows below (see p. 224).

Ardener's papers as presented here are their own evidence, of course, and nothing further is needed. I intend no attempt here at summarizing or introducing his ideas. His work was, however, in many respects a struggle against conventional forms of social scientific understanding, against the grain of common expression. A brief examination of how and why this was may, perhaps, be appropriate here, for it is a question which he does not treat explicitly himself. It is also a question which requires consideration of his work as a whole, in the context of its time, and in the context of his own life.

Ardener was taught, in the 1940s, the empirical and functionalist ortho-doxies of the social anthropology of the time. He carried out very long-term, highly empirical and rigorous research within this framework, and pub-lished three monographs resulting from it, along with many shorter pieces. His field research involved collaboration with statistically minded demo-graphers, and Edwin had great respect for the rigour of the demographic *attempt* at seizing empirical totality. During his early teaching years at Oxford, graduate theses in social anthropology were required to have a 'statistical appendix'. His criticism of this at the time was not of the requirement, but rather of its frequently inadequate fulfilment. If you were going to have a statistical appendix, he argued, then it should be done properly or not at all – the half-hearted appearance of enumeration was useless.

During his long fieldwork, however, it was forced upon his attention that no amount of empirical endeavour could substitute for a *social* under-standing of the reality under investigation. Counting was of little use until you knew *what* you were counting, and once you knew *what* you were counting, then the counting itself often seemed superfluous. And the ques-tion of *what* you were counting, the question of definition, could not be solved by turning with greater assiduity to the researcher's terminology and analytic framework. It was, rather, a question which involved a concep-tually complex meeting of the definitions of the researcher, and the defini-tions of the society under investigation. The complexity of this meeting is now commonly understood, and given titles like 'reflexivity'. Thirty or forty years ago, however, it was scarcely acknowledged. Ardener was studying, among other things, the relationship between divorce and fertility. Studying divorce rates meant studying marriage breakdowns. This presented itself in the first place as an empirical question, with 'marriage' an unquestioned element, holding its common English language meaning. It resolved itself, however, not empirically, but definitionally – the answers to the problems came through a study not of how many marriages broke down, but rather through the study of what marriage *was*, in the terms of the society under study. Many other examples of this kind of problem are discussed in Ardener's papers.

As well as conducting social anthropological research after the habit of the times, Ardener was, and unusually for the period, deeply interested in language, languages and linguistics. The subtle and erudite pleasure in the social life of words, so characteristic of his later writing and conversation, seems to have been present from very early days. While an undergraduate, he taught himself Rumanian in order to read a work otherwise inaccessible to him. He continued, throughout his life, to learn languages as a kind of recreation. These enthusiasms were, it seems, an entirely personal feature –

they were not, at any rate, either required or dictated by the anthropology of the time (and see below, chapter 1, on this). They did mean, however, that Ardener achieved an early version of the now long-fashionable meeting of social anthropology and linguistics – a meeting which proved particularly fruitful, and one that provides the source from which this book might be said to spring. At the time when these concerns were coming together in Ardener's thought, of course, the early works of Lévi-Strauss were already some years past, and were making their first muffled appearance on the British intellectual scene. Ardener's early interests and enthusiasms, although independently developed, made him nevertheless peculiarly well-suited to the task of thinking through the problem that Lévi-Strauss had brought to the fore – how were anthropology and linguistics to come together?

It should be noted, however, that Ardener's early enthusiasm for linguistics was for highly formal approaches – information theory, cybernetics, Chomskyan structuralism and so on. Lévi-Strauss's programme seemed, and in many respects was, a natural complement to this. Ardener's rigorous use of formal models, which remained a feature of his thought, has its origin here (as does the important recognition that models *were* only models, not embodiments of reality – see below, chapters 1 and 2).

Ardener is often thought of as having brought 'linguistic' concerns into the heart of British social anthropology, and this is certainly one aspect of his achievement. Within this enterprise, however, it was not only social anthropology which was obliged to change. Conceptions of language and linguistics have had to be transformed as well, in a way that would not always be recognized or approved of by linguists. The traffic of ideas between linguistics and anthropology was never one-way in Ardener's thought and writing. He never wished to impose inappropriate disciplinary conventions, deriving from linguistics, upon anthropology, and he always recognized both the empirical and conceptual strength of anthropology, covert or unexploited though this strength might sometimes be. As he says, in what is perhaps the central paper of the volume:

The appearance of linguistic examples . . . I know from experience, will lead some readers to a negative reaction. But a close examination will show that we are not dealing with linguistics, or socio-linguistics as normally understood, in such cases. I have had useful discussions on every point with linguistic audiences, but only anthropologists, it seems, easily draw the right conclusions (see below, p. 184).

He has, so to speak, tried to take the pair 'language and society', as it was understood by earlier anthropological and linguistic traditions, and to transform each term by its contact with the other. The result, a possibility of analysis of simultaneities which are at once social and linguistic, material and ideal, is very different from the terms in which the argument might have been structured in the early days of the shift from 'function to meaning' (see below, p. 37; Pocock 1961). Many of the oppositions by which functionalist anthropology defined its virtue, and through which structural and symbolic anthropology found their escape, are dissolved by this kind of analysis – material/ideal, social/linguistic, real/symbolic, behaviour/thought, measurement/definition (and many more).

These dualities, however, and others like them, were the very fabric of thought within positivist social anthropology, and they formed a coherent and powerful framework for the disposition of truth and untruth, relevance and triviality. They allowed older-style positivist thinking to continue on its way, while accommodating newer developments as a kind of optional extra – suitable, perhaps, for 'symbolic' analysis. Ardener's work is a dissolution of this fabric. It is, however, always difficult to express criticism of a structure of knowledge in terms that are outside the structure but comprehensible within it. Social anthropology in later years has contributed much to an understanding of this common human problem, and it is here that the figurative 'voice of prophecy' might be invoked. Argument which cuts across the grain of these dualities, as Ardener's did, was in the first place confusing. It was often received, as noted above, as either perverse or delphic. Because, however, the dominant position within anthropological thinking was built around the first half of each of the oppositions cited above, the apparently perverse or delphic statement was readily assimilated to the second half of the same oppositions. Ardener was attempting to lead social anthropology out of the positivist empiricism of a previous period. He was not doing so from an idealist position, but *criticism* of positivist empiricism, within the dominant contemporary systems of social anthropological self-understanding, could not look like anything else. And the apparently oracular statement, with its apparent waywardness and ambiguity, was only too readily assimilated to idealism, as this was constructed in empirical and materialist critique. This has led, over the years, to a persistent suspicion of idealism, which Ardener came to expect, with a kind of wry fatalism. The charge is refuted by the work in general, and I think it fair to say that Ardener, for the most part, could not be bothered with going over the same points again and again. In one rather unusual aside, he said:

I am particularly desirous to stress the material features of the reality demonstrated, being tired of the naive assumption that we must here be in an 'idealist' discourse (see below, p. 171).

The misunderstanding that led to suspicions of idealism also led, when turned on its head, to something perilously like an espousal of idealism, on the part of those who enthusiastically misunderstood the nature of their conversion. Ardener refers to 'occasional excesses' which 'derive from misinterpretation of the new freedoms' (below, p. 60). This double-edged misinterpretation was a source of some vexation. Ardener knew, from experience across the full range of the human sciences, that positivist empiricism was ever liable to take fright when presented with the goods that he offered. Ingrained distaste had to be overcome, and great circumspection employed. It was no part of this careful preparation that there should be, in the background, a noisy idealist fan-club disgracing itself by riotous assembly, and frightening austere positivism back into the securities of its old faith. Something rather like this did, however, happen from time to time.

It is evident from Ardener's writings, and from his own practice, that the place of empirical material in the 'new anthropology' (as of 1971) was as vital as it had ever been to previous schools. The intricacy of the problems that such material posed, in its gathering and understanding, were now openly expressed; empirical material remained, however, of paramount importance. How could it be otherwise? It began to seem, however, in the immediate locality, that this did not go without saying. There was, I think, a temporary reaction against fact-gathering among some students in Oxford, of which the JASO of the 1970s is some witness. I do not wish to overstate this. There were, however, features of the time and the place which made this a possibility. A rejection of 'naive empiricism' was undertaken, which contained the potential that the empirical material would be rejected along with the naivety – baby and bathwater alike down the drain. All the reality-denouncing enthusiasms of the 1960s still perfumed the air. The structure of Oxford graduate social anthropology meant that many students did a library B. Litt before going to do fieldwork, and it was typically from this group that the editors and contributors (readers as well, perhaps) of JASO were drawn. The rigours and rewards of fieldwork were not, therefore, in certain sections of the student body, appreciated as perhaps they might have been. The sustained intellectual critique in which JASO was involved, valuable as it was, did not in itself contain any impulse to fieldwork. Graduate careers were completed, doctorates finished and tenured posts acquired, within the confines of library research. It is a small matter of notoriety that JASO, in its first invitation to submit papers, asked for papers on 'analysis'. Merely 'descriptive' papers were discouraged. In his article 'Ten Years of JASO', Ardener noted, with something like embarrassed relief, that this admonition was disavowed by a contributor (see Tonkin 1971) very early in the journal's history (the note was changed in 1977). Nevertheless, this editorial requirement, in an intellectual context close to Ardener, is interesting, and bears upon the charge of 'idealism'. Some of Ardener's students at the time did, I think, contrive to persuade themselves that facts *were* vulgar, and that theory was the only work for an intellectual. This was emphatically *not* prescribed by Ardener himself, but it was one, itself rather vulgar, reception of the point that he was trying to get across. No surprise then, that, from the outside, some of the winds blowing from Oxford at the time seemed to contain the whiff of idealism. It has, of course, long been a part of the intellectual sub-culture of British social anthropology that Oxford is 'idealist', and unfavourable assessment of Ardener's work fitted readily into this piece of easy academic folklore.

Ardener had put great effort into trying to persuade positivist empiricism of the virtues of conceptual sophistication. It began to be necessary, however, to put some effort into persuading enthusiastic idealism of the virtues of empirical rigour. He insisted, and had the right to insist, that criticism of empiricism could only come from those that had practised it. He insisted also, and this increasingly as the need for insistence became evident, that conceptual finesse (of whatever kind) could only legitimately grow out of a serious involvement with empirical detail. You could not, as it were, try to be Picasso, without having first acquired the abilities of a competent technical draughtsman. Children's daubs would not do, superficial though the resemblance might be. The image is mine, I must stress, although I do not think that Ardener would have disavowed it entirely.

I do not mean by this that Ardener regarded conceptual dealings as something that could be done *after* the gathering of empirical detail. Or that he regarded empirical detail as something that could be gathered *without* the intervention of conceptual considerations. Rather, the serious attempt to gather empirical material must proceed with a self-consciousness of associated conceptual problems, problems deriving from the meeting of the 'world-structure' of the observer and the observed. Conceptual advance and empirical advance would come together, not necessarily predictably or comfortably, but always inalienably joined. You could not, as JASO hoped in its optimistic youth, have the excitement of the 'analysis' without the tedium of the 'description', for 'analysis' and 'description' had started to look much like one another. Much of Ardener's work has been an attempt to integrate mensurational considerations of human affairs, with conceptual, categorical, classificatory and symbolic approaches. Such approaches are often regarded as being in direct opposition to mensurational approaches, or are treated as essentially different – alternative, optional or additional. Ardener wished to show that measurement (mensuration) and definition (category and so on) were *simultaneously* present in the understanding, apprehension and generation of events. He speaks of the 'collapse of measurement into definition' (below, p. 149). I am anxious not to tie his work up with clichés, for its essential openness was one of its most attractive features. Nevertheless, this phrase usefully characterizes some of the problems with which he was dealing. From Sir Henry Sweet's route to the phoneme (below, p. 28), to the understanding of marriage stability (see Ardener, E. 1962a; below, note 33, chapter 1), concerted attempts at measurement in human affairs, led to a new and more refined understanding of problems of definition, classification, category (and so on), which in their turn illuminated empirical data.

I have noted that thematic grouping of the papers below failed, and this is because the categories of analysis of traditional ethnographic writing are dissolved by Ardener's approach. Maryon McDonald, in her postscript to this volume, discusses this rather radical point, in the context of some of today's developments. Ecology, population, economy, law, politics, symbolism, ritual and language (to name only a few) no longer retain either empirical or analytical integrity. The 'ecology' is no longer an observable complex of biological features, from which understanding can be built. It is, rather, already a part of the 'world-structure' under study, which gives it form and meaning. Population groups are no longer head counts, statistical conglomerates of blood and bone, but semantic phenomena, defining and self-defining, with the features that characterize all human classification, of whatever degree of materiality. There is no natural ordering of the results of ethnographic enquiry, therefore, which would allow one area of study to be isolated from another, or allow an ethnographic construction from the lowest material foundations to the ideological or symbolic peroration. There can be no self-evident beginning in, say, ecology and population size, for a 'collapse into one another of the definitional and the material' (below, p. 185) has been achieved. There can be no natural end, either, in the heady uplands of symbolism; language is no 'refuge from materiality' (below, p. 173), for we are now dealing with a 'semantic materialism' (ibid.).

I have drawn attention to Ardener's ethnographic and empirical achievement, and also to his theoretical and conceptual effort and innovation, because these need to be appreciated together. Ardener had worked in West Africa over a twenty-year period, and his 'research', in this sense, was as much a part of his ordinary life as was teaching in Oxford. The 'fieldwork' hat was not one that he wore on special occasions, but one that he always had on – so much so that one risked not noticing it at all. As I have said elsewhere:

He made constant use of material from this fieldwork throughout his life, but he also carried it very lightly. It was perhaps not always clear to those who knew him primarily as the author of later theoretical papers, that there lay behind these such an unusually complete involvement in long-term fieldwork and empirical endeavour, and such a large body of published ethnographic writing. There was no fieldwork swagger, but rather a complete confidence in the material – a confidence so secure it needed no announcement. To many students, who did not refer to the ethnographic writings directly, Edwin's involvement with the Cameroons might have seemed to consist of a series of hilarious and absurd events, recalled and recounted at length, and with relish. It took some time before one noticed that every tale had its moral, that in Edwin's telling gravity and hilarity always came together, and that there was never need for distinction between the absurd and the profound (Chapman 1987).

It is, perhaps, worth noting that many of those who might have felt disposed to assume materialist or empirical virtue, in criticism of Ardener's position, were building on much shakier foundations.

Ardener's work has, of course, developed over the years. In his decennial note in the *Journal of the Anthropological Society of Oxford*, he observes that the contributions to the journal over the decade from 1970 to 1980 move 'in the direction of less and less trust in formalistic approaches and increasingly towards more simple expositions' (see Ardener, E. 1980: x). The same might be said of his own work, as a comparison of, say, chapter 2 with chapter 13 will readily show. The adjective 'simple', however, needs to be properly understood. Certainly, there is a marked tendency to dispense with formal models and technical language. Ardener became increasingly impatient with the often unwieldy, wordy, modish, grandiose and borrowed theoretical and conceptual apparatuses, so lamentably common in the social sciences, which only obscured the material they were supposed to reveal. He said, in 1973, 'I try to lighten the heavy load that specific terms lay across the analysis' (below, p. 86); in 1980, that 'it is my desire to constitute the problem from the anthropological subject matter, and not to import or impose theories developed from other puzzles and other concerns' (below, p. 160); and, in 1984:

we would often be best advised to 'cut the painter' linking us to our stimulating authors, and to let the doomed *Titanic* steam on its way, while we row our own course. That advice is easier to give than to take, it would seem: hitching a ride from these impressive vessels is extremely tempting to many (see below, p. 195).

The apparent simplicity of the later papers is, I would venture, evidence of a greater intellectual command and sophistication, features that are all the more powerful for being unobtrusive. The simplicity represents a step *beyond* the earlier formal and technical expressions, not a retreat from their complexity.

I have noted that chapter 1 was written between 1969 and 1971, and must be understood as of its time. It is not only a period piece, however. Ardener was by no means persuaded that what he had said in this piece had been fully received and understood, and several times voiced the view that the greater part of his criticism, as of 1971, was still relevant and necessary in 1987. This was, indeed, a serious obstacle to the intended revision – how to revise with diplomacy, when one major diplomatic problem was that revision seemed in many respects unnecessary?

There have, of course, been significant works inspired by the 1971 papers. The 1982 ASA conference, 'Semantic Anthropology' (cf. Crick 1976), which resulted in the volume of the same name, edited by David Parkin, is a clear example. At least two other recent ASA conferences, in 1984 and 1985 (which resulted in the volumes *Reason and Morality*, edited by Joanna Overing, and *Anthropology at Home*, edited by Anthony Jackson), are mulling over many of the same concerns.

Ardener was always interested in currents of opinion among educated people (those that he called, with mild irony, 'the thinking classes'). He was interested in the social and intellectual conditions which lay behind the production of academic disciplines. In this sense, his anthropology, however exotic some of its objects, had always been 'at home'. While he concentrated his thought upon social anthropology, he was interested in a variety of subjects which impinged upon it – literature and literary critic-ism, demography, linguistics, sociology, politics (the activities, one might say, of 'the thinking classes' in general). His views on these all invite lengthy discussion, for which there is no space here. He was, in general, interested in the social activity of the intellect, and often both impatient and critical of its slow reactions. It may help to give some idea of the genuine modernity of his thinking, and its speed in relation to much of the sur-rounding environment, if we touch upon three areas that have engendered, and continue to engender, apparently endless debate – Marxism, the 'rationality' debate and the later developments of structuralism. Ardener was deeply interested in the phenomenon of Western intellectual Marxism, and this interest was reflected in the concerns of some of his students, as the JASO of the 1970s was witness (and see Ardener, 1980: x, for a comment on this). Nevertheless, he regarded it as a problem which was subsumed by other developments, and early expressed surprise that it remained satisfactory to a thinker as sophisticated as Althusser (below, p. 61). Indeed, he came to view its very slow disintegration with a mixture of amusement and irritation. He attended an anthropological conference in Amsterdam in 1981, and a notice-board kept conference delegates informed of the programme, and of changes to it. When a sign went up on the notice-board saying 'Marxism cancelled', he greeted this with some amusement, as a long overdue announcement of rather broader significance.

In 1971, he characterized the 'rationality debate' (as conducted, for example, in Wilson (ed.) 1970) as a 'fight in a ditch between the lines' (below, p. 46). In 1985 he recalled this as a 'skirmish between the lines' (below, p. 210), and noted that it was still going on, in much the same terms as before (and see, for example, Hollis and Lukes (eds) 1982). There is no doubt, in my view, that the contribution of *The Voice of Prophecy* is one that can halt (or slow down, at least) the roundabout of problems upon which rationality and relativism ride. Many of the oppositions through which the debate is conducted are collapsed by Ardener's approach. Many of the burning questions, rather than finding answers, simply stop looking like questions.

Ardener studied the emergence of structuralism into social anthropology (indeed, he was part of this emergence), and he noted its move from anthropology to other disciplines. He climbed through structuralism and moved on, however, and came to have little time for what he called the 'cookbook structuralism' which seemed to replace functionalism as the easiest anthropological orthodoxy. Structuralism, as a theory one could carry round and apply to things, had no place in his thinking. It is perhaps not surprising that the tardy efflorescence of structuralism in literary criticism, and the developments that were wrought from it therein, should have excited his amusement. When modish post-structuralism announced its talent for 'deconstruction', he drew attention to the fact that anthropologists had been practising deconstruction as a kind of empirical and logical necessity, long before the term 'deconstruction' was invented in its vogue form (see, for example, Lévi-Strauss 1962a, 1963b; Needham 1971, referring back to Hocart and Kroeber). He observed that 'we may ignore the embarrassing party going on in Criticism around the corpses of Structuralism and its congeners' (below, note 16, chapter 13).

And yet, Marxism continues to structure argument in the 'thinking' press. The rationality debate continues to chew over its bones. The embarrassing party around the corpse of structuralism continues its noisy song and dance of self-announcement. The gauche excitements engendered by post-structuralism and deconstruction continue to render the literary magazines breathless. And Edwin Ardener is, alas, no longer there to smile.

Many have had the experience of trying to follow where Ardener led, and found themselves bumping into things, going very slowly, and making a great deal of noise, where he advanced with speed and silence. It was his pride, laughingly expressed, that he could 'ghost between the interstices', and certainly he had the ability to lead those who followed him closely to intellectual destinations that they might never have found by themselves. It is a legitimate fear, I think, that some of those intellectual destinations may now prove much more difficult of access. Social anthropology, by its very nature, often produces unusual and interesting combinations of knowledge and experience among those who practise it. By any standards, however, the combination of erudition, and conceptual and empirical expertise, that Ardener brought to his thought and writings, was rare and thrilling. This volume will give some idea, at least, of the challenge and the excitement that he could provoke. He was not, however, greatly concerned with reputation even in life, and with posthumous reputation not at all. He would have hoped, perhaps, that his work could contribute to the greater recognition of social anthropology, and to an increased awareness within social anthropology of its own strengths. If *The Voice of Prophecy* can do this, then he would have been satisfied.

One must conclude by adding that there were, of course, many sides to Ardener, and a narrowly professional view of his achievement does not do justice to these, or to the nature and bent of his writings. He had the skill, born at least in part from the profession of anthropology, of being interested in, and interesting to, whatever social and intellectual milieu he might find himself in. St John's College knew him as a full-time college man, tireless in committee, proud and supportive of college reputation, friendly to new-comers, humorous traditionalist, genial wit and erudite raconteur. Jericho, the motley suburb of Oxford in which he lived, knew him as the committed chairman of its residents association. Cameroonians knew him as a full-time scholar of West Africa. I knew him as an authority on European linguistics and ethnicity, of formidable and often completely unexpected insight and erudition. And there are doubtless many other remembered 'Edwins' and 'Ardeners', in the recollections of all those that have, in one way or another, passed close to him, as students, friends or colleagues.[1] It is perhaps as fitting a valedictory tribute as an anthropologist could wish, that, along with obituary notices in learned journals, national papers, and the college record, the local residents' neighbourhood paper, the *Jericho Echo*, could say:

Here in Jericho, we saw the scholarship which made his name in the University put to the direct benefit of the people he lived among.

Malcolm Chapman

Acknowledgements

My principal debt, in the preparation of this book, has been to Mrs Shirley Ardener, who has given generously of advice, encouragement and information, and to whom I extend warmest thanks. Among the rather extensive diaspora of those whom Edwin Ardener taught or influenced, I am indebted particularly to David Parkin and Kirsten Hastrup, who both provided valuable criticism and comment.

I am grateful to my wife, Jane Chapman, who has provided a wide variety of technical help and literary criticism. I also extend thanks to Sean Magee, and through him to the publishers, Basil Blackwell, for help and encouragement.

Malcolm Chapman

1

Social Anthropology and Language

EDITOR'S PREFACE

The 1969 conference of the Association of Social Anthropologists of Britain and the Commonwealth, held at Sussex University, was convened by Edwin Ardener. As was customary, the proceedings were subsequently published as a monograph, with an introduction by the convenor. The following is Ardener's introduction to the volume *Social Anthropology and Language* (ASA 10), published in 1971. Most of the piece stands independently of the volume, and is reproduced here unchanged. It contained, however, an introductory section relating to the conference, and a concluding section, called 'the present volume', relating specifically to the papers included in *Social Anthropology and Language*. These are not, in their entirety, relevant in the present context, and they have been edited accordingly. Some parts have been omitted, some incorporated into the main text, some put into notes, and some, particularly relating to the purpose and context of the conference, are summarized below. This introduction must be regarded as having been only roughly torn away from its surroundings, with many loose ends left hanging: only a substantial critical appendix could fully tidy these up, and no effort has been made to provide this – brevity was the object, which any such appendix must have defeated. The ASA 10 volume still exists, for those who wish to follow up particular points. Where the text refers to articles in the ASA 10 volume, these have been included in the references section at the end of the book.

A number of editorial notes have been added to the text (in chapter 1 alone, not elsewhere). They have been incorporated into the original note sequence (with the consequence that there are now differences in numbering between the notes here and in the original). No distinction has been made, in enumeration in the text, between notes added by the editor, and those originally provided by Ardener. Within the notes themselves, however, editorial notes are clearly distinguished. The first editorial note is a list of contributions and contributors to the volume for which this introduction was written. Some of the others supply material which, for brevity, has been taken out of the main text; some contain material from the section 'the present volume' which has no obvious place in the main text, but which Ardener was anxious to retain; some note other small changes and omissions.

The 1971 volume had, according to Ardener, three aims: firstly, to be read by social anthropologists 'not as a merely specialist branch of their subject, but as an illustration of certain post-functional trends of general relevance'; secondly, to give a perspective on earlier trends in social anthropology and linguistics, and an introduction to work that had been done (and it is this aim which is largely fulfilled in Ardener's introduction); and thirdly, to offer some collaborative insights, from social anthropology to linguistics (see 1971b: xi).

The conference brought together social anthropologists and linguists, in what was undoubtedly a timely conjunction, at least for British social anthropology. As Mr Ardener noted, between the time when the conference was first planned in 1967, and the appearance of the volume in 1971, there was a great increase in linguistic interests among anthropologists, and apologies were made for a general approach – 'much of this introductory essay . . . will restate a number of linguistically well-worn themes in what may at times be a rather elementary manner' (ibid.). The introduction was 'directed rather closely to illumination of the failings of the past, while leaving itself open to more serious criticism from social anthropologists who take its purpose for granted, but may doubt the skill of its achievement' (ibid.). Ardener also noted that, since 'in the United States anthropological linguistics flowed from decade to decade' (ibid.: x), the sudden and apparently novel coming together of social anthropology and language for the ASA might well 'be received across the Atlantic as yet more evidence of past and present "insularity" and "parochialism", charges which are seemingly now inseparable from the American view of British social anthropology (Murdock 1951; Firth, R. 1951; Harris, M. 1969)' (ibid.: xi). These comments and reservations must be borne in mind, *a fortiori*, for republication in 1989.

Ardener also noted the absence, from the conference and the volume, of two subjects which might have been thought of particular relevance – philosophy, and the social anthropological study of kinship. The latter, kinship, was certainly at the time the major arena within which the relationship between 'language, thought and reality' had been discussed, and its omission was justified because it was to be the subject of the next volume in the ASA monograph series – *Rethinking Kinship and Marriage*, edited and introduced by Needham (1971). The relationship with philosophy has since been much discussed in the same monograph series (see, for example, Parkin (ed.) 1982; Overing (ed.) 1985).

Obviously, had Mr Ardener rewritten the entire piece from the standpoint of 1987, it would have looked very different. No such rewritten version is available, however, although many of the themes are developed and transformed in the later papers. No editorial attempt has been made to dress this piece up in the fashions of today, great though the temptation was. The main editorial changes have been in the interests of brevity, not of modernity. It may still seem, however, that editorial decisions about which sections to relegate to footnotes have a modernizing or tendentious feel, and this is probably so. It is important to stress, however, that no concerted effort has been made in this direction. For the following text, the ethnographic present is sometime between 1969 and 1971.   M. C.

The failure of the great middle generation of social anthropologists to respond to the challenge of language has long been one of the curiosities of the British school of the subject; and possibly nothing today so clearly exemplifies that sadly widening rift between the older and the newer social anthropology than the different attitudes to language to be found on either side. This is in great contrast to the 'cultural anthropology' of the United

States, in which the study of language has never lost its place. There, indeed, even linguistic anthropology has developed far beyond the proportions of a mere sub-field of anthropology – its vast literature is beginning to exceed what anyone but a full-time specialist can assimilate. Of course, the autonomy as an academic discipline of linguistics without special labels has everywhere been long established, and it might therefore appear both economical and logical that its study should be left to specialists. This may once have seemed a reasonable view to take. During the 1940s and 1950s, however, when British theoretical social anthropology often gave the impression of resting after the exertions of the Malinowskian period, scientific linguistics made one or two striking advances of sufficient importance to begin to bear upon thought in neighbouring disciplines. As far as British social anthropology as a whole was concerned, it became aware of these advances with the growing influence of Lévi-Strauss. It is something of an irony that this situation should exist: that the influence of thought purportedly derived in some part from linguistics should have come to be so important in British social anthropology, when the direct study of linguistics had for so long lapsed.

The importance of Malinowski for the London school of linguistics obscured this situation. As Miss Henson shows (see Henson, 1971 and 1974), British social anthropologists have been ill at ease with language ever since the nineteenth-century beginnings. The early developments in comparative philology were, it is true, in many ways a hindrance rather than a help to theoretical development, encouraging as they did some of the less fruitful speculations on race and primitive origins. At Oxford the German Max Müller tried to express before his time, although in a form subsequently much criticized (Evans-Pritchard, 1965d: 20–3), some of the links between language and myth, which were not explored again in this country with official approval for another half-century.[2] The philological movement of the 1870s under Brugmann and his colleagues seemed to make no impact. As far as British anthropology was concerned, the neogrammarians lived and died unnoted. Ferdinand de Saussure lectured in the first decade of this century on topics such as synchrony and diachrony, and subsequently remained uncited by anthropologists whose treatment of these subjects was less skilful. Malinowski taught his pupils to 'learn the language', and it is a tribute that many so successfully made the attempt with what seems in retrospect so relatively little awareness of the main advances in descriptive linguistics in the 1920s and 1930s. In the United States anthropological linguistics flowed from decade to decade, from Boas to Sapir, up to the present day, almost unremarked. Glottochronology rose and fell. Information theory appeared in 1948, fructified linguistics and psychology, and slowly went out of fashion, while few British anthropologists noticed. Chomsky flourished for a decade before many could haltingly spell his name. Only in the one or two academic centres that had preserved links with a wider intellectual world was it possible in the later 1950s and the 1960s for influences from the French and American schools to be gathered together and fed into the British tradition.

Had all this truly been the expression of supreme disciplinary self-confidence, it might have been wholly admirable. But in fact, after 1960, at the same time that the most lively issues were being raised as a result of the newer movements, the image-makers of the profession seemed to be sunk in a mood of breast-beating (below, p. 43) which ran the risk of being taken at its face value by the growing 'social science' establishment. The idea of the relevance of theoretical linguistics to social anthropological theory never made much practical headway in anthropological circles in London after Malinowski (despite pioneering efforts by Milner 1954, and more recently by Whiteley 1966).

The long absence of British social anthropology from linguistic concerns has not been entirely to its disadvantage, as the 1969 ASA conference demonstrated. Indeed, absence from the direct study of language seemed to have conferred some positive advantages. Social anthropology had independently developed insights that have some relevance to linguistic movements, and as a professional subject in its own right it is perfectly well equipped to evaluate the 'social' component of any socio-linguistics. The subject has its *Junggrammatiker*, even though Leitner's view of the early neogrammarians ('literary terrorism exercised by a set of Sanscritists', see Leitner 1874, cited Henson 1971: 25) serves as the prejudicial model for much anthropological comprehension of the 'neo-anthropological' movements. For linguists, it may be sufficient to offer as our justification, and aspiration, a text suitably amended from Hjelmslev:

A temporary restriction of the field of vision was the price that had to be paid to elicit from [society] itself its secret. But precisely through that immanent point of view and by virtue of it, [social anthropology] itself returns the price that it demanded (1963: 127).

SOCIAL ANTHROPOLOGISTS AND LINGUISTICS: LEVELS OF RELATIONSHIP

We may as well begin with Lévi-Strauss's three levels of contact between the subject-matters of the two disciplines: (1) the relationship between a [single] language and a [single] culture, (2) the relationship between language and culture, and (3) the relationship between linguistics as a scientific discipline and anthropology (Lévi-Strauss 1963a: 67–8; Firth, J. R. 1957b: 116; Hymes 1964: xxi; Whiteley 1966: 139). These divisions are hardly exhaustive, however, and problems of definition proliferate from them – is 'language' to be classed as part of 'culture', to be opposed to 'culture', to be a determinant of 'culture', or what (as if 'culture', and 'language' too, for that matter, were not in this context terms of art obscuring any solution)?

I prefer to introduce the matter here from a somewhat different point of view, by taking three levels on which social anthropologists in Britain have viewed the relevance of linguistics to their subject over the last generation or two. The idea of levels here derives from the observed tendency of British social anthropologists to *isolate* pieces of the study of language for their own purposes. They may be labelled in this way:

1   A *technical level*: on which social anthropologists might seek and receive help in actually learning languages, especially those exotic and unwritten languages with which they characteristically have to work.
2   A *pragmatic level*: on which they might seek what help, if any, linguistic data can give in the interpretation of anthropological data in a given region or among a given people.
3   The *level of explanation*: on which they might seek the relevance, if any, of theories *about* language, even of theories about linguistics, to theories *about* society, or about culture, or about the place and aims of social anthropology.

In this country, as I have said, the three levels tend to have been treated separately. At all times there has been some interest at level (1). Sometimes there has been interest at level (2). Nowadays there has been considerable interest at level (3). These split relations with linguistics have correspondingly split the apprehension of language as a whole, especially among post-Malinowskians. These levels, then, form a useful starting-point for discussion on the way to disposing of them.

The technical level

Among the main body of social anthropologists since Malinowski a knowledge of the language is taken for granted as a *sine qua non* of good fieldwork. As it has been summarily put:

Sociologists usually speak the same language (more or less) as the people they study, and they share with them at least some of their basic concepts and categories. But for the social anthropologist the most difficult task is usually to understand the language and ways of thought of the people he studies, which may be – and probably are – very different from his own. This is why in anthropological fieldwork a sound knowledge of the language of the community being studied is indispensable, for a people's categories of thought and the forms of their language are inextricably bound together (Beattie 1964a: 31).

This view, with its stress on categories of thought, was an important advance on the more mechanistic attitude of many writers, among whom there was often an unreflecting faith in the linguistic ability of the average social anthropologist. Interpreters seemed to be abhorred – even hated. Now, there are many very good reasons why interpreters should not be relied upon in social anthropology. No doubt most writers had in mind the khaki-uniformed figure (frequently corrupt) used by the colonial administrations. We must only comment on the surprising insouciance to be found among social anthropologists on the subject of what is possible in adult language-learning. Professor Fortes exemplifies the problems involved very clearly in his introduction to *The Dynamics of Clanship among the Tallensi*. He says:

As there is no linguistic literature for the Tallensi we had to learn their dialect from scratch, with the assistance of a semi-literate interpreter and the scanty literature on Mole-Dagbane.

So far so good.

It took us about six months to learn enough Talni for workaday communication with the people. By the end of the first tour we became proficient enough to dispense with an interpreter. Nevertheless, I know only too well that we reached but a moderate standard in our vocabulary and in our appreciation of the finer shades of thought and feeling that can be expressed in Talni (1945: xii).

Let us abstract the sense of this statement: for six months the anthropologist had no 'workaday communication' except through a semi-literate interpreter. He finally, after a 'tour' (eighteen months?) dispensed with an interpreter when he still had only 'a moderate standard of vocabulary' and could not fully appreciate the 'finer shades' of Talni. This is the linguistic mesh through which it is purported that Tallensi culture is given to us. To say this is, of course, not to impugn Fortes's fieldwork. One may confidently take this writer as an example, precisely because his technical linguistic ability shows on every page. We are dealing with a mode of expression: in the ideology of that period, which from that point of view can only now be said to be ending, interpreters were always 'dispensed with' as if sucked dry and banished. The notion of the language well and truly learnt belonged with the lean-jawed traveller of the 'I-rapped-out-a-few-words-of-Swahili' type, and had romantic rather than realistic origins. One suspects Malinowski of encouraging this particular brand of naivety, although the American Boasians were not free from it either. It should be emphasized that anthropological practice was evidently vastly superior to the view of language that purported to direct it. Nevertheless, to regard language as a tool of research presenting very few problems was mistaken, and it is no coincidence that the most delicate work of modern social anthropologists in the fields of myth, belief and symbolism commonly rests upon firm foundations of sound education outside social anthropology in languages, philosophy, classics or one of the other rigorous humanities.

Technical courses in linguistics were taken by many fieldworkers, but they did not, despite the mechanistic views current, have the effect of producing general familiarity among social anthropologists with the ordinary jargon of descriptive linguistics. This contrasts with the American case. It is not entirely unadmirable, to be sure. The point is made here merely to emphasize that a technical view of language has not necessarily led to any common familiarity with language technicalities. Indeed, even among graduate students the signs used in ordinary phonological transcription of no great sophistication tend to awaken much the same revulsion as those used in mathematics (or in elementary statistics). This must be due precisely to a mechanistic view of both: the elements of technical linguistics (as, for many, those of statistics) are to be mugged up for special purposes, the principles perhaps only barely understood. They go with travel inoculations, not to be seriously thought about until necessary. The post-Malinowskian view of language worked with an abiding faith in 'field-workers' modified Berlitz' – a kind of 'look, listen and say'. In an important sense Malinowski's 'context of situation' was a theoretical charter for this faith: as if context would tell all if you really had eyes to see. In practice there was commonly recourse to bilinguals or, rather, partial or inadequate bilinguals, as we should expect. It was not that social anthropologists failed to learn the languages, but that they did not accord their achievements the intellectual status they deserved. They clearly learnt something, but they never examined how they did it, or publicly exchanged detailed ideas on it, or built up their experience from one another's mistakes.[3] Even an other-wise excellent and up-to-date fieldwork symposium like Epstein's (1967) has no chapter on language (and no reference to it in the index). Malinow-ski's own contribution is discussed in this volume; we touch here on the failure of his most representative pupils to regard the study of language, even at that technical level upon which modern fieldwork might be thought implicitly to depend, as more than another subject to remain necessarily naive about – like psychoanalysis or macro-economics (Gluckman 1964).

The truly formidable problem of communication between the field-working social anthropologist and the members of the other society lies at the heart of traditional social anthropology, although few untutored readers would have guessed this from the blander monographs of the last thirty years. There are exceptions: the classical account of Evans-Pritchard, for example (1940), or, more recently, the linguistically candid statement of Maybury-Lewis (1967). Generally, in the monographs themselves the struggle is over. The contradiction between the scale of the task of inter-pretation and the supposed linguistic apparatus involved is remarkably great, as we have seen. It may be resolved in this way. Even the most exemplary technical approach to language would not in fact have solved the basic problem of communication. The anthropological 'experience' derives from the apprehension of a critical lack of fit of (at least) two entire world-views, one to another. The crudity of the functionalists' linguistic tools did not therefore impede this insight. On the contrary, the experience of *mis*understanding is crucial to it. Had all social anthropologists been really thoroughly trained in (say) the phonemics of their day, it is even possible that they would in fact have become far less quickly aware that transcriptions are not enough. The problem might have been obscured, as it is in some Western sociology, by an apparently detailed, but really superficial, comprehension. Post-Malinowskians talked as if they used lan-guages as a 'tool' for the understanding of societies, but in fact they were forced to attempt this understanding by the imposition upon their material of various 'structures', of which the intuitive and observational bases were only partially open to examination. By the 1950s the existential status of such structures had become a worry to the thoughtful. The stage was set for the discussion of 'models', cognitive categories and the like. The study of language had, of course, a real relevance to social anthropologists concerned with these subjects, not primarily at the technical level but, on the contrary, at the more general levels of linguistic theory and practice.

These remarks are certainly not intended to turn into a virtue a wrongheaded approach to language. French and American social anthropologists arrived at similar ends without detachment from the study of language. They do, however, suggest why the functionalist ethnographic monographs of the post-war period contain few classics, and why on the contrary the most interesting recent work has lain not in traditional ethnography but in the analysis of primitive (and scientific) models of the world.

The pragmatic level

The second level of contact between social anthropology and linguistics has been essentially one at the level of 'data'. There was a time when much of the most fruitful interaction between the two disciplines could be placed under this head. It has always been common, for example, for anthropologists, especially in America, to be concerned with the historical implications of linguistic material. Where well-established literary and linguistic specialisms have existed for certain cultures and regions, social anthropologists have turned to them with gratitude (for example: for Indian studies, Dumont and Pocock 1957–66; for Sinology, Freedman 1963). The general revival of historical interests in British social anthropology since the 1950s (Evans-Pritchard 1950, 1961a) has also directed attention to linguistic work in more traditional ethnographic areas. Thus, classifications of the languages of Africa which have thrown new and frequently confusing light on the history of the continent (Greenberg 1963b; and Guthrie 1948, 1953, 1962) have led to some concern with the nature of the classification of languages and its relation to tribe (cf. Ardener, E. 1967a: 293–9; Chilver and Kaberry 1968: 9–12). Similarly deriving from problems in the classification of exotic languages there has been awareness of the work of Swadesh and of the theories associated with the names 'lexicostatistics' and 'glottochronology' (Swadesh 1950; Hymes 1960). The native tradition for these historico-linguistic interests goes back through administrator-anthropologists like Meek (e.g. 1931), Talbot (e.g. 1912), and Northcote Thomas (e.g. 1914). Such men were, however, out of fashion for a long time, and were later frequently accorded the reduced style of 'ethnologist'.

At this level, there is a sense in which social anthropology has been able to 'take or leave' the contributions from linguistics. The two kinds of data, social and linguistic, did not always mix well, and it is paradoxically because of some contacts at this level that the dissatisfaction with linguistics characteristic of the majority of post-war functionalists has been confirmed. The workers in the two subjects inevitably build numerous working theories on detailed data which do not necessarily hold much insight for each other. It is at this level also that ideals of 'teamwork' or even of common seminars between working social anthropologists and working linguists sometimes fail to be effective. As we shall see, Lévi-Strauss spent years struggling with linguistic terminology on this level, and did not begin to clarify his notion of the relevance of structural linguistics until he had in effect abandoned the pragmatic level for the level of explanation. The best recent work in socio-linguistics does not restrict itself to one level of operation: it looks for unifying principles within which the specific methods and data of social anthropology and linguistics can be used, each to its own best advantage. Nevertheless, a good modern field in which pragmatic contacts can be made lies in work concerned with the way in which members of societies classify their environment. A discussion here will serve to introduce in a practical way some of the implications to be further considered at the level of explanation.

Classification and category   This field of linguistics abuts squarely upon the concerns of social anthropology. Long ago, Durkheim and Mauss (trans. 1963) drew attention to certain unifying principles linking the social and mental categories of a people. Many well-known names in American linguistic and cultural anthropology (for example, Sapir 1921; Whorf 1964; Pike 1954; Conklin 1955; Lounsbury 1956; Goodenough 1956; Frake 1961; and others) have made contributions in different ways in this field (sometimes inadequately called 'cognitive'), as well as European social anthropologists like Lévi-Strauss (in much of his vast corpus), Leach (e.g. 1964), Douglas (1966a), and Needham (e.g. 1960b). Some of the developments have become very intricate. Broadly speaking, most of this work confirms Saussure's conclusion that language is not simply a labelling device for elements of the 'real' world. Rather, there is some relationship between the categories through which the world is experienced and the language used to express them. Propositions phrased loosely in this way are not a matter of serious conflict of opinion, but the long-standing philosophical and metaphysical questions they raise are far from solved (Cohen, L. J. 1966; Hook 1969: 3–47). The extreme view that language actually determines the world-view in a quasi-independent manner is usually attributed to Whorf, and this version is commonly rejected (see Hoijer 1954; Cohen, L. J. 1966: 82–94). In some respects the work of the German semanticists is nowadays more stimulating because of their more truly structural approach, deriving from Saussure. A debt is owed to Ullmann (1951) for making their works more familiar in this country.

For those social anthropologists to whom the general implications of this body of work are still new, they may be best illustrated by taking the usual elementary example: the classical case of colour terminology. That is: the manner in which the physical colour spectrum is divided in different languages. We may take the example, first popularized by Hjelmslev (1943: 48–9; trans. 1963: 52–3), of the different range of reference of certain colour terms in English and Welsh, whose reprinting yet again I justify by adding,[4] for my own purposes, columns for modern colloquial Welsh and for Ibo, and extending the spectrum to include 'black' (see figure 1.1).

How we interpret the relationship between the underlying reality and the 'imposed classification' is controversial. The Newtonian colour labels for the divisions of the spectrum do not provide such a reality, for they

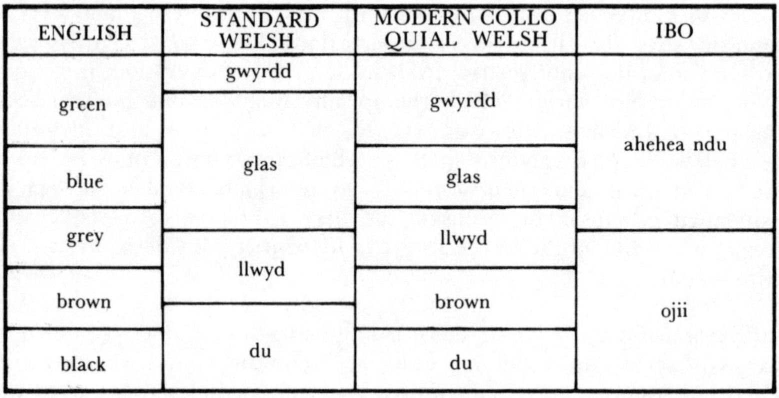

ENGLISH	STANDARD WELSH	MODERN COLLO QUIAL WELSH	IBO
green	gwyrdd	gwyrdd	ahehea ndu
blue	glas	glas	
grey		llwyd	
brown	llwyd	brown	ojii
black	du	du	

Figure 1.1   Certain colour categories

classically exemplify the same process. It is recorded that Newton called in a friend to label the colours of his spectrum, because he himself was not skilled at distinguishing hues. He wished that there should be seven colours, and the term 'indigo' was used to make up the number.[5] This quite extraordinary tale reveals much about the category 'seven' in Renaissance scientific thought, and about the importations of indigo dye to Europe in the same period. Work has been done, nevertheless, suggesting that there are certain essential details given in any colour classification which make for universals in the classification of colours at a much deeper level than that revealed by a simple comparison of different systems. There is in none of these respects any true difference in principle between the commonplace, but always striking, example of colour classification and various other categories imposed upon the social and physical environment by different socio-linguistic communities.

The intuition that a total relativism is unproductive has been supported by the evidence from comparative study, which suggests that a necessary relativism *vis-à-vis* (for example) the categories of English need not lead us to assume a total arbitrariness in all human categorization. I do not intend to enter far into this debate as far as kinship terms are concerned. Lounsbury (1969: 18) has referred to some positions taken by colleagues of mine (e.g. Beattie 1964b) together with that of, for example, Leach (1958), as examples of the 'extreme relativist view'. These and some apparently similar approaches (Needham e.g. 1958) in fact avoid his charge since their effect is to attribute to the kinship structure homologies with other symbolic structures (not necessarily genealogical) which are or may be attributed to universals of another sort – those of the human classifying processes. Furthermore, certain classifications at least are likely to be closely calqued upon basic physical and biological realities in the human condition, from which the different socio-linguistic categorizations of various communities may deviate perhaps only in their degree or direction of 'spread'. The 'relativism' in such cases occurs only in the determination of the boundaries. Nevertheless, the demonstration of those classifications which have a 'universal' core, and those which do not, is by no means easy, and cannot be assumed in advance. A degree of relativism must then have the status of a heuristic hypothisis. There seems no pressing need to fear it, although a social anthropologist cannot avoid the comment that, in all societies, any tampering with the boundaries of categories does awaken the fear of anomaly – generating pollution beliefs, inversion phenomena, and taboo (Douglas 1966a). It is the thought categories of our own tradition that are tampered with in such studies. 'Relativism' may then sometimes appear as a fundamental philosophical danger.

In any event, it is generally agreed that the everyday hypothesis that common categories are entirely universal would not (even in the absence of comparative material) survive evidence that changes may occur in such systems. The most striking thing about Hjelmslev's Welsh colour categories is that they are *not* used, for example, in explaining to the Welsh-speaking public certain changes in the colour code for electric cables (*Y Cymro* 25 March 1970). The modern forms have been lined up with English, as in the third column of figure 1.1. Furthermore, *gwyrdd*, we learn, was an old loan category from Latin *viridis* (Lewis, H. 1943: 10). This intruded on the domain of *glas*, which would formerly have had a 'blue-green' range even closer to Ibo *ahehea ndu* (Ardener, E. 1954b). Further comparison with the Ibo system may help to elucidate some of the issues, through which a kind of universalism emerges from anthropological relativism. The basic colour opposition in Ibo is *ocha/ojii* (brightness/darkness). In this respect the language falls into a well-recognized class. Beyond that there are terms for 'red' (*obara obara* or *uhye uhye*), 'blue-green' (*ahehea ndu* or *akwukwo ndu*), and 'yellow' (*odo odo*), with concrete referents ('blood' or 'camwood', 'living vegetation' or 'leaves', and 'yellow dye-plant'). There is a battery of other descriptive possibilities for specific hues, but except for the addition of 'yellow' the basic system rather resembles Conklin's account of the Hanunóo (1955), a well-known type-case. The single axis of comparison between English and Ibo in figure 1.1 thus completely breaks up the continuum *ocha/ojii*, which lies along the axis of brightness, while *ahehea ndu* lies on the axis of hue (see figure 1.2).

There is a similar opposition in Welsh *gwyn/du*. The 'grey' term *llwyd* also belongs in the middle of the *bright/dark* axis, thus making a triadic division, compared with the Ibo dyad. The terms referring to hues: *glas* 'blue-green', *coch* 'red', and *melyn* 'yellow', are similar to the basic Ibo ones. The factitious continuity of the 'spectrum' from 'green' to 'black' in the second column in figure 1.1 is merely dictated by the first column for English. It results from certain documented English discrepancies with Welsh: e.g. 'grey' mares in Welsh are 'blue': *glas* (*caseg las*), while 'brown' paper is 'grey': *llwyd* (*papur llwyd*).[6] In the first case English uses a *bright/dark* term against a Welsh hue term, whereas in the second the situations are reversed. The Welsh colour terms are therefore best elucidated not in terms of

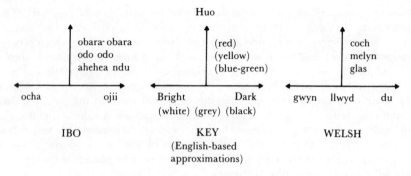

Figure 1.2   Brightness and hue

'perceptual grids', arbitrarily placed over the spectrum, but in structural terms, which would see the Welsh historical transition as matching that of other systems towards more and more differentiation of terms along the hue axis without losing the *bright/dark* opposition.[7]

Such structures clearly intertwine 'mental' and 'natural' phenomena, yet they are linked, through their symbolic expression in language, with the 'social'. Furthermore, such structures are embodied in further meta-levels of symbolism, 'calqued' (to use a linguistic metaphor) upon them. Thus, among the Ibo, the *ocha/ojii* opposition is associated with oppositions like *beautiful/plain, ritual/secular, female/male, weak/sturdy* (Ardener, E. 1954b), in which the *ocha* category bears the aspect of 'purity and danger', while *ojii* is homely and reassuring. This kind of polarity is of course very familiar in social anthropology. The Welsh usages invite many speculations. For example the *bright/dark* axis as a whole (*gwyn/llwyd/du*) seems to symbolize the 'sacred', 'anomalous' or 'dangerous' (*gwynfa*: 'paradise'; *llwyd*: 'holy' of priests; *dubwll*: 'black pit', 'the grave') – in opposition perhaps to the axis of hue as a whole. Despite the basic analogies between the Ibo and Welsh systems, the symbolism of the hues themselves is much more developed in the latter, and the field is a rich one. We need look no further than the thirteenth-century 'Dream of Rhonabwy' (in Jones and Jones 1949) to appreciate this. Nevertheless, our elucidation of the placing of anomalies on the *bright/dark* axis provides an unexpected structural explanation for the so-called 'Celtic twilight'. As the ancient Welsh poem, 'The Spoils of Annwn', puts it:

> *ygkaer pedryfan ynys pybyrdor*
> *echwyd amuchyd kymyscetor*
>
> *(In the Four-Cornered Fortress [of the Otherworld], the isle of the strong door,*
> *Noonday and jet blackness are mingled)*
>
> (Loomis 1956: 136, 165).[8]

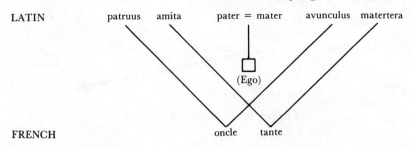

Figure 1.3 The fates of some Latin kin terms

In social anthropology the relationship of colour structures to other structural features in society has been analysed by, for example, Turner (1966: 'red', 'white', 'black'), Tambiah (1968: 203–5) and Leach (1970: 21–35: 'red', 'green', 'yellow'); for the psycho-linguistic background see e.g. Brown and Lenneberg (1954), Lenneberg and Roberts (1956) and Berlin and Kay (1969).

The great interest of the work of the German linguist von Wartburg for social anthropology lies in his useful demonstration of change in structures of interlocking categories. Where such change occurs we are hard put to determine whether the change is essentially one in 'language' or in 'culture' or 'society'. Any attempt at rigid distinction becomes in fact hair-splitting. This is a field in which linguistics and social anthropology frequently overlap totally in their subject-matter, and one therefore in which the analyses of each will be of interest. Once more a familiar example will help us. Whereas Latin distinguished 'father's brother' from 'mother's brother', and 'father's sister' from 'mother's sister', this distinction has been lost in, for instance, French (see figure 1.3). Linguistic analysis shows us that 'parent's male sibling' (*oncle*) and 'parent's female sibling' (*tante*) are reflexes of the Latin terms for 'mother's brother' and 'father's sister' (the latter being more easily seen in our own word 'aunt', which derives from Old French). Linguistic analysis might also suggest reasons why this pair of terms should have been preferred to the alternatives. Thus it might be argued, for example, that the reflexes of *martertera* and *patruus* would fall together too closely in French with the reflexes of *mater* and *pater*. This will not do, however, because the empty slots, instead of being filled with new terms (as they were in other systems of classification), were absorbed. Von Wartburg (1969: 156) points out in an essentially anthropological way that we are dealing with a weakening of the difference in legal status of patrilateral and matrilateral relatives in relation to ego, which had been so important in the older Latin system.

In the medieval world the French solution was accepted by other peoples including the Germans, who had retained the patrilateral/matrilateral distinction (FB *Vetter*, FZ *Base*, MB *Oheim*, MZ *Muhme*). Behind all such major category shifts there no doubt lies a social revolution. It is, however,

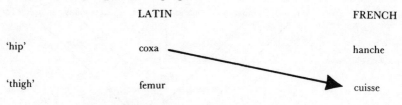

Figure 1.4 'Hip' and 'thigh'

likely that at some period the old and new terminologies coexisted; thus breaking the simple direct calibration between terminology and social organization maintained by Radcliffe-Brown. Furthermore, Malmberg (1964: 130) notes that the distinction is still retained in Swedish, despite analogous jural changes.[9]

It is precisely the diachronic aspect of human category systems that even modern social anthropologists have for the time being tended to neglect. In the naming of bodily parts, 'hip' in Latin was *coxa*, and 'thigh' was *femur*. In French the reflex of *coxa* (*la cuisse*) has come to mean 'thigh' and a new term of Germanic provenance, *hanche*, now fills the category once occupied by *coxa* (see figure 1.4). The situation in Italian, French and Portuguese is similar. The linguist says:

The explanation lies in the awkward situation which had arisen in Latin: *femur, -oris* had become homonymous with *fimus* 'dung' following the modification of *fimus, -i* to *femus, -oris* under the influence of *stercus, -oris*. In order to avoid the now unacceptable *femur*, speakers had recourse to the name for the next nearest part of the body, *coxa*, which henceforward designated the region from the hip to the knee. And as this extension inevitably led to confusion, they turned in case of need to German **hanka*, which they had sometimes heard used by Germanic mercenaries and colonists (von Wartburg 1969: 118).

The anthropological problem lies precisely in the last sentence. The acceptance of **hanka* is not a self-evident further step. It had social as well as linguistic aspects. As von Wartburg himself notes, 'apart from *titta* 'female breast', no other name for a part of the body was borrowed from Germanic at this early period' (p. 118). This arouses the suspicion that what appears to be category slip, caused by adventitious homonymy, may be in effect the merging of portions of two different registers pertaining to the body: a 'polite' and a 'sexual'. (Wartburg's 'German wet-nurses' can surely be only part of the story?) *Coxa* was borrowed into Late British, and survives in Welsh (*coes*: Lewis, H. 1943: 23) for the whole leg. The conservative nature of British Latin (Jackson 1953: 109–12) tends to confirm the evident politeness of *coxa*, rather like Victorian 'limb'. In C. A. Ferguson's (1959) H/L classification, *coxa* belongs to the 'H diatype'. The 'polite' body has many fewer subdivisions than the 'sexual' body. The 'medical' body may have more divisions than either and can be ambiguously polite or sexual. The Romance 'lower leg' took on a Greek veterinary terminology: *camba*, and in French this became 'the whole leg', thus subsuming *coxa*, as *jambe* does *cuisse* to this day. The present French bodily classification contains the debris of all classifications – a veritable *bricolage* (Lévi-Strauss 1962b), which still continues while the *soutien-gorge* exists (to support a 'throat' which includes 'the breasts'). The linguistics of bodily categories would benefit from links with the social anthropology of bodily symbolism (Douglas 1966a).

At a more complicated cognitive level: there was the division in Middle High German, analysed by Trier (1931) and his pupils, between *wîsheit*, *kunst* and *list* (which now mean approximately 'wisdom', 'art' and 'artifice') *Kunst* was at the time, however, used for 'higher' courtly skills, and *list* for 'lower' non-courtly skills (von Wartburg 1969: 157; Ullmann 1959: 166). *Wîsheit* covered both, plus all human wisdom. By about 1300, however, *list* had fallen out (having become 'craft' or 'trick'), and *wîsheit* had become restricted to mystical experience. The field was now totally restructured by *kunst* and *wizzen* (a new term), the former now acquiring connotations of 'art' and the latter of 'knowledge' (von Wartburg 1969: 157–8). The change represented not an autonomous category shift, but 'an abandonment of a social assessment of the field of knowledge' (ibid.: 161), resulting from the collapse of the courtly structure. An abandonment, a social anthropologist would insist, in favour of another.

The notion of the 'linguistic field', the 'semantic field', or the 'conceptual sphere' was expanded by Trier until it has excited criticism:[10]

He postulates that the entire world-picture, which the individual and the linguistic community carry within them, can be completely and organically subdivided, from the whole downwards, into fields of ever-diminishing size. And he believes that, within these fields, the semantic domains of the individual words fit together in the same way to form an unbroken mosaic (von Wartburg 1969: 164).

A major defect of Trier's approach is that it does not express the multidimensionality of human category-making. Nevertheless, the independent development by the German semanticists of theories close to those of Sapir and Whorf is of great interest. The former stress vocabulary whereas the latter are also concerned with grammatical determinants. Similarly, culture and language were conceived by Pike (1954) as combining to provide a 'conceptual grid' through which individuals regard the world. Others speak of a 'filter'. Capell (1966) gathers together much useful material in this light. The static implications of these particular analogies are obvious, as is the positivistic assumption of a stable underlying reality.

Whorf, himself a 'total relativist' if ever there was one, had nevertheless a firm grip on reality. His account of his work as a fire-insurance assessor is a classic (see Carroll 1964: 135–7). For him, 'empty gasoline drums' exploded because they were classed as 'empty' (so that people smoked near them) instead of as 'full' (of gasoline fumes). 'Spun limestone', and 'scrap lead' from condensers, burst into flames, neither being as non-flammable as the classes 'stone' and 'lead' would suggest. Whorf's 'reality' was inextric-

ably intertwined with human classifications. Physical explosions were produced by a careless mixture of categories as well as of chemicals. All the
foregoing discussion obviously raises important implications for social
anthropologists in the interpretation or translation of the categories of one
society in terms of another. It is clear, however, that this task is not likely
to be effectively tackled even in 'empirical' conditions with a merely 'technical' approach to language.

A complex problem in this field, in which various levels of analysis and
various disciplines fall together,[11] concerns the well-known process whereby
loan-words from Norman French produced the parallel terms in English for
'live' and 'slaughtered' farm beasts: sheep/mutton, calf/veal, pig/pork, and
cow/beef. Sir Walter Scott drew the conclusion that the split in the English
categories reflected the fact that the English knew the product on the hoof,
whereas the Normans received it cooked. The perpetuation of the division
when the Normans and English became one speech community is less easily
explained. It is here that what would appear to be a simple marriage
between social anthropology and linguistics through the notion of 'social
stratification' appears totally inadequate. Other distinctions on class lines
vanished, frequently by the supersession of the cruder English by the politer
French. The structuring of this regular series of oppositions is quite other,
and is likely to express certain classifying propensities among the speakers
of English, through which they turned a fortuitous bilingual treasure to
their own ends. The study of such structures has, so far at least, been
mostly the work of social anthropologists (Lévi-Strauss e.g. 1962b and
passim; Leach 1964).

The level of explanation

I have considered the question of classification under the heading of
'pragmatic' contacts between social anthropology and language. In fact, it
is clear that these matters raise theoretical issues of some moment. I shall
examine here the contacts between the explanatory theory of social anthropology and linguistics mainly under headings relating to Ferdinand
de Saussure and Claude Lévi-Strauss. In the time of the former, principles
were stated which have come clearly to the fore (as far as social anthropology is concerned) only in the time of the latter. The discussion of these
writings will form a framework for the consideration of a number of other
theoretical positions and analytical themes in the past and present contacts
between the two disciplines.

Ferdinand de Saussure   The total neglect of Saussure by British social
anthropologists for so long is at first sight incredible. It can be explained in
part by the intellectual isolation, and preoccupation with ethnography, of
the inter-war period. In mitigation, however, it should be said that J. R.
Firth, the functionalists' own linguist, was not a truly sympathetic interpreter of Saussure, and that Malinowski never understood him. Even in the
more enlightened conditions of recent years many social anthropologists

seem to have discovered Saussure backwards, as it were, through Roland Barthes and Lévi-Strauss, both of whom in their different ways insert a barrier between the reader and Saussure. Yet his thought lies behind many of the ideas we have just discussed. Obviously, with over fifty years of debate behind us, the following remarks can be only the merest sketch of even his purely anthropological significance, but since I am addressing myself primarily to social anthropologists the task is worth undertaking.

Ferdinand de Saussure made great contributions to comparative philology at an early age (1878). He taught Sanskrit in Paris from 1881 to 1891, but he is known chiefly for his lectures on linguistics given at the University of Geneva 1906–11. In 1916, after his death, his pupils Charles Bally and Albert Sechehaye published a reconstruction of his lectures,[12] as the *Cours de linguistique générale*.[13]

For anthropologists the significance of Saussure's own approach is that his analytical ideas were 'socio-linguistic' rather than purely linguistic. His central distinction was of course between *la langue* and *la parole* (which may be translated as 'language' and 'speech', or 'speaking' – Engler 1968: 54). *La langue* for Saussure is the system that is abstracted from the whole body of utterances made by human speakers within a speech community. *La parole* is susceptible of acoustic measurement, of tape-recording, and of other physical tests. *La langue* is not, because this is a system abstracted from, and in turn superimposed upon, *la parole*. This distinction *langue/parole* can provide a master exemplar for other distinctions: such as the colour category versus the physical spectrum, or the kinship category versus the biological relationship measured by the study of genetic structure and mating patterns. Yet *langue/parole* is used by Saussure in several different ways. This basic antinomy between 'form' and 'substance' (where 'form' at one level may become 'substance' at another) has been frequently hardened into typologies: types of *langue*, types of *parole*, intermediate forms (e.g. Sechehaye 1940). Yet its essential character derives precisely from this supposed source of confusion (Hockett 1968: 15; Householder 1970: 130). We can now see that its interest lies for social anthropology in its original intuitive form, and the antinomy deserves a place among those ideas that are part of the 'intellectual capital' of the subject (Evans-Pritchard, introduction to Hertz 1960: 24; Needham 1963: xl–xliv).[14]

Also of central interest to us is Saussure's vision of language as a system of signs. His contribution here was to stress that language is not a simple labelling device (*une nomenclature* – 1922: 34): as if there were only objects in the real world waiting to be given 'names'. He did this by talking of a linguistic sign as consisting of two components: the 'signifier' and the 'signified'. The English term *tree* is such a linguistic sign, consisting both of the acoustic chain rendered as /tri:/ and of the range of phenomena that this sequence signifies in English. One could not therefore equate two signs in different languages (say, *tree* in English and *arbre* in French) without taking into account differences in the 'signified' component. Saussure's 'signified' is, however, not reality but a 'concept'. The sign is not a combination of a set of acoustic measurements with a botanical organism (Malmberg, 1964: 44). 'Both parts of the sign are equally psychical' (Saussure 1922: 32; 1964 trans. 'psychological' p. 15). The 'arbitrariness' of the linguistic sign is a Saussurean notion of some complexity (Benvéniste 1939). It was clearly designed to answer adherents of the view (supported incidentally by Tylor) that all language had a representational origin – like 'sign' language. The acoustic chain may not in fact be entirely arbitrary in its association with the 'concept' (e.g. Jakobson 1960; Firth, J. R. 1957a: 192–3). Like Durkheim and Lévi-Strauss (and Chomsky), Saussure wishes to stress the objectivity of his psychical entities:

Linguistic signs, while being essentially psychical, are not abstractions; the associations ratified by *le consentement collectif*, of which the totality makes up language, are realities which have their seat in the brain (1922: 32; my trans.).

Saussure was aware of the very broad implications of his theory of signs. He thought that there should be a special discipline to take into account all systems of signs (*une science qui étudie la vie des signes au sein de la vie sociale*) – under the name 'semiology'.

Semiology would show what constitutes signs, what laws govern them. Since the science does not yet exist, no-one can say what it would be; but it has a right to existence, staked out in advance. Linguistics is only a part of the general science of semiology; the laws discovered by semiology will be applicable to linguistics, and the latter will circumscribe a well-defined area within the mass of human facts (1922: 33; trans. 1964: 16 – where *humain* is translated as *anthropological*).

And further:

If we are to discover the true nature of language (*langue*) we must learn what it has in common with all other systems of the same order: certain linguistic factors that might seem very important at first glance (e.g. the role of the vocal apparatus) ought to receive only secondary consideration if they merely serve to set language apart from other systems. In this way, one will do more than clarify the linguistic problem. By studying rites, customs and the like, as signs, I believe these facts will appear in a new light, and one will feel the need to include them in the science of semiology and to explain them by its laws (1922: 35; trans. 1964: 17, which has been heavily amended here).

These prophetic remarks, published while Malinowski was still in the Trobriands, and no doubt formulated some time before 1911 (thus being blocked off from us by a whole generation of functionalism), are the ultimate source of many of the more general influences, coming from linguistics and the French school, which have penetrated through various cracks in the foundations of empirical social anthropology since 1945 and have gradually become part of the climate of thought. Saussure himself, like Bloomfield, the most eminent American linguist of the next generation, was most concerned with the links between his study and psychology. But Saussure does ask the question: 'must linguistics then be combined with sociology?' (For him *anthropologie* is not yet 'social' anthropology.) 'Language,' says Saussure, echoing Durkheim, 'is a social fact' (1922: 21; trans. 1964: 6).

Doroszewski (1933), who clearly demonstrates the Durkheimian nature of Saussure's *langue* (Durkheim's social/individual = Saussure's *langue/parole*), makes the interesting point:

> F. de Saussure – as I know from an exact source – followed the philosophical debate between Durkheim and Tarde with deep interest. If one takes into consideration not only the idea, essential for Saussure, of *langue* but also the complementary one of *parole*, the Saussurean doctrine as a whole then appears as a curious attempt, undertaken by a linguist of genius, to reconcile the opposed doctrines of Durkheim and Tarde. In the opposition of *langue* and *parole* one glimpses the opposition of the idea of Durkheim to that of Tarde (90–1, my trans.).

French linguists have generally retained a 'sociological' viewpoint since Saussure's day. Vendryes (1921, 1952) and Sechehaye (1933), for example, reaffirmed his aims. Meillet contributed to *L'Année Sociologique*. Marcel Cohen (1948, 1955 edn: 40), while finding Durkheim's school *plutôt idéaliste*, mentions Saussure in the same breath as Marx and Engels (the latter's *Der Fränkische Dialekt* was published in Moscow in 1935).

Another parallel between Saussure's thought and that of French sociology, and of the social anthropology of Radcliffe-Brown and Evans-Pritchard following it, is his use of the terms *synchronic* and *diachronic* to describe two basic approaches to his subject-matter. Saussure was concerned to show that the historical study of language, which had dominated linguistics until his day, was not the only mode of investigation. He likened this to the study of a longitudinal section along the stem of a plant (1922: 125). He demonstrated that a cross-section of the stem – his analogy for a synchronic study – would also show a system. The Malinowskian advance in social anthropology, which occurred soon after Saussure's death, took a similar form. The 'structural-functional' position stressed the synchronic *pattern*, in contrast to the historicist approaches – the preoccupation with origins – of the preceding period. Saussure was, however, a more flexible thinker than Malinowski, or, at least, than the latter's immediate successors. He recognized the significance of both synchrony and diachrony, although he argued that the two approaches were to be clearly separated. He speaks of 'laws' for both approaches, but achieves an important insight which leads him far beyond Radcliffe-Brown, another believer in laws, who died only in the 1950s. He says: 'the synchronic law is general but not imperative . . . the synchronic law reports a state of affairs'. Synchronic patterns contained no indication of their own stability or lack of it: 'the arrangement that the law defines is precarious, precisely because it is not imperative' (1922: 131; trans. 1964: 92). Sometimes, as we shall see, Saussure loosely uses the term *équilibre* for a synchronic state, but there is here no sideways slip into a view of a self-perpetuating equilibrium of a quasi-organic type, such as has dogged social anthropology into our own days.

It is worth citing directly some other statements of Saussure despite their familiarity to linguists: for example, his likening of language to chess.

But of all comparisons which might be imagined the most fruitful is the one that might be drawn between the functioning of language and the game of chess. In both instances we are confronted with a system of values and their observable modifications (1922: 125; trans. 1964: 88).

(Not a system of valuations, 'moral values', but a system in which all parts have a certain weighting, a *valency*.) In what follows it may be worth reading 'society' for 'language':

First: a state of the set of chessmen [i.e. the state of the board at any one time] corresponds closely to a state of language. The respective value of the pieces depends on their position on the chessboard, just as each linguistic term derives its value from its opposition to all the other terms (1922: 125–6; trans. 1964: 88).

(Note the word 'opposition'. Here we have clearly stated the now fashionable anthropological view that elements in the system define themselves in opposition to all other elements in the system.)

In the second place, the system is always momentary: it varies from one position to the next. It is also true that values depend above all else on an unchangeable convention: the set of rules that exists before a game begins and persists after each move. Rules that are agreed upon once and for all exist in language too; they are the constant principles of semiology (1922: 126; trans. 1964: 88).

(We may note here the insight that the very positions of the pieces, and their values, embody the operation of rules.)

Finally to pass from one state of equilibrium to the next, or – according to our terminology – from one synchrony to the next, only one chess piece has to be moved: there is no general rummage. Here we have the counterpart of the diachronic phenomenon with all its peculiarities (1922: 126; trans. 1964: 88).

In particular, Saussure notes that changes affecting single elements (as with the movement of only one chess piece) have repercussions on the whole system:

Resulting changes of value will be, according to the circumstances, either nil, very serious, or of moderate importance. A certain move can revolutionize the game, and even affect pieces that are not immediately involved (1922: 126; trans. 1964: 89).

Saussure had in mind linguistic phenomena of the type (say) of the loss of Indo-European *p* in Common Celtic. All modern Celtic languages do have *p*. Sommerfelt and others said, in effect, that the whole phonological system shuddered, as it were, and rebuilt itself (Hamp 1958: 209–10). The *p* in Welsh, for example, is frequently a reflex of Indo-European *qu

(Jackson 1953: 413). But we may extend this to those socially more signifi-cant sections of language that we have already noted, as when a term drops out from a slot of a system of classification. Diachronically, two of the pieces in the Latin kinship set *avunculus* (MB), *matertera* (MZ), *patruus* (FB), *amita* (FZ), disappeared. The synchronic values of *tante* (MZ, FZ) and *oncle* (MB, FB) as members of a two-piece set are quite different from those of their diachronic 'sames' *amita* and *avunculus* which existed in a four-piece set. So also with the loss of *femur*, in our other example, with its bilingual repercussions.

Saussure says, further: 'In chess each move is absolutely distinct from the preceding and the subsequent equilibrium. The change if effected belongs to neither state: only states matter.' This last is an aphoristic remark which is expanded as follows:

In a game of chess any particular position has a unique characteristic of being freed from all antecedent positions: the route used in arriving there makes absolutely no difference; one who has followed the entire match has no advantage over the curious party who comes up at a critical moment to inspect the state of the game . . .' (1922: 126; trans. 1964: 89).

We now come to a feature of Saussure's thinking that many have found unnecessarily rigid. He insists not only that a *synchronic* study of phenomena must be conceptually distinguished from a *diachronic* study, but that the 'facts' elicited belong in effect to two different universes. Diachronic formu-lations cannot be reduced to synchronic ones. There is an 'opposition' between the two modes, which derives from his conviction that the methodologies of the two modes are not interchangeable. Saussure has been criticized for this by some who wrongly think that they are making a stand for linguistic holism by denying that the synchronic and the diachronic can be separated.[15] We are, of course, concerned here with models drawn upon different selections of data, and Saussure's instinct was sound in recog-nizing that rigour demanded that they be not confused.

Saussure states the intuitive problem of such critics much more effec-tively when he envisages (as a purely speculative hypothesis) the possibility of a 'panchronic' viewpoint. In this he is particularly advanced. 'In linguis-tics,' he says, 'as in chess, there are rules that outlive all events' (1922: 135; trans. 1964: 95). The way in which a panchronic view might be developed may be clarified as follows: we say that synchrony equals a state of the chessboard. The observer will deduce some of the rules, even most of the rules, of chess from sequential states of the board, the 'values' of the elements (the pieces) embodying in their positions the rules. But certain of the rules can never be deduced from either the game so far, or the present state of the game, e.g. the rule for mate. It is the rules in this total sense that Saussure would exclude from synchrony and diachrony and assign to the panchronic field. Saussure's refusal to build these rules into the lin-guistic phenomena themselves is an index of his determination to main-tain a distance between language and the *study* of language. We have seen that the diachronic model for him depends upon the 'opposition', the contrast, of each element with another in a series; while the synchronic model depends upon the opposition of elements to one another in a system at a single state in time. The rules that link the two analytical modes of opposition do not appear in either mode separately. He correctly perceived, despite the obscurities of his expression, that their methodological opposition was resolved not *in* language, but in what is now commonly termed metalanguage.

Whatever criticisms may be advanced against Saussure (Collinder 1968 makes a spirited attack on Saussure's 'polemic' claims) it is now the essential 'modernity' of his propositions that comes through the lecture-notes of his students.[16] It is all there, not only synchrony and diachrony, but the idea of opposition, later to be further developed by the Prague School, and thence bequeathed to Lévi-Strauss. Much modern toying with games theory is made to look jejune before Saussure's early-twentieth-century analogy. (He was always aware of its pitfalls: 'in order to make the game of chess seem at every point like the functioning of language, we should have to imagine an unconscious or unintelligent player' – 1922: 127; trans. 1964: 89). His chess analogy, of course, reappears in Wittgenstein (for example, 1963: 15),[17] in the jurist Hart (1961) and in Ross (1958) (see also Ardener, E. 1971c: 215–17). If Saussure is the true father of structuralism, we must, however, pay tribute to the influence of the French school of sociology in stimulating his thought. Saussure, as it were, channelled into linguistics parts of the new *sociologie* which lacked concrete application, given the paucity of systematically collected social data available at the time. The more copious linguistic data served as a testing-field from which the analytical concepts were returned to Durkheim's successors in a later generation, added to and enriched. Lévi-Strauss frequently speaks with Saussure's words:

Anthropology aims to be a *semiological* science ... This is yet another reason (in addition to many others) why anthropology should maintain close contact with linguistics, where, with regard to the social fact of speech there is the same concern to avoid separating the objective basis of language (sound) from its signifying functions (meaning) (Lévi-Strauss 1963a: 364).

Hjelmslev of Copenhagen now seems to us, as he did years ago to Bally (Hjelmslev 1959: 31), to be the most clear exponent of the Saussurean vision. He cites (1943 and trans. 1963: 107–8) Czechoslovak 'semiological' work of the 1930s on folk costume, art and literature which is not easily accessible, as well as Buyssens (1943).[18] He is aware of the relevance of logicians like Carnap, and sees sign systems as 'abstract transformation systems' (p. 108), bringing us, in 1943, into the world of modern social anthropology, and, as elsewhere (see Ardener, E. 1971c: 228), using the terminology of generativeness fourteen years before its American incarnation. He remarked in 1948 (in Hjelmslev 1959: 34) that semiology did 'not appeal to linguists'. Even he did not seem prepared to pursue further the fact that 'in Saussure's *Cours* this general discipline is thought of as erected on an essentially sociological and psychological basis' (Hjelmslev 1943: 96; trans. 1963: 108). Yet his system does not close in upon itself to subsume only linguistic data: 'in practice a language is a semiotic into which all other semiotics may be translated – both all other languages, and all other conceivable semiotic structures' (1943: 97; trans. 1963: 109). Of which, more later.

This is different from Barthes (1967: 9), who says that, contrary to Saussure's expectation, semiology must form part of linguistics because: 'it is far from certain that in the social life of today there are to be found any extensive systems of signs outside human language.' This remarkable mis-apprehension leads Barthes only into the semiology of minor systems (the Highway Code, fashion). His basic problem, however, going back to Hjelm-slev's observation, is that linguists could not actually see in the sociology or anthropology they were offered in the generation after Saussure any real evidence of what Saussure meant. The sociology of Durkheim had, as it were, gone underground. Only now, through Lévi-Strauss, has a semiotic of wide social relevance begun to emerge. Barthes's semiology, like that of Buyssens (1943), is much too closely calqued on detailed linguistic example to fill the role. It is a *semiologia minor* of small iconic systems. To understand Saussure's semiology aright we must see that its principles will be only partially derivable from language; a semiotic of society will derive its own principles which would be conjoined with those of other systems. Barthes's difficulty is akin to that of anthropologists who attempt to apply the pragmatic operational concepts (data-laden) of another discipline to their own.

Saussure's panchronic (or panchronistic) approach, on the other hand, which for him remained merely a programme, because he could see no model or method to do justice to it, has passed as far as language is concerned into the hands of the transformational generative grammarians. Chomsky states that rules can be deduced from the study of language in a given state, such that, for him, a grammar can predict all well-formed sentences in a language, including those that no one has uttered. It has been frequently said that the 'competence' and 'performance' of the genera-tive grammarians are analogous to the opposition *langue/parole*, although Chomsky's own view has not remained consistent on the matter (1968). It has been further recognized (King 1969: 11) that the strict Saussurean principles make comparison between two dialects impossible: for the 'values' of elements in the two systems are not the same. Thus *o* in a dialect with a five-vowel system is not comparable in value with *o* in a dialect with a seven-vowel system. This problem is not unlike that presented by di-achronic linguistics: in what sense does /ai/ in the Modern English vowel system 'correspond' to Middle English /i:/? The transformationalist solu-tion is, nevertheless, implicit in Saussure's rigorous perception of the use of models. The evident connections between the values in two systems can be described only at the level of oppositions between rules themselves in a system of rules. This is what transformationalist treatment in terms of 'rule-loss' and 'rule-acquisition' really means (Chomsky 1968, and Ardener, E. 1971c: 232). The 'grammars' of the transformationalists are models of 'competence'. They are seeking in effect transformational 'meta-rules' for the linking of Saussurean 'states'. Just as Saussureans (and Saussure) frequently mistake the model *langue* for a reality greater than the model, so too do many transformationalists speak as if their programmes for a model of 'competence' are already achieved. The panchronic approach may, then, be said to be in process of formulation – in principle at least. We shall not be surprised if its practice presents great difficulties.[19]

Semiotic and society[20]   Why should social anthropologists think again about Saussure? Apart from his significance in having anticipated the discussion of diachrony and synchrony, and having shown the way to the notion of system and opposition, and the rest, his ideas contain a generality that simplifies the task of even the most empirically minded. I will take one example. We commonly find that ritual signs have contradictory poles of meaning. Turner (1964: 30–1) expresses this distinction in different ways. Thus a symbol may refer to 'emotions, blood, genitalia' (at the 'sensory' pole), and at the same time to 'unity, continuity of groups' (at the 'ideological' pole). Sapir's division of symbols into 'condensation' symbols (with unconscious roots) and 'referential' symbols (signals, flags) corresponds, in Turner's view, to these two poles – save that ritual symbols combine both. Some social anthropologists restrict the term 'sign' to Sapir's referential symbols, and 'symbol' to Sapir's condensation symbols. These distinctions are not too easy to defend from a Saussurean point of view. Take a Ndembu linguistic sign, the *signifier* – *mudyi* (an 'acoustic image'); the *signified* – 'a tree with milky-white sap' ('the concept'). Now, the association of 'milky-white sap' with 'mother's milk' is so salient that the equation might even qualify for immediate inclusion in the Ndembu dictionary as part of the 'concept' (ibid.: 21–7). The more 'biological' or 'sensory' aspect may thus qualify by a lexicographical definition as 'conscious'. The 'unity of the matrilineage' or the like might well be shown to be, on the contrary, unconscious. The emotional, biological ('sensory') pole may then possibly appear more clearly part of the linguistic sign than the 'ideological' pole.

It would seem more useful to turn to the distinction between a linguistic sign and a ritual sign. Now a ritual sign is not expressed *as such* in language. The '*mudyi* tree', as a member of a set of ritual signs, forms part of a semiology distinct from the lexical element *mudyi*, as a linguistic sign in the Ndembu language. The ritual tree is, however, no less a 'concept' than the signified of *mudyi*. The botanical tree thus generates two 'concepts'. One is tied to the acoustic chain *mudyi* and is a linguistic sign. The other is tied to ritual images, and is a ritual signifier, in a ritual sign (see figure 1.5).

In principle, such a sign exists without any 'label': its label (that by which it is known) is its 'value' as an element in a system of like elements. In practice, ritual signifieds overlap linguistic signifieds. Elements termed 'sensory' and 'ideological' can fall into either field. The linguistic signifieds can nevertheless be consciously 'unpacked' in language. The ritual signi-

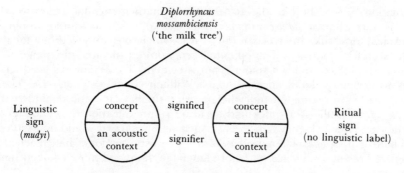

Figure 1.5   Linguistic and ritual signs

fieds by definition contain elements that no one has as yet unpacked into the semiotic of linguistic signs. We may translate the ritual semiotic into language, but if we are not careful we end up with the heaps of polarities in which Turner's many valuable treatments leave us knee-deep. A 'meta-semiotic' which will deal with the structure of all signs must make for a greater simplicity than does the laborious rendering of ritual signifieds into natural language. The polarities within symbols may be at least pro-visionally understood by placing their elements in different sign systems. What has been said about ritual semiotic in relation to linguistic semiotic is applicable to all semiotics that we may define. We may agree so far with Barthes that language will often provide an index to some of these systems, as in his own study of fashion – but, interestingly enough, this is just where language as a semiotic is most obscure. These hints of other systems often subsist as 'redundancies' in language. The semiotic of the human body has already been mentioned here. Its continual 'interference' with the linguistic classification of the body is one of the daily problems of ordered social existence, although it has been illustrated above from traditional linguistic material.

Blank banners   We might visualize a semiotic system that depended, in the absence of the power of speech, upon the apperception by the human participants of contextually defined logical relations among themselves in space. Let us say: the relative position of each participant to another in a gathering, and to items in a fixed environment. The 'elements' of the semiotic would be stated by their existential presence and would acquire 'meaning' ('value') through the 'relations', which would themselves be apperceptible as some kind of syntax. The possible range of such separate semiotics without speech is great. Careful structuring of the bio-physical environment would be required, for the actors themselves are symbols in the semiotic, and a recognizable set of theatres for action must be provided. The whole set of semiotic slots is empty in linguistic terms, for there is no speech. The 'acquisition' of language (if one may use such a word in such a situation) would be like the acquisition of mathematics for zealous early measurers who had *ad hoc* units for every class of object measured, stored in physical form (like the wooden tally sticks which long provided fuel for the Houses of Parliament). The potential generality of the acoustic image as a substitute for multiplex signifier-types is evident. These remarks need have no evolutionary significance (although William Golding's novel, *The Inheritors*, has his retreating Neanderthalers using the new acoustic semiotic with only partial skill – for quick and accurate communication they show each other 'pictures'). If they *were* to have such significance, it would undoubtedly be to tell us (*pace* Chomsky) that non-linguistic semiotics had reached a high degree of sophistication before language more and more codified their realm.

The similarity of my hypothetical case to 'primitive' semiotics, which actually coexist with language, suggests that the need for careful structuring of the environment is the greater where language does not purport to translate all semiotics. The chief feature of archaic, folk, 'minority' and certain other forms of society – a factitious conformity – thus acquires the aspect of a channel-holding mechanism. Furthermore, if new movements occur even in highly 'linguistic' societies they may, perhaps can only, be expressed at first in a non-linguistic semiotic. To that extent the political movements of the 1970s are demonstrations with blank banners, whatever may, for the nonce, be inscribed upon them. At a more detailed level: the supposed 'restricted codes' of Bernstein's working-class drop-outs are best understood as a local variant of the 'primitive' case.

Finally, the ancient and still flourishing human apperception of non-linguistic semiotics, through the structuring of the bio-social environment at all levels, provides a suitably non-mystical 'locus' for Durkheimian collective representations, and other 'cosmological' entities, which long ago roused the revulsion of Malinowski, as they still do of others in those departments of social anthropology where his orthodox tradition was transmitted unbroken. It must be admitted that Durkheim himself (1898, trans. 1951) struggles with the relationship between individual and collective representations. He is reduced to a declaration of faith, and some hopes for telepathy! (1951: 18–23.)

The French school bases itself upon the notions of *extériorité* and *extériorisation* – terms that English-speaking commentators do not always comprehend. For Saussure, *extériorité* was a feature of *langue* (Doroszewski 1933: 89). Sechehaye (1933: 63), his pupil, saw language as 'like' customs, beliefs, political organization: 'Comme toutes ces choses, elle constitue un objet extérieur à l'individu . . .' How appropriate that Cassirer should, in the same journal in the same year, speak of the linguistic construction of the world of objects as 'l'extériorisation des simples états du moi' (1933: 30). That Simonis should speak of Lévi-Strauss's work as expressing the 'exteriorisation of man' (1968: 335) is thus natural and expected. It is not just that Saussuro-Durkheimians see collective representations as 'outside' the individual: the individual is somehow part of them. It is of interest that McLuhan (1970: 37–40) reproduces the essential notion of *extériorisation* as 'outering' – although I am not aware of the process by which he thus incorporated seventy years of French thought.[21]

The terminology of semiotic can be expressed more mechanistically through communication theory. We have to visualize that the message on one channel becomes itself the channel for meta-messages. Lévi-Strauss (1963a: 61) implicitly states the general case, from the particular case of women: *human beings speak, but they are themselves also symbolic elements in a communication system* (see also below, chapter 4). When language fails or lags in its task, as is clearly to some extent the case in social life today, we shall be glad of our attempts to unravel the general semiological principles, to which Saussure so long ago directed our attention.

Claude Lévi-Strauss and the phoneme The original essays in which Lévi-Strauss set out his inspiration from linguistics are far from uniform in their view of the subject. The first statement was published as long ago as August 1945, in the opening issue of *Word*. His introductory remarks gain additional interest in view of the time of their publication:

Linguistics occupies a special place among the social sciences, to whose ranks it unquestionably belongs. It is not merely a social science like the others, but, rather, the one in which by far the greatest progress has been made. It is probably the only one which can truly claim to be a science and which has achieved both the formulation of an empirical method and an understanding of the nature of the data submitted to its analysis (1963a: 31).

He speaks of its 'privileged position' and of psychologists, sociologists and anthropologists 'eager to learn from modern linguistics the road which leads to empirical knowledge of social phenomena' (ibid.). The praise of linguistics is, at least in part, a conventional praise of one's host in a new journal, and a certain disarming of criticism of trespass. Nevertheless, 1945 was early days indeed for a vision that is hardly fully accepted by the majority of functionalist social anthropologists after a quarter of a century. One might, of course, say 'old days indeed', for Lévi-Strauss refers to an article of Mauss (1924) for the statement: 'sociology would certainly have progressed much further if it had everywhere followed the lead of the linguists . . .' (in Mauss, 1950, 1966 edn: 299). Lévi-Strauss believed that the position had changed in degree: linguists and social anthropologists had kept an eye on one another, but if the latter had not followed the linguistic example as far as they might, 'after all anthropology and sociology were looking to linguistics only for insights; nothing foretold a revelation' (1963a: 33).

What was this revelation, in 1945? He says: 'the advent of structural linguistics completely changed this situation' and goes on to the apocalyptic:

Structural linguistics will certainly play the same renovating role with respect to the social sciences that nuclear physics, for example, has played for the physical sciences (ibid.).

A statement published in the month of the explosion of the Hiroshima and Nagasaki atomic bombs would reach an audience that would not under-estimate the contribution of nuclear physics: nuclear physics was not then old hat. The revelation referred, in fact, to Prague School linguistics (then emigrated to the United States) to which Lévi-Strauss had been introduced by Roman Jakobson. The statement is curious, and shares the quality of so many programmatic utterances by men of genius – so apparently inade-quate and undocumented at the time; and yet brought eventually to a kind of realization.[22]

The generation after Saussure had led to a new phase of consolidation of linguistic theory (broadly in the period 1920–50), during which many of the developments loosely describable as 'structural linguistics' of different schools came into existence. This period is marked by the achievement for Saussure's synchronic linguistics of a *method* which offered the same rigour as that of 'comparative philology' (Trubetzkoy 1933: 242–3). The method and the period are marked by the discussion of the so-called *phoneme*, an essentially common-sense idea which awoke a great deal of discussion while enabling a mass of detailed linguistic work to be produced. It was broadly contemporary with the high Malinowskian period in social anthropology, and it showed much of the same productive endeavour. It was, however, basically the least 'anthropological' of the linguistic movements. Looked at from the Saussurean view (which had a message for diachronic as well as synchronic linguists, and for the study of all signs, not merely of linguistic signs), it was an inward movement.

The structuralists concentrated most characteristically on one of the essential elements: synchronic linguistics (cf. Wells, R. S. 1947). The phoneme was at home only in the detailed data of linguistic description. To see the early Lévi-Strauss and even Pike (who was a linguist and an anthropologist) struggling with it – Laocoön-like figures coiled up in ser-pents – to apply it to social phenomena is quite astonishing. The relation of the phoneme to Saussurean principles is like that of the roller-skate to the concept of the wheel – a particular and specialized application. To those ignorant of the wheel the roller-skate may appear to be a beautiful object, as no doubt it is. We should look very foolish if we built a carriage in the form of a roller-skate. To some extent this is what our anthropologists have been up to, even demonstrating it with simple pride to linguists. In short, it was the Saussureanism of the phoneme that was transferable – not the terminology. By its 'Saussureanism' I mean its relationship to the opposi-tion *langue/parole*, and to the notions of 'system', 'opposition' itself, 'value' and the like.

The common-sense aspect of the matter is best approached by our most characteristically British contribution to linguistics: the almost single-handed development of the study of phonetics during the lifetime of Henry Sweet (1845–1912). Phonetics could be very simply defined for a long time as the study of the *acoustic features of speech and modes of their accurate transcrip-tion*. The rub lies in the second part. For, to some extent, the study of phonetics derives from an interest in the discrepancy between the spoken and written forms of language, and the assumption originally was that acoustic features = 'sounds' = letters in an alphabet. It is no coincidence that phonetics in this country developed when it did. The situation with English in England exemplified, and still exemplifies, some of the best stimuli for such a study: (a) a discrepancy between the orthography of the written language and its received pronunciation; (b) a discrepancy between the received pronunciation in its turn and the dialects of English; (c) a discrepancy between the social statuses of different forms of speech, including received pronunciation and the dialects. British phonetics, so often scorned as old-fashioned by American linguists (Gleason 1955a), was a true exercise in socio-linguistics. Henry Sweet was dramatized as Professor Higgins by Bernard Shaw in *Pygmalion* (and set to music in *My Fair Lady*), and Higgins's problem is essentially that of Bernstein (1958, 1960, 1961, 1965): one of social engineering.[23]

By the 1880s there was also a strong international interest in phonetics. In 1886 the International Phonetic Association (IPA) was born (at first under the name of the Phonetic Teachers' Association) with the early and admitted aim of producing a phonetic alphabet capable of writing any 'sound' in any language, an aim that turned out to be, in its narrowest sense, either impossible or misguided (IPA, 1949; Firth, J. R. 1957a: 92–120). Nevertheless this search for a complete alphabet of sounds led the phoneticians by a meticulous and highly empirical route to the same conclusions as Saussure. They started off by thinking that there was only a difference between 'writing' or 'spelling' and the sounds of speech, and that if more 'sounds' could be written orthography would be more correct. In fact they discovered, when they precisely analysed 'sounds', that speakers acted linguistically as if only a certain number of sounds existed. The rest they classed together with these few. Each language classed them differently. Here, then, came the first perception of linguistics working at the level of *parole* that the *langue* structure extended into the 'phonetic' sphere. Thus the category we may mark /r/ in Japanese has an acoustic spread that covers a particular 'band'. This overlaps with the conventional /r/ of English (just as the terms for colours in the two languages overlap in their subdivisions of the visual spectrum), but part of the realization of /r/ in Japanese also overlaps with the realization of /l/ in English. All that remained was to give a name to the 'conventional sounds' of a language to distinguish them from the 'real sounds': discovered by the phoneticians. Sweet was quick off the mark. The 'real sounds' were recorded in 'narrow' transcription and the conventional ones that speakers recognized were those recorded in 'broad' transcription (Jakobson, 1966). Had the matter remained there we should have realized sooner that the supposed 'real' sounds were as much an abstraction as were the conventional ones.

But the term needed was supplied as we know: the 'native phonological categories', the conventional sounds that the speakers recognized, came to be called *phonemes*. In the terminology that was later accepted, speech sounds were called *phones*. The acoustic phones, which a language's speakers called 'the same', were called *allophones* of the *phoneme*. The basic term itself was later the subject of dispute. It was claimed as having been invented, or first used, or first 'properly' used, by numerous schools. Most workers in general linguistics in the period from 1870 to 1912 had, however, come to see the need for the distinction between the 'significant' sounds and the 'insignificant' sounds used in speaking a language. Trubetzkoy (1933: 227) attributes the basic distinction to J. Winteler in 1876. As for the term: it was used at least as early as 1876 in France (*phonème*) by Havet, although only in the meaning of 'speech-sound' (that is, just what, in modern usage, it is not). The first person to use it in print in the sense it has today (as *fonema*) was Kruszewski, a student of the University of Kazan in 1879, who derived the idea from the Russo-Polish linguist Baudouin de Courtenay who had been working on it since 1868. Sweet never used the term, but by 1915 de Courtenay's term was in use with the students of Sweet in London (Jones, D. 1964: 4). Sapir, the American linguist, did not use it consistently until the 1930s. It fully entered American usage with Bloomfields's book *Language* (1933). On the continent, Trubetzkoy, Karcevskij and Jakobson received the phoneme concept from Baudouin de Courtenay, although none, as it happens, was his pupil (Trubetzkoy 1933: 229).

The story of the phoneme is thus two separate stories: the story of an idea and the story of a term. The term for some time overwhelmed the idea. Broadly, two main approaches developed.

1   The Bloomfieldian or American view. According to this: the phoneme could be abstracted from a language by a careful methodology, if you had enough actual utterances, by merely noting which sounds actually distinguished one meaningful unit from another. There were numerous 'discovery procedures' purporting to achieve this. They were so apparently good that bigger and better units were attempted. After *phonemes* came *morphemes*, and so on to a large number of other *emes*. Structural linguistics of the post–Bloomfieldian school had become a pseudo-observational science. Suffice it to say, as I said earlier, that there could hardly be a term more firmly tied to linguistic data than the post-Bloomfieldian phoneme.

2   The Prague version developed the theme differently. Its adherents attempted to go to more universal principles through which the phonemes themselves were to be constructed. They did this by developing the concept of oppositions at the phonological level: the so-called 'distinctive features'. Trubetzkoy (1933: 227) saw that Saussure's theory remained incomplete until phonology made this advance, and that the 'phoneme' linked Saussure's (and de Courtenay's) programme to the facts. He nevertheless remained clear that the definition of a phoneme was its *place* in a system. With this we find the phonemic idea breaking into Saussurean generality again. After all, the 'value' of a phoneme derived from its position in a phonological system (as Hjelmslev always saw). The universals that lay behind the phonemes were the universal rules of opposition: those rules whereby the 'values' of single elements in systems of elements are determined.

The 'distinctive features' of Trubetzkoy and Jakobson were of an acoustic or articulatory type (*'tense/lax'*, *'grave/acute'*, and the like). The binary mode of distinction and its notation could be applied to the precise determination of the values of elements in other systems – not only those of language. To perceive this was, as I have said, laboriously to re-create the generality from which the Prague phoneme derived its distinctive features. It was Prague's and especially Jakobson's phonemes that stimulated Lévi-Strauss (for a later statement: Jakobson and Halle 1956; for the stimulation: Simonis 1968: 163–6).

Linguists spent a long time looking at phonemes, and there was much controversy as to whether they were 'real'. They had reached the stage the comparativists had reached in the nineteenth century. Their phonemic reconstructions were as rigorous (and often as outlandish to the eye) as those of comparative philology, but their principles and problems were alike (Ardener 1971c). Since Bloomfieldians had supposedly 'objective' ways of discovering phonemes, they usually thought that they were there ('God's Truth'). The counter-view was that they were in the mind ('Hocus Pocus'). These were Householder's terms (1952). The confusion between model and reality represented by this debate is now obvious. Essentially, phonemes were formulaic statements for the abstraction of significant units of speech. The analyst simplified the initial 'phonetic' data by using fewer terms but at the expense of requiring a book of rules to interpret them. We may put it: *emic* + rules > the *etic*; or, at a different level: model + reality conventions > the corpus of data. The English phoneticians must be admired for their refusal to become mixed up with the metaphysics of the phoneme (Jones, D. 1962; 1964: 15). In the imagery of formal systems: their theory was restricted to the generation of 'adequate' systems of transcription.

It is an irony perhaps that the phoneme debate accounts in part for some of the revulsion of post-war British social anthropologists from linguistics. To many of them it seemed alien, and fraught with transcription symbols. Somewhat similarly did the kinship debates of social anthropology strike members of other disciplines. In 1945, then, Lévi-Strauss's act of will was remarkable: the wedding of the phoneme to kinship. The paper in *Word* shows the process of his thought as he tried to map a Prague School view of system upon kinship. His well-known *élément* or 'atom' of kinship (1963a: 48) was the result. The symbols (+) and (−) derive by direct analogy from the marking of 'presence' or 'absence' of distinctive features by which Prague School phonemes were analysed. To appreciate the unexpectedness of the endeavour, we should place ourselves in the United States at the date. Linguistics was still in the full post-Bloomfieldian phase, now highly empirical and 'behaviourist'. For another ten or fifteen years, the introductory literature will still be full of references to 'discovery procedures' and the like (Gleason 1955a and b; Hockett 1958). When Zellig Harris *will* write his *Methods in Structural Linguistics* (1951, preface signed in 1947), the high-water mark of these trends, Noam Chomsky will merely be acknowledged as having given 'much-needed assistance with the manuscript'. We are three years before the publication of the crucial papers in communication theory (Shannon 1948; Shannon and Weaver 1949) which gave the later Jakobsonian linguistics its special form.

Lévi-Strauss was not even looking to American anthropological linguistics, which was also essentially Bloomfieldian, although the influence of Sapir was strong. Voegelin and Harris (1945) referred to Lévi-Strauss's article in their contemporary paper 'Linguistics in Ethnology', but its approach was totally different. Although unexceptionable ('talk and non-vocal behaviour together constitute an ethnolinguistic situation', p. 457), the spirit was resolutely pragmatic. Their later paper (1947 – 'the data of linguistic and cultural anthropology are largely the same', p. 588) is similar in drift. The immigrant Prague School structuralism, like European linguistics as a whole, was certainly not then over-valued by Americans (Householder 1957: 156, notes that 'European' was equivalent to 'pre-scientific'). All this was changing, and extremely rapidly, but Lévi-Strauss's declaration for Prague was not along the grain of the relationship between the fieldwork-oriented anthropology and the descriptive linguistics of the day. No wonder he had difficulty in expressing the exact nature of the revelation. He quotes Trubetzkoy's view of the aims of structural linguistics ('discovering general laws either by induction "or ... by logical deduction, which would give them an absolute character"'), and of its demonstration of the concept of system. Lévi-Strauss shows no sign of being really at home with the Prague concepts. He says: 'Thus for the first time, a social science is able to formulate necessary relationships. This is the meaning of Trubetzkoy's last point.' All this is very jejunely expressed in view of the previous statements about nuclear physics – and in the light of what follows:

But when an event of this importance takes place in one of the sciences of man, it is not only permissible for, but required of, representatives of related disciplines immediately to examine its consequences and its possible application to phenomena of another order (1963a: 33–4).

The direct application, when it comes, illustrates Lévi-Strauss's major problem: what he wanted from Prague was the notion of 'opposition', which he intuitively grasped to be of great importance. Unfortunately, the principle was obscured by its expression in the garb of the phoneme. As we have seen, it was an operational concept in linguistics: one that made it possible to link Saussure's *langue* and *parole* – the principle of the wheel realized in the specialized roller-skate. The idea of the (+ −) notation was the technical contribution deriving from Lévi-Strauss's 1945 contacts with Prague linguistics. It is, however, interesting to note that in so far as his (+ −) analyses bore any relationship to the phoneme at all, his usage implied that the infrastructure of kinship relations (the source of oppositions equivalent to the acoustic and articulatory ones in Prague analysis) was largely affective in nature. This was in some ways rather unexpected, given the general views of the French school. Simonis (1968) shows that his concern then with the 'unconsciousness' of underlying systems owed much to Freud. Mauss had, however, long ago asked of psychology: 'Donnez-nous donc une théorie des rapports qui existent entre les divers compartiments de la mentalité...' (1950, 1966 edn: 305).

I have discussed the implications of this first paper of Lévi-Strauss's at some length, to show that the 'linguistic' nature of it was ambiguous. The difference between my treatment of the paper and that of Simonis (1968: 12–32) is obvious. *Later*, Lévi-Strauss did express himself more clearly on the subject, but in relation to a rather different linguistics. Simonis reads back the essential Lévi-Strauss into the first paper, justifiably in one sense, for it is truly Lévi-Strauss and not linguistics that speaks there. But as Simonis himself admits, 'Certes, les détails manquent' (p. 19), and his own excellent 'Annexe' on 'Le modèle linguistique' has to be placed much later in his book (pp. 159–68). He shows us that the answer to the implied question, 'why did Lévi-Strauss see social anthropology and linguistics as related in that way, so early?' is that Lévi-Strauss was already thinking in that way. The publication of *Les Structures élémentaires* in 1949 showed more clearly his assimilation of the notion of a structure as a formal system. This, however, derived from Mauss as much as from linguistics.

By 1951 the scene had changed: in that year Lévi-Strauss published 'Language and the Analysis of Social Laws' in the *American Anthropologist* (53 (2): 155–63; 1958 and 1963a, chapter 3). In the interval the communication theorists had come into notice, and this time the phrase: 'a recent work, whose importance from the point of view of the future of the social sciences can hardly be overestimated' turns out to refer to Wiener's *Cybernetics* (1948). The paper is a similar exercise to the first: the working-out through a welter of suggested analogies of some way of applying a stimulating idea. One of Wiener's points was that social studies, being made by beings on the same scale as the phenomena studied, could not be treated usefully by the methods of natural science. This is related to the 'Maxwell's Demon' question: whether a being of the size of a molecule might be able to reverse entropy (Maxwell 1871, 1872 edn: 308–9; Wiener 1948: 57–8). Lévi-Strauss suggests, on the contrary, that the facts of language are distantiated from the observer. It 'lives and develops as a collective construct' (1963a: 57). Further, the 'long runs' that Wiener thought inaccessible to social studies were available to students of the historical linguistic families (Indo-European and the like):

We thus find in language a social phenomenon that manifests both independence of the observer and long statistical runs, which would seem to indicate that language is a phenomenon fully qualified to satisfy the demands of mathematicians ... (ibid.).

For similar cases in anthropology, Lévi-Strauss cites Kroeber's work on fashion and his own on the interpretation of kinship systems through the circulation of women. It is here that he achieves the essential insight of the paper: that Maussian systems of exchange and reciprocity are analogous to systems of communication, of which language is also one. The subsequent importance of this insight for social anthropology has obscured the fact that, in the original paper, it is overwhelmed by a premature and mis-guided attempt to correlate kinship structures with structural features of the languages of families established by comparative philologists. He takes the Indo-European and Sino-Tibetan families, as well as 'African', 'Oceanic' (both unattested) and 'American Indian'. At this grand level the attempt collapses. Possibly he was influenced by unacknowledged echoes of Saussure, whose tentative correlations between language families and social and psychological factors are more soundly documented (*Cours* 1922: 304–17; trans. 1964: 222–31). Lévi-Strauss's reading of Wiener at this time is the source of his distinction between 'mechanical' and 'statistical' models, one that has not always been clearly understood by social anthropologists (see Ardener, E. 1971c: 233). This rather uncertain paper was criticized, although not always perceptively, by Moore and Olmsted (1952).

In 1952 he presented, at a Conference of Anthropologists and Linguists at Bloomington, Indiana, a paper entitled 'Linguistics and Anthropology' which was first published in 1953 (appearing later as chapter 4 of Lévi-Strauss 1958 and 1963a). By now the communication engineers had fully made their mark and this stirred him to say, about the relationship of anthropologists to linguists:

For many years they have been working very closely with the linguists, and all of a sudden the linguists are playing their former companions this very nasty trick of doing things as well and with the same rigorous approach [as] was long believed to be the privilege of the exact and natural sciences. Then on the side of the anthropologist there is some, let us say, melancholy, and a great deal of envy (1963a: 69).

Once more, then, a revelation. In 1945 it was the Prague phoneme, in 1951 it was Wiener, in 1952 communication theory proper. Like the conductor of a circus orchestra, signalling loud chords for the acrobat to appear, he may well be relieved when on the third crash the acrobat actually does so.

Now what connexions are possible with linguistics? I cannot see any whatsoever, except only one, that when the anthropologist is working in this way he is working more or less in a way parallel to that of the linguist. They are both trying to build a structure with constituent units. But, nevertheless, no conclusions can be drawn from the repetition of the signs in the field of behaviour and the repetition, let us say, of the phonemes of the language, or the grammatical structure of the language; nothing of the kind – it is perfectly hopeless (1963a: 73).

This rather surprising recantation of the 1945 and 1951 papers occurs on the very eve of Lévi-Strauss's achievement of a homology between social anthropology and language. The views expressed in the body of this paper are indeed already clearer. He sets out his three levels of relationsip between anthropology and linguistics, which (although they have been departed from here) contain useful insights. He looks ahead to *La Pensée Sauvage* when he refers to 'this uninvited guest which has been seated during this Conference beside us and which is the human mind' (ibid.: 71).

Finally, in *Anthropologie structurale* (1958), in which Lévi-Strauss reprinted the 1945, 1951 and 1952 papers, he inserted a 'Postcript' (1958 and 1963a, chapter 5) which presents at length analogies with Jakobsonian linguistics in anthropological terms. In particular, the publication of Jakobson and Halle (1956), in which the implications of communication concepts ('code', 'message') had been assimilated into the Prague system, now shows its influence. Lévi-Strauss, through Benvéniste's discussion of the linguistic sign (1939), also returns to broad Saussurean principles. The Prague-type method is now used to distinguish ideological oppositions, not affective or kin-based ones. His approach to symbolism as pervading all domains (foreshadowed in his introduction to Mauss, 1950) leads to his remarkable citation of Marx ('who cannot be suspected of idealism') on the symbolism of gold and silver. After this the elements for the structural study of myth and symbolism are all present, to be fully developed in *La Pensée Sauvage* (1962b) and afterwards. The return to Saussure was finally expressed in its most unequivocal form in the *Leçon inaugurale*:

What then is social anthropology? No one it seems to me was closer to defining it – if only by virtually disregarding its existence – than Ferdinand de Saussure, when, introducing linguistics as part of a science yet to be born, he reserved for this science the name *semiology* and attributed to it as its object of study the life of signs at the heart of social life . . . I conceive, then, of anthropology as the bona fide occupant of that domain of semiology which linguistics has not already claimed for its own . . .' (trans. 1967a: 16–17).

Evans-Pritchard and Malinowski We had had by 1958 a mental Odyssey, thirteen years of Lévi-Strauss reflecting upon linguistics. The ideas are those of the great Saussurean development, inspired with Durkheims's *sociologie*, passed through Baudouin de Courtenay's phoneme, rendered linguistic flesh by the Prague School and post-Bloomfieldian structuralists, scientized by the communication engineers, perceived intuitively by Lévi-Strauss, and reunited with Durkheim through Mauss. In this extraordinary personal achievement, linguistics, as a discipline, became, as his frequent admiring statements express, an ideal type. He was nevertheless the only social anthropologist equipped to perceive intuitively the analytical and explanatory, rather than the pragmatic, implications of linguistics in the period 1945–55. The American anthropological linguists failed to do this, perhaps because of their empiricist, even behaviourist, preoccupations. In 1948 Greenberg was brilliantly aware of the significance of semiotics from the work of Morris (1946). Goodenough too (1957) reacted against the Bloomfieldian structural linguistics, through Morris. Yet both wrote of sign 'behaviour'. So, too, Pike's comprehensive approach (1954, 1955, 1960 – see also 1956) to the notion of *emic* and *etic* was a theory of 'behaviour'. And so, as Casagrande says:

It is a paradox that the anthropological approach most closely approximating the methods of present-day structural linguistics, that of French-British social anthropology, was developed abroad rather than in the United States, where linguistics and anthropology have had such close relations over the years (1963: 294–5).

The French part of this paradox we have considered. He rightly adds: 'It is further remarkable that, except for Malinowski, British social anthropologists have shown so little interest in linguistics' (ibid.).

It may be appropriate here to pay more attention to this latter question, which has been alluded to earlier. For its answer we must look towards a British social anthropologist who, without being a linguist, did encourage a fruitful interest in language at all levels, and in those subjects and writers now of great interest to both social anthropology and linguistics: that is E. E. Evans-Pritchard. It is true that many of his writings have had an explicit linguistic basis (e.g. 1934, 1948, 1954b, 1956b, 1961b, 1962c, 1963b, together with the large number of Zande texts: 1954a, 1955, 1956a, 1957, 1962a, 1962b, 1963a, 1963c and others). This is not, however, so much the point. His social anthropology has itself tended to be informed with an approach that was consonant with that of the continental schools of linguistics. His famous phrase about 'relations between relations' independently echoes Hjelmslev. His notion of 'opposition', as originally developed in *The Nuer* (1940), was Saussurean in type. No doubt his readings in French sociology prepared him for this realization (cf. Evans-Pritchard 1962d: 61). Nothing could be further from the later euhemerization of the idea as 'conflict' in the works of Gluckman. Pocock (1961: 78) cites Adam Ferguson as an intellectual ancestor, who wrote, for example: 'The titles of *fellow citizen* and *countryman* unopposed to those of *alien* and *foreigner*, to which they refer, would fall into disuse, and lose their meaning' (Ferguson, A. 1767: 31). In the Oxford period we may also note the influence of Dumont upon his department.

With Evans-Pritchard's encouragement, several of his pupils and colleagues continuously engaged themselves in translations of mounting and daunting complexity from the French sociological school (Pocock: Durkheim 1951; Cunnison: Mauss 1954; Needham (with Needham, C.): Hertz 1960; Needham: Durkheim and Mauss 1963; Needham: Lévi-Strauss 1963b; Needham (with Bell and von Sturmer): Lévi-Strauss 1969). This technical linguistic task was accompanied by the important exegesis and creative interpretation of the works themselves that characterized Oxford-trained social anthropologists. In addition, original works of the first importance reflected aspects of this tradition, for example: Lienhardt 1961; Needham 1962; and Douglas 1966a. Evans-Pritchard's interest in orally derived texts found further expression in the volumes edited by himself, Lienhardt and Whiteley (1964: series), an interest which was also exemplified by Finnegan (1969a, 1970) and other recent students. For further concern with themes of linguistic relevance from the same milieu, one may cite Beattie (1957, 1960, 1964b), Needham (1954, 1960a), Beidelman (1964), Ardener, E. (1968), Beck (1969), to name a selective but representative range. Finally, in his own department Evans-Pritchard encouraged his colleagues to teach in the field of social anthropology and language.

It was Evans-Pritchard, then, rather than Malinowski, who provided the secure pedagogical conditions for a serious if belated participation of British social anthropology in the problems of language – a participation that by-passes the Malinowskian tradition. Only Leach among Malinowski's students followed a similar path, and still maintains an innovating position, with contributions bearing on the linguistic field (1957, 1958, 1964, 1970; see also Tambiah 1968 and Humphrey 1971, in the new Cambridge tradition). Pocock perceptively said as long ago as 1961 that Evans-Pritchard's work effected for British social anthropology 'a shift from function to meaning' (p. 72), and added: 'there is some indication that the full implications of this movement . . . were not drawn by all social anthropologists in the post-war period' (p. 77).

In one respect Pocock was perhaps over-optimistic in his appraisal:

[Evans-Pritchard's] refusal to make explicit the shift in emphasis had certain tactical advantages. No storm blew up which might have obscured the presentation under a cloud of dust, a sense of continuity was preserved and many younger anthropologists were able to see the deeper relevance of language to their studies (p. 79).

It may well be that it had strategic disadvantages: a reviewer (Blacking 1963) wrote of Pocock's book:

It is too easily within the reach of young and enthusiastic minds in search of new information about the human condition; and as such it can do irreparable harm . . . the book is very narrow and parochial . . . it does a grave disservice to Social Anthropology (pp. 194–5).

The same reviewer believed that Malinowski's *Coral Gardens* 'implicitly' achieved the shift from function to meaning. This was, of course, the point: it might have done, even should have done, but did not – and there were thirty years of tedium in the homes of orthodox functionalism to prove it. It may be noted that Evans-Pritchard never practised that brutal suppression of contrary opinion that biographers, with surprising tolerance, cite so often of Malinowski (Firth, R. 1957: 1; Kardiner and Preble, 1961: 167–8). Malinowski's position as the great linguistic anthropologist of the functionalist school is touched on further below. The slightly less favourable view than usual that I express may easily be balanced without seeking far in the literature. I have, however, come reluctantly to the conviction that it was exactly because of Malinowski's personal influence on social anthropology that the functionalist interest in language withered, together with much else, in the climate of rather provincial anti-intellectualism that fell like a drought upon his empire at his death.[24]

Malinowski's role in introducing language to social anthropology was ambiguous and disappointing, as we have indicated, as far as his own subject was concerned.[25] Professor Robins (1971) discusses the present status of the concern with 'context of situation' which the London School of Linguistics has shared with him. From being largely neglected by transatlantic theorists, this able group of scholars has recently been the subject of 'positive vetting' by transformationalist emissaries (Langendoen 1968). To a social anthropologist, however, it sometimes appears that our linguistic colleagues (Berry 1966, is an exception) are very generous in apportioning the credit for their present renown, the major part of which must surely go to J. R. Firth, who trained linguistic successors who looked for long in vain for any sign of interest among their anthropological coevals. With the exception of Whiteley, no post-war social anthropologist for many years was trained in this tradition. Such persons were usually referred to by Malinowski's successors as having 'gone over to linguistics'. J. R. Firth's (1957b) excellent account of Malinowski's views (in R. Firth, 1957 and Palmer, 1968) is a tribute more often to the insight of the author than to that of his human subject. Many social anthropologists remember clearly ideas of Firth's in his lectures which are now in current fashion. For example, his account of the 'myth' of 'the lion' in Luganda compared with that of the English ('the lion-house', 'Red Lion', 'lions in Trafalgar Square', 'social lion'). His long interest in possible phonological correlates of meaning (in Firth, J. R. 1957a: 43–5, 192–3) became respectable with Jakobson and Halle (1956), Jakobson (1960) and other writings. Although he, and also Ullmann (1963: 226), cited the countervailing examples, certain distinctive features ('lax'/'tense', 'grave'/'acute' and the like) clearly have correlates with other sensory patterns (e.g. Firth's classic *oombooloo* and *kikiriki* drawings – rotund and spiky respectively, see now Leach 1971a). Firth says:

I know from personal association with Malinowski that those parts of de Saussure's general linguistic theory which led [in the direction of French sociology] he found not only unattractive but of little practical value in the study of meaning, which was his principal interest (p. 95).

Firth sees Malinowski as fulfilling certain views of Sweet's, who said: 'Our aim ought to be, while assimilating the methods and results of German work, to concentrate our energies mainly on what may be called "living philology"' (Firth, J. R. 1957b: 100). It is significant that J. R. Firth himself refers to the Bloomington Conference of 1952 and remarks that it did not 'face the problems stated by Lévi-Strauss' (ibid.: 116, referring to Lévi-Strauss's paper there: see Lévi-Strauss 1963a, chapter 4). The move back from phonemics to meaning, which was asked for by the Conference, was squarely in line with Firth's interests. Malinowski's concern with 'meaning' was, of course, his great contribution at a time when only the German school of linguists was still actively concerned with the subject (it is unlikely, however, that the work of Trier and von Wartburg would have appealed to him).

As Leach points out (1957: 130, 1958), Malinowski totally rejected any attempt to relate terminological labels to systems of categories, and some of his denials border upon the absurd. Malinowski thought he was defending the Trobrianders from imputations of 'pre-logical' inferiority, a magnanimous error, rooted however in his own ethnocentric assumption that Western 'reasonableness' provided the only possible 'rationality'. Malinowski believed in 'homonyms', established by accidental coincidences. The historical falling together of 'different' words in the documented languages may well have been in his mind. He would not have understood, however, as von Wartburg did, the way in which homonyms produced by phonemic change may *fail* to survive when they cross an important category boundary (cf. above, *femur* 'thigh', *fimus* 'faeces' → **femor-*). Malinowski's extreme statements are, of course, a useful reminder against equally extreme views of 'category'. His view of context, properly argued, would even provide a structural basis for certain sub-category boundaries within 'homonymous' categories. This is best achieved by a Saussurean view of 'value' and 'system'. Thus the systematic 'values' of Trobriand *tabu* 'grandmother', *tabu* 'grandfather', *tabu* 'father's sister' and the like (Malinowski 1935, II: 28, 113) *might* be argued to differ from each other because of the disparate linguistic and non-linguistic elements present in the 'context of use', in each case. But, of course, we cannot prejudge the nature of any such contexts simply on the basis of these prior English glosses chosen by Malinowski. He was not really a kind of componential analyst (Lounsbury 1965). Leach's re-analysis of the *tabu* term (1958) is in fact ethnographic 'context of situation' raised to professional levels. The term is shown to refer to a category of marginal relationships, and one that is not exhausted by the 'homonyms' Malinowski himself cites (Leach 1958: 121, 144). Lounsbury (1969: 18) has asserted that Leach's analysis is one of extreme relativism. I have touched upon this earlier (p. 10). In fact the underlying 'universal' is transferred from an ethnocentric notion of kinship to a category of 'marginality' or 'liminality' inherent in the relations of human beings to each other, here mapped upon a set of genealogical references.

Hocart (1937, Needham (ed.) 1970: 173–84) effectively demolished Malinowski's approach in his own time. The recent demonstration that Trobriand *tabu*, 'taboo', falls into a different etymological set, by the rules of proto-Austronesian, from the *tabu* kin term (Chowning 1970) does not restore Malinowski's own argument. It does, of course, raise the largely ignored question of the diachronic aspect of cognitive categories. Furthermore, as far as the contemporary valuation of the Trobriand term *tabu* is concerned, the problem presented by the confrontation of 'neogrammarian' etymologies with the folk-etymologizing propensity (Ardener, E. 1971c) is brought into focus. In oral cultures there are no privileged historical etymologies. When Hocart asks, 'how can we make any progress in the understanding of cultures, ancient or modern, if we persist in dividing what the people join and in joining what they keep apart?' (1970: 23), we must apply this principle equally to the effects of phonetic change – provided such changes are in fact assimilated, for (as we have seen) they are capable of being by-passed if they prove to be semantically unacceptable to 'the people'.

If we are to accept such a view, however, we should not forget its corollary that a people's own linguistic glosses provide a significant mode of analysing a lexical category. What the people keep apart we should also not join. For example: the 'risible' features of the 'strange' must once have been evident enough to make the ambiguity of English *funny* of no folk interest in one period of colloquial English. It was then a unit category. The social conscience of the middle classes later created the (now whimsically old-fashioned?) division 'funny-peculiar/funny-haha', thus creating a conscious semantic taxonomy (how shall we unravel the recent 'not queer-*queer*, but queer-funny'?). A careful study of socio-linguistic categories must take into account popular semantic and etymological exegesis. This would be a true 'ethno-linguistics' (that is, a linguistics produced by 'the people', parallel in formation with 'ethno-medicine') – or even an 'ethno-metalinguistics'.

At his best Malinowski did perhaps strive after something like this. In general, however, he bequeathed, on the one hand, a behaviouristic view of context (which even the well-disposed Firthian linguists had to shrug off) combined, on the other, with an intellectually ethnocentric mode of analysis. In so far as Malinowski contributed to the vitality of the London School of Linguistics, whose creativity is undiminished, he must be accorded full recognition for it. On pedagogic grounds I have already suggested that his contribution (in contrast with that of J. R. Firth) may nowadays be viewed with a more muted enthusiasm.[26] Langendoen (1968) separates the Malinowski of the early 1920s from the Malinowski of *Coral Gardens* (1935). Early Malinowski holds (for him) views such as: 'that social structure is a psychological and, hence, not a directly observable reality, and that behaviour can only be understood in terms of it'; and that: 'categories of universal grammar must underlie categories implicit in non-linguistic human behaviour' (pp. 35–6). This is to do much more than justice to a rather unreflective psychologism, and a school-book view of grammar. The picture of Malinowski as a proto-Chomskyan 'rationalist', whose later views were distorted by contact with J. R. Firth, would have its attractions were it not in contrast with all we know of Malinowski the 'empiricist' anthropologist.

'Structural' or 'transformational'?   *Anthropologie structurale* (1958) appeared a year after *Syntactic Structures* (1957) by Noam Chomsky, in total independence. In the next ten years the mature system of Lévi-Strauss, applied to the detailed material of myth, was directed towards the generation of models reflecting 'fundamental structures of the human mind'. Chomsky's linguistics set out to generate models (grammars) mapped upon human linguistic 'competence', which was likewise firmly seated in the human mind. Lévi-Strauss's corpus of data, 'myth', was all versions of the myth, including, it is implied, versions yet to be formulated (1963a: 216–17). Chomskyan grammars set out to generate all well-formed utterances in a language. Both systems used notations inspired by the mathematics of formal systems. Both advanced old problems by the application of the notion of 'transformation'. In this respect Lévi-Strauss's final message was, ironically enough in linguistic terms, not 'structural' but 'transformational': as if by seeking St Brendan's Isle he had truly discovered America.

There are considerable differences, of course. The two approaches are authentically of their own disciplines, but Lévi-Strauss is much less rigorous, as well as less lucid, in his expression than is Chomsky. The latter concludes from a reading of *La Pensée sauvage* only 'that the savage mind attempts to impose some organization on the physical world – that humans classify, if they perform any mental acts at all' (1968: 65). Chomsky is also, more justly, sceptical about Lévi-Strauss's Prague School model:

The significance of structuralist phonology, as developed by Trubetzkoy, Jakobson, and others, lies not in the formal properties of phonemic systems but in the fact that a fairly small number of features that can be specified in absolute, language-independent terms appear to provide the basis for the organization of all phonological systems . . . But if we abstract away from the specific universal set of features and the rule systems in which they function, little of any significance remains (ibid.).

Chomsky makes the telling point that linguistic structures are the 'epiphenomenon' of 'intricate systems of rules'. He speaks of 'systems of rules with infinite generative capacity' (ibid.: 66). Finally: 'if this is correct, then one cannot expect structuralist phonology, in itself, to provide a useful model for investigation of other cultural and social systems' (ibid.). Just so. Yet, as we have seen, the improbable was achieved by Lévi-Strauss – by intuition more than by logic. Chomsky's strong drive in favour of a distinction between human systems and non-human systems, and between language and other semiotics, makes him loth to open his system to the possibility of a general semiological anthropology. He would not support the hypothesis of a prior non-linguistic semiotic (cf. Chomsky 1968: 60 and 70–2) if it were to encroach on the privileged position of language. It may be the prejudice of an anthropologist, but it seems that in this, and in some other respects, Lévi-Strauss has more to say to humanity as a whole than has Chomsky. Their different modes of approach to contemporary problems are also instructive: the one providing what Simonis calls a model of the 'exteriorization of man', and, as I believe, a method of interpreting the inarticulate, even anti-articulate, movements of our time; the other more limited, even (behind the social criticism) less revolutionary. This would be natural, perhaps, for anthropology is still the study of man, while linguistics, even transformational generative grammar, is still the study of language.[27]

The Chomskyan movement as a historical phenomenon is of great anthropological interest. Intellectually, the inevitable and even praiseworthy arbitrariness of the first Chomskyan models has been succeeded by an accretion of partial models loosely articulated to the original; or at best, to cite the analogy so frequently used (Wiener 1948: viii; Leach 1961a: 26), 'epicycles' are added. The imperialism of the Chomskyan system, which once lay firmly within the domain of *langue* ('all well-formed utterances'), now takes its seat in the brain, and seems at times to wish to break right through the domain of *parole* itself, and to require the generation of the very acoustic wave-forms. This Faustian aim is beyond the competence of any single model; with the computer engineers, we should remember that ultimately the only effective store of the natural order is the natural order. The original notion of formal generativeness is submerged, as of too limited a range, and the originally rigorous terminology with its new philosophical outriders begins to take on the appearance of a set of procedures to distinguish the orthodox from the unorthodox. Lévi-Strauss throws light on this process: the Chomskyan movement as a whole is now beginning to work as a mythical system with its own (anthropological) transformational rules. In due course, no doubt, these will become explicitly recognized ('unpacked', as the philosophers say), the system as we know it will be 'exploded', and a new system will be set up by others by *bricolage* from the remains, starting another cycle with similar consequences. Thus it is not truly a criticism, and certainly not an exaggeration, to say that it contains mythical elements; this is the power of all great human systems: the models are, at least in part, *ex post facto* justifications. It is, however, an index of the richer quality of Lévi-Strauss's structuralism that it is able to become conscious of this very process. 'That is why,' he says, 'it would not be wrong to consider this book itself as a myth: it is the myth of mythology' (1964, trans. 1970: 12).[28]

The relationship between aspects of the transformationalist approach and the broadly 'structural' trends in social anthropology, both in their rigorous phases and in their creative expansion, is the more interesting since, as we have seen, the two movements are only very indirectly linked. There is no certainty that they will not turn in very different directions; they are in no way dependent upon each other. Hockett's critique of Chomsky (Hockett 1968) far outshines any critique in social anthropology directed against the newer movements, but the message is the same: the models are too rigid and are imposed on reality; the 'facts' are twisted to fit.[29] But, as we have seen, the nature of a model is to define out and to establish rules of relevance. All new models thus appear supremely open to such charges. As I have shown (Ardener, E. 1971c), the generativeness of the neogrammarian model was preserved by three rules, of which one was that of 'analogy'. The criticism made of this rule by the earlier comparativists was exactly that 'analogy' was a fact-twister, and Osthoff and Brugmann had to answer the charge of 'arbitrariness' as early as 1878. Their critics were of course trivially 'right', as Hockett is 'right', and as the functionalist and neo-functionalist charges in our own subject are also 'right'. No answer could be made to the critics save that the power of the new model finally developed was a guarantee of the status of the new protective rule. None now will doubt the productiveness of the approach. The shears that protect a model are not 'arbitrary' in the common-sense usage, but in a particular technical sense. It would have been no compensation to the nineteenth-century critics, had they lived, to learn that we agree with them.

Reflection on the situation of British post-functionalist 'neo-anthropology', however, shows how relatively weakly placed it is compared with the newer movements in linguistics. We must note the relatively small number of its practitioners, and their relative isolation. The voluminous work of Lévi-Strauss was, it seems, not enough to establish it on the one hand, nor was the detailed research of its native exemplifiers and developers on the other.[30] As late as 1970, most senior anthropological posts were filled by continuators of Malinowski. The latter nevertheless showed a sad lack of confidence in their own discipline.[31] Even while, one after another in the 1960s, practitioners of the older social anthropology declared the death of the subject, the new one already existed at both the programmatic and the empirical level. Of many a rider then lamenting the death of his horse, it could perhaps more justly be said: "'Twas not the horse that died.'

Inarticulate Rationalities[32]   The question of where structures are *located* is still raised by 'positivist' social anthropologists, as it was in the original oral discussion of this paper. It is the old 'God's Truth' or 'Hocus Pocus' argument raised about the phoneme (Householder 1952), as well as about componential analysis (Burling 1964) and the 'grammatical' rules of household composition (Burling 1969), all over again. Once more the question is not a real one, as we saw above. Semantic patterns are only one class of structural patterns. Human minds can use, as comparative experience shows, any evident structural regularity upon which to build the most unexpected and varied semiotics (e.g. left/right, male/female – Hertz 1960; Needham 1960b, 1967). The logical sums need not even be totally consistent. They form a kind of indexing device, and provide a stylistic which can even dress up irregular forms: like Stella Gibbons's *Cold Comfort Farm* pseudo-wisdom ('If sukebind do blow: we shall have snow'), in which the logical sum, if any, is vacuous. These are the imaginary games that have never been played (see Ardener, E. 1971c: 226), which defeat attempts to generate all the human order from single models. The *bricoleur* is always at work.

The relating of one semiotic to another in the manner of one model of a formal system to another, through transformations, provides that check upon interpretation which worries well-disposed social anthropologists of an empirical bent. It reminds us, and them also, that the empirical or observational system upon which they rested so happily in the past for verification is itself one set of linked models, consciously or unconsciously formulated. Tests of fit have been therefore the demonstration of connections between this 'base' set and all other models. The great development of the positivist set obscures this situation. Symbolic phenomena have not been 'correlatable' or 'calibratable' directly with 'behaviour' or the like, because 'behaviour' is already symbolic. There are always paradoxes and inconsistencies because, instead of distinctly separated 'observable' and 'symbolic' orders, there is a range of structures: some conscious, some unconscious. The analyst is attempting to bring more and more of them to awareness. He is hampered by the 'unaware' elements in his own procedures.

The Maxwell's Demon problem in social anthropology is less that of the scale of the observer (Wiener 1948: 57; Lévi-Strauss 1963a: 56) than that of the equivalence of his method of structuring the natural order with that of the actors he hopes to observe. They continually restructure his material;

they are living chessmen. The necessary recognition of this does not lead us into solipsism: the natural order is still 'there' even in society, as the continual source of unprogrammed events, which demand incorporation, or as providing certain basic structural givens. The social anthropologist, with the help of the linguist, may be just beginning to get the hang of handling some of this. For that reason the delineation of the symbolic and semiotic structures of society and culture is likely for some time to look more 'real' in human terms, and in the end is even likely to 'predict' more, than are the hundreds of social surveys daily undertaken. For social anthropology the challenge is that of the 'demonstration with blank banners' to which I have referred. It is the continuation of the work (begun by Durkheim, Mauss, Lévy-Bruhl and Evans-Pritchard) of eliciting the inarticulate as well as the articulate rationalities of human beings.

2

The New Anthropology and its Critics

Is there a 'new anthropology'? And if there is, is it sufficiently established or recognized that it can be truly said to have critics, rather than perhaps mere sceptical detractors? And how new is it? Let me say at once that my title is intended to convey that such original novelty as there may have been about it is largely over. I do not wish to argue here whether it was born in Paris, Oxford or Cambridge or somewhere else, ten years ago, twenty years ago, in this century or the last century; while philosophically it is, of course, as old as the hills. I mean by 'new' that something has already happened to British social anthropology (and to international anthropology in related ways) such that for practical purposes text-books which looked useful, no longer are; monographs which used to appear exhaustive now seem selective; interpretations which once looked full of insight now seem mechanical and lifeless. It is also new enough that these changes are understood (or misunderstood) by some in quite a different light: that monographs have given way to lightweight essays; where once was reason, unreason reigns; for verifiable postulates speculation is substituted; instead of 'reality' we have the cosmological order.

Social anthropologists do not much like ideological labels, but that is not why I do not wish to describe the division as between 'functionalists' and 'structuralists'. The old anthropology has its claim to be called 'functionalist', but the new anthropology is not necessarily accurately termed 'structuralist' unless that term is given an even wider connotation than it has already acquired – indeed I shall be suggesting that the old 'functionalism' is subsumed by it. Furthermore, since the idiosyncrasies of individuals count for so much in a small subject like ours, the situation has become confused by various declarations and rejections of theoretical allegiance.

The confusion derives from the extraordinary range of positions from which debate begins. First we have criticism of the newer positions from an orthodox Malinowskian viewpoint. Then there is a set of differences of view among the core of 'new anthropologists' themselves. This turns often on the nature of 'structuralism', and on whether they are structuralist or not. Then there are certain useful debates on rationality, and the like, which represent a kind of offshoot of the main debates – or a fight in a ditch between the lines. Then there are criticisms of the structuralist position by Marxists, cultural materialists and others, and of British structuralism by adherents of the purer Lévi-Straussian position. There are parallel debates within the American cultural anthropology, where Sturtevant (1964) has already referred to the establishment of 'a new ethnography' (although this development is narrower than the one I have in mind). Somewhere in the middle of it all comes a genuine split. It runs like a crack in an Arctic ice-floe separating colleague from colleague, department from department. Some on one side leap back to the other. Not all those who led the debate end up on the same side. There has occurred an epistemological break (a *coupure* as Althusser (1969) would have put it) of an important kind. So far, and in that sense, there are now a new and an old anthropology. There is a position, acquainted with neighbouring disciplines, which sees the new anthropological movements as part of a change of mind in science itself.

The new is not then a merely speculative and anomalous subdivision of the old. The field of social anthropology is totally restructured: the old field and the new field form different conceptual spaces. A rapproachement cannot therefore be made just by adding an extra course of lectures. Nor does the answer lie 'somewhere in the middle'. To compare our trivial concerns with greater: a course in Boyle's Law cannot be accommodated to a syllabus in phlogiston theory. The restructured field does not abolish previous empirical results – it generates them, plus some more. So if I refer to a new or 'neo-anthropology', the terms cannot represent a permanent situation. Their temporary use draws attention only to the fact that anthropology has 'rethought' itself willy nilly, leaving the subject at least as 'empirical' as it ever was, as well as much harder to do well (a point that its more thoughtless friends as well as its detractors might remember). As a result it is no longer possible to 'get on with fieldwork', using *ad hoc* 'concepts' in the subsequent analysis.

I can hardly deal with all of this in an hour. This lecture is in part a simplification and generalization of arguments advanced and documented in a recent publication (see above, chapter 1 and Ardener, E. 1971c), to which the reader is referred for the most important references. I shall present the position now as some have asked, by avoiding any merely fashionable terminology, and leaving out linguistics. I shall discuss three interrelated themes: 1) the empirical contradiction in social anthropology; 2) the confusion between paradigmatic and syntagmatic structures; and 3) the relationship of the neo-anthropological trends to problems in positivist social science.

There was a central contradiction in the theory of Malinowskian fieldwork, in so far as it was thought to be essentially 'observational' in nature. There was always a certain confusion between statements of frequency based on observation, and statements about frequency. Thus, before statistical measurement became common in the subject, Barnes (1949) drew our attention to the obscure empirical content of statements like 'divorce is frequent' in anthropological monographs. There was a sort of merging of 'observations' of a certain number of actual divorces, with assessments of frequency by supposedly well-informed subjects. It was a combination, as it were, of an unrandom sample of marriages with an unrandom opinion poll about the state of marriage. Sociologistic criticisms of anthropological method were well taken on this point.

But my criticism of the later stages of functionalism is not that it failed to be an accurate observational, probabilistic science, but that it stubbornly saw itself as empirical and observational when any strength it had lay in its failure to be so. The symptoms were soon obvious. Certain members of the Central African/Manchester school of anthropologists did set out to improve the observational methods of fieldwork. Barnes, Mitchell and others made it possible to apply advanced statistical methods where they had been previously regarded as impracticable. The result was unexpected: such studies were not much welcomed even by avowed empiricists. The more 'statistically rigorous' seemed to mean, in some way, the less 'anthropological'. We may not necessarily deny the soundness of this instinct. Let us be clear, however, that the works of many of those who charge the post-functionalist tendency with being 'metaphysical' or 'speculative' fail themselves to satisfy even those elementary criteria of evidence which are known to the humble marketer of soap-powders. Not for them the laborious unpeeling of layer upon layer of probabilities: rather the wide sweep of the brush and the unrepresentative statistic, the unspecified informant, and the underemphasized or unmentioned colonial background. If 'empiricist' stones are to be thrown, the old functionalist house, be it as imposing as the Crystal Palace, is made of glass just the same.

Most post-war anthropologists failed to come to grips with this problem at the heart of their subject – neither truly 'mentalist' nor 'behaviourist', neither consistently 'idealist' nor 'materialist'. We should be grateful, therefore, to those who made the effort to draw attention to the topic, and recognize how surprisingly hard it was to achieve a hearing without resort to a certain polemic tone and even to acts of symbolic violence, among which the detonation of Needham's *plastique*: *Structure and Sentiment* (1962) must remain the classic of our time. Let us recall that Saussure's criticism of Bopp and those linguists who preceded the unruly neogrammarians was very applicable to the later functionalists: 'this school, which had the indisputable merit of opening up a new and fertile field . . . never set itself to seek out the nature of its object of study' (1922: 16, my trans.). Of the neogrammarians themselves, Pedersen was able to afford the luxury of regretting, in the retrospect of calmer days, that they had felt it necessary to operate with such 'clamour and strife' (1962: 292).

Let us suppose, for sake of argument, that functionalist empiricism had been consistently aiming at the honourable task of close and accurate observation, through careful statistical investigation. We can nowadays appreciate the many genuine objections to any attempt to apprehend the nature of structure from close measurement. For example: having chosen some elementary observational problem such as the structure of the movements over time of a group of chairs and a certain table, we find that the micrometer readings at floor level turn up variations which offer puzzles of interpretation. A rather banal statement that 'this is a dining room' not only brings order into the variations, but renders the micro-measurements superfluous. Such a statement has the status of a *programme*. It is sufficient to account for the movement of individual chairs; it condenses the essential relationships within the most flexible limits of measurement. Indeed, as the first lecturer in this series pointed out (Leach 1961a), no relationships of quantity are necessary. In contrast, the refinements of micro-measurement lead the observer below the level of significant phenomena, to delicate precautions to account for the wobble of individual chair-legs, unevenness of floor, slipperiness of linoleum, or variations in woodgrain and so on. As if those were not problems enough, the measurer is always at the mercy of an arbitrary change in the programme, 'this is a dining room', which may be modified without his knowledge, in some such way as 'except on Thursday from seven until eleven when it is a dance hall'. Wherever human beings intervene we are in this scientifically undignified position. In the world of social formations we do not, as it were, even know where the chairs and tables are. In refining our statistical surveys a point comes when we realize this. We know that the definition of the categories that we use for our measures is the true problem (Ardener, E. 1962a: 68–9).

The interest of a preliminary approach through the analogy of the *programme* lies precisely in the field of prediction and verifiability/falsifiability. This is a great irony, for the only kind of prediction which has been accepted as 'scientific' in positivist social science has been the statistical statement of probability. Yet the statement 'this is a dining room' which is devoid of any mensurational component, is quite adequately 'predictive' of future movements of furniture at floor level. The predictivities are, however, of two different kinds. Thus micro-measurement may tell us that if chair-leg X touches point Y on the floor (where there is, say, a knot of wood) it will with a quantifiable probability move off at a certain angle for a certain number of millimetres, according to its previous velocity. Regularities of this sort are remarkably specific. In contrast the programme is predictive rather of *kinds* of movement, including some kinds that haven't happened yet, because (say) the Queen has not yet dined, or the haggis has not yet been piped. We might use a better terminology, and say that the programme is totally 'generative' as to kind of event, but it is not necessarily predictive as to when the events will occur. Furthermore, the programme itself is finite: it may be amended or rejected. As a result it may never, even will never, generate all the kinds of events for which it is the programme.

The image of the programme is also useful, since the very term embodies the empiricist contradiction. When a theoretician, say a philosopher, offers a programme it is essentially *uncalibrated* to events. Yet a computer programme is just the opposite, it is *precisely calibrated* to events. When the term *programmatic* is used of some of the writings of Saussure, of J. R. Firth, of

Hjelmslev, of Lévi-Strauss, the pejorative overtones suggest: 'unverifiable', 'untested', 'unapplied'. When *programmed* is used of computer output any pejorative implication would be expressed as 'strictly predictable', 'mechanistically derived'. A parallel difference in evaluation occurs in the uses of *redundancy* in the different senses of stylistics and communication theory. In stylistics, redundancy is superfluous and unmotivated, leading to an inefficiency, an inelegance in the utterance. In communication theory after Shannon (1948), redundancy is an essential, measurable element in the message, the elegance of which lies in its direct relation to the amount of noise on the channel which it has to overcome. The terms bear different values: they do so because they belong to two different systems. The computer programme and Shannonian redundancy are precise, because of the abstraction from natural events that they represent. Yet why should the imprecise literary equivalents be quite so unlike them: not merely different in degree but in kind?

The programmes for human events are self-transforming. They embody innumerable meta-levels. We may visualize a computer programme for a calculation in which there was an instruction to stop, rewrite all preceding x as y and then to proceed with the calculation as if all x had been y from the beginning. Or we might imagine a programme for an output of music in which an instruction occurred to transpose to another key, or start at the twentieth bar of a new composition. Let us go on to imagine that the tape does not clearly show us the code for the transposition instruction, and imagine further that the transpositions are many and various, and that we do not even possess that tape: merely the output. Are all these strings of figures part of one calculation? In the case of the musical output the question of whether the music was all 'the same' would be even less real. In terms of any one analysis the output would contain apparently unmotivated redundancies, the programme would not be properly calibrated to any single consistent model of events.

Should all the systems to which the different stretches of the output refer be separately stated? Or should some be regarded as false starts? Should only the final stretch of output be referred to a specific system? Do the transpositions themselves express a meta-system? And so on. Shannonian information theory once appeared to offer a model for a view of the output as essentially probabilistic. Given enough 'message', a copious enough output, the code might be determined. The Shannonian transition probabilities for English did actually derive from war-time code-breaking. Jakobson and Halle (1956), however, made an essential distinction between *cryptanalysis* and *decoding*. The cryptanalyst lacks the codebook. He is the outside observer. The decoder (here my possessor of the programme) does not function like a cryptanalyst. The codebook as restored or reconstructed from probabilistic examination of the output can never contain rules for kinds of chains which have not yet been generated.

To see why, let us return to our elementary discussion of predictivity. An empiricist may plausibly assert that the statement 'this is a dining room' can be looked at as probabilistic. It may be seen as summarizing probabilistic statements about the nature of the use of dining rooms, from which its predictivity derives: as if the statement is in effect a statistical assessment, a 'folk statistic'. It is here, in my view, that the basic change in approach derived from Lévi-Strauss, backed up by thought in neighbouring disciplines, becomes clear. If our observer were to deduce certain probabilities from his measurements of a sufficiently large corpus of furniture movements, he could, it is true, express them in a formula such as 'this is a dining room', in which the statement is now a term of art for these probabilities. It bears a 'family resemblance' to the statement in the programme of the informant, and in addition the statistical statement is 'testable' in terms of how accurately those probabilities continue to be realized. There are, however, important differences between the two statements. They derive from the critical importance of the mode of derivation itself. The native statement, as a programme for non-verbal events, has not been apprehended statistically. All the arguments of Chomsky (e.g. 1969: 63) about the apprehension of language apply with equal force to the acquisition of the programmatic structure of society. The 'native actor' has been presented with highly restricted data, 'a highly degenerate sample, in the sense that much of it must be excluded as irrelevant or incorrect'. Yet his 'competence' will always exceed that of the anthropological observer. Thus, if we 'test' a programme statement statistically and it is 'wrong' statistically: this is because it is simply not a probabilistic statement. We sometimes confuse ourselves and our informants, because in all societies the programme is subject to a greater or lesser degree to discussion in statistical metalanguage: nowhere so often as in the positivist West.

The elementary example I have used so far, expressed through a verbal statement, will not, however, take us safely far, without leading us into purely linguistic side-issues. Let us, therefore, quickly go over the question of 'prescriptive' versus 'preference' from this point of view, for it really is important. I do not need to say to this audience that these technical terms as applied to marriage alliance raised controversy (Needham 1962). Whatever be the rights or wrongs of the application of this distinction to specific marriage systems, the *kind* of distinction cannot be denied analytical validity. It will emerge more clearly if we leave the contentious ethnography, and take the category 'marriageable woman' in English society. The only dimension I can think of along which the 'prescribed'/'preferred' distinction clearly emerges is that of age, in this way. The method of probabilistic measurement may well show us that most English women contract their first marriages between ages eighteen and twenty-eight with the peak somewhere near age twenty-one. Native informants like myself may also make statements to the anthropologist that the preferred age of first marriage for women also lies between certain limits – possibly the same limits, or different ones.

In most functionalist fieldwork these two approaches are essentially all that is necessary. There is a 'real', measured, or notionally measurable situation, and a set of statements about it by natives. The latter are 'norms', 'values' or the like. One tests these for their predictivity by the former, the only true observational yard-stick. Many of the commentators on Lévi-Strauss have interpreted these two kinds of statements inaccurately as his 'statistical' and 'mechanical' models (Ardener, E. 1971c: 233–5). Let us accept that the native is confronted by the observer with a discrepancy. The observer may ask: 'What about these other women in unions which they contracted at the age of forty?', or the like. The reply may be, 'Oh yes, those are still marriages'. In dealing thus empirically with a preferred criterion of marriage there is no conflict in *mode* of observation between native and observer. The observer might say that, in fact, most of the ages of wives in marriages contracted this year fell outside those limits. The native may reply, 'Well that's unusual', or 'What can you expect nowadays?'; but he will not deny that these are marriages. The *preferred* category (here defined by age) is like that. Now, if, on the contrary, the observer says, 'Why, you were absolutely right, every woman first married this year did fall within these age limits', it is easy to make the mistake, as many have done, that we are in the presence of a '*prescribed*' category: as if prescription were essentially a 100 per cent prediction by a lay statistician.

The objections are:

1 Not all 100 per cent predictions are prescriptions: thus in the case of the preferred age of marriage a 100 per cent realization is not really more convincing than an 80 per cent or a 50 per cent realization, since other ages of marriage are not excluded.
2 In so far as prescriptions incidentally appear to claim to make 100 per cent predictions, or are cast in such a form, their predictivity is not probabilistic: they generate the nature of the event.

Here lies the point. Consider our English criterion again. You are still 'testing' the preferred age. You now ask: 'what of marriages at age fifteen?' The reply this time is that there are none. 'What,' you ask, 'of that young woman whom I have ascertained to be fifteen and who is married?' The reply is this: 'Either you are wrong about her age and she is married, or you are right about her age and she is not married.' No amount of the sort of empirical demonstration that worked for the *preferential* category can now shake the native statement, for there is in fact a *prescriptive* age category of marriageable women (all women of sixteen years of age and over) which is different in kind from the preferential category we have discussed. A prescription thus defines the category itself.

Now the only lively attack on this surely self-evident position (cf. Maybury-Lewis 1965) has come from the cultural materialist Marvin Harris. He remarks in ironical disbelief:

There is nothing to be shocked about in the proposal that the existence of the prescribed system depends upon whether or not an appropriate 'conceptual' distinction is made by the cultural carriers ... Let it be recorded then that in this fashion, the structuralists climb up ropes and disappear off the tops of them (1969: 509–10).

The rope trick is an illusion all right – a glint in the behaviourist sunglasses. Since we are educated in the positivist tradition – in which prescriptions must be re-encoded in probabilistic terms – we have confused the whole matter with norms and law and ethics. For this reason even the pioneer theorists could only approach the matter through the existing legalistic term 'prescribed'. In non-literate societies the terms of a prescription need no adventitious support. The supposed 'empirical' facts are what is amended. Thus while 'prescribed' numerical minimum age is not a typical feature of non-literate marriage, in some societies no marriages occur before menarche. If there is evidence that the menarche has not occurred, the marriage has not occurred. If there is evidence of a marriage, then the menarche has occurred. Do not imagine that a skilled positivist could convince them otherwise. He will find the terms *menarche* and *marriage* stretch to meet any objection, like that very elastic rubber-sheeting to which Leach once directed our attention. In comparison, the prescription of a genealogical category like 'cross-cousin' is obviously child's play. Whatever the ethnographic mechanics of a prescriptive category in any single case, the possibility of a difference in principle between a prescribed and a preferred category seems to be clearly established and is worth the whole debate. It does not rely on that red herring: the problem of choice – unless Hobson's is also included. This contribution we owe entirely to Needham (1962), since Lévi-Strauss now surprisingly denies his own part in it (1967b).

Harris, indefatigable critic, had no sympathy with Homans and Schneider (1955) for getting involved in this. He sees clearly that they, as well as by implication the English functionalists, were only half-hearted empiricists to start with. They do not object to the absence of statistics:

They are content instead to grapple with the phantoms of idealized rules and idealized marriages, from which beautifully logical idealized exchange cycles result. Innocents abroad! They are prepared to deal with phantoms, but not with *elementary* ones. They do not realize that among professional idealists, as distinct from the eclectic American amateurs who have rubbed shoulders with logical positivism and behaviourism too long to know how to really get off the ground, a rule which is manifest in a hundred cases is no better than that which is manifest in one (1969: 505).

Beautifully put, from the point of view of a micro-measurer at floor level. Harris confuses the genuine outcome of the debate. The peculiar features of prescriptive categories are of the very essence of what I have called the programme. The zone of empirical observation (as normally misunderstood) contains the behaviourist's statistical picture of the facts. The middle zone of native discussion about probabilities contains much of the functionalist's material labelled 'values', 'norms', 'preferences' and the like (to which 'charter' beliefs were once brutally conjoined). Since folk statements of this type could be statistically proved to be predictively inefficient, the anthropologist has tended to miss or ignore the categories which are not so discussable – despite the early warning from Evans-Pritchard, whose study of Azande witchcraft (1937) showed that empirical unfalsifiability was the defining characteristic of their thought system. It is surely the contribution of the new anthropology to be more consciously aware of the primacy of the programme; to state that in understanding society, the native's *as well as* the observer's probabilistic statements are at the mercy of the programme.

It is not its contribution to deny that close measurement and probabilistic dialogue will uncover regularities that are relevant to the programme, and occasionally some, usually ecological, which are central to the programme, as well as lots of *ad hoc* regularities which are irrelevant to the programme, but which are the subject matter of other fields of discourse. Let this all continue, but ever more skilfully.

We are in the position of one person who imitates another. While person X performs some repetitive or patterned activity, person Y, the imitator (in computer terms a *simulator*) acquires some degree of skill in predictivity. When X changes to another mode of activity Y flounders. The predictivity fails at the only moment at which it is truly important. It seems quite likely that human beings in society do tend towards periods of repetitive inertia for varying lengths, along various measurable parameters. The pattern of these stretches may then be recoverable by observation. The biological and environmental infrastructure will impose regularities such that a resolute attention to these in particular is an honourable study. Even with their help, however, the mere 'observer' of social events, even with the further assistance of some probabilistic dialogue with the participants, is truly (as Wiener 1948 says) in a position comparable to a Maxwell's Demon, a being on the same scale as the molecules in a thermal system. The Demon's problem is, essentially, that he cannot command the information to map the system of which he is a part. He is a goal-keeper in the fog trying to intercept footballs kicked from all directions.

I have proceeded so far with the notion of the programme, in order to hold the attention of those of you who thought you were dedicated empiricists. In order to think more about it we shall have to drop the mechanistic analogy, but we have not quite exhausted it. Lévi-Strauss's myth-logic does resemble that of a self-amending programme such as I sketched earlier. A piece of myth looks like nonsense. A myth statement transforms, inverts, adds, subtracts, performs unions upon sets, all in a mishmash of operations, imposed upon images of bits of experience. A myth statement is of the nonsensical order of:

$$\text{apples} + \text{pears} = \text{bananas}$$

Yet this would be a 'reasonable' output of a programme with two transpositions. We could write out an untransposed programme like this:

Programme: 1   Exemplify that the union of two subsets of a set is part
        of the set.
        2   Let the set be *apples*.
Output: apples + apples = apples

Imagine, however, that certain rewrite instructions intervene:

Output: apples + [apples . . .]
Programme: Rewrite *apples as pears*
Output: . . . + pears = [pears]
Programme: Rewrite *pears as bananas*
Output: . . . = bananas

In effect we can 'restore' three linear 'logical' statements which the output
exemplifies in different phases.

        1   apples + apples = apples
        2   pears + pears = pears
        3   bananas + bananas = bananas

So three exemplifications of a 'logical' definition of identity appear in the
output as an 'illogical' confusion of identities. The 'message' is, in the one
case: 'the union of two subsets of a set is part of the set.' In the other, it is
'subsets of different sets are not part of the same set.' The human capacity
to 'receive' the nonsense output is striking. This is achieved through a
'symptomatic' reading, as Freud (and Althusser) would put it. The detailed
write-out, into three logical statements, is the equivalent of Lévi-Strauss's
method of analysis in *Mythologiques*, although he has set himself an enormous task. You are free, of course, to say that the 'myth' of the apples and
pears *symbolizes* a disquisition on identity. Lévi-Strauss's formulae are a
kind of science-fiction, perhaps – a set of possible methods with a set of
guessed answers. They show us, however, that rationality can be restored in
part to the 'nonsensical' output, by a set of rewrite instructions. It is at this
very abstruse point that his thought intuitively meets Chomsky's: it would
be misleading to pursue their separate onward courses.

The condensed statements of myth can be in principle teased out as
totally 'rational', totally 'logical', provided we perceive the self-transforming nature of the programme. The 'rewrites' that are necessary to
restore rationality are generated within the programme itself. Nevertheless
in that part of the output which is symbolized in behaviour they are the
programmatic homologues of 'adaptations' to the infrastructure. At the
level of myth, however, they are least directly calibrated to the natural
order, and the mental structures can be most clearly shown. As Lévi-
Strauss says (1970: 10): 'when the mind is left to commune with itself and
no longer has to come to terms with objects, it is in a sense reduced to
imitating itself as object.' At the level of the adaptations, structures of a
different kind based on observation may be imposed or elicited by the
analyst, as we shall see. But what is all this about the 'restoration' of

rationality? Human 'rational' apperception of symbolic systems may well be evolutionarily older and more developed than the ability to unpack them endlessly into linearly expressed notations (see above, pp. 25–6). Let me remind you of Ortega y Gasset's (1921, my trans.) description of the richly programmatic power of metaphor as 'an instrument necessary for the act of creation, which God forgetfully left . . . in the inside of one of his creatures, as an absent-minded surgeon sews up one of his instruments in the belly of his patient'.

The unpeeling of possible sequences involves their hypothesizing first. Hence, the problem of validating 'structures': the suspicions of arbitrariness and the like. In comparison, those annoying cross-cousin categories begin to look like bleeding chunks of the natural order. You will see that my initial distinction between 'output' and 'programme' is, at the next meta-level, exactly the same kind of analytical 'linear' dissection of a simultaneous concept as is the distinction between the linear logical statement and the condensed, transformationally rewritten, mythological statement. The programme and the output are simultaneously present. We may argue, therefore, that the same kinds of rewrite arguments are implicit in the output of social events. The final rewrite when action occurs will be into the symbolism of behaviour itself. Now this is nothing to do directly with correlations, probabilities, or polling, but I find no 'paralysis of reality' in it (Harris 1969: 497).

In any case, certain programmatic distinctions are 'calques' upon divisions in the most behaviourist reality: sex differences, bodily laterality, geographical directions. Nevertheless, establish one level of categorization and human beings build a metaphorical level upon it, then upon this level, yet another. The number of possible structures nested one inside the other is thus bewilderingly great. It is no wonder that concentration instead upon the plane or field of social events, as they are generated, was for long so attractive. Functionalists have in fact been used to ordering this plane through rudimentary structures of another type, call them 'syntagmatic' if you like, in opposition to the 'paradigmatic' structures of the programme (see below, appendix). Functionalists did not always grasp their arbitrary nature, for syntagmatic structures frequently approximate to our positivist analogues for reality itself. The situational logic of Popper, the functional inter-relationships of Radcliffe-Brown: they 'feel' real.

It is not surprising that those wearing syntagmatic lenses do not see paradigmatic structures. Two cases from Evans-Pritchard will suffice. As Douglas has pointed out (1970b: xiv), *Witchcraft, Oracles and Magic* was about knowing. The structures were paradigmatic. Yet the contribution was seen by most anthropologists as syntagmatic: as about 'social control' and the like. Again, *The Nuer* proposed a model of the opposition of segments in a system of segments. This was a paradigmatic statement: a truly Saussurean vision, but 'opposition' in a paradigmatic statement was apprehended as 'conflict' in a syntagmatic statement. Again: 'exchange' (Mauss)/paradigmatic; 'transaction' (Barth)/syntagmatic. So too: 'alliance'/ 'descent'; 'prescription'/'preference'; and my 'programme'/'output'. The interlocking planes of interpretation show us something of what is meant by the problem of calibration of programme to event. A human being in society experiences an event as an expression of both modes. He and it are united in a unique *valeur* (Saussure 1922: 153–4).

You will think that this lecture is now retreating into an arcane terminology. Let me reassure you. Whatever terms we use, they merely state that the structures of the so-called 'structuralism' are not more 'speculative' (whatever else they are) than the structures of the so-called 'functionalism'. Furthermore, not all formulations derived by 'structuralists' are paradigmatic, although what appears novel is the immanent paradigmatic awareness. Conversely, not all formulations derived by 'functionalists' are syntagmatic, but what appear old and familiar are the syntagmatic assumptions.

The method of structures is indeed already being applied, as yet in an early way, to the syntagmatic plane. I have already suggested (note 32, chapter 1 and Ardener, E. 1971b: lxxv) that Barth's transactions, Barnes's, Bott's, Mitchell's networks and such developments, can thus be designated as steps towards the highest stage of functionalism: 'that is: a functionalism become aware (or about to become aware) that the field of behaviour or action, even when arbitrarily isolated from the ideological programme that determines its meaning, must itself be structured by the observer before it can be "observed".' Syntagmatic models 'work' until a paradigmatic change occurs. They generate only events of the kind which have already happened. Nevertheless, a complementary and fully conscious syntagmatic structuralism is much to be desired, and we may hope for a functionalist revival or transmutation in this more rigorous form, as part of any truly new anthropology. So far, however, the 'syntagmatists' are wrestling with a hundred *ad hoc* terminologies, due to their inexperience of the nature of the paradigmatic dimension. Not the least confusing effect is their tendency to label their 'syntagms' with the term 'paradigm' itself.

The paths to the eliciting of the rationality of paradigmatic structures have meanwhile led through the painstaking examination of symbolic expressions of all kinds: myth, ritual, folklore, legend, riddles, gestures, jokes, lateral symbolism, totemic classification and the like. The American anthropologists of the 'cognitive structure' school, despite a difference of emphasis, must be regarded as part of this. Others have examined the oral literature, the problems of the onomastic process and so on. The recent attention to the philosophical implications has also been valuable. The nature of the 'mentalistic' portion of society is now moderately well known, because of all this work. We are out of the range, however, of probabilistic testing. At different stages the most brilliant European exponents of the new lines of approach have, because of this, found themselves faltering. They have all been highly sensitive to the charge of empirical inadequacy. Lévi-Strauss thus recoiled from the implications of his own analysis of prescription, and resorted to other denials of his own work, which some take too literally. Leach has reaffirmed his functionalist allegiance (how like that Galileo he summoned forth in *Rethinking Anthropology*!). Douglas has been accused by him (1971b) of a retreat into Roman Catholic apologetics.

Needham has come to despair of a future for social anthropology except through disintegration or 'iridescent metamorphosis' (1970). All assail Lévi-Strauss. Like the characters in Sartre's hell the new anthropologists care about each other's faults. Nevertheless, these honourable contradictions derive from the location of their characteristic works in the *coupure epistémologique* itself, although only Lévi-Strauss exemplifies all phases of it.

It is no surprise that in remote university departments anthropology has continued, because of the absent consensus, to be taught more or less unmodified since 1955 to new generations of students. Or a course in 'cognitive anthropology' or the like is patched on. The feelings of some anthropologists are echoed in the jeer of Harris about 'mysticism, cynicism, and miniskirts', and some may agree with him that '... what is most distressing to view is the veritable debauchery of method which has succeeded Radcliffe-Brown's puritanical reign. This weakening of the empirical fibres (can it be the same influence which has made London the exporter of all manner of musical and sartorial novelty?) stands out in morbid contrast to the utilisation of the linguistic model by American cultural anthropologists in the study of emic categories' (Harris 1969: 544–5). (Rather unfair on London in this case!)

Whatever deficiencies of presentation may have occurred in the heady 1960s, we have already seen that the apparent collapse of method was a behaviourist illusion. Isolated and frequently scorned although they have been in functionalist circles, we must thank the neo-anthropologists for showing us the way. It is true that anthropologists will need to be even more widely educated and even more scholarly than at present if they are to make the transition to the kinds of applications that now await us. There will be no short cuts.

We saw that the question of the evaluation of the 'truth' of paradigmatic structures is the hard one. There are three kinds of system that science in its censorious adolescence reacted firmly against, or has come to distrust since: 1) pre-positivist systems – like religious cosmologies; 2) quasi-positivist systems – like Marxism or psychoanalysis; 3) pseudo-positivist systems – like Rosicrucianism, flat-earthism and so on. We now enter a tangle: systems of all these types can be the subject of structural analysis; yet 'structuralism' is like them.

The scientific positivist rests on experimental verification, or the Popperian piecemeal falsification, which is the same thing. The model physical universe expressed in this way was the great achievement of the last few generations, and it easily renders implausible both the pre-positivist systems and the pseudo-systems where they bear on physical phenomena. The quasi-positivist systems are not in quite the same case. Neither Marxism nor Freudianism, although products of the scientific revolution and empirical in orientation, nowadays rest on a truly *positivist* basis. These systems are like scythed chariots which slice away positivist reality around them. In principle there is no way that they can put themselves into a position in which they can be totally falsified as systems. Their use of positivist language, and the common cause that they made against the old religious dogmatisms, at first disguised the fact that these were systems parallel to positivism, not aspects of it. Pseudo-scientific systems like flat-earthism are disreputable, in contrast, because they compete with positivism: they attempt to build a non-positivist superstructure upon essentially positivist premisses. They assert, if you like, the existence of miracles by resort to experiment. This century is littered with the corpses of such hybrids: they run from spiritualism, through sacred mushrooms and beyond.

The quasi-positivist systems on the other hand do not, in their mature forms, any longer need to compete in this way. They are almost as well protected from total experimental disproof as is the system of positivism itself, but they are in no way dependent on positivist procedures. If we look now at Lévi-Strauss's structuralism, stripped of all trendy accretions, we can see that it truly has affinities with Marxism as well as with various versions of psychoanalysis. It is certainly *not* either, but it is an entity of a similar sort – not homoousian (of the same substance) but homoiousian (of a similar substance). These fourth-century theological terms convey the flavour of theological discussion that has grown up around French structuralism. Now if structuralism is 'like' Marxism and psychoanalysis, it is certainly not like flat-earthism. We may drop the fear of that. Are all three not therefore more like the pre-positivist dogmatic systems? The simple answer is that the latter notoriously include propositions which positivism itself can subject to falsification. They were in fact the earlier (of course the original) flat-earthisms. It is, however, instructive to recall again the very sophisticated mode whereby witchcraft typically verifies itself. No amount of positivist measurement would invalidate the system. The witchcraft believer accepts as given that disasters have a statistical probability. He merely has to explain the individual incidence of the rate, and sudden changes in it. He accepts that 'twenty people will die on the road today.' He has to explain the death only of particular persons. Every day particular persons die. The greater the scientific care with which the incidence is mapped, the more grist to his mill. So: Adelabu, a Nigerian politician, died in a motor accident. In his home-town, eighty miles away, his political enemies were massacred for willing his death. In such a scheme Johnson truly killed Kennedy.

The causality in witchcraft beliefs lies in an attempt to explain the incidence of randomness. The believer is Maxwell's Demon, with a theory. It is an essentially 'social' theory; it recognizes that probabilistic approaches are simply not securely predictive. It has a *practice*: a mode of intervention in the syntagmatic plane. The subordinate syntagmatic analysis might well include a specification of 'benefiting' individuals by diagnostic criteria as of 'marginality' or the like. The number of variants, as we know, is enormous. In its economic aspect it states that those who benefit from random events should pay a social tax (Ardener, E. 1970c). Other systems parallel to positivism attempt similar tasks less destructively than witchcraft. They all move causality from the chain of events to unconscious structures. They are 'guesses' about the programme. Thus, the systems of

Marx and Freud achieved a revolutionary return to positions supplementary to positivism. It is significant that both passed through flat-earthist phases, and had to trim off excursions into fields which positivism had made its own: the linguistic theories of Marr, and the biological beliefs of Lysenko were notorious; as were many of the misapprehensions of Freud.

Positivism begins, then, to be clearly visible as a powerful method for the examination of causality in systems on a *non-human* scale, a calque, as it were, upon the stars, the earth and the dice. Yet it too has suffered the metaphorization of all human structures. In this century, the system has more and more begun to be apprehended as a metaphysical one, that is: as independent of genuine scientific method. Thus the human incidence of a statistical rate now comes to be translated into the responsibility not of witches, but of self. People are statistical 'losers' or 'winners', with all the implications that flow from this. More and more they become victims of social engineering based on elaborate non-measurements. But this lay positivism, as a new belief system pertaining to human affairs, is not validated by scientific method. It is no *more* true than Marxism or Freudianism; it is even less true. It should be clear by now that rejection of this ghost image of 'positivism' should not be a rejection of rationality, positivist or otherwise, but a rejection of the privileged status of metaphysical positivism: which is itself immune to test by experiment. A 'positivist religion', if not that of Comte, has certainly won the compulsorily educated masses.

The emergence of 'structuralism' at this period has serious implications. The earlier systems of Marx and Freud could be seen in certain carefully oblique lights as marginal to scientific inquiry, and concerned with politics and mental health. The structuralist approach encroaches upon an established mythology about ordered thought itself, and echoes bigger battles in the philosophy of science. For this reason, there is, I suggest, a life-or-death note about the various debates. That the small subject of anthropology should have been called upon to house its most powerful statement in the humane studies may be an accident of academic history. It is evident that we are not merely concerned with an internal 'revolution', like Malinowski's discovery of fieldwork, from the world-wide intellectual interest not only in structuralism itself, but in almost any writing that reflects or resembles it, even in corrupt and distorted forms. The preparedness of social anthropology derived from the continental schools of Durkheim and his followers, from Saussurean and Prague linguistics, from Evans-Pritchard, and his characteristic pupils – including the Oxford translators and developers of the ideas of the French school – even Dutch anthropology: all welded to material collected in parts of the globe very often only lightly trod by the Malinowskians, among whom Leach, however, rectifies the balance in an important manner. Malinowski himself, despite an interest in language, would surely have rejected it all as some kind of topsy-turvy Radcliffe-Brownianism? We can see at once that the confusion in the present state of anthropology is rather like that of a quiet suburban gardener whose pots have sprouted some illegal but valuable herb. A rag-tag-and-bobtail thrust his geraniums aside, and offer enormous sums for the illicit weed. Shall he be respectable or rich? No wonder he vacillates.

Where I think that Lévi-Strauss's structuralism is in advance of some supposed modern masters, is precisely in his continual hold on a vision of empirical data, even though the precise definition of 'empirical' is no longer simple in the present age. Some of the occasional excesses derive from misinterpretation of the new freedoms. Lévi-Strauss's system contains at its heart an outline of modes whereby individually arbitrary systems can be matched to each other. The data of a structuralist approach are in fact *all other systems*. This is, after all, only a making conscious of a kind of game we have always played. We have validated, tested, systems against 'reality'. By this we have meant our analogues for reality. Logical positivism and the scientific method refined these analogues. We have matched system against system, in the faith that the positivist analogues have a privileged position. In the world of the unrecovered programme, the lack of a privileged set of analogues must provisionally be assumed. The objectivity of a system can then only be found in its contrast to other systems. The bringing of one system into relationship with another by transformational links is the nearest thing available to testing. When a system is offered which is subsumed totally or in part by another, falsification of a kind has occurred. Insofar as the core of positivist analogues for reality rests on more stable structures than human life, many provisional analyses may be properly rejected as flat-earthism, so we must be good at some hard scientific ideas. In zones where positivism cannot reach, the testing of system against system is the only hope of advance. The maintenance of a strategy of provisionality is essential, for only in this way can the fatal obsessing effect of 'unverifiable' systems be finally loosened. 'Let a hundred models of formal systems contend': this is far superior to the present intellectual practice, whereby a generation of scholars is 'converted' to a system for a lifetime, leaving the rethinking to the next. Many people, one suspects, mistake 'provisionality' for 'relativism', whereas it is clearly quite the opposite. By denying an absolute truth-value to systems of good fit, we become aware of what such systems slice off with their shears of relevance. As a result new kinds of 'universals' become accessible. This is to move well beyond structuralism of the facile kind, but not, I think, beyond the programme of Lévi-Strauss himself, frequently contradictory although it is.

It is interesting, finally to take two views inspired by Marx. Marvin Harris is a rather old-style materialist who rejects the Durkheimian tradition *in toto*: 'Every pore [he says] of Durkheim's theory is filled with mentalistic and idealistic images and predilections' (1969: 473). In the *Elementary Forms* Durkheim 'returns us to an idealism patterned after the worst of Hegel's "geists"' (Harris 1969: 478). As we know, Marx said: 'for Hegel, the process of thought . . . is the demiurge of the real, which only represents its external phenomenon. For me, on the contrary, the ideal is nothing but the material, transposed and translated in man's head' (Althusser 1969: 89). Harris is no doubt taking a common interpretation of this when he says that Lévi-Strauss 'found Comte, Durkheim and Mauss standing on their heads, and he joined them' (1969: 513).

The Marxist position is, however, no longer as simple as that. Louis Althusser (1969), who is aware that his modern rethinking of Marx can look dangerously 'idealist', is at some pains specifically to avoid the notion that Marx simply turned Hegel on his head. Furthermore, under Althusser the crude errors of Marxist materialism are averted. His system does not compete with positivism.

Lenin himself criticized Engels and Plekhanov for having *applied* the dialectic externally to 'examples' from the natural sciences. The external application of a concept is never equivalent to a *theoretical practice*. The application changes nothing in the externally derived truth but its *name*, a re-baptism incapable of producing any real transformation of the truths that receive it. The application of the laws of the dialectic to such and such a result of physics, for example, makes not one iota of difference to the structure or development of the theoretical *practice* of physics; worse it may turn into an ideological fetter (Althusser 1969: 170).

Althusser's terminology is applicable to all developed ideological systems parallel to and including positivism. They all differ from 'flat-earthisms' in their generation of reality-transforming practices. 'So ideology,' he says, 'is not an aberration or a contingent excrescence of history: it is a structure essential to the historical life of societies' (232). Again, 'it is profoundly unconscious' (1969: 233). Again, 'men "live" their ideologies as the Cartesians "saw" . . . the moon two hundred paces away . . .' (1969: 233). Again: he speaks of the 'overdetermination of the real by the imaginary and the imaginary by the real' (1969: 234). Finally 'the men who would use an ideology purely as a means of action, as a tool, find that they have been caught by it, implicated by it, just when they are using it and believe themselves to be absolute masters of it' (1969: 234). Harris would thus gain little comfort, as Marxists now disappear up ropes as well.

Althusser (1969: 106) moves the old Hegelian contradictions into the same universe as Lévi-Strauss's elaborate transformations, by the concept of *overdetermination* (itself borrowed from the system of Freud): 'What can this mean but that the simple contradiction is *always overdetermined*? The exception thus discovers in itself the rule, the rule of the rule, and the old "exceptions" must be regarded as methodologically simple examples of the *new rule*.' A strange bedfellow for our friends Douglas (1966a) and Turner (1969)?

The new Marxism can hardly ignore the new anthropology, but at present the two systems only chew at each other. Althusser's science of 'social formations' can demonstrate the ideological status of structuralism as an overdetermination of a contradiction in the late capitalist period. For structuralism, the new Marxism is itself an advanced system of the type of its own privileged subject matter. Harris, an old-liner, might be brought in to warn, in effect, that the new Marxism is meddling with elementary phantoms and cannot come off best. I must confess to some surprise that

Althusser's brilliance is satisfied with the limited ends of the Marxist problematic, unless he is hoping slowly to wean his audience away from its old mythology, towards the much more revolutionary implications of the dethroning of metaphysical positivism (the 'ghost image') as a social practice. As he says: 'we know that a "pure" science only exists on condition that it continually frees itself from the ideology which occupies it, haunts it or lies in wait for it' (Althusser 1969: 70). The anthropological core of structuralism has its own 'theoretical practice' generating the rationality for the supposed unreason of the present age. A Marxist critic of British anthropology (Banaji 1970) specifically exempts Lévi-Strauss's work from simple criticism as an ideology. He over-sternly delineates some confusions of modern British anthropologists, but after all Marx and Engels themselves declared that history always progresses by its apparent mistakes!

In directing this lecture mainly towards positivist anthropologists, I do not feel the need specifically to adopt the label 'structuralist'. In the new conceptual space we have only different kinds of structures, not 'structuralism' *and* 'functionalism'. I have tried to make clear that an empirical approach and a procedure for testing need not be of a positivist type. I re-assert (in agreement here with Harris) that, in fact, European social anthropologists have only been pseudo-positivist anyway. For that reason they have for so long had the germ of a science despite its lack of statistical proofs, in contrast (dare I say it?) with sociologists, whose statistical proofs have over the years almost destroyed their science. Nevertheless, careful documentary or field research, using every technique in our armoury, should proceed with greater conscientiousness, not less. The return of our subject to fellowship in the wider intellectual world, after the rather hearty dominion over palm and pine bequeathed to us by Malinowski, need not blind us to the tradition of meticulous research which his great pupils established, and to which I am glad to pay my tribute in this Memorial Lecture.

I have spoken of the 'new anthropology', rather than of a 'new social anthropology': this I confess is deliberate, although not of substantive importance. Few branches of anthropology fail nowadays to wear a social aspect. The cultural anthropology of the US also provides parallel modes of looking at our problem: the linguists and analysts of categories of cognition and the like. The behaviourist obsession characteristic of the American school sits ill upon them, while we may agree for our part, that the British and Continental schools can benefit from some of their methods. But, in particular, our old anthropological links with students of the biological and environmental infrastructure begin to look very important again, since our analyses start with events in their zones. Furthermore, the return to 'anthropology' as a term may well symbolize the end of that period of one-sided special relationship with conventional social science which has obscured the true development of our subject. From conversation with many scholars in neighbouring fields it seems that they may well be moving in similar directions. Anthropology will then, we may think, survive into the next generation, both empirically and analytically, with a little help from its friends and some bright students, provided that we recognize that the long years of simply patching up the old consensus are happily over.

Appendix

The distinction between 'paradigmatic' and 'syntagmatic', I take ultimately from Saussure and his school, and Jakobson, although I realize that there are already rather many uses of these terms, some over-elaborate. 'Paradigm' is also a term (deriving from a more traditional usage) which is important in the modern discussions of the history of science. I do not necessarily see my uses as inconsistent with these, but the distinction I am making lies both in the opposition with 'syntagm', and in expression of this opposition at a particular meta-level. The essential linguistic distinction is succinctly presented by Milner (1971: 254–5), where he shows the two axes lying at right-angles (and defining the 'paragrammatic space'). The acoustic chain of Saussure is generated linearly along the syntagmatic axis. The paradigmatic axis defines the classes of grammatical relationship in the syntagmatic chain.[1] Again: Lévi-Strauss rearranges his myths by imposing a paradigmatic axis vertically, in opposition to the 'linear' generation of the myth content, which is thus 'syntagmatic'. Finally, my own usage moves a step further from the notion of linear generation. Socially apprehended events are generated in a multi-dimensional space. If we see them as merely generated in ordinary space, this conceptual field I call the 'syntagmatic plane'. Events in this plane can be apprehended by an observer through the eliciting of syntagmatic structures either in space or over time, or both. The same events are, however, generated paradigmatically. Every event in a syntagmatic structure is also an event in a paradigmatic structure. The former is a structure in the 'output'; the latter is a structure in the 'programme'; terms which are too mechanistic for more than analogical use.

To recapitulate briefly the calibration of the two planes. In a specific society, the paradigmatic 'witch' is generated as an apperception (say) of random incidence of disaster. The link to the syntagmatic plane is provided by a 'theoretical practice' which specifies the 'witch'. The common features of such specifications in a given society are syntagmatic structures. Again: paradigmatic 'oppositions' among the Nuer, specify, through a theoretical practice, events which, in the syntagmatic plane, may be labelled 'conflicts'. The pairs of terms I quote here and in the text above are certainly not intended to represent universal analytical oppositions. They are meant to indicate that anthropological concepts have tended to be separately labelled according to the primacy of the syntagmatic or paradigmatic structures in the thought of the analyst.

As I have already indicated, the regularities of syntagmatic structures are usually confusingly called 'paradigms' instead of 'syntagms' by functionalists. As I see it, the Manchester workers, for example, are constantly analysing syntagms, without understanding that the specification of their 'networks', 'ethnicities' and the like, lies in paradigmatic structures (in the precise sense) which are inaccessible to their mode of analysis. It will be necessary to present a detailed example from actual fieldwork in order to take the matter further; this must await a subsequent paper. Meanwhile, it may be noted that the terms used by Needham (1963: xlii–xliii), to express the 'theoretical capital' of social anthropology from the French school, are all paradigmatic in nature, which accounts for their intuitive richness.

The multiplicity of *ad hoc* terms in functionalist social science, all ultimately unsatisfactory, and mostly outmoded as soon as invented, derives from the relatively short repetitive life of so many observed patterns of events. The reason why I have accorded the term 'transaction' the status of a syntagmatic concept, is not because of its particularly great power, but because it labels something near a minimal pattern in that plane. Nevertheless, the primacy of the paradigmatic structures provides the source of any ascription of meaning or 'value' to such transactions.

The primacy of the paradigmatic structures is still maintained when an unprogrammed event intrudes from an infrastructural source – say an event in the natural order, like an unprecedented earthquake. The syntagms may be totally shattered in such a case. No predictivity from previous syntagmatic patterns may survive during the disastrous circumstances. Yet it is evident that in the crisis itself 'when the skies rain blood', certain paradigmatic structures still generate the human apperceptions of the events. Eventually it is they that generate new syntagms. They are thus equivalent to what in an earlier paper I have called (at the level of belief) the 'templates' (1970c: 155, 159). Since both syntagmatic and paradigmatic structures are simultaneously delineated through events, the 'paradigmatic primacy' probably derives from a basic and systematic, 'event-oriented', adaptive capacity in the mentalistic structure of human society. It would thus be both truly primitive as well as primary.

I do not like to leave the matter there without taking up certain questions about the 'location' of structures:

1   The relationship paradigmatic/syntagmatic is an expression of relationship between dimensions. Structures in two dimensions are paradigmatic to structures in one dimension; structures in three dimensions are paradigmatic to structures in two dimensions; structures in four dimensions are paradigmatic to structures in three dimensions; structures in five dimensions are paradigmatic to structures in four dimensions: and so on. In normal linguistic usage the syntagmatic chain is seen as linear (in one dimension) and the paradigmatic has to be represented through a model in two dimensions. Yet any reality to which it corresponds must be conceived of as operating in four-dimensional space-time: the one-dimensional linear chain representing an output generated in three space dimensions over one dimension of time. If this syntagmatic continuum is four-dimensional, then the paradigmatic dimension is a fifth dimension.

2   There is nothing wrong with five dimensions; the time (t) of a given dimension (d) must be expressed through co-ordinates in a space (s) of a dimension one higher. So:

$$\text{In } d_1, \ t_1 \text{ is expressed through co-ordinates in } s_2$$
$$"\ d_2, \ t_2\ "\qquad "\qquad "\qquad "\qquad "\ s_3$$
$$"\ d_3, \ t_3\ "\qquad "\qquad "\qquad "\qquad "\ s_4$$
$$"\ d_4, \ t_4\ "\qquad "\qquad "\qquad "\qquad "\ s_5$$

The relationship *t* between spaces of succeeding dimensions is thus of the same logical order as that between syntagmatic and paradigmatic.

While I am concerned here with logical dimensions, we can hardly ignore the fact that Einstein has already mapped them on to the natural order. Thus t_3 is our naive experience of Einstein's four-dimensional continuum. 'Time three' then is 'syntagmatic time', the time of human historiography, whose vulnerable and relative nature I have shown (1971c) in the terms of structure. The nature of 'time four' is apprehended by us through its contradictions: rendered in Einstein's thought through the concept of the speed of light, through which intervals in space as well as time in s_4 are shrunken to simultaneity. The native of four-dimensional space-time could only be expressed by Einstein through a meta-level one higher: a fifth conceptual dimension.

There is nothing mysterious then about any of this. 'Paradigmatic structures' are conceptually s_5 structures. The relationship t_4 may then be expressed for our narrow purposes as 'paradigmatic time', for which the co-ordinates will lie in s_5. The 'predictivity' of the programme is in t_4 therefore, not in t_3 (syntagmatic time), but 'predictivity' in the narrow sense is a t_3 concept. We must presume that social events occur in the same conceptual world as that in which the physicist lives, but one would never believe this from the low-dimensional models used by conventional social science – as if social science reality were truly pre-Newtonian, let alone pre-Einsteinian.

These further refinements are outlined here in order to express my keen dissatisfaction with Lefebvre's addition of a 'third' *symbolic* dimension to the opposition *syntagmatic/paradigmatic* (1966: 227, 247), thus obscuring the formal properties of 'dimension' as well as those of the syntagmatic/paradigmatic opposition.

3

Language, Ethnicity and Population

It may seem difficult at first sight to understand exactly the relationship between the three terms: 'language', 'ethnicity' and 'population' in a conference at which the focus is primarily on the third. We are, of course, used to some doubts about the precise application of the first two in African circumstances. For example, as far as 'language' is concerned, even a simple list (let alone a classification) of linguistic units leads to hoary problems of 'language' versus 'dialect', 'cluster', 'family' and the like, or to discussions of criteria of 'genetic' or 'typological' or other sorts. With 'tribe' or 'ethnicity', discussion turns on the overlap with 'race', 'culture' or 'language' itself (however ultimately delineated). We are less used to doubts about the third term 'population'. As is common in human studies, we confuse different ideas. Thus we imagine that population is a reality, 'infrastructural' to the other two. Population measures have all the earmarks of objectivity and, for many, the reality of the term 'population' is itself an expression of the various indices used by demographers: birth, death, fertility and nuptiality rates, and enumerations and samplings of various kinds.

Yet what is a population? What is, in each case, the unit to which the demographic measures relate? In a study of the Bakweri of Cameroon, some years ago, for example, a central question began to emerge. Were the Bakweri a declining population? Now the Bakweri tend to think that those of their number who live in modern centres are not quite 'real' Bakweri. The Bakweri picture of themselves made a clear distinction between those inside their village fences (leading a 'Bakweri way of life' as it were) and those outside them. The modern centres (*par excellence* outside the fence) were ethnically mixed, cosmopolitan, un-Bakweri. There was a sense then in which, if the rural heartland was losing population, the Bakweri were also declining in *toto*. The definition of the target population as rural, in an area notorious for a vast 'multitribal' migration to an adjacent plantation industry, moved the question of Bakweri 'decline' out of the realm of demography into that of ideas. For the rural population was not, as it stood, a self-perpetuating population. Demographically it was marked by 'distorted' age-structures and sex ratios – and probably fertility patterns too (see Ardener, E. 1962, 1972b, below, chapter 4).

This did not prevent us from usefully wearing out a demographic armoury on the mensurational aspects of the problem, and learning a great deal of value thereby. The most valuable lesson was that, in the discussion of the dynamics of a population, your unit – 'the population' – is not merely subject to a statistical determination on the part of the observer; it is also dependent on the subjective definition of that population by the human beings concerned. Over time, therefore, population series are continually affected by changing definitions on the part of both the measurers and the measured. This factor has received less general emphasis than it deserves, in part because of the dogmatic, even ideological, definitions of populations that accompanied the development of the nineteenth- and twentieth-century nation states.

In Africa, the assumption that ethnicities were entities of the type that would yield a 'population' has always been too easily made, in both linguistic and biological studies. For that reason the figures for 'tribal' membership and for language-speakers are really even more difficult to evaluate than we usually suspect them to be. The extreme North-West corner of the Bantu-speaking area (I adhere for the present to the boundary according to Guthrie 1948) illustrates this problem with remarkable clarity. We are presented with some two dozen entities, usually called 'tribes', but which also form the elements of the linguistic classification of the area. These entities are marked by very small individual populations from 300 or less to about 30,000, with 6,000 or so being the mean. They are surrounded by 'groups' of quite another scale: Efik, Ekoi, Bamileke and so on. What are we to make of discrepancies of this sort? We are in a difficult area of analysis, which belongs to a field of wider interest than our more limited regional concerns. The classification of human groups will exhibit features common to the classifying of all phenomena. Some part of the question of the particular scale of the North-Western Bantu ethnicities lies in the criteria of the Bantu classification itself – determined, if you like, in arm-chairs in Europe.

First, then, the scholars. It is easy to start with the recognition that the tribal and linguistic classifications were not independently arrived at. Even so, in what sense is it true that the speakers of Nigerian 'Ekoid' languages are more linguistically homogeneous than the West Cameroon group of Bantu speakers? We may answer this in different ways, but we should note that any scholarly or scientific classification occupies a specific taxonomic space. Its confines are to some extent coercive and they must be taken into account when problems of relationship within the space are being examined.

The conventional units which make up the taxonomy of the Bantu languages are defined, on the face of it, by fairly clearly determinable criteria (e.g. Guthrie 1948). The North-West Bantu entities belong, of course, to this taxonomy. If these criteria are strictly applied we shall not be surprised that the taxonomic space of the Bantu classification does not correspond with that independently set up for the West African languages, since the latter notoriously depends on a much less rigorous set (even a mixture) of criteria, and belongs on a different plane of analysis from that which is feasible in Bantu studies (Ardener, E. 1971c, 218–19).

Secondly, the 'people'. We have to consider here the nature of self-classification or self-identification. For the 'people' themselves play the part of theoreticians in this field. Here we touch on the close match of the classifying process with the workings of language itself. It has frequently been noted that the Bantu languages have 'overdetermined', as it were, precisely along the axis of classification. The smallest differentiation of humanity can immediately be linguistically labelled, with a *ba*-form, homologous with that used for the largest ethnic entities. The Bantu taxonomy is continuously self-amending.

In the interaction between insider and outsider, the Bantuizing tendency has aided the differentiation and discrimination of units. The multiplication of 'separate' Bantu languages was even an overt aim of nineteenth-century scholars. For the North-Western Bantu area, it is a fact that many of the divisions now in existence lean on classifications in which the scholar-turned-administrator or the administrator-turned-scholar (German, British and French) played a not insignificant part. There was a feedback to the people, so easily achieved through interpreters and others, to confuse the matter further. After all, one of the more inaccessible 'populations' of the zone is quite content to be called, and to call itself, 'Ngolo-Batanga', a hyphenated form which owes its existence to classifying for the convenience of scholars and foreigners[1] – thus joining the select but expanding company in which are found 'Anglo-Saxon', 'Serbo-Croat' and some others.

The Bantuizing tendency itself belongs to that well-documented domain of structure in which language and reality are intermingled. It is also something of a special case of the more complex phenomenon of 'taxonomic scale'. This is underlined when we consider the neighbouring Ekoi case. The intervention of British-style, ethnically minded, Native Administrations had given, by the 1930s, a local reality to general classifications whose autochthonous basis was originally limited and contradictory. The search for one Ekoi ethnicity, rather than a series of ethnicities, must be brought into relation with the particular scale of the main elements of the Southern Nigerian ethnic space. Dominated as it was by the entities labelled Yoruba, Edo, Ibo and Ibibio, it became virtually determined that 'Ekoi' would be set up homologously with these – despite the possibility of establishing several Ekoi 'tribes' (Talbot 1926; Crabb 1965).

The effect of two essentially different taxonomic spaces in this zone upon tribal divisions can be seen in the usage of the German and British administrations. The former, 'Bantuizing' in tendency, used three 'ethnic' names to divide up the relatively small Ekoi-speaking area which overlapped into its territory. On the other hand, when West Cameroon came under British administrators, some of the latter (e.g. Talbot), being more at home on the Nigerian scale, classified the whole 'Bantu' group together, for population purposes. This did not become general, but the ethnic 'diversity' of the area always remained a source of classifying malaise to them.

In the colonial period, then, the scale of the units in the prevailing ethnic taxonomies was far from uniform. The accepted scale was, in a sense, a result of arbitration between the foreigners and the politically important groups. The Yoruba and Bini kingdoms set the scale for Southern Nigeria, but this was itself set in some ways by the imperial scale of the Fulani-conquered North. It should not be forgotten that the still unsuccessful search for Ekoi unity was preceded by the Ibo case, the successful outcome of whose progress from label to population was not self-evident. It is by continuous series of such contrasts and oppositions (to which, I repeat, both foreigners and Africans contributed) that many (and in principle all) populations have defined themselves.

Much of the discomfort of West Cameroonians in the Federation of Nigeria derived from the discrepancy between their 'Bantuizing' taxonomic scale and that of the Federation as a whole. This led to the paradox, noted at the time, of the growth of a new 'Kamerun' ethnicity of Nigerian scale, covering this 'artificial' political unit – which actually, despite its internal diversity, was, while the taxonomic constraints existed, one of the most homogeneous-looking of the units of the Federation. The Bantuizing scale of the new Cameroon state clearly suits West Cameroon better at present. The West Cameroon area nevertheless still preserves elements of the newer and broader 'ethnicity' generated by the Nigerian phase of their experience (Ardener, E. 1967a, 293–9).

The position of minority peoples in a zone of 'large populations' is thus more complicated than it seems. I wish to bring out of the discussion so far these points, as they relate to the African situation. I think they have more general validity.

1   The ethnic classification is a reflex of self-identification.
2   Onomastic (or naming) propensities are closely involved in this, and thus have more than a purely linguistic interest.
3   Identification by others is an important feature in the establishment of self-identification.
4   The taxonomic space in which self-identification occurs is of overriding importance.
5   The effect of foreign classification, 'scientific' and lay, is far from neutral in the establishment of such a space.

'Tribes are not permanent crystalline structures, belonging to one "stage" of historical or social development . . . the process of self-classification never ceases' (Ardener, E. 1967a: 298). There is a true sense in which the human populations ascribed to some of these entities do not therefore represent demographic units with purely demographic pasts or futures.

Take an entity such as the Kole, one of the labelled units on the border of the Bantu and Efik linguistic domains. This was ascribed a population in 1953 of hundreds. The Kole, or some of them, speak a dialect of Duala, and are traditionally offshoots of the latter people, who live some 100 miles down the coast. Something corresponding to the Kole entity has been attested for 130 years, and on some interpretations of the evidence it could be 200, even 300, years old[2]. This small population always seems to be on the brink of extinction. What is meant by the demographic continuity of populations of this sort? Do we assume they are all the rump remnants of larger groups in the past? For various reasons, the evidence for ethno-linguistic continuity on this coast tends to suggest the opposite – that we are dealing with populations bumping along in exiguous numbers over fifty or a 100 or even several 100 years. With populations of millions, extrapolations back and forward in time using demographic indices may not generate truth, but they contain plausibility. With small hunting and gathering bands an ecological balance is at least a hypothesis (although Douglas 1966b, has called it into question). The populations of the type to which I refer are not at this elementary technological level. In the Kole case, it may well be that the whole dynamic of the 'population' is linguistic or socio-linguistic.

The Kole environmental interest is a border interest – between the Efik and Duala trading zones. The 'Kole' coast probably always had a mixed population. Kole may have always used a trading dialect, whose structure may reflect several neighbouring Bantu languages. Kole, as identifiable people under that label, were probably those members of the commercial group who maintained some connections with the Duala and perhaps with the intervening Isubu. The category 'Kole' may have been filled according to different criteria at different times. Perhaps sometimes, the Kole were mostly Efik. Perhaps sometimes the Kole speech was learnt by all in the zone. Perhaps sometimes it was spoken by nobody of social importance. In all these coastal areas the expansion and contraction of slave or client communities, and their relationships to their masters and hosts, must also be borne in mind. In a case like this the dynamics of a 'population' with a certain label over the centuries are not the dynamics of cohorts, and of fertility or mortality rates. They are the dynamics of an economic, social and linguistic situation.

Who, or what, however, determines the preservation of the classification itself? We can easily hypothesize a situation in which everyone can point to a Kole, but no one calls himself Kole. Labels of this sort are fixed to what may be termed 'hollow categories'. In the actual case, the Efik no doubt maintained the category of 'border coastal Bantu peoples' without much concern for the exact constitutents of the category. The Bantu-speaking Duala, Isubu and others might equally have maintained the category of 'those like us, nearest the Efik'. I suspect that the Kole were, in part, a hollow category like this. They were fixed as an 'ethnic group' in the British administrative system. No wonder many were puzzled by the tiny number of 'linguistic' Kole among a welter of Efik and other migrants. No wonder too that linguistic Kole itself was so hard to pin down, a language of aberrant idiolects. Perhaps it had never been any different?

In order to summarize the population characteristics of a hollow category, we may express the matter so: since the category is filled according to non-demographic criteria, the population's survival or extinction, growth or decline, age-structure or fertility, are not determined in demographic space.

A close congener of the hollow category is the entity maintained by continuous replenishment from a home area. Thus the ethnic map of Cameroon contains stable, growing or declining concentrations of Ibo, Bamileke, Hausa (and the like), which are demographically not necessarily self-perpetuating. This type of unit is familiar now in Africa, as well as in most of the urbanized world. Such concentrations were, however, also known in the past. Nomadic groups such as the Fulani, or economically defined groups such as the Aro among the Ibo, and others elsewhere shared some of the features of such continuously concentrated but demographically unstable groups.

Their close connection with hollow categories lies in their tendency to *become* hollow. Thus the supposed Bali settlers on the Cameroon Plateau are now, in their main settlement, an entity which under close examination turns out to look like a representative sample of all of their neighbours. Their present dominant language is a kind of average Cameroon Bantoid. In Northern Cameroon the category 'Fulbe' has become 'hollow' in this way. In various places and times the categories 'Norman', 'Pict', 'Jew', 'Gypsy', 'Irishman' and many others may have become, or be becoming hollow – a mere smile surviving from the vanished Cheshire cat. Thus not only can a hollow category become a 'population', but a 'population' can also become a hollow category. Indeed, this process need never stop: the category may become a population again. Certain peculiar features in the supposed continuity of certain ethnic, even 'national', groups may well be elucidated in this way.

It is essential to make this effort to separate the concept of 'population' from those of language and ethnicity. In the past the separation has been urged in biological terms. A biological population, it has been pointed out, may coincide in its history with the affiliations of its language or of its culture. I am not repeating this truth, or truism. For we are not able to be so confident about the concept of a biological population. We are concerned with continuities whose processes are only in part biological. Fulbe, Jews and (as we know) Britons are created by definition as much as by pro-creation. We are dealing with 'structures' of a clearly recognized type whose transformations may be documented in statistics, but whose dynamics lie outside the field of statistical extrapolation. I have made this assertion of principle without the important modifications and qualifications in order to highlight its importance in African studies. We may, in the West or in the global context, avert our eyes from these contradictions. Our largest units of human classification have reached such a scale that population dynamics now form the tail that violently wags the human dog.

This is not so even with smaller Western units or sub-units. It was rarely so with African ethnicities.

I have kept these remarks brief. I have not alluded more than sketchily to the topographical, ecological, economic and political elements which enter into identification and self-identification. Ultimately, among the things that society 'is' or 'is like', it 'is' or 'is like' identification. The entities set up may be based upon divisions in empirical reality, or may be set up on reality by the structuring processes of the human mind in society. In such statements 'reality' is, however, frequently only a compendium of 'positivistic' measures and approximations. We experience the structures themselves as reality: they generate events, not merely our experience of events[3]. Anthropologists would argue, I think, that this process is analogous to language, possibly subsuming language, rather than a process of language. But all agree that language acquires a position of critical empirical importance in its study.

For population studies, the most impressive advances have occurred in the study of entities of a macrodemographic scale to which statistical and mensurational indices are central. Nevertheless, *changes* in these indices come back to the differentiation of entities ('minorities', 'classes', 'sects', 'ideologies') within the mass population which redefine or restructure population 'behaviour' and thus, the population. This differentiating process is of exactly the kind which, in our more parochial field of interest, is associated with the waxing and waning of 'ethnicities' and the like. I have used only two or three elementary formulations (' the taxonomic space', 'taxonomic scale' and 'hollow category'), but the basic approach is a small part of recent movements which restore scientific validity to the mentalistic framework within which human societies shape and create events. Thereby, population studies themselves may be given back some of the intuitive life and colour that their subject matter deserves.

4

Belief and the Problem of Women

The problem of women has not been solved by social anthropologists. Indeed the problem itself has been often examined only to be put aside again for want of a solution, for its intractability is genuine. The problem of women is not the problem of 'the position of women', although valuable attention has been paid to this subject by Professor Evans-Pritchard (1965b). I refer to the problem that women present to social anthropologists. It falls into (1) a technical and (2) an analytical part. Here is a human group that forms about half of any population and is even in a majority at certain ages: particularly at those which for so many societies are the 'ruling' ages – the years after forty. Yet however apparently competently the female population has been studied in any particular society, the results in understanding are surprisingly slight, and even tedious. With rare exceptions, women anthropologists, of whom so much was hoped, have been among the first to retire from the problem. Dr Richards was one of the few to return to it at the height of her powers. In *Chisungu* (1956) she produced a study of a girls' rite that raised and anticipated many of the problems with which this paper will deal.[1] While I shall illustrate my central point by reference to a parallel set of rites among the Bakweri of Cameroon, through which women and girls join the world of the mermaid spirits, this paper is less about ethnography than about the interpretation of such rites through the symbolism of the relations between men and women.

The methods of social anthropology as generally illustrated in the classical monographs of the last forty years have purported to 'crack the code' of a vast range of societies, without any direct reference to the female group. At the level of 'observation' in fieldwork, the behaviour of women has, of course, like that of men, been exhaustively plotted: their marriages, their economic activity, their rites and the rest. When we come to that second or 'meta' level of fieldwork, the vast body of debate, discussion, question and answer, that social anthropologists really depend upon to give conviction to their interpretations, there is a real imbalance. We are, for practical purposes, in a male world. The study of women is on a level little higher than the study of the ducks and fowls they commonly own – a mere bird-watching indeed. It is equally revealing and ironical that Lévi-Strauss (1963a: 61) should write: 'for words do not speak, while women do.' For the truth is that women rarely speak in social anthropology in any but that male sense so well exemplified by Lévi-Strauss's own remark: in the sense of merely uttering or giving tongue. It is the very inarticulateness of women that is the technical part of the problem they present. In most societies the ethnographer shares this problem with its male members. The brave failure (with rare exceptions) of even women anthropologists to surmount it really convincingly (and their evident relief when they leave the subject of women) suggests an obvious conclusion. Those trained in ethnography evidently have a bias towards the kinds of model that men are ready to provide (or to concur in) rather than towards any that women might provide. If the men appear 'articulate' compared with the women, it is a case of like speaking to like. To pursue the logic where it leads us: if ethnographers (male and female) want only what the men can give, I suggest it is because the men consistently tend, when pressed, to give a bounded model of society such as ethnographers are attracted to. But the awareness that women appear as lay figures in the men's drama (or like the photographic cut-outs in filmed crowd-scenes) is always dimly present in the ethnographer's mind. Lévi-Strauss, with his perennial ability to experience ethnographic models, thus expressed no more than the truth of all those models when he saw women as items of exchange inexplicably and inappropriately giving tongue.

The technical treatment of the problem is as follows. It is commonly said, with truth, that ethnographers with linguistic difficulties of any kind will find that the men of a society are generally more experienced in bridging this kind of gap than are the women. Thus, as a matter of ordinary experience, interpreters, partial bilinguals or speakers of a vehicular language are more likely to be found among men than among women. For an explanation of this we are referred to statements about the political dominance of men, and their greater mobility. These statements, in their turn, are referred ultimately to the different biological roles of the two sexes. The cumulative effect of these explanations is then: to the degree that communication between ethnographer and people is imperfect, that imperfection drives the ethnographer in greater measure towards men.

This argument while stressing the technical aspect does not dispose of the problem even in its own terms, although we may agree that much ethnography (more than is generally admitted) is affected by factors of this type. It is, however, a common experience that women still 'do not speak' even when linguistic aspects are constant. Ethnographers report that women cannot be reached so easily as men: they giggle when young, snort when old, reject the question, laugh at the topic and the like. The male members of a society frequently see the ethnographer's difficulties as simply a caricature of their own daily case. The technical argument about the incidence of interpreters and so on is therefore really only a confirmation of the importance of the analytical part of the problem. The 'articulateness' of men and of ethnographers is alike, it would appear, in more ways than one. In the same way we may regard as inadequate the more refined explanation that ethnographers 'feed' their own models to their male informants, who are more susceptible for the same technical reasons, and who then feed them back to the ethnographer. That something of this sort does happen is again not to be doubted, but once again the susceptibility of the men is precisely the point. Nor is it an answer to the problem to discuss what might happen if biological facts were different; arguments like 'women through concern with the realities of childbirth and child-rearing have less time for or less propensity towards the making of models of society, for each other, for men, or for ethnographers' (the 'Hot Stove' argument) are again only an expression of the situation they try to explain.

We have here, then, what looked like a technical problem: the difficulty of dealing ethnographically with women. We have, rather, an analytical problem of this sort: if the models of a society made by most ethnographers tend to be models derived from the male portion of that society, how does the symbolic weight of that other mass of persons – half or more of a normal human population, as we have accepted – express itself? Some will maintain that the problem as it is stated here is exaggerated, although only an extremist will deny its existence completely. It may be that individual ethnographers have received from women a picture of a society very similar to the picture given by men. This possibility is conceded, but the female evidence provides in such cases confirmation of a male model which requires no confirmation of this type. The fact is that no one could come back from an ethnographic study of 'the X', having talked only *to* women, and *about* men, without professional comment and some self-doubt. The reverse can and does happen constantly. It is not enough to see this merely as another example of 'injustice to women'. I prefer to suggest that the models of society that women can provide are not of the kind acceptable at first sight to men or to ethnographers, and specifically that, unlike either of these sets of professionals, they do not so readily see society bounded from nature. They lack the metalanguage for its discussion. To put it more simply: they will not necessarily provide a model for society as a unit that will contain both men and themselves. They may indeed provide a model in which women and nature are outside men and society.

I have now deliberately exaggerated, in order to close the gap in a different way. The dominance of men's models of a society in traditional ethnography I take to be accepted. However, men and women do communicate with each other, and are at least aware of each other's models. It has been furthermore the study by ethnographers of myth and belief, collected no doubt, as formerly, largely from men, that has provided the kinds of insights that now make it possible to reopen the problem of women. Much of this material still discusses women from a male viewpoint. Women are classed as inauspicious, dangerous and the like. But models of

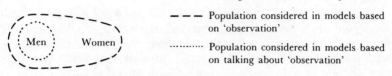

Figure 4.1 Models of observation

society as a symbolic system made from this kind of data are (it is no surprise to note) of a rather different type from the ethnographic (male) models deriving from the older type of fieldwork (e.g. Needham 1958, 1960b, 1967). So much so that many social anthropologists are unable to accept them as 'true' models, that is 'true to reality', where 'reality' is a term of art for what fieldwork reveals. I suggest, on the contrary, that a fieldwork problem of the first magnitude is illuminated. Indeed the astounding deficiency of a method, supposedly objective, is starkly revealed: the failure to include half the people in the total analysis.

STATEMENT AND OBSERVATION

At the risk of labouring the obvious, but to avoid being buried in a righteous avalanche of fieldnotes, I say this yet again with a diagram (figure 4.1).

Because of an interesting failing in the functionalist observational model, statements *about* observation were always added to the ethnographer's own observations. To take a simple case: typically an ethnographer 'observed' a number of marriages and divorces, and heard a number of statements about the frequency of divorce, and then cumulated these quasi-quantitatively into a general statement about divorce frequency. The same process also occurred in other less easily detectable ways, and continues to do so. This confusion had many serious consequences; in particular the difficulty of dealing with statements that were not about 'observation' at all (relegated to 'belief' and the like). For our purposes here, it is enough to note that statements made by the male segment were *about* both males and females. The functionalist confusion of the two levels at any time obscured the inadequacy of the total analysis as far as women were concerned. Since the analysis was always thought to represent observation, or to be checked by observation, it was hard for anyone with field-notes on women to see that they were effectively missing in the total analysis or, more precisely, they were there in the same way as were the Nuer's cows, who were observed but also did not speak.

The students of symbolism cannot be accused of any functionalist bias towards the primacy of observation. Functionalist fieldwork was unhappy with myths precisely because they made statements that conflicted with, could not be cumulated to, objective measures of economic or political status. Not being faced with this mistaken necessity, the symbolists, almost incidentally, rediscovered women, who loom rather large in their material.

In view of the absence of conscient women from the older models, this gains further significance, and suggests a further step, which is taken here. The study of symbolism uncovers certain valuations of women – some of which would have made more sense if women, not men, had made them (they conflict with the social models of men). Old women ('old wives' tales') or mothers (we may extend this analysis even to the lore and language of children) acquire in the world of symbolism something more like their demographic conspicuity. Furthermore, in a field situation poor communication with women in this area is not so often complained of. I here contend that much of this symbolism in fact enacts that female model of the world which has been lacking, and which is different from the models of men in a particular dimension: the placing of the boundary between society and nature.

I suppose in Lévi-Strauss's terms this would place women in an ideologically more primitive position than men. It is not a necessary conclusion. It means something like this: the notion of themselves in society is imposed by its members upon a relatively unbounded continuum in ways which involve the setting up of a multitude of bounded categories, the bounds being marked by taboo, ridicule, pollution, category inversion and the rest, so ably documented of late by social anthropologists (Douglas 1966a; Leach 1961b, 1964). The tension between 'culture' and 'nature' (the 'wild') is to be understood as an outcome of this struggle, from which no human beings are free. The appreciation of the symbolic stress on the division between society and nature derives from Lévi-Strauss (1949), and lies behind much of his later work, including the three volumes of *Mythologiques* (1964, 1966b, 1968). Lévi-Strauss now prefers the terminology 'nature' and 'culture' (1967b: 3; trans. 1969: 3). Of late he has also been concerned to state that the distinction lacks objective criteria (1967b: 12). This concern seems surprising since it is easily resolved as Lévi-Strauss himself shows:

The contrast of nature and culture would be neither a primeval fact, nor a concrete aspect of universal order. Rather it should be seen as an artificial creation of culture, a protective rampart thrown up around it because it only felt able to assert its existence and uniqueness by destroying all the links that led back to its original association with the other manifestations of life (1967b: xvii, trans. 1969: xxix).

Within this wider task men have to bound themselves in relation both to women and to nature.

Since women are biologically not men, it would be surprising if they bounded themselves against nature in the same way as men do. Yet we have seen that the men's models are characteristically dominant in ethnography. If men are the ones who become aware of 'other cultures' more frequently than do women, it may well be that they are likely to develop meta-levels of categorization that enable them at least to consider the necessity to bound themselves-and-their-women from other-men-and-their-women. Thus all such ways of bounding society against society, including our own, may have an inherent maleness. The first level is still recognizable, however, in the tendency to slip back to it from the meta-level: that is, to class other men and their wives with nature; as the Germans say, as *Naturmensch* (cf. Lévi-Strauss 1967b: xvi). If men, because of their political dominance, may tend purely pragmatically to 'need' total bounding models of either type, women may tend to take over men's models when they share the same definitional problems as men. But the models set up by women bounding themselves are not encompassed in those men's models. They still subsist, and both sexes through their common humanity are aware of the contradictions. In the social anthropologist's data the process can be more clearly viewed.

MAN, MOUSE, APE, AND WATER SPIRIT

According to a story of the Bakweri of Cameroon (in a male recension): 'Moto, Ewaki, Eto and Mojili were always quarrelling and agreed to decide by a test which of them was to remain in the town and which should go into the bush. All were to light fires in their houses in the morning and the person whose fire was still burning on their return from the farms in the evening was to be the favoured one. Moto being more cunning than the others built a fire with big sticks properly arranged, whereas they only built with small dry sticks, and so his was the only fire that was still alight on their return in the evening. Thus Moto remained in the town and became Man. Ewaki and Eto went into the bush and became the Ape and the Mouse. Mojili was driven into the water and became a water spirit.'[2] *Moto* (Common Bantu **muntu*) is the ordinary Bakweri word for 'human being of either sex', and thus includes 'woman'. Ewaki, Eto and Mojili, who are opposed to Moto by reason of his special skill with fire, lack of which relegates them to the bush, are in Bakweri belief all associated with women and their children, whom they attract into their domain. Mojili is responsible for young girls becoming mermaids (*liengu*, plural *maengu*) who are dangerous to men, and whose husbands are *eto* (pl. *veto*), the rats; while the attraction of human children to the apes of the forest is so great that the word *ewaki* must not be mentioned in front of children under seven, in case they fall sick and die. Mojili's name has the same effect. Rites exist to control these manifestations (Ardener, E. 1956).[3]

The possible marginality of women when men are defining 'the wild' is evident. Thus the idea of the denizens of the wild, outside Moto's village, being a danger or attraction to women and their offspring is comprehensible in a male model of the universe, in which female reproductive powers do not fall under male control. This is, however, inadequate. Bakweri women themselves bound their world as including the wild that Moto excluded. They go through rites by which they become *liengu* mermaid spirits, or spirits of the forest, generally in adolescence, and retain this feature of womanhood throughout their lives. The story of Moto gives the clue, for the three excluded 'animal' brothers all have the human gift of fire. Although the men bound off 'mankind' from nature, the women persist in overlapping into nature again. For men among the Bakweri this overlapping symbolic area is clearly related to women's reproductive powers. Since these powers are for women far from being marginal, but are of their essence as women, it would seem that a woman's model of the world would also treat them as central. When we speak of Bakweri belief we must therefore recognize a man's sector and a woman's sector, which have to be reconciled. Thus the myth of Moto states the problem of woman for Bakweri men: she insists on living in what is for them the wild.

MERMAIDS AND THE WILD

The wild for the male Bakweri is particularly well differentiated, because of the many striking forms in which it expresses itself. This people occupies the South-Eastern face of the 13,000 foot Cameroon Mountain, on the West African coast of Cameroon – an environment of romantic contrasts. The mountain rises straight from a rocky sea coast through zones of forest, grass and bare lava to the active volcanic craters of the peak. The Bakweri proper occupy the forest, and hunt in the grass zones. A deity or hero, Efasamote, occupies the peak. Congeners of the Bakweri (Mboko, Isubu and Wovea Islanders) occupy the rocky strand, and fish. The Bakweri proper are agriculturists; the staple crop was traditionally the male-cultivated plantain banana, although since the introduction of the Xanthosoma cocoyam in the last century, this female crop has become the staple (Ardener, E. 1970c). It should be added that the whole area is now greatly fragmented by plantations and a large migrant population now lives in the Bakweri area (Ardener, E. Ardener, S. and Warmington 1960). The mountain is an extremely wet place, and visibility is often reduced to a few yards because of the clouds that cover it for much of the time.

The villages are traditionally fenced – people and livestock living inside the fence, the farms being outside the fence. This way of looking at it is not inaccurate. In the light of the subject of this paper it is, however, just as true to say: the men live inside the fence with their livestock (goats, cows and pigs) and most of their plantains; the women go outside the fence for their two main activities – firewood-collecting and farming the Xanthosoma. The men and their livestock are so closely associated that the animals have characteristically lived in the houses themselves. I have myself visited in his hut an elderly man on his bed, so hemmed in by dwarf cows (still the size of ponies) that it was difficult to reach him. The women are in the forest outside the fence all day, returning at evening with their back-breaking loads of wood and cocoyams, streaming with rain, odds and ends tied up with bark strips and fronds, and screaming with fatigue at their husbands, with the constant reiteration in their complaints of the word *wanga* 'bush', 'the forest'. The Bakweri men wait in their leaking huts for the evening meal. It is no wonder that the women seem to be forest creatures, who might vanish one day for ever.

At the coast, the 'wild' *par excellence* is the sea, and its symbolism is expressed through the *liengu* water-spirits. The Cameroon coast provides a kaleidoscope of beliefs about *liengu*. They are found among the Kole, the

Duala, the Wovea, the Oli, the Tanga, the Yasa and many other peoples. Ittmann (1957) gathers together material from numbers of such sources.[4] The common theme is, however, used in the different belief systems of the various peoples in different ways. As I have tried to demonstrate elsewhere (1970c), from a consideration of the Bakweri zombie belief, the *content* of a belief system can be analysed as a specific problem, by methods of the type used by Lévi-Strauss in *Mythologiques* (1964, 1966b, 1968), as well as through those of more humdrum ethnographic aim. Among the latter, it is possible to discuss the geographical distribution of parts of the content of the belief, and consider, in the *liengu* case, questions such as whether the mermaids 'are' manatees or dugongs, which will not concern us here. The *realien* of the belief for each people are the elements plundered by the *bricoleur*: dugongs, mermaids are all to hand, but what dictates the particular disposition of elements in each system, the 'template' of the belief?

The Bakweri incorporate the *liengu* mermaids into a damp tree-ridden environment in which the sea is not visible, or is seen only far off on clear days, and in which the forest is the dominant external embodiment of the wild. The *liengu* beliefs and rites are in detail marked as a result by the inconsistency of a marine iconography with a non-marine environment. We have various different combinations producing a patchwork of several women's rites all of which are linked by the name *liengu*, some of which have content that links them with certain other West African rites. They are all enacted, however, as a response to a fit or seizure that comes mainly upon adolescent girls but also upon older women. For those men who participate in the rites, the stress is laid upon the 'curing' of the women. For, as we shall see, the men have their own view of the rites. *Liengu la ndiva* (*ndiva*: 'deep water') appears to retain the closest connection with the water-spirits.[5] The sickness attacks a girl or woman, characteristically, by causing her to faint over the fireplace, so that she knocks out one of the tree stones that are used to support the cooking pots. A woman versed in this form of *liengu* then comes and addresses her in the secret *liengu* language. If she shows any signs of comprehension, a *liengu* doctor (male or female) is called and given a black cock, on which he spits alligator pepper; he then kills it and sprinkles its blood in the hole made when the girl knocked out the hearth-stone, and replaces the stone. The patient then enters a period of seclusion. Drummers are called on a fixed evening, the girl herself staying in an inner room, dressed only in a skirt made of strips of bark of roots of the *iroko* tree, hung over a waist string. The doctor then makes her a medicine which she vomits, bringing up the black seeds of the wild banana; these are then threaded on a string and worn like a bandolier. The drummers stay all night and they and the doctor receive a fee. There are usually a number of visitors, especially *liengu* women, and these are given food.

During the period of seclusion which then follows, the girl has a woman sponsor who teaches her the secret *liengu* language, and gives her a *liengu* name. She is subject to a number of conventions and taboos during this period, which will be summarized later. After several months, the *liengu* doctor is called again, and, in the darkness before dawn, she is picked up and carried in turn, one by one, by men chosen for their strength, until they reach the deep part of a stream where the doctor pushes her in. Women who accompany them sing *liengu* songs, and the company try to catch a crab, representing the water-spirit. After this rite, the girl is regarded as being a familiar of the water-spirits and one of the *liengu* women. On the return of the party, the *liengu* drummers play and food is provided for the guests. After the visit to the stream the girl stays in her house for a further period. On the occasion when she finally comes out the doctor and the drummers, and other women and visitors, come to the house, where she is dressed in new clothing. Traditionally she was rubbed with camwood. There is another feast, and she is regarded by the men as finally immune from any attack by the water-spirits.

Liεngu la mɔngbango differs from *ndiva* in several respects. For example, the first symptom is sometimes said to be the girl disappearing into the bush as if attracted by spirits. She is then sought by a group of female relatives singing to her in *liengu* language, and when she is found, is taken to the seclusion room. There the doctor makes the vomiting medicine as in *Liεngu, la ndiva*. Details of the seclusion show little difference, but in this case it does not last the whole period of the rite. After a few months, a feast is made which is traditionally all eaten on the ground, after which the girl is allowed to go out, although still subject to taboos. After a further period of about nine months, a sheep is killed and a similar feast made, the girl and her *liengu* woman sponsor being secluded in an enclosure in the bush. She is now dressed in fern-fronds (*senge* or *njombi*) rubbed with camwood, and led through the village tied to the middle of a long rope held by her companions in front and behind. Outside her house, both sets of people pull the rope, as in a tug of war, until the rope comes apart, when the girl falls down, as if dead. She is revived by being called nine times in the *liengu* language, after which she gets up, and is dressed in new clothing. A few weeks later, she is washed in a stream by the doctor to show that she is free from the taboos she observed during the rites. Both with *ndiva* and *mongbango* the rites extend over about a year.

A third version of the rite, *liεngu la vefea*, reduces the procedure essentially to the killing of a goat and a young cock, and the drinking of the vomiting medicine followed by food taboos. The medicine is the same in all three rites. Among the upper Bakweri who live furthest from the sea, an even more generalized *liengu* rite seems to have existed in which the simple *rite de passage* aspect is very noticeable. It is said that formerly every daughter was put through *liengu* at about eight to ten years of age so that she would be fertile. She would wear fern-fronds and be secluded for a period, apparently shorter than in the above examples. Other variations in detail appear to have existed in different places and at different times.[6]

The reduced rites were, at the time of my first acquaintance with the Bakweri (in 1953), the commonest. The people had, during the previous generation, been overwhelmed by their belief that they were 'dying out' – a belief not without some slight demographic justification. Their economy was stagnant. Public rites of all kinds had gone into decline. The people blamed the general conditions of their country on witchcraft. The decline of the *liengu* rites was further blamed by many for the fertility problems of Bakweri women. Nevertheless, a celebration of the *mongbango* ceremony occurred in that same year. In 1958 a Bakweri *liengu* girl was even brought, with a *liengu* mother, to grace a Cameroon Trade Fair. Since then there has been a revival of all kinds of *liengu* rites (I was asked to contribute to the expenses of one in 1970). However, the great rites of *mongbango* and *ndiva*, because of their expense, were probably always relatively rare, compared with *vefea* and other reduced rites. The latter are also common now, because so many *liengu* celebrations are 'remedial', for women who did not pass through them in their adolescence – during the long period of decline. Nevertheless, even such women are told the ideology of the great rites: the immersion (of *ndiva*), the tug of war (of *mongbango*), the seclusion and the secret language. Since we are concerned here with the dimension of belief, it may be added that the image of the *liengu* is a powerful one even for the many Christian, educated and urban Bakweri women. Scraps of the secret language are common currency. It is as if the *liengu* rites are always 'there' as a possibility of fulfilment; and also as if the rites are themselves less important than the vision of women's place in nature that appears in them: the template of the belief.

Despite the fact that *liengu* is a woman's rite, men are not immune to the precipitating sickness, especially if there are no women left in a man's extended family, and rare cases are cited in which men have gone through at least part of the rite. The fertility associations of the rite are uppermost in such cases, and the *liengu* mermaids have had to work through a male in the absence of viable females. *Liengu* doctors may be men or women. As we shall see, the participation of men does not obscure the symbolism of the rites for women. It does assist their symbolism for men. Thus the men who carry the *ndiva* girl have to be strong. Although men from her matrilineage (in practice, perhaps, her full brothers) would be favoured, a man from her patrilineage, or just a fellow-villager would be acceptable. Men see themselves as helping out with the treatment of morbidity (social and physical) in women. The domination of men as doctors in Bakweri medical rites means that the specialization as *liengu* doctors by men presents few problems. The major rites (*ndiva* and *mongbango*) have a public aspect, because of their relative expense, and a male doctor is likely to be involved. The female *liengu* doctors are associated with the less expensive, reduced, rites. The 'medical' aspects of the rite have thus a somewhat 'male' aspect.

The female significance of the rites lies in the girl's acceptance by her fellow *liengu* women. In the fuller *ndiva* and *mongbango* forms, as already noted, it is customary for her to have a sponsor (*nyangb'a liɛngu*, '*liengu* mother') to teach her the mysteries. For the periods of seclusion, in both rites, the girl is not allowed to plait her hair but must must let it grow uncontrolled, and rub it, as well as her whole body, with charcoal mixed with palm-kernel oil, so that she is completely black. This is supposed to make her resemble a spirit. She is forbidden to talk to visitors, but greets them with a rattle, of different types in *liɛngu la ndiva* (*njola*, made of wicker-work) and in *mongbango* (*lisonjo*, made of certain tree-seed shells). This is also used night and morning, when she has to recite certain formulae in the *liengu* language. While in the house, the *liengu*, as the girl herself is now called, treats rats (*veto*) with special respect as they are regarded as her husbands (compare the story of Moto above). If a rat is killed she must cry all day and wash it and bury it in a cloth; killing rats in her compound is forbidden. No man or boy can enter the *liengu* house wearing a hat or shoes, or carrying a book (all introduced by Europeans) or she will seize them, and return them only on the payment of a fine. If a person dies in the village the *liengu* must not eat all day. In *liengu la mɔngbango*, after her period of seclusion, and before the completion of the rite, the girl may go out only with her rattle, and should turn away if she sees any person not a Bakweri. If anyone wishes to stop her he has only to say the word *yowo* ('magical rite') and she must do whatever he says. However, the *liengu* has an effective retaliation if molested, as any male whom she knocks with her rattle is thought to become permanently impotent. The *liengu* may not go into any room but her own and dogs must not go near her. She should always be addressed by her special *liengu* name. Truncated forms of these requirements are also followed by women in the *vefea* rite. After all rites the participant is henceforth known by one of a standard series of *liengu* names.

SYMBOLISM OF THE MERMAID CULT

It has been the intention here merely to indicate those aspects of the symbolism that are peculiar to the *liengu* corpus. This is not the place for an extended analysis, which I hope to attempt elsewhere. The male interpretation is that the *liengu* rites cure a spiritual illness. That is why male doctors take part. The women nod at this sort of interpretation in male Bakweri company, but there is a heady excitement when the *liengu* subject is raised in the absence of Bakweri men. It is accepted that the *liengu* mermaid spirits do 'trouble' the women, and cause them physical symptoms. The trouble is solved when a woman becomes a *liengu*. The mermaid world is one of Alice through the looking-glass – no manmade objects, garments only of forest products; no imported goods, traded through men.[7] For the edible plantain banana, a male crop and consciously seen as clearly phallic, we find the inedible seed-filled, wild banana – a total symbolic reversal whose effect is a 'feminization' of the male symbol. The male doctor, who is perhaps only a half-aware participant in this, makes the medicine in an integument of (male) plantain leaves to hem in its harmful effects. The rites see the women as attracted away into the wild. The domestic hearth-stone (*lio*) is the popular symbol of the household (a unit in the essentially patrilineal residence pattern). It is dislodged. In *mongbango* food is eaten on the earth, and not on the customary (male) plantain leaves. The mermaid's rattle destroys the potency of males. The men are reduced to the scale of little rats, her 'husbands'. She returns to the world through the symbolic tug of war at which she is in the middle. She falls senseless. The men assume the world has won. Yet she is revived by nine calls in the *liengu* language. There is surely little reassuring to men in her final incorporation in the wild outside the fence of the village.[8]

The interpretation of the Bakweri *liengu* rites as 'nubility rites', because they often (but not always) precede marriage, is not exactly an error, since it does not say anything. It merely draws attention to the question 'what after all *is* a nubility rite?' Passage through *liengu* rites shows that a girl is a woman; her fellow-women vouch for it. The men feel a danger has been averted; she has been rescued from the wild and is fitted for marriage with men. But she still continues to bear a spirit name, and converses with fellow-women in the mermaid language. The term 'nubility rite' implies for some that the rites have a social 'function'; the girl takes her place in the system of relations between corporate kin-groups. The rites no doubt can be shown to 'validate' this and that aspect of the structure in the normal 'functionalist' manner. Alternatively they prepare the girl for the role of exchangeable unit in a system of alliance. These are good partial statements, but we are left asking questions like 'why did she vomit the seeds of the wild banana?' The terms 'puberty rite' and 'fertility rite' would be just as useful and just as partial. 'Puberty' stresses the biological basis that 'nubility' obscures, but of course even when the rites are not delayed until after marriage, they may take place some years after the onset of puberty – the rigid association of puberty with the menarche is a result of our mania for precision. 'Fertility' at least takes account of the association of the rites with a whole period of the woman's life. They are also 'medical rites' because they 'cure' sickness, and share features in common with Bakweri medical rites for men and women. A set of overlapping analyses such as Richards makes for *Chisungu* (1956) would clearly be equally fruitful here.

The rites are open to analysis in the manner of Van Gennep as classical rites of passage. They fall like all such rites into stages of separation, transition and incorporation, but the notion of passage is either self-evident (through the rite) or inadequately defined. An analysis in the manner of Turner (1967) could also be attempted, and it is evident that there is the material for such an analysis. The Turnerian method assumes that symbolism is generated by society as a whole. This is of course in a sense true: the very contradiction of symbolic systems, their 'multivalency', 'polysemy', 'condensation' and the like, derive from the totalitarian nature of symbolism. But as the Moto story shows, its surface structure may express the male view of the world, obscuring the existence at deeper levels of an autonomous female view. I feel also that Turner does not perceive the 'bounding' problem that male/female symbolism is about, and which introduces an element of ordering into the symbolic sets.

I have argued that Bakweri women define the boundary of their world in such a way that they live as women in the men's wild, as well as partly within the men's world inside the village fence. In modern times the world outside the fence has included the 'strangers', migrants who are allowed to settle there. Sometimes the strangers' quarter is larger than the Bakweri settlement. Bakweri women have long travelled from stranger-quarter to stranger-quarter, entering into casual liaisons, while the men have complained (Ardener, E., Ardener, S. and Warmington 1960: 294–308; Ardener, E. 1962). This fortuitous overlap of the old wild with the new urban jungle may well account for the peculiar sense of defeat the Bakweri showed for so many years, which made them come to believe that zombies were killing them off (Ardener, E. 1956, 1970c). For the women's part, it is possibly not sufficient to account for their notable conjugal freedom, as I have argued elsewhere (1962), merely on the grounds that there are nearly three males to every woman in the plantation area. The Bakweri system of double descent similarly expresses the basic dichotomy. The patrilineage controls residence (the village), the inheritance of land and cattle, succession to political office – the men's world. The matrilineage controls fertility, and its symbolic fertility bangle is found on a woman's farm outside the village fence (Ardener, E. 1956).

MANKIND AND WOMANKIND

The Bakweri illustration can only briefly document my theme. Men's models of society are expressed at a meta-level which purports to define women. Only at the level of the analysis of belief can the voiceless masses be restored to speech. Not only women, but (a task to be attempted later) inarticulate classes of men, young people and children. We are all lay figures in someone else's play.

The objective basis of the symbolic distinction between nature and society, which Lévi-Strauss recently retreated from prematurely, is a result of the problem of accommodating the two logical sets which classify human beings by different bodily structures: 'male'/'female'; with the two other sets: 'human'/'non-human'. It is, I have suggested, men who usually come to face this problem, and, because their model for *mankind* is based on that for *man*, their opposites, *women* and *non-mankind* (the wild), tend to be ambiguously placed. Hence, in Douglas's terms (1966a), come their sacred and polluting aspects. Women accept the implied symbolic content, by equating *womankind* with the men's wild (see figure 4.2).

The topic of this paper is 'the problem of women'. Women, of course, have 'a problem of men', who may indeed live in a part of the wild that women bound off from themselves. With that world of hunting and war, both sexes are familiar. The men's wild is, of course, a threat to women. The *liengu* taboos of the Bakweri express some of this. The secluded mermaids hate European goods, which have increased male power. The tabooed 'male' animal, the dog (used in the chase), is an added danger because it can see the spirit world. Dogs walk purposefully on their own, although they have nowhere to go, and they frequently stare attentively into space. Bakweri men have their own symbolic zone of adventure and hunting beyond that of the women, on the mountain-top away from all villages and farms. This is ritually expressed in the men's elephant dance (Ardener, E. 1959a). Elephants sometimes emerge from the remote parts of the mountain and destroy the women's farms. Men and boys in many villages

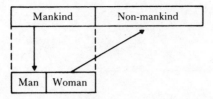

Figure 4.2 The problem

belong to an elephant society, a closed association that claims responsibility for the work of elephants, through the elephant-doubles (*naguals*) of its more powerful members. In their annual dance they enact their control over the elephant world. Women on such occasions form the audience, who clap out the rhythm for the men's virtuoso dancer. Some women rather half-heartedly claim the role of bush-pigs, but like Dames in an order of chivalry or girls at Roedean, they are performing a male scenario.[9]

It is a tragedy of the male life-position that, in the modern age, the men's wild is not now so easily accessible to them. For modern Bakweri as for American males the hunting fantasy at least is no longer plausible. For if women still symbolically live in their wild, men have tried to ignore their own in the official symbolism of civilization. It will have emerged that the argument of this paper as it applies to women is a special but submerged case of the mode whereby self-identification is made. Obviously the different classes of men and of women, and individuals of all ages and both sexes contribute to that totality of symbolism – which merely appears a 'forest' when one fails to look at the trees.

To return, then, to the limited problem of my title, we need not doubt that the societies from which ethnographers come share the problem of all societies. If, as I suggest is the case, men's models of society accommodate women only by making certain assumptions that ignore or hold constant elements that would contradict these models, then the process may be traced further back into the ethnographer's own thinking and his own society. Our women ethnographers may then be expressing the 'maleness' of their subject when they approach the women of other societies.[10] It may well be, too, that their positive reluctance to deal with the problem of women is the greater because they sense that its consideration would split apart the very framework in which they conduct their studies.

5

Some Outstanding Problems
in the Analysis of Events

Recent theoretical developments in social anthropology have moved so fast that it will perhaps at least be helpful to clarify or develop some of my own usages, scattered in various places. I regard most of them as mere stepping stones to understanding. I shall inevitably be touching on the place of the linguistic in the social, but the time has come when social anthropology must reject some criticisms couched merely in terms of the data of other subject-matters. I have exercised almost total self-restraint in citing parallels from other disciplines or from other anthropological writers whose views I have considered to have had priority, or to have matched mine in some respects. Nowadays, so many authorities recant or revise their views (with an admirable provisionality), that instead of referring to them, I shall present my argument from anthropological scratch, and relatively unadorned. I have cited numerous references elsewhere. On this occasion, I shall begin from the point reached in the 'The New Anthropology and Its Critics' (above, chapter 2), and take some of the implications of poststructural theory for our view of the social as a manifold of both *thought* and *behaviour*. In this chapter I try to lighten the heavy load that specific terms lay across analysis.

EVENTS AS OUTPUT

The image of a stream of events that the social anthropologist's initial task was to meter was never far from the minds of early fieldworkers. The journalist's idea of a 'newspaper of record', the old historian's conception of a 'chronicle' or 'annals', and the whole modern development of methods of *documentation* suffice to show that the image of the notionally complete registration of events has a respectable genealogy – respectable enough for its implications to have the invisibility of either the self-evident or the unexamined. Everybody now knows and acknowledges that the 'events' that are regstered are inseparably related to the mode of registration. Yet, as common-sense beings, we are used to identifying an event determined by one mode with an event determined by another, as by sight and by sound; or (at another level) by radio, press and television, or by document and by an oral communication; or (at another level still) by a theory of economics and a theory of psychology. Still, we come at once to an intractability about events; they have to be recognized, detected or picked up by modes of registration. We must know as much as possible about these modes.

Let us suppose that the stream of events is there, 'as advertised'. A simple output model would suffice. The 'events' pass the social anthropologist as on a conveyor belt. He describes them according to selected criteria. He defines the events as if they were carburetors. From records of stretches of output he sets out relations, redefinitions and the like. On a real conveyor belt a sequence from 'carburetors' to 'dynamos' is a more significant one than that from one carburetor to another. In our output of events, however, we pass figuratively from carburetor to dynamo without guidance. The first dynamos are described as aberrant carburetors, or a new term is invented to subsume both types. Given enough 'output', classifications may fit more and more closely to the new units. But it will be seen at once that the view of our subject matter as an output of events leaves us gravely handicapped because of the retrospective nature of our interpretations and our inability to return to check our original specifications, save through our record of them. Nevertheless, even this simple picture enables us to grasp the nature of one use of *significant* as applied to events.

If the output model is now strengthened by the addition of a programmatic component, we see that a discontinuity as between carburetors and dynamos would be discoverable in the programme (see above, chapter 2). On a conveyor belt it is a laborious waste of time to observe the output in order to determine the nature of the units in it, for the programme is available – not only laying down the significant units: carburetors or dynamos, but specifying, perhaps, that ten carburetors will be followed by fifty dynamos. Even the superior combination, 'output and programme' is only of a crude and elementary assistance to us – a temporary crutch – for two reasons: first, our definition of units in the output – the 'events' – depends upon the modes of registration available to us. And second, the programme for the stream of events does not 'exist' in a separate box or office from the output – at least not as far as we are concerned.

This must be the end of that image, therefore. Nevertheless, it throws light on some dilemmas. If you wish to continue to separate the anthropologist observer from the object of his study as heretofore, you must visualize that the programme is located in the output, and generated simultaneously with it. Or if you like, each event is differently 'marked' for programmatic content – some are nearly all 'output'; others are nearly all 'programme'; others in between. Even the anthropologist as observer is thus required to see himself as a being with a mode of registration somewhat more sophisticated than that of a camera. As the *programmatic* content is not crudely observable, we shall need a definition of *event* that includes the supposedly unobservable. Since the so-called observer can himself only register his apprehensions of those events through his own mesh of social and psychological categories, we see that a satisfactory number of current anthropological concerns are before us. Before we leave the conveyor belt, therefore, it is worth noting that social anthropologists even in their most empiricist garb have rarely assumed they were only checking off output. Even when counting stocks of yams they were also charting myths. Thus the 'observed' events always included (for example) linguistic events, even when these events were inadequately delineated.

STRUCTURES

The structures that social anthropologists have hypothesized out of the foregoing are: (1) structures homologous with those of the programme; (2) structures homologous with those of the output; and (for the observer) (3) the modes of registration he has: systems of interpretation and technical and cultural categories of his own, aware and unaware.

Only (1) and (2) will occupy us for the moment. These I have termed elsewhere *paradigmatic* and *syntagmatic*. It is however unfortunate that the term *paradigm* has achieved common conversational currency as often little more than a vogue synonym of *pattern*, sometimes only of *tabulation*. It is already far gone on the road taken already by *model* and *syndrome*. In addition, those of us who have used the *paradigmatic/syntagmatic* terminology have had to cope with the different levels at which this relation can be applied. The relation is an abstract one of great power and importance. Yet it has become data-laden in different ways through its applications, quite legitimate in themselves, to the material of varied disciplines. For that reason, new terms will be used later.

I want here to demonstrate that social anthropologists do not need to turn to any material but their own to express this abstract relation. We shall consider anthropological usages. In so doing we shall discover that we are dealing with matters that are not parasitical on the terminology of other disciplines. We are concerned with certain structural universals that cannot help appearing in all fields concerned with human beings. It is with reluctance then, that I here cut the painter linking our terms with those of other disciplines for the moment. Let no one turn to a dictionary, or to Saussure or Jakobson or Roland Barthes or Kuhn or Lévi-Strauss to elucidate or to 'correct' the following remarks. Erase all images of *paradigms* from the mind.

ETHNOGRAPHY

The necessity for a distinction between 'levels' in structural analysis has been a commonplace. In considering the case of the Bakweri *nyongo* phenomenon, a distinction emerged in this way. Certain kinds of zombie manifestations were correlated with low economic performance of the mass of the population. Yet that which correlated on each occasion was not the symbolic content of the behaviour. This was separately 'assembled' at the different periods of manifestation, or so I hypothesized, through new symbols, or newly arranged old symbols. Thus, at one period, zombie manifestations were caused by persons who had built corrugated iron houses. They were thought to kill their younger relatives and to use them as zombie labour. At another period, the zombie phenomena were thought to be caused by 'Frenchmen'. The content was not continuous over time, but something else was: a repetitive, distinctive, structuring tendency that I called then the *template* (Ardener, E. 1970c: 155).

On another occasion, the Bakweri (who lived on a long-quiescent volcano) blamed a serious eruption upon Posts and Telegraphs engineers who had scraped the mountain's back to build a rough, rock-strewn road to a VHF station. A new rite of exorcism and appeasement was devised by elders for performance on the road, which upon Bakweri representation was barred to vehicles for the time being (Ardener, E. 1959a). The content of the new rite was congruent (we see with hindsight) with other rites, but the new one did not derive from any other. It could not simply be generated from all previously extant rites. Merely to verbalize this distinction requires us to propose at least two structuring processes: one that shapes, and a second that builds. In this case, a 'well-formed rite' for a Bakweri is recognized in terms quite different from one devised by Sicilians for an eruption on Mt Etna. The Bakweri would be able to produce a rite, even in the absence of traditional props and with the use of foreign or modern symbolic elements, that was still 'well-formed'. The building process may be likened to the *bricolage* of Lévi-Strauss.

To take a further example: The Bakweri mermaid (mammy-water) or *liengu* rites for women are built up from elements common to the peoples of the whole Bight of Biafra. The template in this case was peculiar to the Bakweri, with elements derived from the ambiguity in self-classification between men and women as expressed through a characteristic contradiction in the Bakweri view of the 'wild' (see above, chapter 4).

Again, certain peoples like the Ibo show a remarkable lability in their symbolic forms. 'New customs', 'modifications' and 'modernizations' follow each other rapidly. It seemed here that the *bricolage* facility was exaggerated, 'overdetermined'. The new shapes were 'Ibo' despite their frequent transformations of content. The 'novelties' were not relevant to a definition of what was Ibo. This feature seems to be characteristic of highly adaptive, 'strong' but 'modernizing' cultures, of which the Japanese may be a supreme example.

In all of these cases the need for a distinction between two kinds of structures is strengthened by a practical difference in the methods available for their analysis. The former are in one terminology *template structures* and the latter *structures of realizations*. The latter present no problems. All observational and recording devices provide data. In addition, linguistic and textual analyses of many kinds are possible and in order. That point must be stressed, since some 'structuralists' are concerned with these structures in their own data quite as often as most 'functionalists', although with characteristic differences. The *s*-structures then, as we may now call the structures of realization, appear in the normal flux of experience. They are studiable in the 'stream of events' itself.

The *p*-structures, as we may now call the template structures, are a different class, set up as unknowns, posited before identified. As far as social anthropology is concerned, they are its quarks or hadrons. But we can say something about them. We apprehend (or construct) them out of the same world as the *s*-structure, but we can document them only by their reflections, or their *reflexes*.

S-STRUCTURES

In studying witchcraft (for example), it is a commonplace to examine the 'personnel' involved. There may perhaps be an analysis of the sex, age and socio-economic status of the accused. It is no surprise that a category labelled *marginality* or *deviance* may frequently seem appropriate to cover the human constellations revealed. I. M. Lewis (1971) has expressed essentially the synchronic form of such an approach, K. V. Thomas (1971) the diachronic. Explanations of phenomena in terms of the observable characteristics of the participants, their demography, their relative positions in 'social systems' and the like are all explanations based upon *s*-structures. In the Bakweri case of the zombie witchcraft, it would be possible to plot *s*-structures of these kinds.

The problem presented by *s*-structures lies in their contingent quality. That may appear strange since such structures (or more precisely terms, whose only embodiment lies in such structures) form the common basis for conventional sociological analysis, and the 'social structure' itself is simply its most inclusive example. The problem becomes acute where *s*-structures are considered over time. If the phenomenon that an *s*-structure is to explain 'disappears', as for example, witchcraft in late eighteenth-century England, we may be forced to propose that the *s*-structure itself has no longer any validity: the formerly marginal categories no longer exist, let us say, or at least, this kind of marginality is no longer 'significant'. It is obvious that we are soon in difficulties. Few students of witchcraft can nowadays bring themselves to argue that the *s*-structures *are* witchcraft, in some way. They admit nowadays that they are handed the term *witchcraft* 'in advance' as part of a system of ideas – even as a word among words. The question of *whose* system of ideas, a world in whose language, is quite commonly discussed, but more, perhaps, by social anthropologists than by historians.

A *P*-STRUCTURE

It must follow from the argument so far that *p*-structures cannot appear to the analyst by the methods that will generate *s*-structures. It is quite wrong to be asked to be 'shown' a *p*-structure; *p*-structures are unknowns, almost by definition. On the other hand, it has been stated that such structures, if they have any existence, must be revealed in the stream of events. If so,

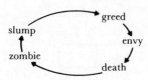

Figure 5.1   Bakweri witchcraft

linguistic problems loom very large in their consideration. The normal terminological and onomastic process ascribes labels to *s*-structures with ease, for most of our categories in social studies are of *s*-type. We can sense what a *p*-structure should have in it, but the terms available to us are either overspecific or underspecific, the result of using an educated discourse brought up on *s*-structures.

For example, one *p*-structure that we require for the specification of a witchcraft system has in it some component for relating persons to misfortune through other persons. In the Bakweri zombie witchcraft case, we can begin to shadow the elements of the *p*-structure with preliminary hints like this:

Individual self-betterment ↔ public misfortune

You will recall that when boom agricultural conditions occurred, the threshold of 'activation' of the *p*-structure rose: no zombie manifestations. In slumps, the threshold fell: zombie manifestations appeared. Bakweri talked of *inona* ('envy') as being generated by *nyanga* ('pride', 'ambitious achievement'). Self-betterment resulted from the killing of fellow Bakweri (particularly one's own children) and using the dead bodies to work as zombies. All these elements present a complicated problem for description by the anthropologist, since what is describable is realized in *s*-structures. String these emotive words together (see figure 5.1). We have an impression of the *p*-structure when activated: the hollow shape of its shadow in language. Nevertheless, this one is rooted in concepts of 'property', and in economic behaviour, as well as in 'affective', even adrenal, matters. For the moment we may just note that this structure may be difficult to express but may be easier to 'locate'. I fear that even this example will have over-concretized the anthropological view of such a structure. Critics should remember then that for the moment we are concerned entirely with generating such structures from purely anthropological data.

THE CALIBRATION OF P-STRUCTURES AND
S-STRUCTURES

P-structures and *s*-structures cause difficulties because their calibrations do not directly match. To make them fit we must propose something between them – a black box, as it were, in which all calibration problems are solved. I will call it a *mode of specification* (see figure 5.2).

p-structures

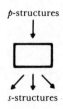

s-structures

Figure 5.2   Mode of specification

MODE OF SPECIFICATION

The black box specifies the particular realization of the elements of the *p*-structures. The mode of specification for the Bakweri zombie witchcraft included a very practical one: 'owners of metal-roofed houses are zombie masters.' Another was: 'all sudden deaths, especially of young persons are caused by zombie masters.' We can list a whole string. When we talk of *witchcraft* as having elements of universality, it is easy to see that we are talking of certain similarities essentially between *p*-structures. Despite the peculiarities of the observable aspects of Bakweri zombie manifestations compared with English witchcraft, the difference between the *p*-structures is much less great. We can hypothesize (the language shadow of) a *p*-structure thus: misfortune ↔ personal cause. We require a mode of specification of the kinds of events that qualify as misfortune and where to find the personal causes. Very similar *p*-structures may have very different modes of specification, thus generating very different *s*-structures. Statements like 'deprived, marginal, persons' belong now in the mode of specification, through which the *s*-structures are generated.

When we look at this phenomenon that we have chosen to call *witchcraft*, we see at once that changes may occur in the *p*-structures, in the mode of specification, and in the *s*-structures. If the *p*-structure changes to: misfortune ↔ *im*personal cause, the mode of specification and the generated *s*-structures automatically change. Witchcraft vanishes. If the mode of specification changes, but the *p*-structures do not, we see different types of grounds for witchcraft emerging, or changes in the kinds of person accused. Again the *s*-structures inevitably change.

Why should not the *s*-structures change independently? This would occur (let us say) when there are no actual events that fit the specifications – no people of the sort heretofore specifiable as witches.

The introduction of the black box, the mode of specification, is merely another mechanical crutch, and we shall eventually dispense with it. It has been necessary because of the confused way in which we apprehend *s*-structures. The contingencies or accidents of reality set up chains of events. The observing social anthropologist may set up *s*-structures that are not 'imperative', that is, not generated by the society concerned. As if the contingencies of reality had produced, for example, a set of temporary correlations in the Bakweri case between ownership of metal-roofed houses and blood-group O. Some such correlations might be well-founded, in the sense that they might be derived from the sorting-out effect of the mode of specification. But even such well-founded structures may be rendered inoperative by a change in the mode of specification. Consequently, certain *s*-structures of 'observers' may seem to have 'explanatory' value, for a time, and then to cease to do so. It was precisely the interest of this question that led us to hypothesize *p*-structures in the first place, in order to help the conceptualization of what is essential, continuous and 'imperative' in the structuring of society, and to separate it from the merely contingent and from the realization processes themselves.

The resolution of simultaneities into linear chains is a mode of exposition with many practical advantages. It is important, however, to grasp that the $p \rightarrow \Box \rightarrow s$ levels are present together in our experience. Questions that leap to the lips like, 'is not the black box (the mode of specification) part of the *p*-structure?' should, strictly speaking, be stifled immediately. The black box does not exist: It merely shows the relationship diagrammatically.

We have already gained something in clarity by this stretching out of a simultaneity. It is helpful, for example, to see in passing that the term *paradigm* is used by various authors for quite disparate parts of the sequence. The key to their differences lies in the placing of the black box. For some scholars, *s*-structures plus their modes of specification are commonly called the *paradigms* (they fail to register *p*-structures at all). Many structuralists, on the other hand, collapse *p*-structures and modes of specification together as paradigms. It is an irony that the processes in the black box, which was only a temporary hypothesis, should loom so disproportionately large in analysis. It is as if the zone of calibration between *p*-structures and *s*-structures was disproportionately magnified, was specially enlarged because of its critical importance.

A SIMULTANEITY

It is a strain upon our language to express the nature of a simultaneity in practical anthropology, such that the *p*-structural, the specificatory and the *s*-structural elements can be all shown to be present at a stroboscopic instant. Examine this sequence:

> A crowd howls at an old man hiding under a bed. Dismantled sheets of rusty corrugated iron lie in the vicinity.

That is already part of a record masquerading as a real instant. Suppose it to represent an instant in the wave of detections of zombie masters. Everything in that scene can be set up into *s*-structures by behaviourist-empiricist methods: therein lies the power of the latter. (Count the crowd; find the age of the man and the structure of the bed; locate iron; analyse rust; measure the site; record the speech, etc.) Yet the participants 'know' the significance 'at a glance'. Only the iron sheets can be assigned to the mode of specification, by which the old man was also specified. Thus, they are also a link with the *p*-structure. The 'corrugated iron' then in the tiny, inadequate stretch of time is mysteriously lit up. It is a 'marked' element. It is simultaneously (for that snapshot instant) part of the evidence for the *p*-structure, a part of the mode of specification, and an element marking the *s*-structure so specified – the group of builders of metal-roofed houses, the zombie masters.

We seem to be gaining some fleeting reflected insight into *symbol, association, metaphor, metonymy* and the rest. Once more we have only a language-shadow, this time of the articulation of *p*- and *s*-structures.

DEAD STRETCHES

Most of our analyses are done upon dead stretches of experience, upon data as recorded. The problem that was alluded to at the beginning of this chapter, of the intervention of the recorder into the process, now emerges more clearly. We do not possess those successive instants, only our records of some of them, and from instant to instant we select aspects only. These are our 'events'. With the naive and unreflectingly ethnocentric observer, the General G. Custer or H. M. Stanley, events he records or registers are totally structured by specifications from the *p*-structure of his own society (see below, chapter 7). There can in such a case be no records of the other society that would yield material for the reconstruction of any *p*-structures save his own.

The step from experiencing society to analysing a record of the experience is thus a crucial one. Unlike the historian the social anthropologist does both the living and the recording. The ethnography is a kind of slaughter of the experience and a dissecting of the corpse. That increasing modern preoccupation with attempts to understand the generative elements of a living society, which is now becoming apparent, requires some appreciation of the exact point at which the opportunity for such an understanding both exists and vanishes – the exact moment of the slaughter, as it were. That moment was exactly when we wrote: 'A crowd howls at an old man hiding under a bed, etc.' The opportunity existed of a record that would separate the programmatic from the accidental, read the marking on the signs, determine the signs and note the dispositions they reveal for particular subsequent events to occur. The opportunity vanished because the language for that record has been beyond our normal powers. The language of the record quoted is merely blocked together (*bricolé*, it might be said) out of the categories of English. The resulting petrification of the Bakweri experience that is given us has a different kind of weight in a normal English experience. For example, those sheets of corrugated iron strike a banal note – surely no drama could rest on them? A tinge of the ridiculous creeps in.

The good ethnographic observer must therefore use categories and labels in an ambiguous manner, or use some that have a degree of ambiguity already in his own language, and hope that by applying enough of them,

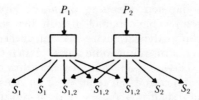

Figure 5.3 *p*-structures: observer and observed

he will enable the reader to create from their elements new combinations that will be closer to the 'native experience' being recorded. I call this the method of language-shadows.

THE MODE OF REGISTRATION

The condensation of concepts to illustrate the instant at which the anthropologist apprehends his 'event', has enabled us to answer questions that were raised in dispensing with the 'conveyor belt' or output model. We left over from the discussion of structures the problem of the 'structures of the observer': the modes of registration at which we began. We now see that the reference to the definition of events according to the mode of registration of the observer is to set up another black box. Indeed, it is not a new black box but a different aspect of our old friend the mode of specification of a $p \to s$ sequence. The registration of the simultaneity that has just been discussed is the matching of the *s*-structures of the observer to the *s*-structures of the event. If the *p*-structures of the observer come from the same set as the *p*-structures that generate the event – then the *s*-structures of the observer may be 'imperative', 'will match'. If not, the *s*-structures will be contingent, *not* imperative. Once more that enlarged portion of the relationship, the purported 'black box' area, is a curious complication. The highly self-conscious observer figure is a manipulator of some *p*-structures and their modes of specification into *s*-structures, but he may still fail to match those of the participants.

We may generalize the relationship as in figure 5.3. Where p_2 is a *p*-structure of the social anthropologist (or of his society or culture), p_1 is a *p*-structure of the other society; s_1 are the *s*-structures of events specified by p_1; s_2 are the *s*-structures of events specified by p_2; $s_{1,2}$ are *s*-structures of the observer that are 'imperative'; s_2 are *s*-structures of p_2 that are not 'imperative', are contingent and are not generated by p_1.

I have had to put it in this lengthy way in order to show that the third element in understanding the event, the mode of registration of the event by the observer, is analysed in the same way as the event itself. We have also been brought to consider that the *p*-structures of thinking individuals and those of the social continua in which they live will require some differentiation. (See the section below on 'world-structures'.)

So far we have progressed from the data and necessities of social

anthropology itself, to the step of setting up *p*-structures. We have suggested that such structures have homologies in the reality with which
anthropologists work. An analytical device that the anthropologist needs to
make sense of social events turns out to be a usable image of the way social
events are generated. Having said that, we may like to dispense with
p-structures and *s*-structures and tell it as it is. Dispense with the terms
though we may, 'telling it as it is' requires more than ordinary skills. Most
anthropologists end up by still telling it in terms of such structures, disguised as technical terms, *ad hoc* jargon or expressive language. That is why
I must now leave these mechanical formulations, and repeat (to the regret
of many) that *p*-structures and *s*-structures, embedded although they are in
the particular data of social anthropology, are related as the *paradigmatic* is
to the *syntagmatic*, and the properties of this relation are all available to help
us from the unwieldy language of structure. The path we have followed,
however, was necessary to show us that these terms, as used in linguistics,
are expressed in a different reality. I want to explore some of these differences. In order to do so I must allude to some elementary linguistic
matters, although many social anthropologists may wish to turn straight on
to the section headed 'Why linguistics is different'.

PARADIGMATIC AND SYNTAGMATIC AGAIN

We know that, in language, at each stage of a sentence the morphemes fall
into place unbidden, as it were, into sequences, the structures of which are
demonstrable, by examination, over the length of the sentence. Yet, simultaneously, paradigmatic relations determine the kinds of morphemes that
must be selected. Where are the paradigmatic relations? No one asks that
question in linguistics, any more than one asks 'where is the ten-times-
table?' Yet such questions are asked in social anthropology, as if our
audiences cannot hold abstractions in their heads. Still, some linguists
might try to reply that they are in a paradigmatic rulebook, a kind of
Liddell and Scott, just as words are conceived of as being in a lexicon,
and the syntagmata are in a book of syntax. We might say, then, that in
social anthropology the *p*-structures exist in the appropriate section of an
ethnography.

There is no doubt that the ordinary grammarian is aided in his mental
imagery by the external representations of his abstractions in real volumes,
indexes and dictionaries. To such an extent does this occur that the syntagmatic chain of utterance is commonly visualized as already in its 'completed' state, as the discipline's version of 'a dead stretch': that is, as a
recorded sentence, or the like. The syntagmata are seen as wholes, as if
taken in at a glance on the page. But in natural speech, syntagmata are
generated 'live', and the same questions that social anthropologists ask
can in fact be asked in the live situation. We could answer then that the
paradigmatic specifications are generated in the same acoustic chain as the
syntagmatic. The receiving brains sort it all out almost without noticing.

But the social anthropologist asks his question because no one as far as he knows is 'uttering' society, and he is not at all sure if there is anyone 'receiving' it. It all gets very complicated when we note that the 'utterance' of events is in three dimensions over time; and that among the behaviour uttered is linguistic utterance – nesting like a small detailed replica of the whole, and yet purporting to render acoustically an image of some of the whole. It is not surprising that to some it seems easiest to see it all as an excrescence of language in the first place. Then the syntagmatic and paradigmatic axes would be co-ordinates inevitably based on language, giving us an artificial horizon and vertical for stabilizing our discourse at all levels. The clear expression of this relationship outside natural language in quite simple mathematics makes it of greater interest than that (see above, chapter 2, p. 64).

DIACHRONIC AND SYNCHRONIC

There is an occasional anthropological misconception that the paradigmatic is diachronic, and the syntagmatic is synchronic; some think the exact opposite. Both are wrong, of course. The linguistic case will be genuinely helpful here. An utterance may be analysed (1) according to the syntactical arrangements between its parts – syntagmatically; (2) according to the kinds of parts that are required (a choice of *I, you, we* etc. among pronouns, for example) – paradigmatically; (3) diachronically – by which the utterance in all its parts is traced historically over time; and (4) synchronically – by which analysis is concerned only with the utterance as a system of parts at any one time.

It will be seen that the terms *diachronic* and *synchronic*, which to some seem simpler to grasp than *paradigmatic* and *syntagmatic*, are really much more confusing. It has been pointed out elsewhere that both *diachronic* and *synchronic* as terms applied to systems are *static* in nature. This is a result of looking at our data as dead stretches. Set the system moving (even in very slow motion) in natural time: utterances are generated lineally, specified paradigmatically, unrolling well-formed syntagmata. The synchronic is a freezing of this process. The diachronic is an examination of successive freezings of the process (Ardener, E. 1971c). Once more the tremendous weight of the conceptualization of language in terms of kinds of records lies heavy over even Saussurean linguistics. That is why we cannot always take the usually welcome advice of linguists in examining these matters. Fictions convenient on the scale of language become cumbersome and misleading at the scale of social events.

In natural time both the paradigmatic and the syntagmatic change continuously. Consider the sequences (see figure 5.4) over three centuries (the change from an impersonal construction in the use of *like* in English illustrates all four terms: synchronic, diachronic, syntagmatic, paradigmatic.) 1, 2 and 3 are each a sequence from a *synchronic* state of English (dates are only illustrative). Together they form a *diachronic* sequence. Each sentence is analysed from left to right *syntagmatically*. Each may be divided into *paradigmatically* selected units. The arrows show the changes in paradig-

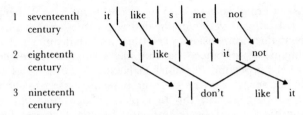

Figure 5.4   English 'like'

matic selection over time. The sentences are staggered to the right to suggest the element of syntagmatic change over time. Once the system is visualized in continuous operation (Saussure's *panchronic* (1964) was groping towards this; see above, chapter 1, p. 23), it begins to cry out for devices like rewrite rules and transformational analysis. This is still a 'dead stretch' nevertheless. In order to visualize the process in natural time we must put in all the speaking individuals, and all the versions of the utterance. Modern linguistics moves rapidly off on its own here.

Such a moving diagram for the three-dimensional grammar of even a single *ritual* over time would be a 'model' worth having indeed. Some research is already in hand on this. For the living grammar of the whole set of systems that is loosely labelled a *society*, we have quite a task before us. It is because the homologies between language and society are so many and so varied that it is necessary to point out that the social expressions of the common principles involved are working through much more intractable material than the linguistic.

WHY LINGUISTICS IS DIFFERENT

The social homologues of utterances churn themselves out very burdensomely compared with speech. Were language to be like that, the significant units would be occurring at generally long and always very irregular intervals, among contingent events, and on a time scale of the same order as the normal rate of deterioration of the system. As if the telephone wires had time to corrode away, or the vocal cords to mortify, before the speaker got it all out. The 'system' is one of permanent emergency routing. That is why there cannot be the cosy meshing of paradigmatic with syntagmatic that occurs in speech. Circumstances so change between successive 'utterances' that the actual mode of expression may have radically changed in the meantime. A kind of memory of what the system is about is stored in *ad hoc* ways. These are the *p*-structures, that are so difficult to locate. Since there is no homologue of the speaker, however, the *p*-structures must have a certain unconscious, blind or automatic quality. They are not all open to awareness. They are in some direct relationship to the 'infrastructure'. It is no surprise, then, that we find ethologists, ecologists, biologists and psychologists converging in separate dogsledges upon this zone, where the theologian, the philosopher and the social anthropologist already pace the ground.

The old 'template' for the zombie belief of the Bakweri was a combination of infrastructural (agricultural productivity) and bio-psychological elements and theories of causality. Looked at now as a *p*-structure, it behaves in the appropriately immanent manner: generating an *s*-structure at one time of zombies and corrugated iron roofs, and later on of Frenchmen and deep-sea wharfs (see Ardener, E. 1970c: 155). If this were any language studied by linguists, it would require some exaggerated form of continuous restructuring, a series of repeated and unpredictable creolizations. That is why I have related it in another study to the logic of a programme with continuous rewriters. We are much closer to systems as diverse as the language of infants, of the insane or of animals. We may take a cue from this, to ask ourselves whether there is lacking a 'metalinguistic' faculty in the social system, or whether if it does exist it is of only a haphazard function. The matter is a serious one because successive realizations of a *p*-structure may be so different in their *s*-forms that the supposed 'actors' do not easily link the sets of events together. Once more I remind you that the successive 'zombie' manifestations were apperceived as separate by those that lived through them. We are rather like high-grade aphasics of the type studied by Luria.

STORAGE AND LOCATION

These terms from warehousing have since moved into computer studies, but perhaps they are more literally appropriate when they are applied to society as a system of structures. It is beginning to appear as if what may be treated as abstractions in language have for society to be 'stored' separately and 'located' in the unstable series of social events. Human beings even build physical structures and rearrange the environment, and thus incorporate physical events into the system. Society is thus a 'brain' trying to be a 'language'.

When we tried to understand *p*-structures, we found that their *location* and their evidence for existence were linked problems. The *p*-structure homologues in language (the paradigmatics) are in the last analysis 'stored' no doubt somewhere in the brain – that is, outside the acoustic chain. That is one of the great steps forward we took with language. In the 'social' the separation of media is rudimentary and unstable. Having asked about the 'metalinguistic' faculty, which is so difficult to detect in the grunting, noise-ridden, idiot-tongue of society, we may then ask whether it is separately 'stored' or 'located' (I would emphasize here that the *p*-structures do not provide a 'metalanguage', they are part of the 'language'.) A 'black box' for a metalanguage of the system will require a device for monitoring the whole system, reporting on it, substituting in it and modifying it. The only social phenomenon that is a serious candidate turns out to be real language – that is, language, properly so called: the system of acoustic speech. If so, it shows that the social is not like real language in its detailed structure. In real language the metalinguistic faculty is expressed *in* real language, not in an independent system. We have to get used to seeing different analytical levels expressed in different media, and separations between media in ways that are momentarily surprising.

Consider the social as a surface composed of receptors operating on the slow-moving scale that I have tried to depict. Real language operates like a system of comparatively instantaneous links between receptors: real language deteriorates more slowly than the surface. It is not surprising then that in this aspect real language is (or was) the only thing fast enough to provide a meta-system for the social. It can hardly be efficient: when we speak of the difficulty of 'unpacking' non-verbal semiotics into language, we are using another terminology to express the lag in awareness that the 'infrastructural' source of so much of the social 'output' (leading to unconscious, automatic features) makes difficult to overcome.

The language-like continuum of society cannot be apprehended without recognizing that real language is such a great improvement on society, in some particulars, that it cannot be a perfect mirror of society. It can usefully map a lot of the social into a medium that can delineate and label structures. Thus far it stores. It is not at all bad at storing language images of *s*-structures. It is not good at imaging and storing *p*-structures. We can suggest reasons why not, but it is sufficient to note the phenomenon. To demonstrate a new *p*-structure through language, we have to run through metaphors, analogies and symbols of multiple reference, until we have created a 'language-shadow' of it. Those who can express the process in other than natural language – possibly mainly mathematicians – are at a great advantage, but it appears that this faculty is not widely spread in any society. Language certainly creates its own problems. Furthermore, it adds some new automaton-like processes, out of its own peculiar 'wiring', even as it helps us to plot some of those due to the peculiarities of the social. The totality of action and partial awareness may be termed a *world-structure* (see below, chapter 7).

WORLD-STRUCTURES

A *world-structure* is a manifold of the relations we have discussed; it is also a system of people. It is like a communication system in so far as it has certain properties shared by systems that have a transmitter and a receiver. It is also like a homeostatic system, insofar as the chief receiver of its communications is itself. This duality comes from the position of individuals both as elements of the system and as communicating beings themselves. There is a high degree of automatism in the world-structure, and human beings, by investing their fates in it, sacrifice a great deal of their freedom of action. They cease to experience events, and instead they experience 'events' – where the quotation marks express the transformation of experience through the world-structure. In another place I have discussed, for example, the reduced capacity of a world-structure to respond to its own demographic changes (below, chapter 7).

In confronting the 'unaware' parts of the world-structure, we may recognize (with the strongest possible emphasis) that human beings as individuals are much more complicated than they are as parts of the structure. Those expensive and sophisticated intelligences may serve in their social aspect to signal relatively simple messages – many no doubt of on/off binary type (e.g., acquiescence/non-acquiescence). With certain conventions a small structural chain can be set up generating behaviour in a way that is 'unconsciously' constraining on each individual. Such chains are set up every day in laboratory experiments, not only with rats, but in studies of human behaviour. The structure, as such, is not stored in individual nervous systems. We can, for a game, devise a bureaucracy that will work with no single individual knowing the whole structure. We can go further and say that a mature bureaucracy may work for long periods in that way. From the useful evidence of the Watergate enquiry, we note that two major 'decisions' – to enter the building and to cover-up the affair – each took place in automatic sequences. Mr Jeb Magruder said of the latter that, on the news of the Watergate arrests, the cover-up simply began: 'I do not remember any discussion that there should not be a cover-up.' The sleep-walking effect was very noticeable when individuals were asked to examine their consciousness of the events.

We need not jib, therefore, at accepting that human beings in a world-structure will not be conscious of all of it. We may be glad just to be able to conceive that we may be in one. The Watergate case illustrates another way in which we see events as 'significant' from outside. If the Nixonian White House is taken as a convenient model of a world-structure, the two events mentioned earlier were 'significant' in the light of that world-structure's subsequent collapse. To the participants, 'event' followed 'event', linked with syntagmatic logicality, while certain triggers set themselves unnoticed. Such 'triggers' belong in the p-component. (For those who still need the 'black box', they reset the mode of specification of the s-structures.)

Simple predictivity in human science is revealed as a misguided goal when we consider the discontinuity of p- and s-components. A p-change may release a 'trigger', leaving a disposition in the structure that does not realize itself because the precipitating conditions simply do not occur. Or, given a major social entity, over time, triggers may be released, or thresholds overridden, that are realized in the s-structures only a generation later. There seems no doubt that p-structures are labile, and may set or release triggers under the influence of infrastructural changes. We have discussed problems of 'storage' and 'location' and deterioration. We have hinted at the demographic problem as a modifier of the human content of the system (for details see below, chapter 7). The major outstanding problem in the analysis of events is to spot the triggers moving – to catch the p-component in events.

The world-structure occupies a space that is neither 'idealist' nor 'materialist'. Looked at through language it is the one; looked at through 'events' it is the other. I have always thought that Whorf – the fire-insurance assessor who found he could not stop fires without correcting language – well understood the world-structure as a sometimes dangerous generator of reality (Whorf 1956).

WHAT IS A WORLD-STRUCTURE LIKE?

At various stages in this chapter, we have set up 'black boxes' to help to solve problems, and we have then dispensed with them. The whole language of structure is ultimately a process of that type, and the world-structure is the biggest black box of them all. How might it work? We have suggested that it may be like a surface with particular properties. Let us compare it with a special memory surface. That surface both 'registers' and 'recognizes' events by fairly simple principles. The traces of different events reinforce each other only in the parts that overlap. Old traces die out if not reinforced. This creates a continuous movement across the surface. The configurations on the surface are stable or change shape, become 'deeper' or 'shallower', according to the degree to which they are reinforced. The newer or the rarer the event, the less readily will it be registered. Only those aspects that reinforce existing configurations will register; indeed, a deficiency of such a surface is that those configurations are thereby further strengthened.

It is unlikely on the other hand that the world-structure as a surface would work with such relatively simple excitation rules as De Bono (1969) suggests for individual perception. It is both more rudimentary and more complex; for example, the surface itself has important discontinuities caused by the irregular demographic distribution of the human elements of the surface. On an ideal memory surface, the flow across the surface is uninterrupted save by the processes of the surface itself. Still, it is probable that any degree of mutual sensitivity between enough like organisms could set up some elements of a memory surface. Two bonding attractions would be enough: one into the physical world (say hunger) and one into like elements in the surface (say sex). A simple pair of p-structures (using our previous terms) would generate the activity of the surface. The continuity of the 'social' through animal species to man may, indeed, merely exemplify this kind of proposition. Thereby, we confront once more the prospect of some automatism in our subject matter.

The rudimentary form of the surface is importantly modified by incorporating ways of scanning the surface supplementary to the operations of the surface itself. We can do this by superimposing on the surface a second surface (surface 2), which will register events on surface 1. What has been said of surface 1 applies *mutatis mutandis* to surface 2. This time it is configurations newly established on surface 1 that will not register easily. The configurations on surface 2 would tend to overdetermine the most deeply reinforced parts of the configurations on surface 1. If, furthermore, surface 1 now has the faculty of registering the configurations of surface 2 as well as physical events, we have some of the properties of a world-structure. Surface 2 is like the scanning effect of language, and exemplifies some defective features in that scanning. The mutual registration of surfaces 1 and 2 creates a duality of configurations on surface 1, some registering the 'environment', some the scanning process. The elaborate new surface thus registers 'markers' indicating some of its own states. Some of the events that are thus registered can be said then to be 'symbolic' of states of or in the surface.

To translate this back into the terms of the social anthropological subject matter, language (that is real language) provides a map of some of the main regularities of the social. I have suggested elsewhere (see above, chapter 1, p. 25), that multiple semiotic systems must have prepared the way, and must still coexist with it. Language represents a much fuller exploitation of the human capacities of the surface, but as we saw earlier, whole regions of the automatism in the surface are only inefficiently mapped through it.

We are led to the probability that even the extraordinary complexity introduced into the surface by the rapid transmission of provisional maps of its own configurations still does not utilize more than some fraction of the complexity of the individuals composing it. That may be said, even though over recent millennia the storing of language by recording devices has accelerated the process of *'linguification'* of the surface to the degree that there is now a somewhat greater resemblance between the surface and an elaborate memory surface than there can have been in the remotest past.

We have suggested that this introduces more and more complicated 'automatisms'. The surface registers natural events but generates a welter of 'events' of its own. A state of the surface may well appear such that most events individuals contend with in that strange 'real world' are mere automatisms of the surface. The failure of language to discriminate rapidly or even (as far as untechnical discourse is concerned) at all between its own processes and the processes of the surface becomes critical at this stage. In this condition, *individuals* may make the necessary discriminations, step outside the surface, as it were, but lack a common real language for their expression.

TEMPORARY CONCLUSION

We have tried, in the last section, another way of visualizing how strange a world-structure might look if we were not in one. Even were I to defend the attempt as a mere language-shadow, I would not claim it to be very successful. The capacious terminology of structures is more reassuring to us at the moment, and certainly more closely matches our research capacities. But we should recognize the provisional nature of even these rich theories.

The bringing of world-structures to consciousness is a bigger task than social anthropology on its own can tackle. It has got the small distance that it has because of its privileged experience of a multiplicity of such structures. However, the terminology of 'structure' is itself becoming exhausted. It has had a good life in social anthropology, although in the lay world its vogue is only just beginning. 'Structure' does not always help us to visualize the multiple realizations that we are dealing with. We are, of course, not waiting for new terms for 'structures'. We are simply in a post-structuralist situation parallel to the post-functionalist situation of the 1940s and 1950s. In the post-structuralist period the capturing of the life of events as they articulate with structures will certainly be one outstanding problem requiring a new phase of specially collected data. In this place, it is not necessary to specify the methods that could be used, but they might include the detailed study of what I have called *simultaneities*. As an alternative to the method of definition, the method of language-shadows may be used to delineate immanent structures.

We are in a *post*-structuralist position, however. This means that old Durkheimian problems such as that of the *location* of structures no longer seem to require a metaphysical solution. The problem of *validation* – that is, of determining the 'truth' of structural analysis, derives from the degree of 'match' or 'fit' – a feature I have called imperativeness. We have learned also that the human is a world on a very grand scale indeed: a world in which a consistent and relatively simple set of structuring principles is fleshed out in the most diverse ways. It still appears to me that individual human minds are much more advanced than the structures through which a kind of sleep-walking ratiocination occurs. An awareness of structure is a first stage in stepping out of it.

6

'Behaviour' – a Social Anthropological Criticism

We have been offered the term *behaviour* as a cross-disciplinary concept with applications throughout the component subjects of the Human Sciences degree. It is a strange term to use for it is a genuine product of social life – with a characteristic socio-linguistic history. Like its verb 'behave', it seems to be a fifteenth-century coinage. The verb was originally always reflexive and consciously derived from 'have', (so that a person 'behad' himself), and the force of the *be*-preverb was to denote the imposition of a constraint on the person involved. The substantive was formed upon *havour*, or *haviour*, 'possession', which came straight from French *avoir* at the same period. Although *haviour* and *behaviour* were thus of independent origin, the new substantive was, by its French ornamentation, quite appropriate to expressing a certain conception of deportment, or socially prescribed or sanctioned conduct. It became a semantic doublet of *demeanour*, but differently marked. *Demeanour* had a lower-class application: *behaviour* thus emerges in a period when an expectation of restraint in upper-class behaviour could be regarded as desirable. The positive marking of concepts that referred to courtly life in the late middle ages is well documented by Trier and his successors. *Behaviour* without modifier, was marked as 'good'; the 'behaviour' being watched for was 'good deportment'. Bad behaviour was failed behaviour. *Demeanour* without modifier was marked as 'bad': the 'demeanour' being watched for was 'bad deportment'. Good demeanour was corrected demeanour. Afterwards the semantic field of *behaviour* invaded not only that of *demeanour* but of *conduct, comportment* and the rest.

It is important then to stress that *behaviour* is a term from a set of terms, and a set of terms from a particular historical period. It is strange to social anthropologists, steeped as we are in language, to be shown the term as something quasi-objective: as an 'idea' or 'concept' to be exemplified, even 'defined', in various supposed manifestations in disparate kinds of data.

Behaviour when we meet it first is, we note, a coining and a slightly grandiose one. It thus labels a new kind of component. In that world, there could be no such thing as 'random' behaviour.

The extension of 'behave' and 'behaviour' into scientific discourse is Victorian. The first applications are in Chemistry in the 1850s and 1860s ('It combines violently with water, behaving like the bichloride of tin', 1854; 'In Chemistry, the behaviour of different substances towards each other, in respect of combination and affinity', 1866 – OED). These early examples have still some of the direct living metaphor about them. The very model of orderly discrimination of the conditions under which things acted as they did, was derived from social behaviour. *Behaviour* was marked therefore for its knowability in advance: an image or aspiration for the natural order. When in 1878 T. H. Huxley talked of the 'behaviour of water', he was reducing to orderly terms the activities of a supremely unpredictable element. No doubt it was the continual use of 'behaviour' in contexts in which the activity was far from understood, that led to its association with 'activity in general', and even ('behaviour problems') towards relatively violent activity. The generalization of 'behaviour' to the inanimate world has since then gone so far that we tend to think of it as 'action that is not yet understood' rather than as 'action that is supremely understood' because prescribed.

It is ironical that the use of the term 'animal behaviour' probably owes more to its natural science uses than it does to its original social use. Paradoxically, then, we are offered 'behaviour' as a quantifiable universal, a mere century after its metaphorical use in natural science began. Of course, there has been retained throughout the essential component of 'constraint on action'. At all times 'behaviour' has been conceived of as *rule-governed*: the natural science shift has moved the locus of the rules. At one time behaviour is expressly the subject of rules, at another it is the subject of an aspiration that it will turn out to be governed by rules.

Not all the 'behaviours' we have heard about today are the same. To ask a social anthropologist to treat 'behaviour' as a universal and to relate it to his own subject, is inevitably to miss the point of all recent advances in the subject. To acquiesce in the game for a while, we note that the post-Victorian uses of 'behaviour' do not easily translate into the languages of other peoples. Even in other European languages there are well-known difficulties. Many of the terms in use in them are too embarrasingly close to terms for (social) good conduct. The translation of the American *behavioral* is a perpetual crux in international literature. The situation is then not resolved by appeal to an independent scientific vocabulary. 'Behaviour' turns out to be wrenched from a set of terms in the English lexicon, trailing still the evidence of its old connections.

In more exotic but still reflective societies, 'behaviour' has to be subsumed under various terms indicating acts of a socially appropriate or inappropriate kind. Sometimes there is no lexical link between the terms for 'bad behaviour' and 'good behaviour'. In Ibo, the verb radical *me* ('do, make') appears in words like *omume, ome,* or the like, each of which expresses activity that is marked according to social evaluations; *ome* in the phrase *ome nala* ('*ome* in the country') is what whites usually misleadingly translate as 'custom'. The important point to grasp is, however, that actions in Ibo society are identified *a priori*. There is no objective field of behaviour.

We are different, of course, you will argue. That is why we are 'human scientists'. It does not always look very like it when we tote terms about in this way. Once we enter the human zone, we are dealing with *classes* of action. Unfortunately, we are not the main classifiers. That position is occupied by the human beings who are acting. It is always the major task in social anthropology to find the actors' classification. This is not quite the same as asking him *why* he is acting. Our first task is to agree on what actions are significant for him. For example, when a yam-hole is dug, among a certain people, herbs are added and a quantity of ash. The whole activity may be described by the farmer as done 'to make the yam grow'. It is not uncommon in such situations for the observer to say that some of this action is 'symbolic' – because for instance, the herbs have little or no chemical fertilizing effect. The matter of the ash may however detain him, because it may seem 'really' to have a fertilizer effect (potash etc.). He is thus tempted to subdivide the action sequence into symbolic and instrumental sections. He may still do this when (say) he learns from an agriculturalist that the ash does not have chemically significant effect, for even false attempts at 'science' may be classified differently from hopeless nonscience. That kind of classification is seen in many ordinary monographs. Even Evans-Pritchard came dangerously near to such distinctions at times. They lie in the system of discriminations of the recorder. In this particular case we are not justified in breaking up the planting sequence in this way. To do so distorts the significance of the different parts of the sequence, according to criteria which are irrelevant to the actor.

Presented with 'behaviour' then, we find that we can only speak of kinds of significant action. The markers for that significance are, however, not directly given in the action itself (or if we think they are they require a much more sophisticated theory to detect them). Where human beings are concerned the action is the final output of a very complicated programme. We are not, however, simply in the zone marked 'systems of thought'. Some of our work may have been misleading in this respect. Societies differ greatly in the degree to which they externalize (into action), or internalize (into language) the processes by which they (i.e. the societies) operate. Thus, it is often forgotten that Evans-Pritchard said that the Azande demonstrate their system by enacting it. The Ibo at times seem to belong to a society which 'knows' what it is doing only by doing it. We find richly differentiated rituals and the constant generation of 'new customs'; 'fashions' of all kinds sweep over the social surface in rapid succession. There is little mythological or ideological superstructure, in contrast with, for example, the Bakweri. This people, in contrast, has no rich variety of action: minor events, are, however, charged with enormous significance, which derives from the internalization of an unseen universe of causes, for which a command of the language and its expression of the non-behavioural world-structure is absolutely essential. For the Ibo, events are like a rapid continuous game of draughts, with a plethora of moves, and brilliant sequences leading to few basic changes in the balance of pieces. For the Bakweri events come after long intervals, charged with relational value, like those of chessmen in a master tournament.

The arguments for the view of society as a manifold both of ideas (stored in various linguistic and other 'semiotic' forms) and action, are made more cogent nowadays by the increasing evidence that societies (as in the cases I have mentioned) differ in the degree to which the action component itself embodies cues to its own significance. Historical periods marked by labile social forms may exemplify, in an exaggerated manner, some of the features I have ascribed to the Ibo, and may repay close attention to the 'action', which may embody many of the cues to its own interpretation. It is, however, characteristic that they in their turn frequently become enshrined in the ideas store of a subsequent period. I have in mind unreflective action periods like that of the American West, which store their significance later as mythology. This mythology in its turn generates successive transformations of itself, and in turn generates actions of an existentially different type, in later periods – as it might be street-gang 'behaviour', or even aspects of the Vietnam War.

As a system over time, the social does not yield its essential features through a study of 'behaviour', even though for some stretches 'behaviour' may be more significant than others.

Social anthropologists have long been forced to realize that there is no universal unit of 'action' in society. The general theory is acquiring a certain solidity now. The kinds of empiricism required for its operation are appearing in a variety of disciplinary guises. Socio-linguistic approaches exist (some actions can only be triggered, or even recognized, in specified linguistic contexts). 'Situational analyses' of various kinds, are responses to some of these needs. Elsewhere we hear of 'symbolic interaction', even of 'symbolic interaction*ism*'. We sometimes hear regrettably of 'symbolic behaviour'. The separation of the empirical aspects from the theoretical is somewhat more characteristic of the sociological developments, than of social anthropology. Nevertheless we all have to guard against *over-determining a distinction in our own culture, objectifying it through new data, and then receiving it back, no longer able to recognize our own artefact.* 'Behaviour' is such a case: we may clutch it as those experimental monkey infants clutch their mothers made of wire, and receive precious little nourishment.

7

Social Anthropology and Population

INTRODUCTION

In any series of lectures on population there comes (somewhere between the animal populations and the great population explosions of relatively recent times) the lecture on supposed small-scale, archaic or pre-modern human groups. Formerly these would have been boldly called 'primitive' or 'savage' at one of their extremes and 'peasant' at the other. In this series the title originally offered to me was 'Tribal Communities'. Whatever they are termed, the social anthropologist's contribution is commonly, but wrongly, seen in the present context as in some degree historical or pre-historical. In population studies the anthropological subject matter has been seen as a bridge between biological and industrial man.

It would have been easy today, therefore, to survey briefly the range of demographic studies of exotic populations made by social anthropologists and others. But to do that on this occasion would be to repeat some extremely recent publications indeed. In particular: the contributions to the excellent volume edited by Dr Harrison and Dr Boyce (1972) are, or should be, the essential background reading for much of this lecture series. Fortunately, as far as I am concerned, some of the main topics and many telling ethnographic examples are, as it were, elegantly pre-empted by many of the contributors therein. That leaves me the opportunity to consider some wider questions raised by our researches. There was a time when it was necessary to make some propaganda for quantified demographic studies in social anthropology – for there has been an on-and-off relationship with statistics over the years. That necessity has dwindled away – we are perhaps now in a different danger of mistaking the lessons of the studies we have. Eleven years ago I wrote:

It may be suspected perhaps that in some societies interpreted through institutional and value systems alone, without detailed attention to demographic factors, anthropologists may have sometimes attributed to the fly [travelling on the axle of the chariot] the momentum of the chariot wheel (1962: vii).

There was much talk at that time, for example, of the relative roles of matrilineal and patrilineal kinship systems as determinants of marital stability or instability. Demographic data were brought into the discussions. As time went on the marital stability question was subsumed in more powerful anthropological models of alliance and exchange. Using these approaches it is interesting to note that the recent demographic analyses of Chagnon for the Yanomamö of South America (1972) are totally different in conception from those done, under the stimulus of Barnes (1949), Mitchell (1967), and other pioneer specialists, in Africa. In changes of this sort the definition of what is 'demographic' has also changed. Social anthropologists can see these intellectual processes a little more easily in their studies, because they can take nothing for granted in their subject-matter. But problems uncovered during the critical period of change in anthropological theory, inspired usually by other than demographic pre-occupations, are of quite general interest: are the entities called 'populations' *names* or *numbers*? If names: named for whom, and by whom? If numbers: counted by whom, and for whom? In asking the questions 'by whom?' and 'for whom?' we also ask in particular: by or for the 'people' concerned? Or by or for the anthropologist or other scientific observer?

The problem of the sorts of entity that populations are could not be better stated (in order, unfortunately, to be put aside) than by Dr Harrison and Dr Boyce: 'because there are many factors determining the ways populations are *defined* . . . the situation may be much more like a *continuum of overlapping categories* than a series of clusters.' They continue: 'however, whilst it is possible to conceptualize populations in these terms, in practical considerations populations *are recognized according to some particular component which is of interest.* And the major components on which interest focuses are demographic, genetic, social, and ecological' (1972: 3, my italics). This lecture will occupy the conceptual space between these two sentences. We shall be concerned with the light that anthropological studies can throw on terms like 'determinants of population size', even of 'population' itself. For this week at least, humanity will look slightly more independent of supposed raw demographic trends than I am sure it will look in later lectures, but no less vulnerable because of that. I shall be arguing that all human aggregates have 'folk demographies', on the one hand, and, on the other, that our vast bodies of numerical data do not necessarily build a culture-free or neutral demographic science.

ETHNIC SELF-DEFINITION

I may as well say at the outset then that there is no entity that 'tribal community' consistently labels. There is already a considerable literature on 'tribe' and 'tribalism' (Epstein, 1958; Mitchell 1967; Barth 1969; Cohen, Abner 1969). The term 'ethnicity' has of late risen from the ruins of controversy (Bates 1970; Wallerstein 1960; Ardener, E. 1967a). But new 'ethnicities' are not simply old 'tribes' writ large. To some lay persons they seem to deserve the adjective 'atavistic' rather than 'primitive' – often seated in cities as much as in jungles (Cohen, Abner 1969). So let us begin with the question: if we do not know what a tribal community is, how can we say anything sensible about its population? You might well try the answer that common-sense approximations already exist which at least throw light on the question. For example, General Custer made a supposedly adequate estimate of the number of Sioux. I shall agree that demographic statements have been attached to tribal labels. I shall suggest that it is not accidental that our evidence derives from the preoccupations of Custer rather than from the requirements of Sitting Bull. For there is hardly a 'tribe' of which you have heard, which does not present problems of exact definition. Take the Yanomamö case, that I have mentioned:

They are divided into approximately 125 widely scattered villages. Many... villages have yet to be seen by outsiders [on] essentially unexplored rivers (Chagnon 1972: 254).

Further, there is 'considerable variation in the tribe, in a cultural, linguistic, and biological sense'. They number 10,000 to 15,000 we are told – or 12,500 ± 2,500, a 20 per cent margin of error either way.

There are hundreds of other units whose definition has not truly been attempted. Even an entity such as the Ibo, a West African 'tribe' of 'national' scale, whose definition was laid down in monographs and by indigenous consensus for generations, suddenly saw its Ikwerri section split off during the Biafran war, to declare itself 'not Ibo'. Some of you will know that in the nineteenth century the term 'Ibo' had been acceptable to only a handful of the many millions who later gladly bore it, even after the Ikwerri secession. Nevertheless, the Ikwerri declaration coming in the 1960s, looked rather like a stretch of Southern England declaring itself 'not English'. It is, in fact, this 'arbitrary' feature that is one of the last available minimal criteria of a 'tribe' or 'ethnicity'. Ethnicities demand to be viewed from inside. They have no imperative relationship with particular 'objective' criteria. They have not 'internalized' even such objective criteria as an outsider purports to discover. They are in this sense 'named by the people'. There was much discussion in the Nigerian and even the British press, for example, over whether the Ikwerri 'spoke Ibo'. The very definition of 'speaking Ibo' (which is a continuum of dialects) made this finally a fruitless discussion, but by the Ikwerri criterion even Norway might fall apart tomorrow. It is also of interest that one of the causes of the Biafran war lay in disputations over the Nigerian census. The point is that the pace-setting Western societies denied themselves such easy luxuries many centuries ago. You are supposed to know who you are and what you are – and (exactly) 'stand up and be counted'. On the whole, rational scientists still subscribe to this, despite growing signs of the restoration of the phenomena of ethnicity in those societies themselves (as shown by Cohen, Abner 1969).

MISAPPREHENSIONS OF 'ETHNIC' POPULATION BEHAVIOUR

Ethnicities generate an apprehension of 'otherness' among non-members, and the lay equation of 'tribes' with animal species is old (far older than Custer). In the past, certain steppe-peoples seemed, to settled observers, to resemble animal populations in their frightening apparent tendency to multiply in numbers and to burst out of their bounds. They appeared to 'swarm'. They swept like a terrible plague, suddenly dwindling as rapidly as they grew. The ancient cases of the Huns, Goths and other German tribes, and medieval cases such as the Magyars, Mongols and the like, are deeply ingrained in the historical consciousness of our civilization. The present world-picture does not lack elements that raise these old images to prominence even among members of an audience of this kind. We should take these cases seriously, in order to see how easily alien populations are judged to be out of control. How often have we heard of the desiccation of the inner Asian steppes driving out virile hordes? Yet if we take the classic case of the Huns, we know that the swollen masses under Attila included almost every people from the Rhine to the Urals. The swarm effect, as it was experienced, was a combination of mobility plus accretion. The mobility may be broken down into a combination of technological factors (such as the horse and the bow) and broadly social ones. Gibbon was well aware of some of these. Among the former factors:

The active cavalry of Scythia is always followed, in their most distant and rapid incursions, by an adequate number of spare horses, who may be occasionally used either to redouble the speed or to satisfy the hunger of the barbarians (1787: 5).

Among the latter:

The individuals of the same tribe are constantly assembled, but they are assembled in a camp, and the native spirit of these dauntless shepherds is animated by mutual support and emulation. The houses of the Tartars are no more than small tents, of an oval form, which afford a cold and dirty habitation for the promiscuous youth of both sexes. The palaces of the rich consist of wooden huts, of such a size that they may be conveniently fixed on large waggons, and drawn by a team perhaps of twenty or thirty oxen. The flocks and herds, after grazing all day in the adjacent pastures, retire on the approach of night, within the protection of the camp. The necessity of preventing the most mischievous confusion in such a perpetual concourse of men and animals must gradually introduce, in the distribution, the order, and the guard of the encampment, the rudiments of the military art (ibid.: 6).

And this anthropological insight:

The connection between the people and their territory is of so frail a texture that it may be broken by the slightest accident. The camp, and not the soil, is the native country of the genuine Tartar. Within the precincts of that camp his family, his companions, his property are always included, and in the most distant marches he is still surrounded by the objects which are dear or valuable or familiar in his eyes. (ibid.: 7).

The accretion of subject and allied peoples – even as leaders – derived from certain other peculiarities of an ethnic polity: what I shall be calling its 'recruitment component'. These belong entirely in the cultural sphere. On one aspect – 'fictive' kinship – Gibbon has an interesting early word:

The custom, which still prevails, of adopting the bravest and most faithful of the captives, may countenance the very probable suspicion that this extensive consanguinity is, in a great measure, legal and fictitious. But the useful prejudice which has obtained the sanction of time and opinion produces the effects of truth (ibid.: 9).

The 'swarming' of the Huns could have occurred without any significant numerical change in the originating population at all. We have indeed no certain knowledge of the precise definition of the originating population. When the Attilan entity collapses in AD 454 we catch glimpses of small remnant groups of successor 'Huns' (Utigurs, Kutrigurs) of very limited significance, incorporated in other rolling, swelling ethnicities. A century later the Avars 'swarmed' by incorporating a large Slavonic population (Chadwick 1945: 61). The rapid collapse of their apparent numbers in AD 796 was such that a Russian proverb came to say: 'They perished like the Avars, and there survives of them neither progeny nor heir' (Chadwick 1945: 73). Save, that is, for the Balkan Slavs themselves, whose own expansion occurred (in the view of many authorities) behind the 'Avar' screen.

The process I describe has as much in common with the growth and collapse of a fiduciary phenomenon like the South Sea bubble as it has with any biological one. The sudden shrinking of such barbarian enemies is a function of their presupposed size. Conversely, the rapid increase in effectiveness of the Germanic peoples was certainly connected with the growth of confederacies – that is, ethnic self-redefinitions – which transformed the ethnic map from the multitude of peoples given by the ethnographer Tacitus in the first century to a much more limited number of polities by the fourth century under names new and old, such as Franks, Saxons, Burgundians and the like. Even Custer's fatal Sioux were themselves 'Dakota', literally 'a confederacy'. Ethnicities, as I said earlier, have this powerful quality of self-definition and redefinition. It is not (I emphasize strongly) that population changes played no role at all in any of these matters, but that they were overlaid, and totally reshaped by changes in the mode of self-identification of the ethnicities concerned. As we shall see, this is a little more basic than saying merely that 'the social, political, military or economic organizations changed', for it gives us a way of motivating the changes in manmade structures of such a kind. In any event, we are presented in all this with something surely that animals do not do.

PRESENT-DAY ETHNICITIES: SOME PRACTICALITIES

Let us return to present-day ethnicities, and think about the numbering question: turning these entities into 'demography', if you like. If we remember that most ethnic groups in the Third World present definitional problems, it will be realized that even the determination of population size, in the quite practical sense of a count of people, is a far from simple task. To go on to discuss numerically the dynamics of the population of such entities can be extremely hazardous.

Documented cases are beginning to emerge of relationships between neighbouring peoples – different 'tribes' if you will – which spread the population dynamic over some aggregate much larger than any one ethnicity. Imagine that if you ran away to sea you became a German, or to become a Londoner you gave up your mother tongue. We should find no doubt that the populations of the resulting individual ethnicities were not demographically stable. Work on some very small Bantu-speaking groups of West Africa suggests a situation something like this over a considerable area (see above, chapter 3). Certain ethnicities wax and wane by accretion and loss, according to their economic or commercial success. Paul Spencer's work on the pastoral Rendille and Samburu of Kenya demonstrates a kind of 'classifying symbiosis' between the two ethnicities of a most interesting kind. Essentially Rendille lose population continually to the Samburu. If you do not make it in the rather close Rendille cattle-breeding economy, you merge with the more open Samburu cattle economy, and you are redefined as Samburu. One lineage, the Ariaal, forms a sort of valve between the two (Spencer 1973). We should note that linguistically the two peoples belong to different language families (Spencer 1965). Conversely Hurault (1969) found that the statistics for the *Lamidate* of Banyo bore signs of internal diversities, which suggested that the significant demographic units were certain older ethnicities submerged in the Banyo state. These cases are very important if we are to grasp that a *'population'* as a scientific, demographic bundle of indices need not be the same as an 'ethnicity' or as I shall now sometimes prefer to say: a 'people'.

Suppose we leave aside for the moment the question of the bounds of a given group. We still find the most extraordinary difficulties in getting certain crucial data: for example, the sex of children and the age-structure. Because the demographic survey will usually be the first ever made, the dynamics of the population have to be determined retrospectively, from an accurate construction of the life histories (marital, fertility experience) of the living and (by report) of certain categories of the dead, for example, the deceased children of informants. If the information is properly recorded from a random sample, the treatment of the data can be statistically quite respectable. From this base indeed substantial demographic superstructures can be built effortlessly. The nature of the random sample will of course be affected by the supposed definition of the universe – back to the 'square one' of the definition of the ethnicity. In the end we have to fall back on a kind of compromise with bureaucratic opinion and honest general repute.

So we sample supposed settlements and villages, a proportion of which turn out not to be there any more, or to be in the wrong place, or to be misprints of some sort (unnumberable names). In 1963–5 I had the privilege of assisting brilliant French-trained demographers in the devising of a sampling frame for a stretch of Africa containing eighty or more supposed ethnicities (Turlot et al. 1969). They would agree with me that the actual sample came from a reality different from that of the supposed universe.

The further retreat into practicalities does not solve our problem. We are now face to face with the people. The expectation of candour in reply to questions about 'population' is, when we reflect on it, a surprising one, even if we assume that certain possible fears (about taxation or the like) have been allayed. In an 'ethnic' situation nothing which shakes the self-definition of the group will be easily elicited. An ethnicity is an ideal structure in which hardly any demographic variable is not already pre-judged. In the 'folk-demography' the group is (to take one common example) always expanding in numbers, more boys than girls are born, all women are married at puberty, all wives had maximum fertility, all old persons are extremely old, all men have, have had, or will have several wives and so on. Anthropologists as well as demographers when faced with the challenge of eliciting 'objective' population data from behind this screen of obfuscation, have responded in skilful ways (Blanc 1960). They have achieved stretches, or short lengths, of accurate data. A lot of labour has been put into the precise determination of the sex and age-structures in populations of this sort. Mortality and fertility rates rest upon them. Yet even the best work relies upon model population tables, standard age-pyramids and standard approximations to level out supposed irregularities.

In work on ethnic populations certain structural anomalies could never come to unambiguous light. Some extraordinary but limited imbalance in the older ages, for example: an excess of men aged seventy-eight years or a lack of women aged sixty-seven. Such immanent 'real' phenomena are inaccessible because they are swamped by the margin of error in the determination of ages above about fifty. Either the data would not show the imbalances, or, even if they did, we should not be allowed to believe them. If members of an ethnicity of this type had gone so far as to refrain from sexual intercourse for a year or two in the past, we could not accept the evidence of it in our crudely constructed age-pyramids. Such gross distortions would be smoothed away in our five-year, even ten-year, age-groupings of the data.

If a so-called 'primitive tribe' has had some interesting mode of adaptation affecting population indices we really have to be specifically told about it. And if we are, what then? I cannot help being reminded of the case of Major Tweedy. He reported of the Ngie people of the Cameroon Highlands in the 1920s that all persons over the age of forty were killed and eaten by adherents of a certain 'Kwap juju'. Some elderly persons who could not evade Major Tweedy's eye were, he was told, the parents of Kwap juju doctors; the doctors, it was hinted, being naturally loth to despatch their own old people – even in the interests of population control. The officer's successor reported that the story must have resulted from the (by then) late major's unfortunate gullibility (Buea 1926). But we cannot ever know the facts on the Kwap juju; by this second visit the Ngie were fully apprised of the bad administrative impression that had been created by an unfortunate (surely satirical?) tendency, and they rectified it to everyone's satisfaction. Nevertheless the very outrageousness of the Kwap juju story made it susceptible to an 'averaging-out' operation. The outrageous does occasionally happen, but if it did happen and we were told about it, we still may not know whether to believe it. By the time anthropologists get to peoples of this sort, the last chance of actually observing something as outrageous as that has usually gone. Anthropologists have not unequivocally determined to this day whether or not certain African divine kings were buried alive or not (Evans-Pritchard 1962c). Among one noted people of Africa I lived surrounded by repeated tales of active cannibalism, but I cannot to this day decide whether the events all happened. If the people have deceived *themselves*, by what criterion shall the anthropologist say whether he has been deceived?

The problems of age determination diminish after long personal acquaintance with the demographically surveyed population. But for large-scale statistical surveys one needs 'rule of thumb' methods. In manuals for 'tribal' demography it is suggested that the people should be asked to count certain cycles: of farms cleared, or of age-set membership, for example. Experience shows that these cannot always be related to exact chronologies. Unfortunately even ordered age-set cycles are not found everywhere. So-called 'calendars of events' are set up by the enquirer to help people to pin down birth dates or life histories. To do all this for only 100 people is a task of real complexity, but most anthropologists will achieve this over time. Given enough time they may manage 1,000 people or even more. But the greater the accuracy, generally the smaller the scale of the survey, and the less its extrapolative value. Meanwhile the supposed 'calendar of events' method teaches us more about notions of history and time than about ages. Even big 'colonial' events may make patchy impact. In one group among whom I worked, people could remember noting the end of World War II, but not its beginning. The coming of early 'white men' needs an archival knowledge of casual explorations. Really well-remembered local events, of course, are often no more datable than the birth dates they were expected to elucidate. Generally, the more complicated the political structure, and the older and the more violent the contact with the outer world, the better the dating. But of course, this immediately reduces the value of the results as an index of a population system adapting in its own way. Even studies like Turnbull's (1972) or Chagnon's on elusive groups cannot be taken as providing data characteristic of a supposed 'Tribal Epoch' (1972: 252).

If our difficulties with age-structure in ethnic populations lead us into such ramifications, it is no wonder that we experience problems with sex ratios at birth. So difficult are our studies that if a somewhat unbalanced ratio of say 109 males per 100 females emerges, it is justly viewed as almost certainly due to survey error. We have to rely on reports by mothers who suppress or wrongly report the sex of their deceased infants, or do not distinguish between early infant deaths, stillbirths and miscarriages. But as a result of our necessary caution, we may have underestimated certain real variations in non-Western sex ratios. As Teitelbaum shows (1972: 90), commonly used calculations for the Net Reproduction Rate can vary significantly with quite small differences in the assessments of the female proportion of births. In the midst of all of this a moderate but well-disguised tendency to female infanticide would probably not be detected.

Wherever we look, then, demographic studies make ethnicities look relatively *less* distinctive, for two reasons: when the people are ill documented the material is eked out by model data; when the people are well documented they have by this very fact entered into modern conditions. This very brief survey of some practicalities was therefore necessary to show that as more and more 'good' studies are made, and as Third World statistics increase in quantity, the further we move from ethnic reality.

DEMOGRAPHIC 'CONSCIOUSNESS'

Let us now take the provisional position that if a certain 'demographic consciousness' is a feature of modern societies, the relative absence of it would correspondingly be one aspect of societies thought of roughly as 'ethnic' or 'tribal'. It does not take much examination, however, to show that we are not dealing with two clearly differentiated categories. The ideal type of the modern society, documented to the eyebrows, its own adaptations including adaptations to its own statistical data about itself – this must seem easy to visualize. We contrast this with the group lacking knowledge of even its total size, let alone its growth rates and the like. But some demographic consciousness in our sense goes far back in the history of the old civilizations (Glass and Eversley 1965). Enumerations were made for purposes of tribute, tax and military service. Adaptations of corporate behaviour were attempted in the light of some of these data. Yet, as historical demographers tell us, these data were usually distorted (even 'wrong') by modern statistical standards. Is there then something like a demographic '*false* consciousness' that we have to recognize? But the 'wrong' data are not likely to be randomly wrong in such circumstances. The old folk-statistics document deep-seated hypotheses about the social unit. Thus early parish-registered christenings (Cox 1910) do not yield birth statistics: but were they not, in another sense, the births that counted? Graunt's analyses of the Bills of Mortality gave unbalanced mortality statistics, but the new urban deaths were perhaps the striking social fact (Graunt 1662; Hollingsworth 1969: 145–9; Ardener, E. and Ardener, S. 1965). To go still further, then, the inadequately or erroneously documented pre-modern polities are not easily distinguished in principle from societies in which no statistics are formally taken, but which nevertheless have elicitable images of how their group is constructed and how situated in time and space. This is the essential 'consciousness' upon which attempts at numeration and mensuration may well ultimately depend, even in our own time.

Let us ask another key question: to what extent and by what processes is it possible for human groups to become aware of their demographic structures (Ardener, E. and Ardener, S. 1965: 7). We are not permitted the simple expedient of pressure on food resources. This limitation is too draconian, on the one hand, and uninteresting, on the other. The difficulty is that even a supposedly objective circumstance like pressure on food supply is experienced through remarkable distortions. Thus, even outright starvation might be attributed to the malice of enemies. It is true that the slaying of these enemies might reduce pressure on food, in some gross sense, but in such conditions by the time we have worked out the permutations we soon tire of a simple pressure-on-food model. At all stages we meet direct intervention by human beings in defining the crisis stage itself – to the extent indeed that pressure-on-food seems like a social rather than a biological concept. For a few weeks in 1973 quite affluent middle-class persons in Great Britain began, as a result of a rise in beef prices, to behave as if meat supplies had totally dried up (many even seemed to take on a hollow-cheeked appearance, when asked by television reporters how they were managing to carry on!).

THE DOUGLAS EFFECT

Professor Mary Douglas, in an important paper, had already pointed out that human groups are 'more often inspired by concern for scarce sources, for objects giving status and prestige, than by concern for dwindling basic resources' (Douglas 1966: 268). By examining the cases of supposed population homeostasis in the anthropological literature, she came to the conclusion that these rested characteristically on a clear-cut evaluation of limited social advantage. As she said, the big question is rather why population homeostatis does not occur. One suggestion she made was that certain kinds of social breakdown change the structural (*not* the biological) limitations and permit population explosion. Whatever the specific arguments for or against in individual cases (Spencer 1965), I would point out the degree of complexity that the possibility of such a conclusion reveals. A common lay view of 'social breakdown' sees it as causing population decline. I will not repeat Professor Douglas's lucid and well-documented arguments. Her 'oysters and champagne' (1966b: 271) view of scarce resources is now widely known. The consideration of certain apparently key economic resources in isolation can certainly mislead us.

An example of the Douglas effect can be given from my own material on the savannah Highlands of Cameroon. Among the Esu people, ordinary farming land is quite plentiful. An upper limit to the growth of settlements is set by the relative shortage of raffia-palms (the latter being used for house-building). These are all restricted to stream-valleys. It is not the case, however, that people wait to move away until building materials have actually run out. Rather, raffia-palms are constantly subject to litigation and the jealous definition of rights. Men brood, and harm each other by witchcraft because of conflicts over such rights. Village and ward headmen tend to be powerfully placed. Political power and witchcraft are frequently joined in them. The weak and the young tend to hive off elsewhere. We may decide to put the ecological limitation at the beginning of the chain, but if we do, we are far removed from the simple world of termites who have eaten up their last tree. The Esu migrate at a very high rate, despite an amplitude of ordinary agricultural resources. But no one can doubt that the raffia-palm thicket situation is already a *socially defined* scarcity. Part of the image of an Esu man is that he is independent enough to go off to a private raffia-palm thicket at will, as if he were a ward head. (Vain dream – like the motorist's image of everyone parking his car outside his city destination.) The Esu are to be contrasted with the case of the Ibo heartland, where a very high-out-migration occurs, but with rural densities of over 1,000 to the square mile compared with seven to the square mile among the Esu (Ardener, E. Ardener, S. and Warmington 1960: 212). Later I shall suggest that among the Ibo the Douglas effect has in fact been interestingly overridden, without significant breakdown of the status system.

Even the most deprived human groups are aristocrats in their definitions of scarcity. If animal models are applied, humanity need never feel serious nutritional constraints until the last rat, mouse, cat, dog and recently deceased comrade is eaten up. Once we come to man, we are in a new topsy-turvy world. He lives in an '*as if*' environment of as yet unexploded hypotheses, of '*as if*' shortages and '*as if*' riches. This is no 'naked ape'; this is the ape wearing emperor's clothes – not quite the same thing! In this sense, perhaps, rather than that of Professors Fox and Tiger, he merits the label 'The Imperial Animal' (1972).

Having thus touched glancingly on current 'ethologism' (Callan's terms, 1970), I should add that I am aware that even in the animal models resource-pressure is buffered by some intermediate structuring. But Fox and Tiger do recognize, in a way that some other more popular writers do not, that 'territory' is not enough to understand man.

While humans do have fights over territory that are equivalent to animal conflicts, their fights over property and other focuses of symbolic attachment such as nationality or religion are not so readily equatable. (1972: 227).

There is no time here to examine every way in which even this statement is still inadequate – in particular that fights are 'over' symbolic features. It is sufficient to say that the human being in society simply lives in a different kind of space: what we may call a 'world-structure' (see above, chapter 5). Crude population density plays different roles in different 'world-structures'. In Hamlet's words: 'I could be bounded in a nutshell and count myself a king of infinite space.'

A CLOUD OF UNKNOWING

In the circumstances, we may have to say that a major determinant of population size is the degree of evolutionary success or failure of that fuzzy cloud of unknowing which is a society's image of its own world-structure. This structure is built up by processes of naming – that is of labelling or categorizing – rather than by numbering. This is the insubstantial front along which the supposed social version of 'adaptation' takes place. When demographic changes occur they are 'apperceived', if I may use that term, through that structure. I am not sure that human beings are always in much better case when aided consciously by demographic data. These may merely give us another mode of expression for changes whose 'causality' lies outside demography. In illustrating the 'unknowing' aspect of world-structures I give examples from very different parts of the world.

THE 'LOST GENERATION'

Consider first the peculiar case of the 'Lost Generation' in English society. The nation was believed to be fatally weakened by the losses of World War I. In the words of Mr Baldwin in 1935:

Have you thought what it has meant to the world to have had that swathe of death cut through the loveliest and best of our contemporaries, how our public life has suffered because those who would have been ready to take over from our tired and disillusioned generation are not there? (Barnett 1972: 425).

Mr Corelli Barnett calls this a 'legend', even a 'myth', thus bringing the topic within our present competence. He notes that proportionately Britain lost fewer men than Germany, but that none thought that Germany's national energy was impaired. On the Western Front itself the 512,564 United Kingdom dead was of the same order as the Italian losses on a single front (460,000). Yet the Italians under Mussolini were not felt in the 1930s to have lost military vigour. Most striking of all:

Even the British losses in officers on all fronts – the true source of the legend of the 'Lost Generation' – was, at 37,452 killed, considerably less than the 55,888 lost by the air crews of Bomber Command during the Second World War, and which led to no comparable legend (ibid.: 426).

Finally, even the massive blood-letting of World War I left 46 per cent of males of military age in the population in 1926, as opposed to 47 per cent in 1911. Mr Barnett concluded brutally that 'the truth was that the Great War crippled the British *psychologically* but in no other way' (ibid., his italics). He noted that it was the disproportionate loss of some small number (say 150) of the inner core of the small British governing class, which led to the legend. 'Unconsciously arrogant', the survivors made the error of thinking that 'because their own small circle had been decimated, the vitality of the British nation had been critically impaired' (ibid.: 428). I do not know that any change in our view of the Lost Generation has been the result of anything in the figures themselves. Mr Barnett talks of 'psychological factors': I have been leading my argument to face you with the proposition that the primitive cloud of unknowing, the self-image through which human aggregates experience the world, is still very much with us – deck it about with eroded age-pyramids though we may. We may note the further lesson that not all social experience contributes equally to the establishment of that self-image; knowledge and the interpretation of knowledge are already located in segments of the very structure that it is expected to explain.

'DYING OUT'

Every so often one meets with a people among whom the opinion has spread that it is 'dying out'. I have worked among one such (the Bantu-speaking Bakweri of Mount Cameroon) alone or with colleagues for many years. This is my second example. Their numbers were about 16,000 in the 1950s. We found high divorce rates, venereal disease, prostitution, honky-tonks for male migrant workers, and low completed family size – we estimated in 1957 a net reproduction rate hovering around 1.00 (or stable) for the previous thirty years (Ardener, E. 1962). All that, and *de facto* population homeostasis too! It is remarkable what demographic indices will put up with. But the self-image of the people had been shrinking over the same period. They saw themselves embattled against zombie foes derived from the ranks of their wickedly murdered children, driven on by known entrepreneurs who had profited from the new economy by witchcraft. Even our own findings were swept into the maw. Some of the knowledgeable (teachers and the like) came to aver that it was the Net Reproduction Rate that witches were striking at – an accommodation with science worthy of broad-minded South Bank theologians.

The Bakweri had good grounds for feeling that their population was not expanding, but the experience of rapid *decline* was a complicated one. Houses fell empty. Migrant workers moved into the area in large numbers. Some Bakweri moved out to plantation employment. The relative number of strangers doubled in a generation. Added to which the Bakweri self-definition excluded from the ranks of 'real Bakweri' their members who were living outside the rural areas. The rural population was not demographically stable. By a series of changes more ideological than economic, which are published elsewhere (Ardener, E. 1970c), the zombies were defeated. At present the demographic indices are probably not very different from before, but the Bakweri no longer hold as common knowledge the opinion that they are dying out. Many think their numbers are increasing, but they are probably as 'wrong' statistically as before.

The supposed propensity to 'die out' was, of course, one much associated with the Custer view of tribes – especially in situations of continual harassment, in which the last stages are best called 'killing out'. However, when numbers decline below a certain point, ethnicities in contact with others may finally *define* themselves out – by not recognizing the children of unions with people of other tribes, for example. When numbers are small, an ethnicity with a more open definition of itself may increase faster than through the best available fertility rate. It is not always easy to keep track of these processes as 'fictive' kinship blurs the genealogical record, as Gibbon long ago noted. Jacquard's paper (1968) on the special effect of sheer smallness on the dynamics of a population does not examine such factors.

The more one documented the Bakweri situation, the more 'wheels within wheels' were to be found. Thus the Bakweri set a very high store upon fertility. Certain fertility medicines that were customarily prescribed for pregnant women were regarded as so important that the failure of a husband to provide them was actually a ground for divorce (Ardener, E. 1962: 58). Yet they consisted of purgatives, administered by crude wooden or gourd enemas – which must have added to, rather than reduced, the obstacles to healthy gestation (Ardener, E. Ardener, S. and Warmington 1960). In such ways social entities build in 'double-bind' situations. We simple observers would be hard put to decide the determinants of population size among the Bakweri, but the possibility that one of them has been a mildly abortifacient 'fertility' drug cannot be excluded. This situation has more in common with the great thalidomide error than it has with the behaviour of any animal population we know.

FERTILITY AND THE 'SUCKLING LAW'

Of course, human intervention in demography is everywhere great in the field of fertility (Hawthorn 1972; Devereux 1955). There are direct interventions and indirect interventions, intended or unintended in either case, any of which may be effective or ineffective (Lorimer et al. 1954; Benedict 1972). All have taken place against a background of some degree of ignorance and disease. It is not surprising that maximum female fertility or something approaching it has rarely been documented. Many African societies, even in healthy modern conditions, have total fertility much reduced by the requirement that a woman should not conceive a second or a subsequent child while her previous one is suckling. This period may last one or two years. It is probably one of the most effective direct interventions on fertility documented in African societies. Yet it is clearly in any overt sense 'unintended'. Women (and men) in such societies, when asked what total family size they would like, characteristically say '100', or 'as many as possible'. Yet a mean total fertility of six seems to be that generated by the suckling law – far below the figure for Victorian vicarages. The fixing of a long suckling period may sometimes be directly related to food-types. There may be no suitable alternative to mothers' milk. Yet in many of these societies this is not true. Whether or not alternative foods are taken may even be neutral, so long as the child has maternal milk. A woman's last child may, indeed, stand up to the breast as late as the age of five. The suckling law is often stated to be a powerful support for male polygyny, and this too has been argued to be a net reducer of total fertility, if only on grounds of reduction of average coital frequency per woman. But polygyny does not always lead to sexual exclusiveness. Large harems, in which institutionalized lovers are recognized, may on the contrary provide

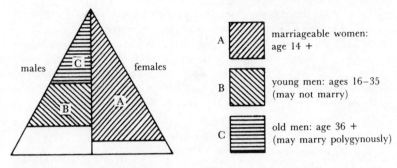

Figure 7.1   An idealized 'gerontocratic' age-pyramid. (Ages only illustrative)

peculiarly favourable conditions for fertility. The Ibo are such a case. The royal harems of the Cameroon grassfields are relatively barren in contrast (Reyher 1952).

It is probable that the suckling law is *grosso modo* of 'beneficial' demographic effect, but it cannot be directly linked to basic resources. On the contrary, a food crisis may lead to an uncertainty, even an ambiguity, as to what is the 'proper food' for children. The painful tragedy of the Biafran infants is still fresh in our memories. The collapse of mothers' milk supply and the disruption of root-crop imports – a source of the mashes made up for young children – led to a totally uncontrolled situation. Protein broths were not socially recognized supplements, and eggs were not eaten. So it was that in many households chickens and goats remained alive while infants imperceptibly wasted away. Long-standing ideas on childcare may thus fail to mesh with a new and unprecedented reality.

GERONTOCRACY

We can sometimes deduce what kind of 'objective' demography a 'folk-demography' would require. Figure 7.1 is the notional age-pyramid for gerontocracies of types discussed by Spencer (1965). Essentially the male age tranche (B) is restricted from marriage – say by service in war camps. This leaves the whole marriageable group of women (A) available for polygynous marriage with males (C) over the age of thirty-five. Dr Spencer's excellent Samburu analysis is very close to this. Younger males may have adulterous relations with the younger married women, so that actual fertility may not be significantly reduced. But the folk-demographies of human societies do not necessarily always fit what we might see as objective facts. Plenty of societies with a folk-demography of a high rate of male polygyny do not in fact achieve the delayed marriage of males that would make this a possibility. In warlike conditions the model may have grown from a kind of external necessity. Where these do not exist, it is a human artefact embedded now in the world-structure, defining behaviour in its own right.

Many lessons may be drawn from this example. The point I am concerned with here is that folk-demographies outlive or transcend their core of reality. It requires a greater effort to see that the Lost Generation was a folk-demography of a similar type, and finally that much of the 'demography' of a series of lectures like this (and especially of the more popular manifestations associated with the enterprise) is the sophisticated folk-demography of Westerners of our historical period.

HOW 'ADAPTIVE' ARE SOCIETIES?

Since we have had to throw doubt on the degree to which crude sociological and demographic restraints can be directly apprehended, it is perhaps useful to point out a neglected area in which something like a direct link between a demographic variable and human world-structures does occur. The accommodation of new generations is an unavoidable feature of even the most technologically simple societies. This particular feature should not be confused with the direct and indirect interventions in fertility that we have discussed. The actual physical arrival of a certain number of new individuals is a reality of a particular unavoidable sort. There has to be an immanent 'recruitment theory' if each newcomer is not to be defined out of the society. A world-structure without an adequate 'recruitment theory' clearly will soon lose its human base. Upon this feature are built the commonest folk-demographies. What are conventionally called kinship systems are for this reason among the finest flowers of human constructions. They ensure that each new person is already a *kind* of person at his birth, and they provide a map of the relationship of kinds to each other (e.g. 'father' to 'son'), and of the transformations of kinds into each other (e.g. 'son' into 'father' through the reproductive cycle). It is a commonplace now to see kinship terminologies as systems that map articulated sets of kinds of person, although differences exist about numerous technicalities.

If we are to relate the 'world-structure' idea of society to conventional evolutionary selection, we see that it is only at this point that failure in a structural component *must* wither the whole structure. As soon as human beings ceased to respond directly to biological constraints, the possibility arose that a group could develop a world-structure which would define babies as alien, or polluting, or as disposable. We may rest assured that none of our ancestors can have belonged to such a group. You may speculate if you wish as to conditions in which a recruitment theory might generate such features over short stretches – but that is not the same as absence of a recruitment theory.

The absolute requirement that there *be* a recruitment component throws some light on the supposed 'fictive' element in kinship systems. The term rests frequently on a misapprehension. The emergence of newcomers to the notice of the world-structure rests upon sets of mainly genealogical categories, which are inevitably homologous in part with the chain of reproduction through which most of the new entrants come; but a recruitment theory that can also recruit and assimilate 'strange' children or active adults is clearly advantageous, since it does not rest exclusively on the chances of biological fertility. We touched on this in connection with 'dying', or very small, ethnicities. There is certainly no reason why a satisfactory theory should have to embody a set of biologically accurate genealogical discovery procedures for who copulated with whom. The fact that this latter distinction has emerged in special historical circumstances underlines the point.

We now see that when Lorimer et al. (1954) and others (Benedict 1972) ask whether a segmentary lineage system is expansionary in tendency, the question is more complicated than it seems. Societies with such systems express the recruitment process through the image of a continually branching genealogy. Placed on its side its branches look like those in a model of successive multiple choices. These genealogies have been long known to be ideal only (e.g. Evans-Pritchard 1940; Bohannan, L. 1952; Ardener, E. 1959b) and the way they are constantly revised in 'fictive' ways, with retrospective effect, is about as well documented as anything in social anthropology. Lorimer's question should perhaps be answered by saying that the expansionism lies essentially in the genealogical image: an open-ended system of nodes of multiple choice. Any real birth is a real addition at one of the nodes. When lines die out they are simply suppressed from the genealogy. All surviving nodes thus imply that additions are possible. In such systems, then, an expansionary self-image may remain in existence, even in conditions of objective stability or decline. The effect is then not to encourage expansion but to neutralize the actual experience of it. If we return to our idea of the space or world-structure in which societies live, we note that the Ibo, a people with an open-genealogy segmentary lineage system, achieved remarkable rural densities of up to 1,600 per square mile, which were tolerated with great resilience. At no time could expansion of the lineage be experienced as disadvantageous by the Ibo, despite growing evidence of exhaustion of agricultural land (Ardener, E. 1954a; 1959b). We may note indeed the appearance of ever greater industry, inventiveness and incentive that the Ibo exhibited through the recent period of growth. The cherished male status crop, the yam, was even abandoned as staple over large areas in favour of the recently introduced cassava. In other words the 'Douglas effect' did not work where we might have expected. Rather it was overridden by an extremely powerful recruitment component, and without any evidence of internal social breakdown of the sort that the Douglas hypothesis needs.

It may be guessed that the adaptation required open migration; another kind of breakdown occurred when this was barred by Northern Nigeria – leading to the Biafran war. Such cases do not refute the Douglas effect – we are even further away from a simple pressure-on-resources model. The Douglas effect is a small-scale and possibly short-term aspect of the more general self-defining phenomenon inherent in the world-structure concept. If you like, the recruitment component itself was paradoxically the point at which the effect occurred. Thus, it could not result in population homeostasis – the 'oysters and champagne' were *people*, which were always, by definition, 'scarce' and always a source of 'prestige'. The Douglas effect, in its proper usage, may then not be expected inevitably to intervene homeo-statically. After all, the 'proletariat' was so called because its wealth lay in its off-spring (*proles*).

CONCLUSION

The way in which the adaptations of human beings have been vested in a partly unconscious social system is one of the marvels of evolution. For there is no doubt that this truly blind, because unsuspecting, abrogation of sovereignty by the individual over his own animal survival lies in the form of the human consciousness itself. If a crisis is sufficiently unprecedented, the social forms all too often grind themselves to destruction, because indi-viduals simply do not 'see', that is, grasp or perceive, the nature of the crisis. To ask about the determinants of population size is really to ask about what I have called 'world-structures', about kinds of consciousness, and their accuracy in helping groups to survive. One fears, however, that we cannot assume that they have a 'purpose' or 'function' to help us survive. All human societies existing today may be soberly stated to have survived in spite of the most grotesque misjudgements of events in the past. The fact that they have only a direct relationship with evolutionary pres-sure through their recruitment component, and that in the direction of more openness, may be a great weakness.

If you are accustomed to say that certain population determinants are 'social', I hope I have shown that we must be very careful to think what we meant by that. It is surprising that many intellectual persons of a scientific bent, whose own minds and lives are a continuum of nuances and subtle-ties, are often easily satisfied with ideas of social systems made up of simple causal chains, which would not safely guide them through ten minutes of real life. Anthropologists are not able to help out by saying that there are 'simple' societies where life *is* like that, as if we can still return to well-tried mechanisms. The contribution of such peoples is to suggest to us that even major variations in population indices may be affected by minor changes in the 'world-structure' of human groups. Furthermore that, if there are changes in basic resources on a scale much greater than that of a given human group, its world-structure will determine how those changes are apperceived, and indeed decide whether they are apperceived at all. Per-haps our danger today resides in the greater specialization and isolation of those groups in our own culture who shape our view of reality and thus our actions. There may be a crisis ahead, but as usual the one we are living in is mixed up with a crisis of interpretation. That is why I have suggested that demographic studies are not necessarily neutral or objective. They rest on too many quasi-realities, among which the term 'population' is pre-eminent. Our main task, therefore, is to restore 'the people' to their central place in the picture, custodians of the cloud of unknowing that got us into the ambiguous situation we are in today.

8

The 'Problem' Revisited

The paper reprinted above (see chapter 4) is now somewhat old, and as composed just antedated the main impact of the new feminist literature. It is important to stress therefore that it was not seen as a contribution to that literature. Most of what it says seems quite commonplace at the present. In its rather long unpublished existence it was orally delivered in various places in the context of a discussion of the nature of dominant structures. It is not exactly the paper I would now write, if indeed I would write it at all. It has been a genuine pleasure to me, as a result, that it has not been rejected in its entirety by women social anthropologists concerned with the social differentiation of men and women. There have, however, been questions, and one or two misunderstandings, most of which occur in a critique by Nicole-Claude Mathieu called 'Homme-Culture et Femme-Nature?' (1973).

First of all, it should not be necessary for a social anthropologist, male or female, to offer any particular explanation for writing on 'the problem of women' as I presented it. One of the greatest statements of it was made by Virginia Woolf in 1928. She noted the great gulf between the saliency of women in symbolism and literature and their position until recently in the official structure. 'Imaginatively she is of the highest importance; practically she is completely insignificant. She pervades poetry from cover to cover; she is all but absent from history' (Woolf 1928: 45). Perhaps there were certain coincidences, for what they are worth, that at least did not place any obstacles of experience to my attempt on the question. My first fieldwork was among the Ibo, in the area in which the Women's Uprising of 1929 occurred. This was followed by studies among the Bakweri of Cameroon, who were portrayed, and who portrayed themselves, as riven by marital conflict. Among the latter, studies from the male point of view (Ardener, E. Ardener, S. and Warmington 1960: part 3) were followed by a study from the women's side (Ardener, E. 1962). The difference in atmosphere was extremely striking. For the men, society was in chaos, even breaking down. For the women, life was a periplus of adventures, in which the role of independent 'harlot' was often viewed as objectively a proud one. I admit that the paper may be affected by ethnographic experiences that particularly highlight the 'separate realities' of men and women. There will be societies in which the gap is greater or smaller, confined to one area of life or another. Alternatively the gap should be seen as an exemplification of all discontinuities in the experience of groups in society, however defined.

Still, the necessity to interview women in such numbers as is required in a fertility and marital survey provides a considerable body of data for an anthropologist, which it has not always been fashionable to see in other than statistical terms. In the general social anthropological world, I do not think it an exaggeration to say that by 1960 studies of women had declined to a fairly low theoretical status. Temporarily even the standard books by Margaret Mead had receded into the background. No doubt my recollection can be contested. Nevertheless, I recall the remark then being made (by a woman): 'no anthropological book with "women" in the title sells.' The writings were there, as some critics point out, but (to modify the pre-nineteenth-century motto of the Russians about their literature): '*De mulieribus – sunt, non leguntur.*'

I have been asked whether women anthropologists 'raised my conscious-ness'. Although this hints at a characteristic modern paradox,[1] the question is relevant and deserves a careful answer. Because in both Eastern Nigeria and Cameroon, women had caused 'trouble' to the male population and to the administration, there had already been women anthropologists in these areas. In Iboland Sylvia Leith-Ross and M. M. Green had been deliberate-ly invited to make studies in the aftermath of the Women's Riots, or what Caroline Ifeka terms the Women's War. It was Miss Green who in later years taught me the first elements of Ibo. In Cameroon, Phyllis Kaberry at one time nearly studied the Bakweri but eventually studied 'women' on the inland Plateau. She had already written *Aboriginal Woman*, and was to write *Women of the Grassfields*. Then through all phases of both the Nigerian and Cameroon studies, the last of which are still not finally completed, I worked with Shirley Ardener who must be the female anthropologist of the most continuous and subtle influence on me. Later she and Phyllis Kaberry and I collaborated on studies in Cameroon history with Sally Chilver – now one of the most distinguished ethno-historians in the study of the region. If in retrospect I note that my first teacher was Audrey Richards, and that the paper appeared in her festschrift, edited in its turn by Jean La Fontaine, there is a galaxy of female talent enough here to reassure any who might view with regret and suspicion the presence of a male anthropologist in this field.

Yet what was the precise nature of their influence on this paper? None of them, certainly of the senior ones, were particularly of a 'feminist' turn of mind. None appeared to be then students of 'women' except fortuitously, as part of their general anthropological work. Thus arose the paradox that a 'problem of women anthropologists' began to present itself unbidden to my mind. It had two components: (1) that they did not seem to be in a much more privileged position in interpreting the women of their fields than was a male anthropologist (2) that the women anthropologists themselves, although they were loth to differentiate themselves from male anthropologists, did have significantly different academic pasts, presents and (it looked likely) futures, in the anthropological profession itself.

It is easy nowadays to criticize me for needing these insights. A critic (Mathieu 1973) has stated that only one who believes in 'woman' as a universal category could have fallen into the error of entertaining such an expectation as is implied in the first point. That reading is not quite exact: the problem was that women anthropologists did not themselves then reject the expectation, even though they were uncomfortable with it. Of course, in the last few years all this has changed – or begun to change. My second point is also a mere commonplace among militant women. Nevertheless, an independent perspective is not without its value. During the sixties it did sometimes look as if women anthropologists had even more academic vitality in relation to their numbers than had their male colleagues. At long anthropological conferences their contributions frequently threw brave, short-lived beams of light into the gloom before being overwhelmed by it. Nevertheless no woman became until recently a Professor of Anthropology in a British university.[2] It was quite apparent, however, that women formed only an easily recognizable part of a class of social anthropologists in the same condition. Yet while male anthropologists of a 'destructured' tendency were generally conscious of the nature of the situation which enveloped them, the women anthropologists seemed 'muted' on their own position. Publicly, at least, they did not 'see' or 'perceive' themselves within the structure of academic anthropology; so, inevitably, they did not 'see' other women clearly in their own fields. That is the reason why 'Belief and the Problem of Women' ends with the challenge to women anthropologists 'to split apart the very framework in which they conduct their studies'. Nicole-Claude Mathieu asks, should not men do likewise? Precisely. No one who knows my general position will imagine that this conclusion was to be seen as an achievement of male complacency. I have taken the 'woman' case in order to *de*sexualize it. When I say that it is a special case of a situation applying to other social classes and individuals, both men and women, this is not a casual aside as Mathieu again seems to think – it is the intended conclusion of the paper, which has been merely illustrated by the case of women.

In the light of the foregoing it may be worth noting for the chronological record that in July 1973 at the Session on Marxism of the ASA Decennial Conference I made an oral contribution to the discussion of class:

If we look at those classes which are usually considered to be the exploiting or dominant classes, and then we consider those others which are supposedly the exploited or suppressed classes, there is this dimension that hasn't been mentioned yet: which is [that] of relative articulateness. One of the problems that women presented was that they were rendered 'inarticulate' by the male structure; that the dominant structure was articulated in terms of a male world-position. Those who were not in the male world-position, were, as it were, 'muted'.

I repeated my suggestion that this applied to other social groups and also to individuals, and stated its relevance to the question of the universality or otherwise of the concept of class:

We may speak of 'muted groups' and 'articulate groups' along this dimension. There are many kinds of muted groups. We would then go on to ask: 'What is it that makes a group muted?' We then become aware that it is muted simply because it does not form part of the dominant communicative system of the society – expressed as it must be through the dominant ideology, and that 'mode of production', if you wish, which is articulated with it (from transcript of discussion 7 July 1973).

Nevertheless, the point must be made that not all phenomena of mutedness can be linked simply and directly to a 'mode of production'. Dominant/muted alternations, as we shall see, occur at too many levels to actualize themselves always in these terms. The definition of 'mode of production' itself would suffer extraordinary transfigurations if it were so. Nevertheless, those alternations which are tied to a mode of production certainly acquire a special kind of salience or stability – an institutionalization – that will be familiar to Marxist analysts.

The approach is already being provisionally applied to other muted groups, such as children (Hardman 1973) and criminals (Maguire 1974). We owe the convenient term 'muted' itself to Charlotte Hardman. But the phenomenon of 'mutedness' (it must be warned) is a technically defined condition of structures – not some condition of linguistic silence.[3] There is also an ambiguity about the term 'muted' in this connection – for in English we mean by it both 'dumb' and 'of a reduced level of perceptibility'. The muted structures are 'there' but cannot be 'realized' in the language of the dominant structure (see Ardener, S. 1975b: xiii–xv).

The operation of a dominant structure from the point of view of a subdominant may be likened to a pin-table in which the very operation of the spring, to propel the ball, itself moves the scoring holes some centimetres to the side. The more skill the operator uses in directing the ball, the more carefully he ensures that the scoring hole will not be there to receive it. The ultimate negativity of attempts to modify dominant structures by their own 'rules' derives from the totally reality-defining nature of such structures. Because of this essential element the manifold of experience through the social may be usefully termed a 'world-structure', for it is an organization both of *people and of their reality*. It is not my intention to appear to confuse the apparently practical aspects of the perception of woman, and of perceiving by women, by alluding in too much detail to these questions, some of which are at early stage of analysis. But a 'world-structure', in these clearly defined terms, is the nearest congener to the 'society' or (and?) 'culture' of traditional anthropology. The characteristic bounding problem that those terms imply ('where does a society begin or end?', 'when are cultures the "same" or "different"? In space or in time?') is solved by its resolution in the chief criterion of a 'world-structure': it is a *self*-defining system.

We are now able to examine an unfortunate misunderstanding of my previous paper. I find it difficult to see how any careful reader can deduce that for me it is a simple case of 'man = culture' and 'women = nature'. The fault lies, no doubt, in my citation of Lévi-Strauss. My readers should concentrate upon the 'defining' or 'bounding' problem presented by women in a situation in which the 'bounds' of 'society' are themselves defined by men. In the conceptual act of bounding 'society' there is a fortuitous homology between the purely ideational field or background against which 'society' is defined as a concept, and that part of the actual, territorial world which is not socially organized – the 'wild'. The 'wild' = the 'non-social'. It is a mere confusion that it may also be walkable into, and be found to contain sounding cataracts and unusual beasts. A 'society', because it has a geographical *situs*, in one of its defining spaces, or along one of its dimensions, therefore projects an equivalent geographical aspect on to its counter-concept – the 'non-social'. If the world were geographically a uniformly barren surface, the self-defining human entities upon it would thereby merely lack a useful set of topographical differentiae for the 'non-social'. Conceptually these differentiae would not cease to exist. In rural societies the equation: non-social = non-human = the wild = 'nature' is easily concretized. There is a powerful metaphor, with a key into experience. This is the source of the triviality as well as the power of the binary opposition 'nature/culture' in Lévi-Strauss's own analyses. Its 'universality' is indeed a powerful triviality. It is 'self/not-self' raised to the level of society's own self-definition, and clothed in 'totemic' and botanical imagery.

My argument was: where society is defined by men, some features of women do not fit that definition. In rural societies the anomaly is experienced as a feature of the 'wild', for the 'wild' is a metaphor of the non-social which in confusing ways is vouched for by the senses (see figure 8.1). A B C D is an unbounded field against which the two intersecting circles *x* and *y* are defined. From the perspective of circle *x* the shaded portion of *y* is part of the field A B C D. The circle *x*, *plus* the unshaded overlap of circle *y*, is the model of society where the male model is dominant (heavy outline and capital letters). In metaphorical terms, A B C D is 'the wild'. In the diagram, the shaded area of *y*, which is classified by men with the 'wild', is

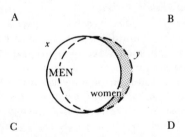

Figure 8.1 Men, women and 'the wild'

not confused by women themselves with the 'wild' (save when they speak in the dominant 'language'). Rather, for them there is a zone in circle x which is ambiguously male and 'wild', a zone which men do not perceive.

This confusion of self-definition with geographical reality is avoided when we think not of 'society', but of a world-structure which defines human reality – if you like 'relevant' reality. In these terms if the male perception yields a dominant structure, the female one is a muted structure. It is an empirical contingency that the immanent realizations of muted structures are so often equated in this way with the nullity of the background, of 'nature'; and also that 'nature' itself should thus contain at its core a common metaphorical conceptualization, appearing in Rousseau and Lévi-Strauss, on the one hand, and the Bororo or the Bakweri, on the other.[4]

Mathieu appears to take my own argument to its extreme when she chides me for mentioning the female biology as one of the features males find difficult to tidy away into the perceptions of the dominant structure. Yes, of course, we can say that the very concept of female biology is a product of the dominant structure. But once more I reply that the un-doubted anatomical and functional differences become a powerful and convenient metaphor for this, possibly the most ancient and surely the most nearly universal, structural dominance. Hertz similarly showed that a pos-sibly slight anatomical ('biological') discrepancy between a right- and a left-handed tendency became a powerful metaphor for all binary discri-minations, including this very one between the sexes; and, as Needham's comprehensive volume on the subject also illustrates (1973), it is also no surprise that spatial concepts (inside/outside, village/wild) should be lined up with these pairs. Mathieu thus is quite mistaken in asserting that I am a 'biological essentialist' and that my analysis demands a theory of biological causation.

Some of her mistakes rest upon subtle difficulties of translation from English into French, and I accept part of the blame for this, as even for an English-speaking reader there are a number of levels of irony and ambi-guous nuance in the style of the paper. Still, when I write of 'women overlapping into [the men's view of] nature again' I do not mean *'refaire le saut dans la nature'* (Mathieu: 107–8). Women do not 'leap back' into nature: they overlap, protrude beyond the limits set for them by men. When I write of a 'propensity' of males to make models of society of a particular bounded type, I do not mean *une capacité* (ibid.: 107) but 'a structural readiness'; nor do I refer to *des modèles bien délimités, modèles discrets de la société* (ibid.: 102), but to models of a society bounded (*délimités) in a particular way*. Further-more, when I say that 'all such ways of bounding society against society ... may have an inherent maleness', the term 'maleness' is of course not here a biological term, a function of male gonads. We cannot draw from it the conclusion that: *'La "dominance politique" des hommes est ainsi conçue comme une caractéristique fixe d'une catégorie biologique fixe: le politique est à l'homme ce que la vertu dormitive est au pavot, une propriété'* (ibid.: 107). It is strange to be suspected of an ethologistic determinism, even greater than Professors Fox and Tiger are normally accused of.

Lastly, nothing but some basic stereotypical error can account for the sternness of Mathieu's response to my interchange with Jean La Fontaine (see below, chapter 4, note 9). She detects an irony on my part. There is indeed one: I certainly do not reject (as she suggests) the validity of a female equation of the wild of 'maleness' with death, destruction and 'non-culture'. I was gently deprecating, however, any hint of a simple 'female utopianism' that would define death and destruction as incompatible with *itself*. But in the end I suspect that 'culture' is for Mathieu an *a priori* category with a high positive marking – whereas, for many of us, a position 'in the wild' (were that actually in question) still has no negative connotations. I am quite prepared to be defined as 'nature' by Mathieu for I detect in her paper the salutary symptoms of one who has begun to 'split apart the very framework of her studies'.[5]

In conclusion I would state my position so: the woman case is only a relatively prominent example of muting: one that has clear political, biological and social symbols. The real problem is that all world-structures are totalitarian in tendency. The Gypsy world-structure, for example, englobes that of the sedentary community just as avidly as that of the sedentary community englobes that of the Gypsies. The englobed structure is totally 'muted' in terms of the englobing one. There is then an absolute equality of world-structures in this principle, for we are talking of their self-defining and reality-reducing features. *Dominance* occurs when one structure blocks the power of actualization of the other, so that it has no 'freedom of action'. That this approach is not simply a Marxist one lies in our recognition that the articulation of world-structures does not rest only in their production base but at all levels of communication: that a structure is also a kind of language of many semiological elements, which specify all actions by its power of definition.

My intervention in the discussion as far as it concerns women was a product of concern with the technical features of socio-intellectual structures which regularly assign contending viewpoints to a non-real status; making them 'overlooked', 'muted', 'invisible': mere black holes in someone else's universe.

9

The Voice of Prophecy
Further Problems in the Analysis
of Events

TIME

When this lecture was first given I had developed the idea of the social as a 'world-structure'.[1] I here attempt to examine some features of the concept and its properties as a 'definition space'. The term 'world-structure' was derived from a consideration of the 'structural' models deriving from various streams of social anthropological theory. This terminology I saw as already outmoded. During this lecture I begin to dispense with the term and to concentrate on the living features of the social space. In particular I consider how discontinuities appear in it over time, and how individuals themselves may be discontinuities in it. The defining properties of the space contain the secret of both its 'determinist' and its 'free' aspects.

The Prophetic Condition

On this occasion I wish to consider more questions about what the social as a world is like. What kind of space is it? I have chosen to start on this occasion from certain paradoxes inherent in the idea of prophecy, in order to discuss aspects of the dynamics of the space: its changes and automatisms and the degree to which individuals are conscious or not of the nature of the space. The first half will be relatively concrete in order to lead into some of the problems through particular data. The second half will be relatively more theoretical.

Let us begin with this quotation from Yeats:

> When Pearse summoned Cuchúlainn to his side,
> What stalked through the Post Office? What intellect,
> What calculation, number, measurement replied?
> ('The Statues', Yeats 1950: 375).

Yeats's question was not rhetorical, nor sceptical: he was perturbed by the uncomfortable implications of certain kinds of event, marked by the transfiguration of the banal into the significant, the collapse of the past into the present, the 'irreal' into the real. For the Dublin Post Office rising of 1916 was a strange fruit of Yeats's own prophetic role in summoning into Irish consciousness such grotesque shapes from antiquity as Cuchúlainn (O'Connor 1967: 7).[2] The times, the man, the event met in . . . the Post Office. Even to our ears, for whom the great Victorian monuments to modernity are receding into the past, certain phrases still retain a comfortable rationality: the Post Office, the railway time-table, the electric telegraph. We can reconstruct their feel for Yeats's time, and his puzzlement. If this was prophecy how did it realize itself in the Post Office? Yeats, still after all a Victorian by birth, asked: 'What intellect, what calculation, number, measurement replied?'

When we speak of prophecies we are not concerned with prediction – I almost said 'simple' prediction. Elsewhere (see above, chapter 2) I have already discussed the essentially repetitive feature of successful predictions. They fail at precisely the moment at which they are required, when the repetition does not occur. All prophets are like Cassandra. They are not believed beforehand. They are not necessarily recognized afterwards. In advance, the prophecies are incomprehensible, afterwards they are trivial. This is a feature of prophetic situations, as much as of prophets as people. It is difficult to capture afterwards precisely the lineaments of the prophetic situation. Prophecy, I shall suggest, is a kind of condition both of individuals and of structures – or an expression of such a condition if you like, although as we shall see the distinction is a tautology. Essentially 'prediction' and 'prophecy' depend to begin with on different definitions of time or on a movement of time into a conceptual irrelevancy. Interestingly, only the latter seems to fit the most modern scientific views of it. Prophecy links language, time and space.

The question of time in relation to structure and to physical space has been discussed often enough in anthropology (I need only refer to Evans-Pritchard 1940 and Leach, E. R. 1961a) but the experience of living in structural time is not easily accepted. For that reason I will make some points on the nature of time as a definition problem. It will also help to examine the various ways that language puzzlingly intervenes in the definition of worlds. As a tribute to the Celtic ambiance of the present occasion, for data to illustrate this half of the lecture we can easily cite a Scottish example.

'Cultural' time: The Scottish Gaelic Example

Discussion of the Scottish Gaelic time system has been overlaid by a fatal attraction towards the reconstruction of hypothetical 'Celtic' systems. Indeed, one of the few extensive documentary remains of continental Celtic is the Coligny calendar (Thurneysen 1899; Lainé-Kerjean 1942–3; Rees, A. and Rees, B. 1961: 84–9). It is moderately unhelpful in the analysis of insular systems, no doubt because there was a loss of ancient astronomical knowledge in the collapse of the ancient world. Furthermore any ancient system suitable for Continental Europe could hardly remain unamended in higher latitudes. The Scottish Gaelic system is in that sense modern, 'folk', eclectic – a system without druids or astronomers. From the general Insular Celtic background we detect a division of the year into a 'light' summer half from 1 May to 1 November, and an opposing winter half. We note that the winter is the 'dark' half, like the annual night, and that the year begins with the winter, just as the Celtic day begins on the previous dusk. The old markers were the feast of the Calends of winter (*Samhainn*) which was fixed historically to 1 November, and the Calends of summer (*Bealltuinn*) ascribed to 1 May. At the mid-points of the main seasons were feasts on 1 August *Liùnasdal* (Lammas) and on 1–2 February *Féill Brìde*, Candlemas (the Old Irish *Imbolc*).

These time points were fixed in the post-classical period, usually matched to Christian feasts, and have remained ever since in some kind of connection with the standard calendar. The festivals of *Nollaig* (Christmas), and St John's Eve (Midsummer) were an additional feature of medieval Gaeldom. The festival of the old Calends of winter (now Hallowtide) has been to some extent duplicated at the present Hogmanay (*Calluinn*: 1 January), whence possibly some Hallowe'en aspects of its customs (Grant 1961: 357–61).

So much for the basic framework. Gaelic time retained no trace of the Coligny Calendar's meticulous month measurements. Feasts were pinned to the current dominant time system, but throughout the nineteenth century the Gregorian amendments (of 1582 but introduced in Great Britain only in 1752) remained ineffective over much of the area. Folk-dates were in Old Style, which after 1900 had moved out of kilter by fourteen days (Dwelly 1920: 426). Some people were still on pre-1900 Old Style, and out by only thirteen days. A third group were on New Style. When even the supposed standard months were out, it is no surprise that native Gaelic time periods showed a welter of varieties when the nineteenth-century scholars began to record them.

This confused mixture of outdated or forgotten knowledge ('hollow categories': see above, chapter 3, p. 69) and 'folk' usage gives a much better picture of the intervention of restructuring into a non-scientific time system than do reconstructions of consistent, 'pure' systems. Our anthropological cases show similar eclectic tendencies as I shall illustrate. The constant brushes of Gaelic time with standard time are thus very illuminating, as an exemplification in a non-exotic milieu of the resistance of a 'world-structural' feature to linearization.

There is now, as is well known, a standard list of Scottish Gaelic names for the twelve calendar months (see table 9.1 for the standard list and figure 9.1 for a representation of the Scottish Gaelic year). In providing such a list, learned Gaels exhibit an excusable failing: an attempt to match up a terminological system developed in specific and highly local conditions against a standard one of supposedly higher status. For the standard calendar is standard in terms of measurement, of mensuration. Time in it

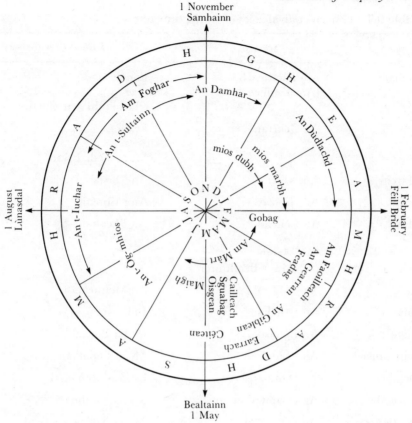

Figure 9.1 The Scottish Gaelic year

is the result of centuries, even millennia, of the search for 'real' time – a search that we in the West fell into *pari passu* with our search for 'real' space (as we shall suggest later).

Let us look at month 1, *Am Faoilteach* or *Am Faoilleach* (the purported 'January'). The Highland Society's Gaelic Dictionary (1828) defined it as 'the season of wolf-ravage' (as if from *faol*: wolf). Armstrong (1925: 239) extends it into February, and it is indeed sometimes translated 'February'. We are told by MacAlpine (1832/1973: 124) that it is 'the last fortnight of winter and the first fortnight of spring...'. Sometimes the two halves were named winter *Faoilteach* and spring *Faoilteach* (*Am F. Geamhraidh* and *Am F. Earraich*). For the best exemplification of the characteristic mismatching of Gaelic system to dominant system, linearized on to fixed time, and fixed time unfixed into Old Style, Dwelly (1920: 413) records that in Lewis, *Am Faoilleach* (the local form) 'begins on the Friday nearest three weeks before the end of January, and ends on the Tuesday nearest the end of the third week of February – *Di-haoine a thig 's Di-màirt a dh'fhalbas*, comes on Friday and goes on Tuesday – three weeks of Winter, and three weeks of Spring'. Six weeks in all. So much for the fixity of purported 'January'.

Table 9.1   Official equivalences of Gaelic time terms

	Scottish	Irish
January	Am Faoilteach (Am Faoilleach)	Eanáir *or* Chéad mhí den bhliain
February	An Gearran	Feabhra *or* Mí na Féile Bríde*
March	Am Màrt	An Márta
April	An Giblean	An tAibreán
May	An Céitean *or* Am Maigh (1st May) Bealltuinn*	An Bhealtaine*
June	An t-Òg-mhios	An Meitheamh
July	An t-Iuchar	Iúil
August	An Lùnasdal*	Mí na Lúnasa*
September	An t-Sultainn	Meán Fhómhair
October	An Damhar	Deireadh Fómhair
November	An t-Samhainn*	Mí na Samhna*
December	An Dùdlachd	Mí na Nollag

* Ancient ritual dates.

Spring	An t-Earrach	An tEarrach
Summer	An Samhradh	An Samhradh
Autumn	Am Foghar	An Fómhar
Winter	An Geamhradh	An Geimhreadh

Turning to month 2, *An Gearran* (purported 'February'), we find periods like: 'from 15 March to 11 April inclusive' (MacAlpine 1832/1973), as well as 'the latter end of February' (Armstrong 1825: 289). More interesting still: 'The nine days after "*Faoileach*"; *Mios faoilich naoidh là Gearrain*.' (Dwelly 1920: 486). There is a further difficulty about two unharmonized periods, *Feadag* and *Gobag*, not accommodated in the standard sequence of pseudo-months. For *Gobag* it is said: 'period of the year, lasting according to some, three days, according to others a week, coming in between the *Feadag* and the *Gearran* and so ending on the 14th March.' (ibid.: 571, after Nicholson 1881: 411–14). *Gearran* is our purported February. As for *Feadag*, that is ascribed by some to the third week of February (Armstrong 1825: 243; Dwelly; 1920: 420). We shall meet some attempts to deal with this confused zone later.[3]

With month 3, *Am Màrt* (purported 'March'), we come to a valuable example of just how complex the relationship of language to world-structure is. For the name *Am Màrt* is an ancient learned borrowing, going back to an early matching with the month of March (*mensis Martis*). Yet the auspicious nature of Tuesday (especially for work requiring sharp instruments – Carmichael 1900, vol. 1: 245) has encouraged the further confusion of the name of the month with the Gaelic name of Tuesday which, also following the Latin tradition, is *Di-màirt* (*Dies Martis*). *Am Màrt* was also the appropriate sowing season. When combined with the auspiciousness of Tuesdays we get structural involutions of super-auspiciousness like: *An ciad Mhàrt de Mhàrt-na-curachd* ('the first *Màrt* [Tuesday] of *Màrt* [March]-of-sowing').

The idea of 'a *Màrt* of a *Màrt*' produced purely linguistic reflexes, echoes or calques such as 'a *Bealltuinn* of the *Bealltuinn*' and 'a *Liùnasdal* of *Liùnasdal*' (Dwelly 1920: 634). These mean '1 May of 1 May' and '1 August of 1 August', or if you prefer: 'a Mayday of a Maymonth' or 'an Augustday of an Augustmonth'. These phrases are basically only a linguistic arabesque, an automatism – if you like a kind of 'disease of language', to modify Max Müller's usage. Meanwhile *Màrt*, we learn, can refer not only to sowing time but to other busy times of the agricultural calendar. We hear then of *three Màrts* which seem to be three Tuesdays in the *Màrt* period, of which only the third is suitable for sowing. Elsewhere we hear of three busy *Màrts*: 12 April to 1 May, 12 August, and 12 September (Campbell, Lord A. 1889; Dwelly 1920: 634).

Dwelly, faced with these difficulties, came to some very modern conclusions. I cite them because they prefigure the definition of a 'prescriptive category', here of time (see above, chapter 2). He says

In the first place the old 'months' appear to have been moveable, and depended for their commencement on whether the suitable weather had already arrived. *If the weather had not come neither had the month* e.g. Luath no mall g'an tig am Maigh, thig a'chubhag, Late or early as May comes (i.e. as May-weather comes), so comes the cuckoo . . . (Dwelly 1920: 634, my italics).

An anthropologist would differ only with the expression: that the old 'months' were moveable. They did not 'move' in relation to their own world. This is an illusion from our alien perspective; as if in measuring a moving body with a fixed rule we were to say that our 'inches' moved. We may add that the so-called months were obviously not of equal length either, or better: that they went on as long as they were perceived to go on, and the determinants lay in 'ecological' and 'social' factors.

Yet there was a living and continuous search to match up Gaelic time to standard time, leading to ever more extreme mismatches, but yielding ever clearer clues to the key elements. For example, we have time segments once keyed perhaps to moons but certainly not to months, specifying cyclical weather periods and agricultural seasons. The 'firsts' of months which inaugurated festivals were probably once the days on which it was announced that the segment of time had begun. We have living examples of this process, elsewhere. Thus, among the Ibo of South-Eastern Nigeria, the months were numbered every year, or perhaps we should say that 'moons' were (e.g. *onwa ato*, 'moon three', etc.). In the course of thirty continuous months of fieldwork, we found that the stated numbers did not coincide from year to year. We were careful, of course, about lunar months – not calendar months – but to no avail. In fact, no one else was counting in sequence at all. Those numbers were not ordinal, but absolute. It is true that every year certain events were connected with certain numbered months. Yet when a certain ritual sequence was due in say, 'month four' the priests looked for a moon at about the time that they wanted to do the rite and called it *moon four*.

The Ibo problem is only a highly concentrated version of that of the scientific system. Our own social calendars will also not permit the system of months to go out of relation to the system of sun-cycles, but in comparison the Ibo are astronomers, if you like, with continuously and poorly revised Old Style calendars. We should try to see the matter that way round for two reasons. First: in order to by-pass, and incidentally de-romanticize, the discussion of 'primitive' science. We see, for example, that an encoding by numbers and a desire to check against astronomical reality – both characteristic of the Ibo – may still only measure *social* reality. Second: in order to help us to see that attempts of such practitioners to use 'modern' science (as did the Gaels) are only to be expected. Thus, it was disconcerting to find that the anthropologist, wanting to know the Ibo system of determining the moons, was expected to know better than his hosts, and to help them to determine the moons. The paradox here is difficult to express: the anthropologist is aware that each world generates a kind of reality, yet within it there may also be ways of accommodating what we think of as 'scientific' reality.

The similar paradoxes in the modern Gaelic folk-system were in fact the result of the constant search by Gaelic thinkers for assistance in expressing their own time system, as if visiting anthropologists had given advice from the outside world over and over again through the centuries. We may suspect that in Celtic times there was an ancient Ibo-like system of announcing the 'months'. Thus the term *Caluinn* (cognate with Latin *Calendae*) covers the concept of 'first day' (now New Year's Day) but etymologically it may well derive from a term meaning 'announcement' or 'declaration'. Furthermore, the 'first day' and its season might be simultaneous categories. Thus *Bealltuinn* is the '1 May' but it was also a period. In the Irish version of the standardization of months *Bealtaine* is used for May, as well as for Mayday. This uncertainty as to whether time labels refer to specific points, or to the period between such points is a commonplace of non-linear time systems. So as *Bealltuinn* was both a day and a season, so *Am Màrt*, despite its impeccable onomastic origin in the Latin for March, was able to become an event, an occasion, or a date, not only in its own month but in other months. Furthermore *Am Màrt*, as if this was not enough, also had its Old Style scientization, so that even when it was matched with standard March, for some it did not begin till modern March was half over (Dwelly 1920: 634).

Clearly the purported months one, two and three covered a period of late winter and spring, more like February to May than the purported January to March. This flexibility is even easier to understand from a backward glance at month twelve, *An Dùdlachd*, purported 'December', which basically refers to the 'depth of winter' as in the phrase *Dùdlachd a gheamhraidh*, 'a time of tempestuous weather' (ibid.: 370). So when *Dùdlachd* ends, be it in January or February or later, can *Faoillteach* be far behind?[4]

As a result of the flexibilities already discussed, canonical month four, *An Giblean* (purported 'April'), and month six, *An t-Òg-mhios* ('The young month', purported 'June'), inevitably have an interpolated appearance, due to the fact that purported 'March' (*Am Màrt*) overlaps April (as we have seen), while purported 'May' (*Maigh* or *An Céitean*, or the month of *Bealltuinn*) could extend into or over June. You will no longer be surprised to learn that purported 'May' under the label *An Céitean* is by various authorities also called the 'beginning of summer' and sometimes just 'spring'. Furthermore, it has its Old Style dating (*Céitean na h-òinnsich*: 19 April to 12 May, ibid: 187).

An influential attempt to put order into this part of the year was Nicholson's. He is clearly somewhat embarrassed by it:

> The season of Spring was more specially a matter of observation and interest to our ancestors than any of the other seasons, on account of its importance as the time of the year on the character of which their existence and comfort so much depended. Accordingly we find it divided into various periods with fanciful names, founded so far as their meaning can be guessed, on the imaginary causes of various changes of weather (1881: 411–14).

Later Carmichael's *Carmina Gadelica* (1900), not uninfluenced by Nicholson, records the sequence which we may summarize as:

A month of *Faoilleach*:	'ravenous' wind (wolf)[5]
Nine days of *Gearran*:	'galloping' wind (gelding)
A week of *Feadag*:	'sharp, piping' wind (plover)
A week of *Cailleach*:	'semi-calm' days (old woman)
Three days of *Sguabag*:	'Soughing blast which ushers in spring' ('brushlet' or small brush)

He has to put the unplaced *Gobag* the day before the *Gearran*. Meanwhile Nicholson (1881: 411–14) had also slipped in *Oisgean* (meaning 'ewes') as '3 days immediately following the *Cailleach*' in the 3rd week of April, Old Style. Last of all came '*Céitean*, foretaste of Summer . . . three weeks up to 12 May.' *Earrach* (the dictionary word for 'Spring') appears briefly in the sequence, until we reach the 'cuckoo on yellow May-day' (*Là buidhe Bealltuinn*).

After these terminological orgies, purported 'July', *An t-Iuchar* (month seven) may detain us only to note that it seems to mean 'the dog-days'. Our authorities refer by a kind of opposition to *Faoilteach*: 'storm month' and *An t-Iuchar*: 'worm month' (where 'warm' is commonly puzzlingly spelt 'worm'). The term *Am mios buidhe* ('the yellow month') is also given by some to July (Nicholson 1881: 25). Not until canonical month eight, *An Lùnasdal* (purported 'August') do we meet the remains of an ancient major time marker like *Bealltuinn* the first of May. It is the 'first of August', as well as (for some) 'a certain epoch only – not the month of August' (Dwelly 1920: 610, MacAlpine 1832/1973). Known today as Lammas, the period is historically the festival of the God Lugh, Old Irish *Lughnasa*. Purported 'September' then follows (*An t-Sultainn* or *An t-Sultuine*). We shall not be surprised to learn that this 'September' can run from 'the second half of October to the first half of November' (Dwelly 1920: 915), thus apparently wiping out month ten, purported 'October' itself (*An Damhar*), which, however, since it means 'the rutting time of deer' (*damh*: 'deer') can occur over its own separate season.

So finally month eleven, *An t-Samhainn*, (purported 'November') arrives. Like *Bealltuinn* and *Liùnasdal* this is another 'first day' of a ritual season (1 November: All Souls or 'Hallowday') as well as the season itself (Hallowtide). After Hallowtide it is 'winter' *An Geamhradh* which might well have been the name for 'December' instead of *An Dùdlachd*. But the standardizers needed four 'seasons' as well as twelve 'months', despite the fact that all the names represented seasons of a sort.[6]

To summarize: the Scottish Gaelic year consisted of overlapping categories of weather and agricultural epochs, into which three or four ancient ritual seasons intruded. The standardizations have attempted to create out of these terms twelve months and four seasons as understood in Rome, London or Edinburgh. The modern Irish system using similar materials is at a more advanced stage of ossification.[7]

SPACE-TIME

Time, Space, and Language

I am not going to tidy up the picture I have presented to you. To do so would lead us into certain high-structuralist failings. To look out of a window and say ' *'S e am Faoilteach a tha ann an diugh*' ('It's *Faoilteach* today') was the privilege of an elderly Highlander: consistency with any fixed sequence of Nicholson's 'fanciful names' based on 'imaginary causes' was not exacted, nor was consistency with other speakers on the same or other occasions. The matter could, of course, be discussed, two or three together mulling the question 'when is/was *Faoilteach*? Or *Gobag*?' Another 'disease of language' if you like, for the question has no solution in those terms. Time systems occupy spaces which are generated by and with the physical and social space. The dominant system for us is a positivistic, mensurational one, its spaces and times are mensurational. Western scientists define the second as '9,192,631,700 cycles of the frequency associated with the transition between the two isotopes of caesium 133'.[8] We may adapt Yeats's lines to our time problem, and ask: when we called January *Am Faoilteach*, 'What calculation, number, measurement replied?'. Those misshapen Gaelic time categories stalk like Cuchúllain through the tidy chronological schemes.

I must repeat that the study of language is not, on its own, the key to these problems, while continuing to assert that an anthropological apprehension of the role of language as well as of its extraordinary limitations is an essential preliminary to their examination. Language, in our example, at one level 'expresses' the system. Yet language becomes a manipulable feature in the system, and introduces arabesques into it, which are due to automatisms in language itself. A system of the sort I have discussed can be viewed as a 'dead stretch' of language and termed a 'semantic field', a 'domain' or the like. It is certainly 'like' a semantic field. It is 'like' a domain of 'colour terms' or of 'kin terms'. We also know that a useful armoury of historical linguistic analyses may also be brought to bear. But in Whiteley's words: 'happy were those who could speak of *the* system' (Whiteley 1971b: 121). For what we are discussing is not founded *in* language, but in a language-like but sluggishly moving continuum of social perceptions of time and physical space, with language both expressing them and intruding into them through its own independent propensity towards change and restructuring.

It is here necessary to reflect that we tolerate a high degree of cultural variability in time concepts, without dreading that we are living in a philosophically 'idealist' universe as a result. It is not unusual for an anthropologist and his people to turn up at a predetermined meeting place at different times. We accept that this failure of a common time-map has essentially practical ('real') consequences. Although an exposition of time categories might enable us to understand why it happened, we should not think that we were in the world of linguistics – we know that language here is the dress not the substance. Imagine similar accidents to occur in space, however. Say that we and our friends continually miss the physical rendezvous itself. We in this modern century would not easily accept this as merely homologous with the time problem. Such space mismatches are likely to be irritably ascribed to language or perversity (call in a linguist, even a psychiatrist). We think we know space: we are the socially evolved products of an epoch of seeking out and defining 'real space'. We are space specialists. We cannot easily see that space notions and the particular world-structure are as mutually permeated as are time notions and the world-structure. We underestimate the improbability of a world such as ours in which the sentence 'see you at Wimbledon' means 'in the Centre Court on 1 July', not (for example) 'in the middle of the town supermarket on Christmas night'. We accept a racing calendar made up of place names. We find it much harder to accept a list of places identified by times.

Among the Ibo the daily calendar is a list of four cyclical market days (*eke, orie, afo, nkwo*). But in addition, the geographical space-map is a map of topographical market-places named by the same labels. You can there-fore walk about an *eke* as you cannot walk about a 'Tuesday'. 'See you at Afo Inyogugu' means 'see you in Afo Inyogugu market' or 'on Afo Inyogu-gu day', or both – unless you specify different locations or different times. The pragmatism and practicality of the Ibo are well known.

To consider our own special view of space is important to us, for many of the misunderstandings concerning empiricism in our structure are bound up in it. We are not required to dissolve the observational world into 'ideas'. A world-structure is neither empiricist nor idealist. Thus a tele-vision prediction of twenty deaths on the roads over Easter is in Abeokuta valuable assistance in guessing how many witches will be active. In rich Saudi Arabia today the commandment to stone an adulterous woman to death, is, I am informed, now effected by emptying a modern tip-up truck laden with rocks on her. Empiricizing our world does not in itself destruc-ture it, nor *a fortiori* restructure it.

I have several times referred to the search by Westerners for definition of 'real space'. This search which received a great boost in the age of dis-covery has perhaps only of late seemed to receive any serious check. The development of ideas of 'real time' occurred in parallel. Our time problems have tended therefore to be space problems (for example: the chronometer was developed to provide a reliable longitude fix for sea navigation). Yet immobile man is to physical space as the season-trapped man is to time. When we ask 'when in exact minutes is the Gaelic *Faoilteach*?' or 'when is the Ibo fourth moon really?', we are very like land-lubbers who ask 'where is Atlantis really?'. Yet, as we know, Brazil was a 'non-existent' place named in advance, but a marvel of the age of discovery was that Brazil was thought to have been discovered. More subtly, the India of Columbus was as 'unreal' as Brazil, despite its existence elsewhere than in the American continent. First the imaginary and the conjectured places were discovered, then the unimagined places.

Nothing better illustrates the broader intellectual effects of this than a peculiar transfiguration of language that occurred as vast areas of 'real space' had to be unpacked into the concepts of a formerly more restricted world. John Livingston Lowes's remarkable analysis of the imagery of Coleridge, in *The Road to Xanadu*, was first published in 1927. Lowes's main purpose was to unravel the imagery of Coleridge's *Ancient Mariner* and his *Kubla Khan*, by using the note-book recording the poet's reading. He opened the books Coleridge read, followed up references in them to still other works, looked on pages opposite or near passages consciously cited by his author, and as he did so turned up passage after passage which showed words, connections and phrases, that had been melted together by Col-eridge into the texts of those two extraordinary poems, which he wrote in their first versions in 1797.

The books in question were virtually all works of exploration and travel, dating largely from the sixteenth and seventeenth centuries – the great period of expansion of Western Europe, which in Coleridge's time was about to embark on its last great century. It is important to note that the authors were practical seafarers. Yet their language has a peculiar 'stretched' quality. As Lowes excellently puts it:

And this common feature of their language is inseparable from the nature of their undertaking ... There was really little else that they could do. They sailed into regions of the fantastically new, and *had words, for the most part, for accustomed things alone. And so the strange assumed perforce the guise of the familiar, and familiar terms took on enchanting connotations through their involuntary commerce with the strange* (1927: 314, my italics).

Thus we read of 'Rose-like-shaped Slime-fish' which 'are numerous in the North Sea as Atomes in the Air' (Lowes 1927: 88, 313, citing Frederick Martens's *Voyage in to Spitzbergen and Greenland*). While at an extreme of transfiguration of what is now the commonplace there is this description – of what? A coconut:

But to proceed further, your Majestie shall understand, that in the place of the stone or coornell, there is in the middest of the said carnositie a void place, which neverthelesse is full of a most cleere and excellent water, in such quantitie as may fill a great Egge shell, or more, or lesse, according to the bignesse of the Cocos, the which water surely, is the most substantiall, excellent and precious to bee drunke, that may be found in the World: insomuch that in the moment when it passeth the palate of the mouth, and beginneth to goe downe the throate, it seemeth that from the sole of the foot, to the crowne of the head, there is no part of the bodie but that feeleth great comfort thereby: as it is doubtlesse one of the most excellent things that may bee tasted upon the earth, and such as I am not able by writing or tongue to expresse. And to proceed yet further, I say that when the meate of this fruit is taken from the Vessell thereof, the vessell remayneth as faire and neate as though it were polished, and is without of colour inclining toward black, and shineth or glistereth very faire, and is within of no lesse delicatenesse (cited from Purchas, Lowes, 1927: 314).

'The glory has departed from the coconut' wrote Lowes 'and a prosaic world has relinquished one delight' (ibid.: 315). Lowes described this stretching of language as one aspect of:

that process of incorporating the unknown with the known, through which ... the adventuring human spirit constructs the never completed, always augmenting fabric of its world. And the language of the adventurers owes a large share of its peculiar savour to the workings of that vast enterprise of assimilation in which the great era of discovery was eagerly engaged (ibid.: 314).

World-structures are located in physical space, and in real aggregates of human beings. It should not be surprising that the extension of physical space, and of the experience of those beings, produces a genuine extension of the structure, with all its co-ordinates in language and thought.[9]

'Real space', 'real time', 'real space-time', 'reality' itself – all these terms were expressed through the expansion and transformations of a particular world-structure over a particular historical period. Can it be wondered that for Western man the maxim 'name it, then go and look for it' has appeared so magically efficient a formula: a basic principle of our very science. No wonder that prophecy was resolved in action. No one noticed that the atom as measured bore no resemblance to the fantasized atom. No one cared that germ theory as proposed did not envisage the later distinction between (say) bacteria and viruses. The failure of the intellectual aspect of our method occurred only when the subject matter became man himself. The wand was tapped, but the rabbits did not appear. Social entities were named but they were not 'discovered'. (Nothing became so outdated as last week's social science terminology). Clearly we were running up against what we may call, in the light of our first example, the *Faoilteach* problem. The reason why vulgar materialism failed with world-structures was because of the paradox that the confrontation generates. If the social as world-structure is reality-defining, by what reality shall it be measured? The successes of *a priori* prediction gave way again to the peculiarities of prophecy. Perhaps we may say that there was a return to a recognition of the normal condition of world-structures.

WORLD-STRUCTURE AND DEFINITION-SPACE

What is a World-Structure like?

Briefly the present position is as follows. It is argued that 'the social' is a space with particular properties.

1   We can say that it is 'like' a store of 'information'; in that sense it is 'like' a brain. The individuals in their relations to themselves and their environment would form the essential physical framework of such a brain-like structure.
2   But we can also say that it is 'like' a language: that a kind of syntax-like regularity pervades it at all levels.
3   We can say that it is like a homeostat: that it adapts itself to infra-structural changes.
4   We can also say that it is 'like' a mind: a system of perception (apperception is better), or of knowing.
5   Most important it is 'like' a reality-generating system with its own events, its own parameters and its own automaton-like features.

All these things (and others) that the social is 'like' have produced separate technical languages for their analysis. The biggest stumbling block to a unified theory of the social space lay for long in a difficulty that anthropologists shared with many humanists, including our Gaelic theorists. They could not visualize more than two dimensions at a time. They indulged in successive linearizations of areas of the space, but found it hard to link the different kinds of subject-matter.

The developments in linguistics that led to ideas like semiotics were only a stage towards a solution. It was, for example, a partial advantage to visualize the social as what we may call a *multi-media space*. The social would then also be like a system of coexisting semiotics expressed in separate, or overlapping, or merging media, and stored in channels of all levels of complexity. The idea of a *multi-media space* certainly helps to dispense with the artificial distinction between 'behavioural' and the 'non-behavioural' aspects of the social, by stimulating the idea of 'behaviour' as an area of semiotics (see above, chapter 6).

The totality (or, in its reality-defining aspects, the totalitarianism) of the space is, however, not completely revealed even in a semiological approach – at least as that is normally expressed in technical practice. Each technical model must hold certain concepts arbitrarily steady, and the idea of the 'semiotic' is itself an *ex post facto* construct – a dead stretch. We need to realize that the space is not merely one in which separate semiotics coexist, albeit with some homologous principles of regularity, but one in which storage is 'cross-semiotic'. I have suggested elsewhere that the acquisition of language has both simplified and obscured our awareness of other semiotics (see above, chapters 1 and 5). We find it difficult to visualize a situation in which different structural features must be stored and expressed in different media: as it were the rule-book in the environment, the morphology in behaviour, the syntax in myth, the metalanguage in speech, interpretation rules in biology and so on. A 'location' (the homologue of a 'concept') in such a space is to the untutored mind a strange phenomenon – somewhat unstable, labile in its storage, never quite the same on each occasion.

Of course a 'concept' in an individual mind is also like that at a microcosmic level, but the time-scales, instabilities and inconsistencies are much different in the social space. Some of you may have seen the documentary film about a spastic who had one handicapped friend who could interpret his normally incomprehensible utterances, but could not read. They set up a chain whereby the spastic told his life-story to the friend who could understand him, who repeated it to another spastic who could write but not type or recite, whose text was corrected by a nurse, then dictated to a spastic typist, letter by letter, by a spastic who could recite the names of letters but could not read.[10] This gives us only a rudimentary inkling of the sort of space we have to deal with. The scanning procedure, for example, becomes cumbersome. To fix or review an 'utterance' one must pass back and forth through multiple transformations between the individual semiotics, channels, or what you will. If we were to extend such a chain through a further set of partial physical disabilities, so that it took twenty differentially handicapped spastics to render the apperception of a fire and to transmit a final hand movement to a fire alarm, we are closer to the situation I wish to convey. If such a sequence took a year the fire itself might consume the system, and such a rudimentary social space would not survive. In fact the social space is not quite so crude and mechanical a structure, in part because of the monitoring or mapping role of language in it.

In a previous paper (see above, chapter 5) I have set out some arguments for specifying the structure of the social space to account for some of these things that it is like. I will merely say here that the cross-media concepts have much in common with those termed *p*-structures, and single medium storage with the so-called *s*-structures. The social space as a reality-generating entity subsumes all these partial aspects: thus it has been called a 'world-structure'. The reason for our stress on the analysis of events is because the anthropologist has no way into an alien world-structure save through his inadequate apperception of the events of that world-structure.

Individuals experience and can generally only express what their world-structure registers, yet individuals can, as it were, 'step out' of the structure under certain conditions, or perhaps individuals are not all equally auto-matized by the structure. We have seen that some individuals are always experimenting with expression (our time theorists, Gaelic and Ibo) or action (adultery and dumper trucks). We note that such interventions, as in those cases, may merely introduce arabesques; further appendices to the structure, whose basic definitions remain unaffected. We are in the realm of *bricolage* – the replication of *p*-structural continuities in *s*-structural seg-ments. The praxis of the structure has not changed. A lifetime of individual freedom of thought and action may be of this sort.

We recognize that another kind of freedom exists for some individuals at all periods, and for more sizable groups at rarer periods. That is: a partial separation from the structure as expressed in dominant ideas, praxis and language. There remains for such individuals the problem of the expression of their own experience in a suitable language – for as we have seen the match between a world-structure and a natural language is virtually a tautology. We have seen that world-structures do change, however, and an old language has to be stretched to perform new tasks. We also know that individuals, scientists, scholars, poets may experience a similar pheno-menon in the expression of a paradigm-shift, or an epistemological break. There is a certain linkage of all these phenomena, as they all form parts of the space we are calling a world-structure. The problem is one of monitor-ing and expressing changes in the ground definitions in a world which defines, as it registers, as it experiences. Such changes will of course very often be closely related to infrastructural, including ecological, and econo-mic changes.

The 'prophetic' condition of structures and individuals occurs I suggest at such periods of singularity. It occurs, if you like, because a category for the registration of the condition then becomes a necessity. At other times 'prophets' may exist but they are not registered: their category is collapsed with that of irrelevant deviants. They are 'muted'. The paradox of the prophetic category can be seen in Evans-Pritchard's account of the Nuer prophets (1956c: 287–310). The normally muted condition of prophets makes their periods of freedom frequently not very helpful. Old language is used in new ways, with multiple connotations of old signs, language-shadowing (see above, chapter 5). When redefinition occurs and the space is restructured, the new world appears self-evident, banal again. 'the glory has departed from the coconut.' The definitions of the old world have gone. In non-literate systems there remain merely memories of the curious events, of the feel of the time, of the paradoxical but opaque utterances and the particular symbols that seemed then so powerful.

A Definition Space

Any model of a world-structure must deal with these phenomena: for if the space defines, it also redefines. What kind of space is required to generate the kind of transformation symptoms we have discussed? A useful beginning is to set up what I call here a 'definition space with parameter collapse', which contains a singularity of an interesting kind.

We may say that cultural categories are 'definitions' of a sort, and that cultural perceptions of significant actions are also of this sort. Yet they are not static. A definition is a space. Across time a definition may be modelled as a circle-like space consisting of two features: content, and bounding criteria. If the boundary criteria are measurable we may call them parameters. Over time, a definition may change. In such a case the values of the parameters form a moving shell to the modelled space. A definition space very frequently suffers from a phenomenon known as *parameter collapse*. Take the two following examples, noted from an address by Professor Braithwaite, which he used to another purpose.

1 In the case of progressive redefinition of the world water-speed record, beyond a certain speed the criteria were so much amended that the question of measuring the record vanished into questions of the definition of water-speed versus air-speed. In the definition of water-speed the surface friction is the point. Once full contact ceases the matter dissolves into definition of the degree of partial contact permitted, and the like.

2 In the past the world altitude record was broken regularly. Not only balloons and aircraft but the first rockets and earth satellites qualified for it. But soon, with space travel, the question of altitude above the earth collapsed into a definitional problem, not one of measurement – the altitude record is no longer interesting.

These particular examples of parameter collapse are valuable because I wish to stress that the collapse of measurement into definition is a common practical experience. The changes can be modelled as taking place in a space in which the parameter shell – the defining criteria – reach values such that the definition ceases to exist. Proceeding with the same criteria produces a singularity in the definition space which produces a new definition space related to the first in a particular way, as shown very simply in figure 9.2.

The bounding parameters α' and α'' meet at a vanishing point and then, as it were, turn inside out. New bounding parameters are created out of the bounded continuum ω, becoming ω' and ω'', and α', α'' collapse into the new bounded continuum α. The parameters (which may be of any number)

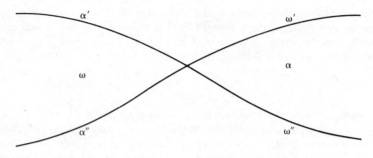

Figure 9.2   Parameter collapse

provide a 'shell' for the maintenance of the space. After the parameter collapse the space is turned inside out. Features of the former shell are diffused over the new space. The old content becomes 'shell'. Beyond the point of parameter collapse the new continuum is restructured, but not arbitrarily.

In the case of example 1, the water-speed record is defined within a shell of speed measures, the α parameters. As the measurements proceed, however, each specification involves a new definition, such that if ω contains 'watercraft', the relevance or otherwise of a speed measure now begins to depend on whether the moving object (hydrofoil, hovercraft) is any longer a 'watercraft'. If it is, then the waterspeed counts, if not it does not. Again: ω begins with the 'water surface' being an unproblematic part of the unchanging content. Later, it must be continually redefined in order to state whether the speed 'counts' as relating to the water surface. Thus the measured speeds were once the α shell of the definition. They now come to represent *'defined'* not *'defining'* entities, enclosed in a set of new defining parameters ω' and ω''.

In the case of example 2, the altitude record (ω) is defined by α parameters related to fixed points on the earth's surface. As spacecraft take orbits to the moon and to the planets the altitude measurements must be specified as relevant or not in those conditions. In the revised space the old α parameters are 'defined', not 'defining', and criteria which were undifferentiated before the collapse (ω', ω'') are now part of the shell that defines the new α space.

Let us consider 'definition spaces' of more complex types. The development of a theory perhaps. We must then assume we have an arrow of time ($\rightarrow$) and a temporal unfolding from left to right. Thus, Professor Gluckman's theory of marriage stability expounded in 1951 postulated a connection between descent-type and high or low marital stability. Parameter collapse in this theory occurred by about 1960. The parameters were a bundle of statements about 'lineality' (non-mensurational) and 'stability' (partly mensurational). The ω space was the category 'marriage', whose content was defined behaviourally, and through, among other things, 'jural' rights and the like. As the analyses progressed towards greater quantification both 'lineality' and 'stability' collapsed into statements about exchange of rights (genetricial, uxorial etc.). Beyond the collapse, 'marriage' became redefined by a new shell of parameters related to 'exchange' (formerly content) while the previous shell parameters were collapsed into the new space.[11] We can thus represent a redefinition of any concept, in the form of a restructuring of a space. We may note, however, that definition spaces of a conceptual nature do not necessarily proceed beyond the collapse. Long and tenaciously held theories very frequently do exhibit the whole process. A reality-generating space would in its turn have material transitions and material redefinitions which would exhibit a similar twist or twists, if redefinitions occurred in it, with material consequences. We also require the notion of a 'twist', of the sort we get in a definition space with parameter collapse, to account for general phenomena associated with 'paradigm shift', which has very similar features. Although the verbal exposition is somewhat cumbersome, homologies with the phenomenon known as the 'epistemological break' already begin to suggest themselves.

Let us therefore proceed to our world-structural space. This is, of course, a multi-dimensional continuum, and human beings 'experience' the space itself. Since a world-structure is for many purposes *like* a definition space, world-structural transformations would require the space to contain or generate twists of a similar sort. The kind of space required is quite a familiar one: in two-dimensional form it is a Möbius strip. We may keep the well-known properties of a Möbius strip in mind. A being moving in a Möbius strip will, when he passes the 'twist' in his space, without any variation perceptible to him, change 'handedness', left becoming right and right left. The abstract notion of a Möbius twist in a definition space would lead us to expect from a world-structural transformation an experiential continuity marked in its symbolic expressions by sign-reversals. This expectation seems to be realized in cyclical definitions of time, in which epochs are marked by behaviour reversals (cf. Leach, E. R. 1961a). It crops up again and again in the structuralist analyses. Where polarity reversals occur in a situation which is in 'real life' experienced as a continuum, a definition space with a 'twist' in it will preserve the conflicting requirements of opposition as well as of continuity. For a multi-dimensional structure we shall more appropriately refer to the twist as a *Möbius-type singularity*.

I have frequently discussed the Nixonian White House as a useful model for an isolated world-structure. Most of the α parameters might be classed as concerned with information control, providing the definition 'shell' of the space. Closer and closer information control took the structure to the point of parameter collapse. The vanishing point on one parameter occurring at some point close to the taping of the President by himself. On another parameter that point was reached at the break-in itself, which although a mechanism of secrecy became unavoidably public. From now on information control continually increased information, destroying the isolate. Those living in the space detected no change, merely that, as it were, the signs were reversed. Procedure in the previously orderly direction now produced contrary results. The brake, if you like, became the accelerator.

No one who has read the transcripts and studied the filmed Senate procedures and the interviews given by the participants, can fail to note the classical symptoms of parameter collapse in a definition space; the bewilderment apparent on passing a Möbius singularity in their world-structure. Had a prophet stood forth in the Nixonian White House, what could he have said? Remember that the language is pre-empted by the structure itself. What impression of babbling tongues would he have presented? Would he have been reduced to crying 'the last shall be the first'? Or 'prepare to meet thy doom'? We should merely read John Dean's attempts to warn the President. There is no language for parameter collapse, because the categories of the language are part of the reality-defining features of a world-structure. We shall push the Nixonian White House case no further, because although an excellent model of a world-structure it was itself merely a specification in a larger one, and its independence was in fact relatively limited.

The Prophetic Condition and the Individual

Prophecy, then, is not telling what will be, but what is. It may well be that individuals may see world-structures clearly at certain critical junctures, or perhaps when their dominant segments are at critical junctures. We may have to hypothesize that the development of a singularity in the structure momentarily frees some individuals from their *enchaînement*, their auto-hypnosis. The idea that women, or excluded groups are prone to don the mantle of prophecy is found in various works (see, e.g. I. M. Lewis 1971). I suspect that we are here in that area of distinction within structures, summarized in the theory of muted in relation to dominant (Ardener, S. 1975b, 1978). The prophetic condition might then arise at several levels: (1) the singularity in the world-structure will affect the definition of muted groups: thus (by definition) unmuting them; (2) the singularity may work itself out first through the dominant structure, under the eyes as it were of individuals in the hitherto muted segments; (3) the singularity may be restricted to the muted groups themselves. But these considerations are not essential to a model of the social space, as they tend to be subsumed under a more general statement: that any individual who stands out from the space, in effect redefines himself, and *there is a theoretical requirement that this should in itself be experienced as a singularity in the space*. The paradox of individual freedom or lack of it in a space of the reality-defining type, is thus placed in a different perspective. The bizarre modes by which the prophet himself is perceived by other individuals are also rendered more comprehensible, even inevitable. Evans-Pritchard says of the Nuer prophets:

According to the Nuer tales about them their behaviour was most abnormal. The first prophet, or at any rate the first to achieve fame, was Ngundeng son of Bung, of the Lou tribe, a prophet of the spirit *deng*, who died in 1906. He acquired his powers by prolonged fasts. It is said that he lived for weeks by himself in the bush, eating animal and human excrement, that he used to sit on a cattle-peg in his kraal and let it penetrate his anus, that he used to wander about the bush for days mumbling to himself or sit in his cattle byre. After he had established himself as a prophet he seems to have given up his solitary wanderings, though he still used to shut himself up in his hut from time to time to undergo long fasts. Nuer say that when the spirit *deng* seized him he could climb into the air without support and could also run up and down from the ground to the top of his byre. His son Gwek, described my Mr Coriat as of squat body, misshapen arms and legs, and a short toad-like head, also had a reputation for daemonic exhibitions. Mr Coriat records that he would spend, and spent during Mr Coriat's visit to his home, all day shouting from the top of what has been described as a pyramid, a remarkable feat both of agility, for the pyramid was most difficult of ascent, and of endurance (Evans-Pritchard 1956c: 305, my italic).

The 'symbolic' mode of apperception of the 'prophetic situation' which gives the prophet his problem of expression, is also the only mode by which the non-prophets can represent the 'singularity' which he embodies. Since language is part of the space we are concerned with, as well as a mode of mapping it, the language of prophecy may well exhibit paradoxical features in the passage through a singularity. Although fresh automatisms of language itself may confuse still further what is already a serious problem of communication, we should recall the effect of the sudden expansion of the European world on the ordinary language of navigators.

CONCLUSION

It is unfortunate that expositions such as the above are not necessarily viewed with much favour nowadays, a side-effect perhaps of the otherwise interesting collapse of the structuralist vogue. Was that vogue itself not rather like a prophetic situation whose lineaments we cannot now easily recall? Sign-reversal, 'transformations', the idea of revolutionary breaks – these give way to the present more humdrum era. Nevertheless, a model is required in which highly reflexive and qualitative human interventions can be encompassed while preserving those undoubted and uncontrovertible tendencies to predefinition, and to typical and sterotypical behaviour and thought, which make much of social life so surprisingly predictable.

I would now dismantle the term 'world-structure', and say that the social space is again a 'world' incorporating material and immaterial defining features. These defining features do inevitably model a 'definition space' and the more controlled the social system the more obvious are the singularities that emerge in it. All units defined in the space are modelled as twisted off it by singularities of the same type as, but of smaller scope than, the singularities representing major redefinitions in the space as a whole. That is why 'contradiction' is a feature of all definition. The model of the space must be simple in principle because it is continually redefining at all levels, by the same general mechanisms. Thus the structuralists' binary oppositions will appear anywhere in the space, at any level, from the mind outward. Lévi-Strauss should appear banal, not merely 'outmoded'. 'The glory hath departed from the coconut', indeed.

I have stressed that the space is truly composed of thought, language and reality, and changes in any feature will affect the others – and the changes will be materially embodied, not in some ideal realm. The deterministic and mechanistic overtones of theories of the social as 'world' should be more sympathetically viewed as undertones. Individuals are in constant contrast to their worlds, from which they never entirely free themselves. The prophetic individuals merely become more and more singular, until those periodic occasions when everyone is a prophet. Nevertheless the world is a construct which is dependent upon the coherent and co-ordinated defining powers of individuals. One of the things it is to be human is participation in the process of construction. Another is to fail to recognize the concrete effects of that participation.

A final word is necessary to relate the definition space to catastrophe theory. The catastrophe model consists of a surface with a discontinuity modelled as a fold. The variables are plotted on that surface. The passage through the discontinuity occurs, however, in a higher-dimensional space than that modelled by the surface. In a solid model of the surface there is a literal 'fall through the air', from one part of the surface to the other. The 'air', if you like, is outside the surface. The singularity in a definition space on the contrary leaves the paths of variables continuous within the model, without a shift of dimension. The Möbius effect is the 'cost' of that continuity. We have no choice but to experience continuously, however. The definition space is the social space in its reality-defining aspect. That is the only reason for choosing it as a model. Catastrophe theory is not appropriate to modelling the social: it is 'mechanistic' and 'deterministic', if you like. The catastrophe surface is a singularity in a world in which definitions remain constant: in such a world it is the variables that are discontinuous. If worlds were catastrophe surfaces, we should literally disappear and reappear during transitions between cusps of the surface, like Flat-landers. We do not experience reality like that, so that excellent as catastrophe theory is for what it is good for, it is not good for modelling the social space. Perhaps this will help to clarify a basic matter which is a source of misunderstanding. 'Ideal' worlds can be modelled 'ideally' – conceptual models need not tie themselves arbitrarily to a single point of view. But the social space is (so to speak) like a conceptual model with a wooden leg. That is: it is a lived space as well as a conceptual space. To model it no feature of experienced reality can be arbitrarily excluded. 'The life-paths of individuals must be preserved as continuous', is an axiom of the space. In *thinking* about the life-paths of individuals this axiom does not operate. Conceptual discontinuities can be introduced at will, hence the metaphoric-al interest of catastrophe models in psychology. Nevertheless, catastrophes are a strange side-view of the world of the human, not a view of that world as humans actually live it.

10

'Social Fitness' and the Idea of 'Survival'

The external aspect of 'social fitness', that is: an intellectual evaluation of societies in terms of their fitness or otherwise to adapt and endure, derives most recently from evolutionist ideas of the nineteenth century. The idea has long vanished from social anthropology in that form. The early evolutionists were concerned with a particular solution of a problem that is of much longer standing, – part of a very general tendency of human beings to bring a moral evaluation to the condition of their social fabric. Long before Darwin there were centuries of European and Near Eastern historical evidence available for reflection on this subject. The facts of conquest, destruction, dispersal and absorption of certain societies by others provided the oldest basic material of human history – a seemingly endless series of tragedies for those directly involved with implications that were supremely depressing. The conditions under which polities survived or failed to survive were of genuine, even urgent, interest.

The Victorian evolutionists, in asserting that it is the 'best' (in some sense) that survives thus added a special optimistic nuance to what had formerly been a more pragmatic accommodation with necessity.

It was a commonplace of historical study, for example, that much which was meritorious was destroyed so that Rome might survive; the idea that its 'peace' was a kind of 'wilderness' goes, of course, back to its own imperial days (Tacitus). In the middle ages the idea of the destroyed beauty now included Rome itself. The trajectories of several of the succeeding political entities (Goths, Vandals, Byzantium) merely confirmed that the survival of social entities could not be guaranteed. The ages before the evolutionists had therefore inevitably to come to terms with the matter. It is important to note then that nothing as simple as a vulgar 'might is right' was then accepted as a moral axiom. For many centuries of medieval time there was no doubt in the minds of many thinkers that there had been an unfortunate decline in most qualities of civilization despite important religious gains. The fact that Rome or classical civilization had not survived was not endowed with the particular metaphysics of survival that we now know.

History in such cases seemed rather to confirm the mythological theme of the 'Golden Age'. It was a feature of Golden Ages that men became unfit to live in them, not that Golden Ages were unfit to survive. The idea of the Renaissance was thus of great significance later. It was explicitly so called because the classical age had been reborn; men had become fit to restore it

It is interesting that it was in the eighteenth century that the notion of the classical civilization having died from a failure of and in itself, became finally fixed in English letters as an ambiguous result of Gibbon's *Decline and Fall*. That work still set out to show that men in some way had not been fitted for the Roman Empire. Yet its weight of scholarship conveyed the simultaneous conclusion that those same faulty men had been produced by the Roman Empire. Gibbon's masterpiece is, in my opinion, an essential literary precursor (placed as it was in every scholar's library) to the geologically, archaeologically and zoologically based social evolutionism of the next century. For although his work was truly about the failures of human beings, Gibbon himself produced the cautious assessment that by the late eighteen century, the modern system in which he lived had despite its faults not yet to face its own fall. The next century was characteristically less cautious.

The raising of the fact of survival to a measure of fitness in itself, arose in the nineteenth century through a sort of undistributed historical middle. The nineteenth century was assessed to have surpassed the past, by the past's own very best criteria. The course that had led to nineteenth-century excellence was retraced back through history – criteria of future promise (not unlike the child Harold Wilson standing outside 10 Downing Street) were selected from the post-classical remains. Contemporary societies were evaluated in the same way: generally as inferior or 'primitive', their 'survival' being related to fitness for certain historical conditions only. This is all familiar enough from nineteenth-century social anthropology, which was merely of its age in this respect.

But the problem of fitness as applied to societies was continued unconsciously into the twentieth century, ironically, by that most antievolutionist school of social anthropologists – the functionalists. Their demonstration of the internal coherence of social institutions in non-Western societies came in the end to lie very close to the simple view: 'if it is there it has a function.' Although the matter of extancy ('is it there?') was at an important level separated from the question of survival, the 'function' of 'function', in Malinowski's and Gluckman's writings at least, seems to be to maintain the society in being. In this surprising sense functionalism was a last triumph of the evolutionary approach, even as it turned it on its head. It demonstrated, in effect, that 'fitness' redefined as 'function' was not a feature of Western societies alone. (This was a source of fruitful and corrective relativism in the best work of the period.) From there the further step to the hyper-relativism which alarmingly removes the word 'alone' from that sentence, was a short one, quickly taken by many of todays ecologists. That is: that Western societies may, on a long view, be less 'fit' than 'simpler' smaller ones.

It is still possible to hear the assertion that for humanity evolution has moved from biology to society. The admission of society into the picture is, however, to produce the possibility of a self-evaluation. There is an internal aspect to the idea of social fitness. For the Victorian, the external and internal aspects – his view of 'biology' and of himself – were able to coincide. 'The fittest survive: fortunately (or as it happens), I am the fittest.' Result: happiness. For the twentieth-century ecologist, it is perhaps rather: 'The fittest survive: although (for my part) I do not feel very fit:' Result: consternation. This is a fault in logic before it is a fault in life. We are not entirely like science-fiction computers to be outwitted by a paradox and made to self-destruct. The nature of survival must be removed to its pre-nineteenth-century position. Any definition of fitness in terms of survival renders the term 'fitness' otiose, for fitness is thus only a property of having survived.

Murdock in this passage thus speaks with the voice of another age:

By and large, the cultural elements that are eliminated through trial and error or social competition are the less adaptive ones, so that the process is as definitely one of the survival of the fittest as is that of natural selection (1965a: 126; first published 1956).

And in particular:

What man has lost, in the main, is a mass of maladaptive and barbarous practices, inefficient techniques, and outworn superstitutions (ibid.: 127).

The modern redefinition of survival as 'adaptive continuity' raises equally difficult questions where society is concerned. With a broad enough definition, adaptation is historically demonstrable through almost any circumstances. Adaptation may follow adaptation, as it were, until a generation suddenly asks (we must imagine) 'whatever happened to the Roman Empire?'. At some time an evaluation is made that a human entity has not survived – it was with us when we set out but it is no longer to be seen. A kind of objectification has retrospectively occurred. The fitness of a social form cannot be assessed as if it were an organism, because of this arbitrariness inherent in the social. Thus, traditionally, it is stated that the House of Commons has 'survived by adaptation' for seven centuries, the monarchy for ten or more. In contrast, although the American Presidency by external criteria may continue more features of eighteenth-century monarchy than does the present British monarchy, the criterion of evaluation that 'the monarchy survives in the United States' is not open to us.

No progress can be expected in this matter until it is accepted that social entities are self-defining systems. Some transformations that are logically possible are defined out of actual experience. Possibly in a certain case only one definitional criterion must remain unchanged to demonstrate adaptive continuity. Frequently this may be only a 'name'. Perhaps in another case there are so many detailed criteria that no significant redefinition is possible. As an example, the Socialist Party of Great Britain, we learn from a recent study, once had a meeting that expelled dissenters by a majority vote. The meeting then voted to expel those who had voted against that motion. It then voted on the expulsion of those who had voted against that. The SPGB has been at times on the brink of biological extinction: a bus-crash or an influenza epidemic might have extinguished the party. The present gathering might have been likely to favour and to stress the ultimate biological explanation had such a tragedy occurred. But in terms of biology the ex-members of the SPGB, like those of the Communist Party, might well be legion. But for the history of the party, what would have been their survival if the SPGB had not survived?[1]

We may make some helpful comments of a sort. A social entity survives ('in name') then if it does not maintain too many (how many?) self-defining criteria. In that sense then fitness has a marginal place even in modern social anthropology. We may imagine that if an SPGB-like entity were in charge of some critical task like maintaining irrigation, the craft might well be accidentally extinguished, to the detriment of a larger dependent population. Perhaps then we may say that a society's survival is related to the criteria of definition of some critically important unit. Priesthoods in charge of 'knowledge' provide possible examples. The Egyptian priesthood was perhaps more critically balanced in this respect than were the European monasteries (or than are modern universities?). Elsewhere it is argued that criteria of recruitment are the only demonstrable link between evolution and society, with only ambiguous implications for 'social fitness' (see above, chapter 7).

We begin to see that the social evaluation of fitness does not make a clear distinction between the social and the biological. High rates of gestatory difficulties among Bakweri women (Ardener, E. 1962) were certainly in part due to the social definition as 'fertility medicines and treatments' of substances (purgatives) and procedures (enemas) of an abortifacient tendency. The social definition of biologically detrimental substances as beneficial is the oldest problem in preventative medicine.

The internal aspect of social fitness thus comes to our notice. Among several peoples the social is itself felt to be potentially healthy, or unhealthy. Places 'spoil', become bad. Witches become more virulent in bad places. Among sailors, bad ships are accident-prone as well as socially divided. The internal aspect of the idea of 'social fitness' still closely resembles the 'external aspect' we associate with the scholarly tradition whereby societies are evaluated for their historical success or failure. The scholarly version turns out to be merely part of that general tendency to externalization common to modern thought. The recognition of the inherent entropy in human structures as not necessarily 'progressive' is, however, both very new and very old among observers of the human.

11
Comprehending Others

ETHOLOGY AND LANGUAGE

Introductory

'... and the darkness comprehended it not'

In previous papers I have described the concept of 'the social' as a space with definitional properties (see above, chapter 9) in which the unit is the event (see above, chapter 5). I do not intend to pursue these discussions on this occasion but to exemplify some intersections of language with events. The particular view of the relation of language to social anthropology that is implicit in it is not necessarily widespread in social anthropology, but it has much in common with various other approaches, which might not express matters in identical terms (see, for example, Crick 1976). The idea of a more 'semantic' approach to social anthropology is far from new, and even in its more recent manifestations we shall soon be speaking of decades rather than years. I have already discussed elsewhere some common concerns of the present age: the relationship between structures of the 'high-structuralist' kind associated with Lévi-Strauss, and those of a more Radcliffe-Brownian type associated with much post-war social anthropology. It is questionable whether we need a very cumbersome apparatus of linguistic theory to discuss the problems of understanding each other. It is worth remembering, however, that the linguistic inspiration of structuralism resulted in the almost accidental discovery that society can be analysed in some ways like a text. It turned out that structuralism in its heyday (or at least the particular anthropologists and others that we may call 'high-structuralists') had no compelling theory that would demonstrate the essential unity of structure and action. Structuralism floats, as it were, attached by an inadequate number of ropes to the old empiricist ground beneath.

It would be a great pity if we had to see 'meaning' become a mere vogue word covering up the same problem. In this paper, therefore, I have analysed certain 'simultaneities', where category and measurement, definition and action are directly generated from experience. It is my wish to demonstrate that the problem of translation is illuminated by this, and that 'comprehending others' cannot be a kind of passive act leaving one or both sides unchanged. Despite the brilliant and almost exhaustive treatment of literary translations by G. Steiner (1975), the translation of culture raises certain questions in a more indirect form. Some part of what follows may be said to be further material to supplement his discussion (Steiner, G. 1975: 353–61) concerning the nature of highly exotic translation. But, as usual, it is my desire to constitute the problem from the anthropological subject-matter, and not to import or impose theories developed from other puzzles and other concerns.[1]

Ethology and Language

We may begin with the point at which social anthropology takes over from what for many is a purely observational subject – the study of primates. I am not concerned here with the particular ethological subject-matter, although the problem of the continuity or not of animal into human both in biological structures and communicational modes, is of the first interest.[2] I prefer to start from a different direction.

Reynolds (1975) lists the differing terminologies used by students of social behaviour of the rhesus monkey, *Macaca mulatta*. He shows that the significant units of behaviour are difficult to define, and that it is far from certain that the 'same' inventory of perceived units can be derived from the analyses of various primatologists. In table 11.1, listing four authors' usages (here I label them A, B, C and D) there are sixteen possible behaviour units. In table 11.2 using three authors only (B, C and D) a further eight units emerge. I do not wish to enter into the technical features of this valuable paper, but to draw attention to some of the broader implications of the variations described therein. From the four-author series I give a characteristic selection of behaviour units, described as follows:

Table 11.1 Units of primate behaviour – 1

unit	A	B	C	D
1	hough-hough	hough	bark, pant, threat, roar, growl	'!Ho!'
2	coo coo	food call	food call	'Kōō'
3	eech	screech	screech	'ēēē'
8	looking directly at opponent	aggressive look	glare or scandalized expression	stares at
11	rigid body posture and stiff legs	haughty walk	slow pacing	holds tail erect

After Reynolds (1975: 282, table 1).

For the three-author series the following is also a characteristic selection:

Table 11.2   Units of primate behaviour – 2

unit	B	C	D
1	feeding hough	food bark	'!Ho!'
2	bark	shrill bark	'Ka!'
3	splutter	gecker	'ik, ik, ik . . .'
4	submissive sit	cat-like sit	looks 'apprehensively' (towards)

After Reynolds (1975: 283, table 2).

These examples bring out clearly some immediate problems in the supposedly direct observation of significant behaviour. First, we may note that the human observer's cultural background penetrates even his description of primate behaviour. It is interesting, for example, that a rendering of rhesus vocalization is attempted in several cases. Authors A and B characterize the monkey sounds by approximations from English folk-phonetics. Author D appears at first sight to introduce a more 'international' standard, but it seems on a closer examination that the '-ōō' and 'ēēē' notations are phonetically [u:] and [i:] or the like, and not, for example [o:] and [e:]. Thus D introduces slightly more graphical confusion than A and B. The impression given by the choices of all three authors is of a conscious, almost literary exoticism. The renderings of authors A and B relegate the rhesus sound to a region of English graphemics which is a by-word for the lack of consistent phonetic reference. Their *hough* (or *hough-hough*) is no doubt felt to be like a *cough* [kɔf], a *hiccough* [hikʌp] or a *huff* [hʌf] rather than (say) like *bough* [bau], or *through* [θru]. There is the further cultural association of Irish words like *lough* [lɔx] (or anglicized [lʌf]). The obsolete archaic spelling *hough* (apparently [hɔk] for *haw* (as in 'hem and haw') or possibly for *hawk* (as in 'hawking and spitting') also exists, although it is uncertain whether the reminiscence is deliberate. We may note that *haw* and *hawk* in these usages themselves occur in restricted, fairly stereotyped, collocations, and are for some speakers nearly obsolete. Further, we may note that for author C the articulation is represented variously by *bark, pant, roar* and *growl*, none of which is normally regarded as synonymous with the others, let alone with *haw* or *hawk*.

For author D (who may be from an American milieu) '!Ho!', with its idiosyncratic exclamation marks front and back, presents an exoticism of a different kind, as does his use of both diacritics and repetition to represent length in other examples. Written English contains among its stylistic conventions a loose but not totally open set for the rendering of the outlandish and uncouth. When speakers of a language attempt to represent non-human, or totally alien sounds, they commonly do their linguistic neighbours (whether speakers of non-standard dialects or foreigners) the honour of acting as models. Such neighbours are like 'nature' rather than 'culture' as Lévi-Strauss would point out (see also Leach 1964). There is certainly an archaic, dialectal or Celtic hint about the descriptions of rhesus monkey vocalizations by authors A and B, and a primitive or faintly folk 'Red Indian' flavour about author D's '!Ho!'. For a hint from another cultural background, Jorge Luis Borges, an Argentinian, in his *Ficciones*, invents an outlandish country which he calls 'Tlön'. Surely only a speaker of Spanish would chance upon this only apparently 'random' choice, containing as it does 'tl' from the exotic Amerindian-derived area of the Castillian lexicon – found mainly in Mexican topography and nomenclature – and 'ö' from the European North – alien in orthography, sound and cultural association.

When we confront the attempt to label rhesus utterances, we may well argue that cultural peculiarities are at their most evident when humans try to represent the *absence* of cultural characteristics. If, as Evans-Pritchard (1940) suggested long ago, we define ourselves by opposition to others, then 'the other' is not an open category of infinite possibilities, but is in turn defined by its opposition to ourselves. Each culture inevitably generates its own perception of what is, either as dream or nightmare, its 'other'. We might be tempted to ask in the particular case, why, since a phonetic approximation was being offered, all the well-developed resources of the International Phonetic Alphabet (IPA) were not brought into play. A Japanese scientist would, at least, then not need to know English in order to understand the representation of a rhesus utterance. The use of the IPA would, however, only confuse the matter further, for rhesus phonetics are not human phonetics. Evidently the only adequate solution would be a special rhesus phonetic inventory. Even when that solution was reached, the labour might be of only academic interest since rhesus utterances are no doubt so stereotyped that a numbered inventory of sample tape-recordings might be more convenient. Any particular written form would then be of merely mnemonic function. In that case whether we write *hough-hough*, *hough*, *'!Ho!'* or *no. 1* is of no particular moment, thus returning us full circle.

There is, however, a difference in consciousness between our conclusion and that demonstrated by primatological practice. For we see that even when Reynolds's authors abandon a quasi-phonetic notation of articulations for a 'description' of behaviour, they draw the same problems with them into this sphere. We meet here *geckering*, a term from the world of English dialect. *Gecker* is meaningless to most modern Southern English-speakers – its basic usage seems to derive from 'a gesture of ridicule' (see *Oxford English Dictionary* s.v. *geck*) I have furthermore heard a primatologist state, no doubt in an unthinking moment, that the 'correct' word for one kind of rhesus grimace was *girning*. *Girn* derives from *grin* by metathesis in South-Western English dialects (Wright 1913: 134). It is known to standard English-speakers (when it is known at all) through the rural folk-custom of holding *girning* competitions, to discover who can pull the ugliest face while looking through the frame of a horse-collar. Nothing could be more culturally specific than the grotesque grimaces of *girning*. Its dialect origin no doubt lends it the association with the outlandish required to describe monkey behaviour.

We may press the matter further. For one unit of behaviour, author C chooses *gecker*, D uses *ik, ik, ik,* but B selects *splutter*. It may be thought that *splutter* at least is a neutral descriptive term, but this belongs to a domain of lexicon which ultimately is as culturally idiosyncratic as *gecker*. For example, translating terms of this sort between languages can be particularly difficult. Informants state that only this, or only that, is a 'splutter', perhaps with obscure demonstrations – and with careful exegesis on the affective implications without which (or with which) it is not (or is), truly, a splutter. The ethologist's problem is that demeanour is rule-governed in human societies (see above, chapter 6). The natural-language terms available to cover animal sounds and acoustic gestures are likely to come dressed in highly emotive cultural associations. Animal behaviour is likely to recall uncontrolled, childish or ill-mannered demeanour, and the terms used bring semantic overtones into the supposedly neutral description.[3]

When we come, therefore, to more elaborate delineations of rhesus activity, as with author C's 'glare or scandalized expression' or B's 'haughty walk' we are in the thick of the ethological problem. If 'haughty walk' is acceptable could we also accept 'sagacious nod' or 'admiring stare' as possible rhesus behaviours? These remarks are not intended to make jests at the expense of ethological description. All the problems of scientific investigation are present in these examples. Ethologists are increasingly aware of these questions (cf. a recent unpublished criticism by Chalmers of the category of 'play'). For a discipline which wishes to determine objectively what animals and humans have in common, it is an issue of critical importance if natural language has already prejudged the issue by 'contaminating' the descriptive instruments with evidence of humanity (see also Callan 1970 and Crick 1976: 100–8, for further discussion). For social anthropologists the important conclusion, always worth repeating, is that the observation and the labelling of 'behaviour' are inseparable from the importation of socially derived meanings – even when observing monkeys. How much the more so when the process is reflexive, when the observers and the observed are both 'meaning-makers' (Crick 1976: 2–3).

SOCIAL ANTHROPOLOGY, LANGUAGE AND REALITY

The study of classification has a long history in social anthropology.[4] At many points this interest has closely paralleled and overlapped with the interests of linguists, both in its general and its particular applications. A classical instance of common endeavour has, for example, been in the field of colour classification. Hjelmslev, for example, long ago noted the discrepancies in colour labels between different languages (1963: 52–3). Anthropology has multiplied such instances, so that both the numbers and kinds of colours discriminated by unit category terms have been shown to be of considerable variety. Later, some order was brought into the variation by (among others) Berlin and Kay (1969). There are some general principles underlying the cultural choices.

These studies raised the issue of relativism versus universals in social anthropology. Thus, insofar as all classifications partake of this feature exemplified by colour classification it became legitimate to ask whether all cultural systems were in principle *sui generis*, even implying in some sense 'separate realities'. Whorf, as generally represented at least, took this question to the point of appearing to argue that cultural perceptions were not simply mediated by language, but that language determined the way in which we experience reality. His examples were drawn in part from the kinds of classification differences referred to already, such as the famous three kinds of snow of the Eskimo (Carroll 1964: 210). He referred also to other more general features of language – for example, presence or absence of grammatical 'tense' or of 'mood' or 'aspect' – as being some kind of determinant of views of time or process in particular cultures. Thus, again putting the matter very simply, a Hopi physics (for reasons of this sort) would differ from a European physics. I think that Whorf has been misunderstood, but there is no doubt that the misunderstanding itself has a firm place in specialist thinking about this knotty combination of language, classification and reality. Consequently much of this work has been judged to have painted itself into a corner, appearing to favour: 1) extreme cultural relativism: 2) separate cultural realities: 3) the cultural determination of both knowledge and 'experience': and even, as we have seen, 4) linguistic determination of cultural experience. These extreme positions (if actually held) would obviously make arguments for the existence of cultural universals more difficult, and stand in opposition to ideas of cultural change, as well as to more subtle views of the relation of language to culture and of culture to reality.

Berlin and Kay's work on colour classification was seen by many as restoring universals to the centre of discussion. Thus cultures were 'relativistic' in detail but there was some kind of limit to their arbitrary, reality-shaping powers. Some went so far as to argue that at a common-sense level cultural differences were greatly exaggerated, and that the major differences were mystifications deriving from ritual specialists (Bloch 1977). For people with any idea of a universal truth to be taught to all mankind, the exact nature of cultural difference is a serious question. Thus at times both missionaries and historical materialists have led violent attacks on the merest hint of cultural relativism. In Miss Mandy Rice-Davies's phrase, 'They would, wouldn't they?' If there are self-evident truths that are to be taught these truths cannot themselves be subject to any law of cultural relativism. 'Cultural realities' must then be rejected on two grounds: 1) if the observer's vision is the truth, then it cannot just be part of the relativity of the observer's culture; 2) if that truth is to be transmitted to others, then cultural 'worlds' that differ from it or reject it must be obfuscations of some kind, obscuring the truth. Whether or not one goes on to attribute the obfuscations to simple error, or to self-interest on the part of some portion of the population concerned, is a detail. Fundamentalist missionaries and some development economists have vacillated between both interpretations, while Marxists and historical materialists often tend to favour the latter.

That is after all the more universalistic position: cultural classifications thereby become the secondary result, or 'artefact', of human universals like power and dominance. As for any kind of role for language – those of 'running dog', or at best of 'handmaiden' or 'lackey', seem to be the most conveniently vacant! So much for any short-lived Whorfian linguistic dreams of empire.

I do not wish to caricature this debate – I think that the oppositions implied are simply false, although it is easy to see why they should arise. It is, for example, quite obvious that 'mystifications' do occur. The literature on the social manipulation of discourse is quite well established: there is really nothing controversial about it. Indeed, it probably seems less problematic to linguists even than it does to social anthropologists. Let us, as it were, assert that when the issues are big enough there is no recourse but to firmly universalistic principles. Yet cross-cultural (or subcultural) misunderstanding on supposedly trivial issues (whatever the possibilities on greater ones) is a very real problem at the level of close interactions between individuals, so much so that it is itself a human universal, and whether we like it or not language looms very large in these situations. This does not only arise in the obvious limiting case, in which the interactors do not share a language. On the contrary, it often seems that the more they *think* they share, the more those 'Whorfian' characteristics arise, and in comes the whole baggage of cultural classifications and the rest, all clothed in rich linguistic detail. It is my opinion (see above, chapter 1, pp. 9–16), not perhaps widely understood, that this is the point on which Whorf's original insight rests. The self-taught fire-insurance assessor was in the possession of the basic facts of the interpenetration of 'language, thought and reality' (Carroll 1964) before he was tempted into the world of the professionals and learned bad habits. The famous programme for linguistic determinism is correctly named the 'Sapir-Whorf Hypothesis', for there was no reason why Whorf in his untutored state should have taken that road.

Whorf's problem as a fire-insurance assessor was a *material* one. The insurance company lost if a fire broke out. Any interpretation of the cause of a fire that reduced the incidence of such fires and the amount of such payments was 'cost-effective'. It might even reduce premiums. We are used to such causes being cast in terms of the physics of combustion. Whorf's insight was to see that the disposition of flammable materials in vulnerable places was often due to a set of underlying linguistic classifications. For him 'empty gasoline drums' exploded because they were classed as 'empty' (so that people smoked near them) instead of 'full' (of gasoline fumes). He found that 'spun limestone', and 'scrap lead' from condensers (both highly combustible materials), burst into flames when left near rubbish fires, because they were heaped wrongly with non-combustible waste. The mistake was due to the classifications with 'lead' and 'stone'. Whorf's 'reality' was inextricably inter-twined with human classifications. Physical explosions (he appeared to say) were produced by a careless mixture of categories as well as of chemicals, (see above, chapter 1, p. 15). It is the *material* nature of Whorf's basic problem that contains the interesting antidote to his own, and other people's, flight into debates on cultural reality. Of course, Whorf's failure to develop an adequate language to discuss his original insight does not absolve him from serious criticism. From any modern point of view it is a great pity that time has frequently to be wasted in denying that this or that study of language and categories of classification embodies merely a culturally relativistic position (see above, chapter 1, p. 10). Meanwhile, from the point of view of linguitics this often leads to the study of cultural classifications being represented as the collection of cultural curiosities.

Some of these points, including the materiality feature, are here illustrated from the classification of bodily parts. It is well known that the human body is divided by different criteria in different languages. In the present exposition I shall treat part of such a classification through a simultaneous analysis of thought, language and action, in order to make clearer my arguments.

Let us consider the shaking of hands in England and among the Ibo of South-Eastern Nigeria.[5] In both languages there are apparently inter-translatable terms for the gesture (Ibo *ji aka*). Although *aka* is usually translated 'hand' the boundaries of the parts concerned are, however, quite different. The English 'hand' is bounded at the wrist. The Ibo *aka* is bounded just below the shoulder. The fingers and thumb are called *mkpisi aka*, in which *mkpisi* is 'any thin somewhat elongated object' (cf. 'a stick' *mkpisi osisi* – *osisi* 'tree', 'a match' *mkpisi okhu* – *okhu* 'fire'). The more open-gestured nature of the Ibo handshake compared with the English handshake is linked in part to this difference of classification. For the English-speaker the extreme, 'formal' possibility of presenting an only slightly mobile hand at the end of a relatively stiff arm becomes a choice reinforced by language. For the Ibo-speaker, even if that is a possible gesture it has no backing from language. On the contrary, for him, gripping the forearm and other variants of the gesture are still covered by the concept of shaking the *aka*, and are, as it were, allomorphs of the common gestural morpheme. For the English-speaker such arm-grips are gesturally (that is, not merely linguistically) separate from shaking hands – they are gestures of a different 'meaning'.

We do not resort to any linguistic determinism if we argue that the gestural classification rests to a certain degree on the labelling of bodily parts. The possibility of a different classification of greetings exists for the English speaker because of the particular placing of a conceptual boundary, which does not exist in Ibo. Thus, on the average of observations, an Ibo in 'shaking hands' may involve the movement of an area greater than the 'hand' more often than does an English person. Consistently shaking the hand alone, with articulation only at the wrist, might therefore seem to the traditional Ibo a slightly incomprehensible restriction of movement, equivalent perhaps in flavour to being, in the English case, offered only two or three fingers to shake. From the opposite point of view, to the English-speaker 'shaking hands' and 'arm-grip' are two *kinds* of greeting. To the Ibo they are degrees of intensity, demonstrativeness, of warmth, of 'the same' greeting. As a result even a 'warm' handshake in the English sense may seem relatively 'cool' as a greeting to an Ibo.

Further light is shed by another collocation. The English 'help' is translated *nye aka* in Ibo, which appears to mean 'give a hand' and thus to be a directly parallel metaphorical usage. Yet in close face-to-face cases when a physical 'hand' is appropriate, such as when assistance over a large fallen tree-trunk on a path, or up a steep slope, is asked for (*nye m aka* 'give me a hand'), a forearm may be offered to be gripped as often as the hand, if in practical terms either may suffice. In an English language context the request 'give (or lend) me a hand' in those exact circumstances would only rarely fail to result in the offer of the literal 'hand'. With regard to the 'degree' of helpfulness it is a 'warmer' gesture for the English-speaker to be offered a hand than a forearm. The apparent deficiency is thus now on the opposite side of the cultural-linguistic divide.

We may easily ask here, following a respectable anthropological tradition, whether the bodily classifications are not simply determined by the social events the body mediates. One chain of argument might develop from the observation that when the hand is engaged in work, or in preparing palm-oil or food, there is a polite reluctance to offer help or greeting with it. The offering of a portion of the 'arm' is, however, still conceptually the 'same' gesture, and not a completely 'substitute' gesture, as it would have to be in English. Thus, in such circumstances, where an Ibo will offer another part of his *aka*, the English person will have to say 'I'm sorry, I can't shake hands.' Socially speaking the more extended Ibo *aka* may be determined, let us say, by an overriding requirement that a physical gesture of greeting be made in the maximum number of circumstances. We shall have cause to revert in a different way to this statistical feature. This view implicitly argues that conceptual boundaries are modified like rules: as if a rule with too many exceptions (anomalies) is replaced by a revised rule to accommodate the exceptions. Douglas (1966a) was very helpful in relating the idea of category anomaly to the study of social categorization. But, as she herself shows, the existence of anomalies does not lead necessarily to the revision of categories – ambiguity at boundaries, she argues, is, for example, commonly marked by taboo.

It is nevertheless proper to consider our case through the eyes of those who see the body as a map of social interactions. For Douglas and for several other theorists the body is viewed as a main image of society. For them, we would be adding a further reason why the images of the body and of society should be able to coincide. It is possible, on the other hand, to accommodate quite extreme pragmatism, or a kind of behaviourism. For example, to take now the particular use of the *aka* as a 'helping hand' it might be that the use of the *aka* as a 'rope' to be gripped in an emergency, with the 'hand' portion clenched, offers more security, the helped one's 'hand' being less likely to slide off – in a hot, sticky and often rainy environment in which all helping hands are likely to be slippery. Such pragmatic interpretations are not uninteresting. They lead us, indeed to enquire why two English-speakers' hands should have to make those wild grasping movements towards each other in a similar circumstance. Perhaps a helping *aka* is really more often needed, and the help more often required in more messy and mildly dangerous conditions, than a helping 'hand' is. We should encourage all such lines of discussion, in order to show that the material and statistical side of this question is a normal subject for examination. It would be misleading, however, to argue from this pragmatically that the 'behaviour determines the language classification'. The *aka* classification ignores a possible intermediate conceptual boundary and thereby, we can argue, removes a linguistic criterion that might introduce the possibility of an unwanted choice into the material situation. Once the classification exists, however, it is part of the total experience of unreflecting individuals. There is no 'arrow of causation' from behaviour to category, since they cannot be separated. They form a 'simultaneity'.

It is quite clear then that the *aka* is not a 'mere' taxonomic label. Some would echo certain philosophers and say: they are not first of all 'objects' and then they are 'used' – they are objects *because* they are used. There is a Yoruba proverb which may be translated: 'in a forest no-one need fail to fight because of the lack of a cudgel' (Ojo 1966: 34). The forest here is defined as littered with cudgels – that is a social classification, not a botanical one. We cannot define 'use' in a pragmatic sense, therefore (by the way, I am not speaking of the use of *words*, for that would be to prejudge the fundamental question). It seems that *aka* is not a 'mere' word in some nineteenth-century lexicographical sense. It is attached to the upper limb, but it is a mnemonic for conceptualizations which are not conventionally linguistic or psychological, and which are actualized almost unconsciously as far as the individual is concerned. This is undoubtedly part of the distinction known by the terms 'signifier' and 'signified' (Saussure 1916). Nevertheless, such a 'signified' is too complex for the traditional 'linguistic sign' to encompass.

It does seem that persons bilingual or partially bilingual in Ibo and English are prepared to tolerate the rough translation of *aka* as 'hand' rather than 'arm'. The reason lies perhaps in a partly statistical judgement of the relative importance of certain kinds of error. The English 'hand' does not easily bear classification as an 'arm', but, as we have seen, it is perhaps surprisingly easy to use 'hand' for some 'arm' interactions. The basic misunderstandings emerge in failed interactions of the rather subtle but materially important kinds that we have been discussing. Different, simpler, more narrowly 'linguistic', misunderstandings also occur when (as is usual) animal front limbs are called 'hands' by untutored English-speaking Ibo ('hand of dog'). This makes a double misclassification, from an English language view, since animal front limbs are generally classed as 'legs', that is as 'rear' not 'front' limbs from a human point of view.[6] I would distinguish between cases of misunderstanding of this sort, which are experienced as apparent if puzzling 'misidentifications' (from the point of view of one or other speaker), and the cases of deeper misunderstanding that I have in mind. In the one case the solution is, figuratively, to call for a dictionary (or to make one if it does not exist). In the other the material problem is not experienced as a 'misidentification'. It is experienced as a social error or a social puzzle, even as some kind of wickedness. Who should be sent for? The difference lies in the fact that only parts of the language-category-object simultaneity are defined as language problems by natural language users. Underestimated as this latter group commonly are, it is worth stressing that such natural users have got the hang of lexical translation. They recognize that there is a common comprehension problem due to using a 'wrong' label. They reach frequently for the nearest lexical solution ('that is not a dog's hand but its leg.') The problems we started with, on the contrary, are not seen as linguistic, but as lying in the realm of action. Whorf tried to call them 'linguistic', but confused everyone including, very often, himself.

I do not wish to add to the complexities of this case. It is, however, important now to take up the further matter of the 'density' of a category. For Ibo-speakers the forearm or lower part of the *aka* is engaged in more socially significant activity than the upper part – as if, as Berlin and Kay argue for colours, the category has a centre of gravity, or a zone most characteristic of its qualities. It may be noted that the Ibo 'shoulder' (which we are not discussing here) bounds the top of the upper limb as does a vest or undershirt with a short sleeve, not (as with the English word) as does a garment without a sleeve; in other words, the *aka* is not quite as long shoulderwards as the 'arm'. It is a fact of common experience that 'unit' categories commonly exhibit conceptual sub-gradings (or shadings). We are, for example, clearly aware of this feature with some 'unit' kinship terms covering various genealogical specifications. Thus the Ibo *nwa nna* ('father's child') refers to 'half-sibling' as well as various 'patrilineal relatives'. There is always felt to be some degree of semantic density about half-siblings within the category even though half-siblings are also indelibly marked as kinds of patrilineal relative, in virtue of their membership of the unit category. It is worth noting that this is not quite the same as saying that the term *nwa nna* is 'extended' from half-siblings to other patrilineal relatives. That is now seen as an ethnocentric error, compounded though it is by the common Ibo–English translation of *nwa nna* as 'brother' or 'sister'.

The 'density' gradients of categories must be related to frequency in some ways – perhaps we may put it as frequency of association or interaction with reality. Categories thus contain or coexist with a statistical feature – it is part of their materiality, and we see that the earlier discussion of the possible influence of certain frequencies of social interaction involving the *aka* category has prepared us for such a view. Our perception of the gradients of semantic density, or the possibility of such a perception, is a main reason for denying any simple view that all reality is exhausted by sets of categories. The statistical figure marks irregularities in experience which are not flattened out by unit categories. This is an important point, accounting as it does for the existence of ways of incorporating experience into the category system. We shall wish to recall this later.

To return to our case, the *aka* is more *aka*-like, the lower down the limb we travel. The denser *aka* of the Ibo still includes the forearm, not just the 'hand'. The next named subdivisions, as we have seen, are the *mkpisi aka*, the 'fingers'. The biological pragmatist would draw attention to the un- doubted saliency of the fingers (and thumb) for all humans. This merely leads us to reflect that the wrist is not anything like so important a subdivision pragmatically, and we may be ready to concede that the real problem may be why the wrist became a boundary in (say) North-West Europe, and not why it fails to be in some other areas (perhaps we shall look forward to a full historical account of these questions from the pens of experts.) To subdivide *aka* into 'arm' and 'hand' is then to reinforce the density gradient at the active end of the limb, but the declaration of terminological independence of the 'hand' still does not eliminate a possible perception of the ambiguity of the wrist boundary. For the moment, we may note that the 'social' extends so far into the 'semantic' here, that the case for a 'semantic anthropology' in these terms (Crick) is only a case for a more delicate social anthropology.

For help in making further important distinctions I will allude to the 'leg' word *ukwu*, which in a parallel fashion includes the English 'foot'. Again there are *mkpisi ukwu* ('toes') to match *mkpisi aka* ('fingers'). I have no absolutely equivalent data that bring the *ukwu*/'leg + foot' relationship into prominence, but it is my impression that the classification is susceptible of an equally detailed analysis. The social interventions of the *ukwu* are not subtle, but the 'foot' part of the *ukwu* rarely suffers any fate not shared by at least the lower 'leg'. There is a strong possibility that the uneventful *ukwu* classification reinforces the *aka* classification by the example of a classifi- catory symmetry. But conversely the forelimb may provide the lively model for the classification of the lower limb. The English system, if we use the new perspective gained from our analysis, is surely *over*-symmetrical? The terminological specification of the 'hand' and its 'fingers' must be the model for the elaborate separation of 'foot' from 'leg', and the further provision of 'toes' as a separate lexical term to balance the 'fingers'. We detect here the entry into categorization of a symmetry feature. The failure to provide a unit category term equivalent to 'thumb' for the appropriate (big) toe strengthens rather than weakens this impression. The big toe is the only one worth singling out ('I stubbed my toe'), so that the limit to the application of classificatory symmetry is marked by ambiguity.

As we examine the *ukwu* classification beside the *aka* one, new suggestions concerning the different experiential gradients of different terms even inside the same set have arisen. Kroeber long ago (1909) noted the tendency for a classificatory symmetry to tidy up such sets. This is important as indicating that some categories may be 'emptier', more decorative, more intellectual, more 'cognitive' perhaps, or just more 'linguistic', than others. It cannot therefore be the case that the statistical ('frequency') feature we have discussed already, actually determines the categories. On the contrary, through at least the symmetry feature, a certain autonomy appears in category sets. Thus we have been able to catch even bodily terms already taking off into realms of abstraction, their materiality giving way to ideality. In all respects, however, the Ibo system is relatively less advanced than the English one on that road.

I started my account at a point where *aka* was neither behaviour nor text, neither social nor linguistic, but a simultaneity, a unit in total experience. It is now possible to see why Lévi-Strauss's structuralism was able to stumble on the discovery that society *is* text, or that the social is homologous with the textual. As we know, the failure of structuralism in practice was to have no theory to account for the homology. Only a microscopic focus enables us to track the way in which 'textuality' peels away from experiential unity. Language is in large measure responsible, no doubt. It is a hybrid medium, its map being partly interior, subjective and rooted in regularities of the 'human mind', and partly exterior, objective, and rooted in materiality. Left to itself it intrudes its own arabesques into the perception of materiality: as if a fungus on a lens were to add a galaxy to a record of the universe.

In making an analysis such as the foregoing, I have no opinion on whether other systems which contain a unit 'arm + hand' category would have similar detailed features. No other has been made in exactly this way. However, Professor Mihai Pop, on hearing a version of this paper, stated that Romanian usages were remarkably similar. *Mînǎ*, although from Latin *manus* 'hand', is a 'forelimb' (the pattern is common in Eastern European languages) and *da mînǎ* to give a 'hand' also (he stated) differs in its realization from the English manner. Dr Andrei Pippidi, the historian, tells me that the use of *braţ* ('arm') has overlaid the *mînǎ* classification only in the recent history of the standard Romanian language. The *aka*-like features of *mînǎ* emerge in many standard collocations. The spread of *braţ* is a Westernizing feature, exemplified by an indeterminacy about the bounds of the member, as well as by the lack of a symmetrical feature in the lower limb. The 'foot + leg' term *picior* is even today undifferentiated. The terms for 'finger' and 'toe' are also not separated *degetul mîinii* and *degetul piciorului*. Such parallels are, when attested, a bonus, but are also in a sense diversions, as the realities must be explored *de novo* in each case. It is interesting, however, that Roman imperial interactions resulted in the Dacian limb, like the Ibo *aka*, receiving in translation the foreign 'hand' term. We cannot pursue these issues here. Even the French terminology bears signs of several reconstructions (cf. von Wartburg 1969: 118, Ullman 1951; see also above, chapter 1, p. 14). The common Romance 'leg' word is a loan in several modern Romance languages (*gamba* > Greek *kambe*). The 'finger' and 'toe' words remain undifferentiated. The *aka*-type terminology is to be detected in Gaelic and Welsh despite the confusions of English models. Certainly linguistic collections of cultural classifications should be dusted off and restored to the social matrixes from which they were untimely ripped. Many rich results lie in wait for the researcher.[7]

The purpose of this paper, has, however, been to illustrate what is meant by the study of 'simultaneities'. I wish to indicate that it is possible to derive a multiplicity of social, epistemological, linguistic and psychological theories from a single case. No prizes are offered for their discovery. I am particularly desirous to stress the material features of the reality demonstrated, being tired of the naive assumption that we must here be in an 'idealist' discourse. A multiplicity of interpretations is possible because all interpretations start off together in a point source. Certain familiar oppositions take on a healthily problematic air: category/object, structure/event, relativistic/universalistic, collective/individual, and yet there is no collapse by this method of analysis into abstraction.

It will be evident that choosing one part of a body classification instead of a whole body classification (let alone a whole social space) reduces the amount of exotic description, so that it can easily be seen what the anthropology is like. The total space is composed of an infinite series of subtleties of that order. It is also important to demonstrate the very close mesh with reality that I have in mind. The particular case has also some useful corrective features embodied in it. Handshakes and the like belong to an area of human social life which are commonly taken to be the most 'observable'. Such behaviour can, it is often thought, be relatively objectively described, in much the same way as we might expect (not, as we have seen, always safely) to describe the behaviour of animals. Indeed, 'greeting' in animals is even considered by some to be the same *sort* of phenomenon.[8] Yet even in this simple zone it is clear that the critical humanization has taken place – such that the handshake and the helping hand are 'sicklied o'er with the pale cast of thought' mediated by language. We may think the actual instance socially trivial, but in fact the relations of naive English-speakers with naive Ibo-speakers have no more characteristic a framework than this. It is commonplace to draw attention to differences between cultures in complex domains (colour terms and the like). The excellence of such work has perhaps led to the too abstracted view of 'cognitive' processes. The classification of the event and the 'event' are simultaneous. That is why language penetrates the social. That is also why, by a paradox, linguistics, including socio-linguistics as commonly practised, does not seem to exhaust its significance.

My treatment of Whorf is introduced to show how the absence of a discourse through which to tell of his insights led him ultimately up one of the many blind alleys that start from his initial position. I have often puzzled over why people tend to see only text *or* life, as if each rules out the other. Malinowski too may have started from a similar insight but his blind alley was the theory of context of situation, and the equation of meaning with function (Henson 1974).

Category contains a statistical feature which I have called a 'density'. This feature accounts for the mathematical possibilities implied in many theories. Start with the extreme view that the cultural categories, linguistically expressed, are the only way we can register experience. Unit categories are then matched to a pattern of frequencies of occurrence which introduces discrepancies both within and between the categories. Thus the *aka* is more involved in interactions the further one travels towards the fingers from the shoulder. The *nwa nna* is realized as 'half-sibling' with a particular experiential frequency, within the general pattern of frequency for other patrilineal relatives. The importance of the statistical feature can be illustrated from its bearing on the Berlin and Kay statement concerning colour universals: that colour shades described by subjects as the most typical within unit colour categories are more similar cross-culturally than are the colour *ranges* covered by the categories. The statement is not without methodologically controversial problems, but it matches the notion of frequency and density. The biological features of perception are not abolished by the grid of category: they appear in the density gradients of categories. For the 'language is reality' people the existence of the gradients does not change the fact that they are not 'present' in the inventory of categories. In addition, as we have seen, the category boundaries intrude their own effects upon the perception of frequency gradients. They are themselves a kind of statistical feature. On the other hand, the 'reality is universal' people will pick up frequency gradients corresponding to pan-human experiences which cannot be held therefore to be culturally derived. The important point is, however, that there is in experience no subdivision. For that reason worlds set up by categories bear all the signs of materiality to the untutored human being.[9]

The major contribution of anthropology results from the experience of trying on a multiplicity of cultural spectacles: the illusion of total truth is amended by the revealed discrepancies. Where all the spectacles agree we have a universal. Is it simply a universal of spectacle construction? To find out we try to deconstruct the spectacles. We have added a semantic materialism to the approaches available for such purposes. It is inevitably in part linguistic, for our worlds are inescapably contaminated with language. It is an important advance to learn that the contamination extends into materiality, for that has long been for some the last refuge from language. Conversely, for others language has been a refuge from materiality.

Total Translation

In dealing with 'other cultures', the term 'translation' is frequently used as a description of the task of the social anthropologist. Not only the translation of language is intended but something more extensive pertaining to the whole practice of ethnography. The relations between translation in the literary sense and in this anthropological sense have long been recognized. The practice of anthropology cannot be quite analogous to literary translation, although the differences are not easy to express.

Let me first exemplify an effect of what has been called an automatism of language. At agricultural shows in part of Cameroon, classes of farm-animal and poultry for which prizes are offered are announced in Creolized English. Some of them are as follows (for simplicity I use an Anglicized orthography):

1 man cow, woman cow, woman cow wey e get bikin for back
   (bull, cow and cow with calf)
2 man swine, woman swine, woman swine wey e get bikin for back
   (pig, sow and sow with piglets)
3 man fowl, woman fowl, woman fowl wey e get bikin for back
   (cock, hen and hen with chicks)

4   man duck-fowl, woman duck-fowl, woman duck-fowl wey e get bikin for
    back
      (drake, duck and duck with ducklings)

We may note in passing the breaking down of the elaborate standard
English categorizations into combinations with 'man', 'woman' and 'bikin'
('child'). It is, however, possible to continue the list so:

5   man hand, woman hand, woman hand wey e get bikin for back (right
    hand, left hand, and . . . ?)

The initial classificatory parallelism in the 'man' and 'woman' compounds
with 'hand' arises because, as is common (cf. Hertz 1960; Needham 1973),
'man' in that context specifies 'right' and 'woman' specifies 'left'. The
parallelism:

      . . . woman hand wey e get bikin for back
      (left hand with children)

has no equivalent reality, but it leads to a respectable Creole question that
we may translate as 'what are the children of the left hand?'. Whether we
treat the question as a joke, a riddle (answer: 'fingers'), a metaphysics, a
poetics or a paradox, the question and sequence 5 are derivable from
sequences 1 to 4 in Creolized English. They are not so derivable from the
standard English sequence. Sequence 5 slips, as it were, under the Creole-
speaker's linguistic guard as a consequence of the particular form of his
language (these sequences are possible also in many African languages). If
the standard English translations are read instead, sequence 5 is merely
bizarre, and has no imperative connection with the others, save in its
sentence rhythm or the like. But an interesting side-effect is that a phrase
such as 'the children of the left hand' has a gratuitously poetic effect in
standard English – the translation sets up resonances *de novo* in the second
language.[10] We may ask 'what in such a case have we "translated"; what
does the translation "mean"?'

Social anthropology confronts such questions at the very beginning of the
attempt to understand another society. They are, of course, also asked of
English texts as various as those of MacPherson's Ossian (see Campbell,
J. F. 1872), Fitzgerald's *Rubáiyát*, and the Authorized Version of the Bible
(Steiner, G. 1975: 356, has an excellent discussion). The anthropologist's
study of even the quasi-textual elements of the field, myths and the like,
cannot be begun without the recognition that his understaneding may be
inadequate and perfunctory, and not up to the standard of the cumulative
criticism of long-established literary works (ibid., 1975: 353ff).

Thus the familiar problem of translating the personal nomenclature of
classical Russian novels has been approached in different ways. A character
named Ivan Ivanovitch Petrov may be referred to or addressed perhaps as
Ivan Ivanovich, as Petrov, as Ivan, or as Vanya, a diminutive of the latter.
In a novel full of characters the use of these variants is very confusing to the

non-Russian reader. Older translators broadly followed the usage of the text. Recent translators try to simplify to something closer to an English usage. It is quite well known that the Russian variants are subtly context-bound, linguistically and socially. 'Code-switching' is also frequently involved, with manipulations of the possible usages by characters and author, to express changes of mood and relationship. All of this is lost in the 'Anglicizing' translation. Since the reader of literature without Russian cannot presumably understand any of it (some argue) he loses what he never truly had. Literary translation is a series of compromises. Possibly an anthropologist without Russian might prefer a more exact, if un-English rendering of the usages, because learning about differences is his job – but then that job would be better carried out in Russia and in Russian, rather than through translations of novels. Nevertheless, our example suggests that as a translator of a culture the social anthropologist will not always be able to place his bounds between the *preserving of differences* and the *demonstration of similarities* in the same places as the literary translator.

The phrase 'translation of culture' is, however, somewhat misleading, since 'translation' is, when we come to life rather than letters, deeply involved in the nature of the contact of the intertranslating entities. During the later nineteenth century, official English texts favoured the use of the English term 'Emperor' for the rulers of Russia and Germany. *Reichstag*, the German Imperial Parliament, was translated 'Diet'. When Japan, whose ruler was already termed Emperor in English, modeled its new parliament on that of Germany it was termed 'Diet' in English also. To say that 'Diet' is the 'correct' answer to the question: 'what is the Japanese Parliament called?' is not a technical matter of translation. 'Diet' in this sense has no non-literary English context whatsoever. To call 'Diet' the 'correct' translation is not different in principle from saying that 'girning' is the 'correct' word for a certain rhesus monkey behaviour.

Still in this field of terminology, in the nineteenth century, English usage did not favour the official use of 'native' terms such as *Tsar, Kaiser* or *Reichstag*. It may be that Victorian usage 'translated' a stable view of the world in which constitutions were open to logical development, despite national variations. There were, of course, constitutional differences between Emperors and Kings, and between Parliaments and Imperial Diets. There were already in the English terms covert implications of degrees of political virtue. To make overt the 'foreign-ness' of the institution would be to rub in the fact, or would remind one of the intractability of the ethnic reality. Later, on the contrary, when it became usual to refer to the *Tsar* or *Kaiser*, something else became dominant, variously attributable to realism, cynicism, loss of political innocence, insecurity, xenophobia or other factors associated with the collapse of the Victorian order. The pejorative use of the 'native' terms was quite explicit by 1914. Since then those particular terms have sunk into a historical perspective, but the same process continues wherever peoples are in uneasy or hostile contact. Winston Churchill directed that 'submarine' be restricted to British or Allied vessels, 'U-boat' to be used for the German ones. At the present time the differentiation between 'regime' and 'government' is applied by not entirely conscious sets of rules. But in general we may agree with Adam Ferguson (1767: 31): 'the titles of *fellow citizen* and *countryman* unopposed to those of *alien* and *foreigner*, to which they refer, would fall into disuse, and lose their meaning.' The work of Evans-Pritchard on Nuer politics (1940) continues this tradition into social anthropology (Pocock 1961: 78; Dumont 1975 and above, chapter 3).[11]

Nomenclature as translation

The question of translation of other 'people' is, then, already much complicated. The 'observer' of others must be aware that his 'observations' of others are, in subtle ways, made for him in advance. The reflexiveness of the process can achieve extraordinary convolutions. The definition of alien persons arises often in the case of translation names. Perhaps the non-Englishness of the Spanish monarchy is emphasized by not calling King Carlos 'King Charles'. It is, if so, surprising to many to see 'Elizabeth II' rendered as 'Isabel II' in Spanish publications. The Hispanic requirement to 'translate' all personal names (Carlos Marx, and the like) is well known (the devising of 'equivalents' can be a difficulty: Kennedy as a forename, for example, may be rendered *Canadio*).

The Gaelic-speaking peoples exhibit an instructive special example. There is for Scottish Gaelic a standard set of dual personal names to be used respectively in Gaelic language and English language contexts. They fall broadly into three classes:

1 Gaelic names with alternative Englished spellings

Aonghas	Angus
Fearghus	Fergus
Ailean	Allan

2 Gaelic names cognate with English versions

Eanruig	Henry
Alasdair	Alexander
Art	Arthur
Iain	John
Anndra	Andrew
Ealasaid	Elizabeth
Seamus	James (Hamish is a false form from the Gaelic vocative 'A Sheamuis!')

3 Arbitrary equivalents

Gilleasbuig	Archibald, Archie
Tormoid (from Norse Tormund)	Norman
Somhairle (from Norse Somerled)	Samuel
Ruaraidh	Derek
Tearlach	Charles
Mór, Mórag	Sarah, Sally
Aoirig	Euphemia, Effie
Raodhailt	Rachel
Beathag	Rebecca

There are in class 3 some approximate resemblances, but the Gaelic names have no direct association by etymology of meaning with the English ones. There are some other pairs, class 2 in appearance, which are linguistically class 3 (for example Eilidh and Helen). Aonghas (Angus, class 1) is also Aeneas (class 3). There are class 2 names misconstrued (Iomhair is paired to English Edward, instead of etymologically to Ivor.) Certain class 2 English cognates follow of course a Scottish, not a Southern standard (Sine = Jean, not Joan; Seonaid = Janet).[12]

Cases like Mórag/Sarah and Gilleasbuig/Archie exhibit most clearly that the whole system is one of what we may call 'person-translation'. Gilleasbuig MacThòmais is not just Archie Thomson in exotic guise (or at least *was* not – nowadays such names can be protective colouring for English-speaking Lowland intellectuals). We may say that the effect is not to equate the Gaelic-speaking person to his English-speaking *alter-ego* but to 'disequate' – to maintain the difference between the two social spaces. There is not one 'person' (Tormoid, say) in two worlds, but Tormoid and Norman. In Ireland an equivalent though different system (based largely on phonetic approximations) is detectable still in the choice of certain English names (Terence = Toirdhealbhach or Turlough (contrast Scottish Gaelic in which the related Tearlach = Charles), Phineas = Fionn; Milo = Maolmuire; Jerry, Jeremy = Diarmaid).

The Gaelic for 'English language' does not involve the ethnic name of the alien *Sasannach*. It is called *Beurla* (Old Irish *Belre*), an ancient term perhaps suggesting 'jargon', 'secret language', even 'gibberish'. If the rhesus monkey's purported *hough* has an Irish flavour, so the 'bird language' (*en belre*) of the Old Irish authors has an English one. The Scottish Gaelic-speakers' 'translation' of their world into that of *Beurla*-speakers (largely in fact Lowland Scots), has been one of continuous revision. Elsewhere (see above, chapter 9) in an examination of the time system of the Scottish Gaels, I pointed out that the folk-terms for parts of the year (purported 'months') did not match the general calendrical equivalents which are now standard. I give above two figures which summarize the difference between the two temporal worlds (see above, pp. 135–142). It can be seen from these that the standard equivalent translations for the 'months' mask rather than reveal the Scottish Gaelic reality.

The Paradox of Total Translation

It is interesting to note the convention employed by Tolkien in his *Lord of the Rings* that his text is a translation from Westron, a fictitious language. The appendixes to the third volume (*The Return of the King*) state that Westron has been treated as if it were English. This involves Tolkien in convoluted fictive philological feats. Thus, a character is called Sam. Since Westron lacks any Juadeo-Christian history (Tolkien 1954: 414), Sam is derived not from Samuel but from Samwise (Old English *Samwís*) meaning 'half-wise, simple'. For this name Tolkien creates the 'real' Westron *Ban* short for the compound *Banazîr* of which *Samwise* is then a 'translation'.

Again, in the novel the inhabitants of the country of Rohan speak an 'archaic' Westron. Since Westron is English, then Rohan's language becomes Old English. The heroes of the novels are called 'hobbits' in English, a term invented by Tolkien, for which he nevertheless skilfully derives an Old English etymology *holbytla* ('hole-builder'), which thus becomes the name for the hobbits in the language of Rohan. Since the novel is a 'translation', we are later told (Tolkien 1954: 416) that the equivalent terms are, in 'real' Westron (Hobbit dialect), *kuduk*, and in 'real' Rohan, *kûd-dûkan* ('hole-dweller'). The whole novel, with every name in it, is conceived on that scale. Yet no 'real' translation would go so far as to remap the very philology of the source into the philology of the receiving language. It is sufficient to state that 'real' translations of the novel into other languages do not attempt the daunting equivalent task – of recreating all this again, in the medium of Danish for example.[13] Such a translation as Tolkien purports to have made would, had it really occurred, have abolished translation. The hobbits *are* English. If there really were to be a translation of an alien world that constructed that degree of Englishness it would have to travel even further along the road Tolkien pursues than even he was conscious of.

What lies at the end of the road of translation, beyond Tolkien's imagination, is a kind of entropy of the translated system – a total remapping of the other social space in the entities of the translating one. At our destination the terrain would, however, be disappointingly familiar. The end of the road is only a journey to the anthropology of our beginning. It is suspiciously like our own homely ethnic world where monkeys 'correctly' *girn*, *gecker* and 'haughtily walk', where the Japanese Parliament is 'correctly' a *Diet*, and where I, Gilleàspuig, am ('correctly') Archie. Tolkien's enterprise (for many purely whimsical), by attempting to disguise creation as translation in so thoroughgoing a fashion, throws much light on both.

Arbitrariness and Automatisms

In other places I have argued that the simultaneity of social action with the definition of the event in which the action becomes significant, means that the attention to language is both essential *and* inadequate. The acquisition of language introduced a variable into the human defining process with its own rules; Wittgenstein rightly called it 'a form of life'. Once we map our world, partially though it be, into a system subject to its own entropy, with its own automatisms, we replace the animal world of events with one in which there are events and 'events', where the quotation marks indicate simulacra embodied in language – a field, if you like, of signifiers.

Thus we may attempt to set up onomatopes to match the sound of an animal or bird. It matters little whether **kuku-* or the like was a good approximation to the sound of the cuckoo in Common Germanic and Common Celtic. It is of moment, however, that it developed by regular automatisms into *gauch* in German and *cuach* in Irish, while cuckoos themselves vocalize in much the same way now, we may be sure, as they did three millennia ago. In French and English, phonetic effects were accompanied by semantic associations: *cocu* (from Latin *cucullus*) and the first vowel of *cuckold* (pronounced [kʌkɔld] by regular development of Old English [u] → [ʌ]) retain the best reflexes of the older 'cuckoo' form. In fact 'restored' onomatopes for the bird itself have been created in German, French and English (*kukuk, coucou, cuckoo* ['kuku:]), and for everyday purposes in Irish too (by 'borrowing' from English). The linguistic behaviour of onomatopes shows certain peculiarities in the lexicon (stress, tone, length features) but we may note that even given the relative specificity of the onomatope vocabulary it too succumbs to the automatisms of the medium of expression.

This phenomenon provides a neglected riposte to those who equate animal calls with rudimentary language on the grounds that by certain definitions they are communicative, and utilize bodily organs homologous or partly homologous with those in man. The systematics of animal calls are closely connected with the systematics of a biological system. The systematics of language on the other hand have taken off from the organism: Saussurean 'arbitrariness' has occurred. Human beings have the faculty, at any level of symbolizing, to 'lock the form' – to use printers' terminology. Once a block of type is set up, all the stages or steps by which individual types are selected or founded, placed, rejected or replaced are rendered irrelevant. On 'locking the form' the block of type as a whole is now subject to the systematics of blocks of type, and not to any systematics whereby the block of type was originally made. This does not occur, as far as we know, in the acoustic semiotic of the mating calls of birds – so cuckoos do not yet cry *gauch*.

If the acquisition of language is almost the model of all models for the humanization of the social space, the social anthropologist must not restrict himself to language. While the generalized semiotic faculty of human beings in society is, as a matter of fact, closely connected with language, every system of conceptualizations has its own particular 'automatisms'. Leroy-Gourhan (1964) deduced that in the Mousterian period a concept we may label 'interment' already existed, for the human remains are not merely 'found buried' but show signs of being formally or funereally buried. For him the existence of such a 'concept' is *prima facie* evidence for the existence of language. The hypothesis is intuitively plausible. Yet the 'language' of physical interments has its own automatisms from then on – dictated by the nature of soil structures, digging tools and kinds and availability of artefacts for grave-goods. If contemporaneously a linguistic sign, or a set of linguistic contexts, also specified 'interment', they too would proceed on an arbitrary course of development, restructuring and substitution. The continuous respecification of the materially realized concept of 'interment', as a definition of whether or not what is done with the body fulfills its minimal criteria or not, proceeds simultaneously with a continuous respecification of the lexical items involved in terms of whether or not they continue to express rather than to obscure the social actions involved, as they pass through automatic processes of phonological and semantic drift. It will be no wonder if we cannot sometimes tease out in real life whether we are dealing with a 'social' or a 'linguistic' phenomenon. Language is to the social as a measuring rod is to the measured, where, however, the inches or centimetres stretch or contract at the same time as the object itself deforms in related or independent directions.

The development of 'arbitrariness' with the countervailing cost of 'automatisms' is clearly a critical development in the humanization of the social space, which comes to be composed of a simultaneous set of systematizations, material and immaterial – each with its implicit rules of arbitrariness, each subject to its own automatisms, and all brought to consciousness by individuals (if at all) only partially and fitfully: principally through the medium of only one of those fallible arbitrarinesses – language – which itself enters into the automaton-like aspects of the space. I have discussed elsewhere (see above, chapters 5 and 9) ways in which the social space may be modelled (for some purposes it may be termed a 'world-space'). Here I am concerned merely to emphasize that linguistics cannot alone unlock the complexities of the social space, despite the direct involvement of language with those complexities at almost every level.

Mama and Papa again

To speak of the automaton-like processes of the social space, is not to imply a necessary automatism in the individuals who form its living aspect. Some authors refer to the human faculty of multi-level 'monitoring' (Harré and Secord 1972). The linguistic example of the 'restoration' of the *kuku:* type onomatope is in this context quite as significant as its arbitrariness and its ultimate mutability. We must assume that the new 'cuckoo' is restored because the onomatopoeic quality is so embedded in the social definition of the appropriate term (as if the bird 'is' in some way its sound) that, for ultimately cultural reasons, the sound-changed lexical item is supplemented by another onomatope. This should not obscure the fact that the new onomatope will be characteristically an onomatope of the language.

A somewhat similar effect seems to occur in another controversial realm. In Indo-European languages (we shall not involve ourselves in the world-wide data) while **mater* or the like has suffered characteristic deformations, some vocable like *mama* has a remarkable stability. Jakobson (1960, 1968), Murdock (1965b) and E. R. Leach (1971a) have thrown light on the possible underlying force of this kind of feature within sets of kin terms. There is probably, as the literature suggests, a basic element of child vocalization involved. To that extent *mama* partakes of some features of an onomatope. It is a linguistic rendering of a 'sublinguistic', organic sound, which is then subject to sound change in its phonetic context. In this case, the term shows evidence of a continuous process of restoration. Traces of regular change can be seen in a once standard pronunciation of English *mama* as [mɔˈmaː] in which the quality of the first vowel is reduced with the loss of even stress on the first syllable. The restressing to [ˈma(ː)mɔ] or the like with restoration of first vowel stress is, however, now found in those

oòmboòloò   kíkíkí [Firth's spellings]

J.R. Firth's phonaesthetic drawings

Figure 11.1   J. R. Firth's phonaesthetic drawings

circles which do not use a version of the now commoner *mum* [mʌm].
Synchronically the latter term shows interesting cross-dialect irregularities.
In broad strokes the situation is that Southern English *mum* [mʌm] would
be expected to produce Northern English [mum] (cf. [kum] 'come') and
North American [mem] (cf. [kem] 'come'). In reality the /a/ type English
[ʌ] is represented by [a] in many Northern English dialects, and by an /a/
type phoneme in North America, expressed in the spelling *mom* (which is
mistakenly reprounounced by Southern English readers of American texts
as [mɔm] or the like). It must be said at once that alternative historico-
regional explanations can be marshalled,[14] but in the context of this peculiar zone of the lexicon it is worth noting that the acoustic impression of the
three dialect renderings for the *mum/mom/mam/* word is remarkably similar,
with an /a/ type phoneme.

It is a possibility that the tension between an 'onomatopoeic' rendering,
and a lexical one in which sound change retains its automatisms, is here
expressed in a 'restoring' or 'monitoring' effect – for remoter reasons, which
may be found in more fields of human study than one. Biological infrastructure lies no doubt behind certain other effects, such as certain phonaesthetic associations. If low-toned back sounds do correlate with large,
rotund, relaxing images, and high-toned front sounds with spiky, thin, tense
images (as in J. R. Firth's blackboard drawings in figure 11.1) then
countervailing examples like Zande *kirikiri* demonstrate that phonaesthetic
phenomena likewise become subject to arbitrarization. We may speculate
that the anti-arbitrary aspect of phonaesthetics derives from a close overlap
of the articulatory with the nervous system. The infrastructure of the
system, as it were, shows up in the system itself. If all such suggested effects
in language were to turn out to be demonstrated it would not change,
therefore, the basic paradox of language – that although it is an acoustic
code it is particularly strained in the encoding of biologically rooted articulations. Its acoustic or generally biological nature must, in a sense, be

reduced to a secondary level before it can become language. This is what 'arbitrariness' means in these circumstances.

When we consider other systematic levels of conceptualization in society, through patterns of action, structuring of the environment and the like, the tension between arbitrariness and the 'natural' meaning is certainly harder to monitor. The Yoruba scholar Ojo in his work on Yoruba culture (1966: 34) quotes a proverb *A kì njà nìgbó, ráùn ópá*, that 'in a forest no-one need fail to fight for the lack of a cudgel'.[15] The Yoruba forest is a domain of cultural artefacts, in this instance of potential cudgels, as well as of trees. If a man breaks a branch it may be, or may not be, a cultural act. With reference to our discussion in an earlier section of different conceptual boundaries, it is noteworthy also that although he writes in English, there is a slight discrepancy between the boundary of culture, as expressed by the Yoruba Ojo, and our own usage. He is quite explicit on this point. Culture begins, if you like, much deeper in the zone of 'environment'. In many non-Western worlds there is more 'meaning' in material, ecological features, because of the high degree of arbitrarization of materiality.

I suggested elsewhere (see above, p. 25) that a stable relation to the environment establishes a series of 'theatres of action' which are in some ways homologous with 'semiotic frames'. Among the Ibo, patches of forest were reserved as *ɔhea ɔjɔɔ*, 'forest of evil' or 'bad bush'. Corpses resulting from certain kinds of death, and the belongings of the deceased, were deposited there (Ojo 1966: 30 discusses a Yoruba variant). The Ibo population has trebled during this century, and what were once patches within a larger forest, now remain isolated as often the only remaining islands of uncleared forest. Uncleared forest is traditionally viewed as 'virgin' land for farming. In the land-use pattern of today *ɔhea ɔjɔɔ* is perspicuous where once it was hidden, potentially valuable where once it was avoided. The environmental 'language' has changed. For many villages the 'dangerous forest' concept has to be actualized in 'dangerous spots' or has become unactualized. Conversely, where *ɔhea ɔjɔɔ* still exists, even in completely Christianized areas, its exploitation is more tentative and less whole-hearted than if it were 'real' forest. The ambiguity that arises when materiality and the symbolic are in tension in a non-linguistic system is harder to conceptualize than in our linguistic examples, but its roots lie in similar general principles.

Universals

Many of the points discussed here have been only briefly exemplified. My examples have been building a picture to suggest that understanding of others, a supposedly social anthropological aim, is impossible with a merely naive use of language (even if monkeys are 'the other'), and yet even under favourable conditions language alone is not an infallible guide. The idea of translation, implicit in much recent social anthropology, involves us in a world of infinite reflexivity, if not of infinite regress. The problems penetrate even realms of minimal physical actions (as in the use of the hands), and indeed the action part of the space is dangerously confusing for this reason. We see that 'others' are already presenting simulacra of themselves to fob off our search to understand them. Understanding, we noted, appears to be about disequation rather than equation.

For these reasons, the early work on 'the structure of social worlds' slid into extreme relativism. Its thrust seemed to deny universals or to render them ever more remote. Whorf, at whose door much of this is laid, was not in my view truly open to this charge (see above, p. 15 and p. 165) but a version of it is now part of the ordinary armoury of debate in this field. Some anthropologists (cf. Bloch 1977) now even appear to assert that the common people, as it were, are everywhere much the same, and that 'separate worlds' derive from the mystifications of essentially ritual special-ists. The view is not without its force for societies with highly elaborate ritual and theological traditions. The control of communications produces patterns of dominance, leading to a 'muting' of subordinate groups (see Ardener, S. 1975a). But, in its strong form, rejection of discontinuities between ethnic world-spaces does not carry conviction.

But if we return to our earlier discussion we note some striking facts. When Leroy-Gourhan detects 'signs' of 'interment' in Mousterian 'graves', he, in common with all archaeologists, does not hesitate to leap a six-digit period of years – and a major change in the human stock – to detect those signs. Is this not methodologically similar to attributing 'girning' and 'scandalized stares' to rhesus monkeys. Perhaps not exactly. Whatever the implicit or unconscious effects of the ethological labels, ethologists will not stand on the point that monkeys are really 'girning' or 'scandalized' in a contemporary human (English) sense. Leroy-Gourhan on the other hand almost certainly would aver that when he says 'interment' he means that Mousterians did 'inter' in some contemporarily cognizable human sense. His assertion then is quite conscious and, if 'wrong', blatantly and un-ashamedly so. 'Interment' is just such a simulacrum of a natural event (the haphazard natural covering of a corpse with deposits of soil), with its 'significant' reductions of randomness, with 'suspicious' reorderings, as is a human utterance compared with the most expressive animal cries. The suspicious taint of order shows that the fight between arbitrariness and automatism has already begun. We claim to detect here the characteristic which equates rather than disequates humanity, regardless indeed of whether it is 'correctly' detected in the Mousterian case. Its rudimentary evidences are like the echo of a human voice. Perhaps that is why Leroy-Gourhan is prepared to state that it occurred together with language.

If we return to the limiting case of 'total translation', in which 'the other' is remapped in terms of ourselves, we reach similar conclusions to those of Steiner in a literary context. The total entropy of the other system to which I have referred refers only to the data. Lest the use of 'only' about data may appear deliberately provocative on my part, imagine that Stendhal's well-known social-climbing hero were rendered as English not French, were a 'vicar' and not an 'abbé', and rendered therefore (since the doings of clerics relate to a particular literary genre) in the style of Jane Austen or Trollope, with consequent root and branch restructuring of plot and incident, possibly even of dénouement. The process would thus reach much further than the Authorized Version of the Bible, the *Rubáiyát* or *Ossian* – where a 'naturalized' (note the characteristic paradox of the term) version is part of the point. What remains, when the otherness has disappeared? (the idea is not so far-fetched: the great Hollywood treatments of literary classics go much of the way). Even in the ultimate case, we have a new entity of our own, a new text, which although it is not 'other' is 'different'.[16]

If we visualize the attempt at 'total understanding' of another society as having led to an analogous dissolution of ethnographic otherness, we begin to perceive the artificiality of our example once we move from art to life. We would, it is true, receive another statement about 'ourselves', but in so doing we would have radically redefined ourselves. The translation of culture occurs at the level of the interpretation of events, within the very complex social space that we have visualized. Even in the tiny handshake case that I have raised, either understanding never occurs, or, if it does, a 'handshake' is never the same again: never again a 'mere' handshake or a 'natural' handshake. The human universal lies in the capacity of both sides to gain that experience.

Summary of the Argument

The appearance of linguistic examples in the preceding text, I know from experience, will lead some readers to a negative reaction. But a close examination will show that we are not dealing with linguistics, or sociolinguistics as normally understood, in such cases. I have had useful discussions on every point with linguistic audiences, but only anthropologists, it seems, easily draw the right conclusions.

We began in the rhesus monkey case right in the heart of empirical observation, without hope of much classifying assistance from the monkey subjects. We found a kind of innocence in those observations. The 'simultaneity' analysed is the act of objectifying the otherness of animal behaviour. Rhesus monkeys appear as already marginally humanized.

The case of the 'hand' classification and the 'hand' action is a good example of a simultaneity as I envisage it. The now somewhat boring and repetitive subject of ethno-classification (here of bodily parts) is given a new life. There is not a static classification and a set of social acts: the classification and act are not 'aspects' of each other – they coexist in an indeterminate quantum package. There is no distinction between the material and the ideal. That is what I mean when I say that the social space is neither idealist nor materialist. Language, and symbolization in general, introduces arbitrary fixings into the depicting of the space, which then develop automatisms of their own. That is a reason why linguistics and semiotics are not enough to aid comprehension.

In the example of the farm-animals and the right and the left hands, I wanted to illustrate how, because of a process of language, an ultimately 'untranslatable' form of life is created. We understand only by an exposition that the anthropologist's cultural 'translation' will wish to retain more of the 'foreignness' than some literary translations. In the other cases of nomenclature we see that some see names as translatable labels, others as markers of totally parallel social persons, as in the traditional Gaelic case. For similar reasons, the paradox of total translation was examined, and we found that total literary translation is either a literary ideal (as in Tolkien) or a total destruction or reconstruction of the 'other' as a new document about ourselves.

The discussions in the last sections are more technical, but attempt to explain through the processes of *arbitrariness* and *automatism* how a system constituted at one level passes into social unconsciousness, and then becomes subject to continuous semi-automatic processes, which ultimately 'unlock' the fit of social classifications. The 'humanness' of this opposition I have summarized as 'cuckoos do not cry *gauch*.'

My intervention in the mama/papa discussion is intended to illuminate the same point, and to propose that the more close to 'biology' are our classifications (shown often by the 'phonaesthetic' feature in the acoustic labels) the more chance there is that automatism is rectified. Yet even such phenomena cannot long resist the process of re-arbitrarization.

These parts of the argument are really much more simply said in the paper itself. They are intended to exemplify further the collapse into one another of the definitional and the material, by exhibiting the nature of the basic process.

On universals versus relativism I have merely stated that this opposition appears uninteresting in the light of what has gone before. The paradox of total translation shows both that we do not want it, and that in life rather than in text (and here is our critical break with high-structuralism) we cannot have it. I rest upon the final remarks in the main paper on this point.

That ending is, however, based on some clear methodological approaches that redefine the nature of the task in less vague terms than to talk only of 'meaning' or signification. The smallest operational problems embody the clues. We should be slow to ossify the comprehension of others into rigid two-dimensional systems, through which (to return to the text from St John with which we began) the word is merely 'comprehended' by the darkness.

12

The Problem of Dominance

At the post-plenary meetings on the 'Visibility and Invisibility of Women', Professor Leela Dube and other organizers kindly invited me to make a few general remarks on themes in various sessions of the main congress concerning women. The remarks I made then were informal and intended merely to provide a basis for discussion. It would not be appropriate now to accord all of them the permanence of print. I was asked, however, to present a note on one of the general points I raised: the problem of dominance.

In the plenary sessions, there were various accounts of male dominance, some of which seemed at the time to be rather mechanical. Whatever the nature of dominance is, to reveal it will require more than the examination of crude, arbitrary cruelties or exploitations. Dominance when applied to women is also only patchily related to the economic structure. For example, the difference between Euro-American women and peasant Asian women economically and socially is so striking that nothing would seem, on the face of it, more inappropriate than the view of apparently privileged women that they are silenced or invisible. Women learn (as do some men) that progress up a social hierarchy may involve the inevitable acquisition of a privileged status in relation to their former fellows which in itself seems to silence the right of complaint. Professor Srinivas's excellent paper, 'The Changing Position of Indian Women' (1977) refers to the increasing 'immurement' of Indian women as the price of the rise in apparent status. We detect parallels with mid-nineteenth-century England. A. J. Munby, a Victorian gentleman, made studies of working women in 'dirty' occupations – miners, glue-makers, fisherwomen and others. He was an odd-man-out among the liberals of his day in that he opposed the loss of working women's independent industrial occupations, arduous as they were. When he visited a new secretarial school for girls, he asked whether the constraining of girls into artificial and protected 'lady-like' ways, and into the straitjacket-like clothing of the period, was a gain or a decrease in freedom.[1]

It is indeed a fact that there is a kind of independence about working women inside the often exploiting work, which is not necessarily preserved as their material position improves.

Nonetheless it is folly to romanticize the lives of such working women: the independence, cheerfulness and vigour of individuals who are young and have their health and strength show only one side of the question. Modern middle-class writers often similarly describe the working *child* of the last century as sturdy and independent, and some imply that a serious loss resulted later from education. Of course, the match-selling boy was frequently happy, master (as he might think) of his fate. At the age of fifty, perhaps by then a pauper or broken in health, he would not have thanked you for admiring his independence at eight years of age. In judging the 'happiness' of people with their lot, the whole life must be taken into account. The happiness of the hardworking, 'independent', industrially employed or peasant woman is likewise precarious and dependent on forces she may not be aware of. In a different way, the lot of elite women in the Third World, whose 'happy independence' depends on servants, is also precarious. This lesson was learnt by Western middle-class women in our time.

It is as if we have to work through the outer defences of the economic and authority systems of the world before we can even *see* the underlying structures of dominance. That is why women so often must become privileged, with a life-style which, perhaps, a peasant woman would gladly settle for, before they perceive its ultimate nature. Dominance then appears like an intricate silver chain that has lain at the bottom of the sea for so long that it has become encrusted with so many particular exploitations that the basic shape has been hidden. Chip away these objective encrustations by social reform, and only at the end is the intricate final chainwork revealed – still intact.

The problem of dominance is, then, a problem of humanity, and no revolution has ever abolished it. Even the most complete and cruel upheavals, destroying authority structures, amending the channels of power, replacing elites and eliminating individuals in every walk of life, have left the 'templates' of dominance unaffected, able to replicate again in new forms, with new accretions, some more superficially attractive but usually strangely the same. It seems then that authority and power, as generally understood, are not dominance. The charisma of dominance comes from a particular power – that of ultimately defining the world in which nondominants live. Nothing could be more practical and 'action-based' therefore than a theory of dominance. Robert Hertz (see 1973), showed many years ago how human populations select what may be a very slight, and perhaps in itself trivial disparity, and build elaborations one upon another, until a complex structure of asymmetries emerges. He notes, in his classic example of handedness, that 'the slight advantages possessed by the right-hand are merely the occasion of a qualitative differentiation, the cause of which lies beyond the individual, in the constitution of the collective consciousness' (ibid.: 21).

If 'an almost insignificant bodily asymmetry' as between the left and right hand can be exploited in this way, similarly very slight imbalances in the relations between individuals have become the basis of dominance structures. If these imbalances are persistent and consistent, they are conceptually polarized and are further built upon until they become 'over-determined'. A slight imbalance is thus raised to an imparity, an imparity to an inequality, an inequality to an exploitation, and so on to become the basis for a whole systematization of power. When a set of specific imbalances coincide, the resulting intricate process acquires considerable momentum. The developments become both symbolic *and* action-based, both ideological *and* production-based. The dominance structure always tends to grow as fast and as far as it can. Those of its aspects which involve processes of production are normally the specialization of the historical materialists, who have made useful contributions to this field.

The theory of dominance is not therefore a theory concerned with women alone. It is a theory of the modes whereby societies create the daily realities that their members experience. It is not a branch of anthropology: it is one of anthropology's general theories. The case of women is thus highly instructive: it is perhaps the oldest structural dominance, which has now acquired both decorative and beguiling as well as harsh and occasionally desperate features.

Here I go on to suggest only one pathway of the structure of dominance as it affects women. There is a certain imbalance of a social kind that occurs between boys and girls in the years about puberty – I say 'social' because it is a mistake to see the imbalance as biological. The 'biological' side lies merely in a set of differences in the chronological age at, and in the physical nature of, puberty. Such differences could be potentially neutral in social terms. For example, boys pass through critical adolescent experiences at different ages and rates. Yet, on the whole, imbalance between youths in strength, kinds of experience, or sexuality, does not become permanently embedded in their later social life. Between the sexes, however, a similar difference does characteristically develop such consequences. It seems to stem from an absolute difference in the socially derived significance of choices made by girls and boys in very young adolescence.

In seeking for the roots of this social difference we may note the degree to which self-identification through identification with the parent of the same sex assists in prejudging the issue. The identification of sons with their fathers differs from the identification of daughters with their mothers in a minor respect which, however, plays its part here. The importance of identification in the first few years of life, when the polarity of the parents' roles and occupations may be very marked, should be noted. In imagining herself as her mother, motherhood becomes the earliest female role that a daughter grasps – so that the onset of puberty is easily seen by the girl-child as the entry to motherhood, even if this may conflict with other roles (such as helicopter pilot) which she will later perhaps be more aware of. In a sense the most demanding human role of all is conceptualized for her first of all – not last of all or simply later on. For the young pubertal male, in contrast, the 'male' roles that impress his imagination are not pre-empted by his merely impregnating role. His hard education in male competition begins at once. The young, inexperienced, pubertal female can be trapped – even mesmerized – by sexual and procreative life. It must be emphasized that we are considering very young girls, aged nearer thirteen than eighteen – an age of choice in which the sexual fate, as wife, prostitute or unthinking follower of an older male, may be embarked upon with a zest which is literally premature. The 'free' pubertal girl is, if you like, readily distract-able from following what the male youth already perceives as a race towards self-fulfilment. It is an injustice to tell her later, or at the time, that this, her first choice, *is* her self-fulfilment.

The problem of according or denying free choice to young pubertal girls is the first problem for women. It is an unfair problem – it is life's first socially derived imbalance between the sexes in their fully human role. A conscious humanistic feminism therefore is dependent on a certain structur-ing of society in advance – that is, on a willingness to encourage the female to forego a particular freedom on the very threshold of adult life. This is like the child which loses its eight-year-old independence as a street-trader by opting for the disciplines and subjections of education, to avoid paupery in old age. But the harsh dialectic of dominance begins at once. The require-ment of special assistance for very young girls through the sexuality trap requires the co-operation of males as well as of older females – neither of whom necessarily find it in their immediate interest to provide it. The assistance required may be minimal, but the dominance process has begun. Over-elaboration occurs, assistance becomes protection, which becomes over-protection. These begin to develop their own momentum. The males, potentially equal playmates of the girls before puberty, proceed over the hill to participate in the society at large. They can devote energies and time to the sheer excitement of 'creating' society for better or for worse. Girls who were delayed at the trap struggle up later, and try to learn the rules, in which they are already by now allocated their place. No wonder that, even in. enlightened days, many generations of being first into the fray have bequeathed males a world which speaks to them without interpreters, which is their own club.[2]

It is unlikely that any group difference of strength between males and females would have affected the issue of dominance between the sexes if the sexuality trap did not tend to introduce an imbalance into the adolescent age-group as a whole, preventing its maintenance as a continuous social entity. The humane 'protection' of girls from a premature sexual choice, leading to 'over-protection' generates an equal and opposite image of female 'vulnerability' on the male side. The males become ideologically stronger and stronger, the females weaker and weaker. The idea becomes event, and daily evidences of its physical manifestation confirm its apparent 'natural' reality. It is quite characteristic of human social semantics that arabesques and detailed elaborations develop from quite simple 'simul-taneities' of definition and action. The one chosen here to illustrate this proposition is a minor 'hiccup' in the differentiation of males and females at puberty: that 'absolute' freedom of choice produces totally different ultimate social results between pubertal females and males; requiring, in order to restore parity, some positive social action.

Since this is simply the first of many imbalances in life-trajectories[3] introduced by the reproduction cycle, it would still be likely that structural dominance in the defining of society, and of the cognitive experiences within it, would tend to favour males. Nevertheless, the puberty trap by being the first imbalance sets the structure askew from the beginning. It is suggested that social reform and material betterment, by reducing the 'encrustation' or crude elaborations of dominance, begin to reveal the ultimate 'silver chain', and that that is why Western women are more concerned than peasant women about the subject. Peasant women may not even question that the reproductive choice at puberty is the only life-choice. In the West it is a paradox that 'freedom' has left the 'puberty trap' relatively unattended. 'Reformed' sexual mores have left choices of pubertal females highly imbalanced *vis-à-vis* those of males.

Yet the dialectic can work in other ways. If the particular effect of the identification of daughters with their mothers introduces a slight disparity between males and females with dangerous possibilities, the identification of fathers with their daughters has its own ambiguous effects. It is often the unexpected source of some female emancipation, providing one reason why changes *do* occur – why, for example, girls' education becomes permitted. Some fathers treat their daughters as surrogate sons. Human love (or ambition) is thus a great emancipator, although the emancipation of daughters in any historical period can expand only as far as the vision of the most indulgent father. It may be that when other historical conditions are favourable, these 'surrogate sons' are poised to be the first to take advantage of them.

It seems that life imposes many kinds of handicaps and disadvantages upon us all, rather like hands of cards for a game we did not choose. Perhaps taking all in all, as far as peasant societies were concerned the supreme importance of progeny and the hard life of everyone in subsistence economies made the power-play of men of little interest and even a thing of fun for women. Perhaps it was the growth of literacy and the storage of information that exaggerated the imparity of the sexes. When the women woke up, the men's game had become a serious matter – they had changed the world. There is surely no need, however, for women to be continuously represented as downtrodden 'invisibles' – a simple mental act of confidence in every situation, as many have discovered, may be all that is required. By something more powerful than that 'bloodless decree' which Engels quaintly imagined to have led to the 'world-historical defeat' of women, both sexes may so act as to reduce each inequality to an imparity, each imparity to an imbalance, and then to dissolve the imbalance into a simple, unmarked, difference. The world would then still contain the empty shells of dominance, but that particular game would be truly over. The problem of dominance within human beings as a whole would not disappear, but perhaps it too would be illuminated.

13
Social Anthropology and the decline of Modernism

The discussion of modernism as a Western cultural movement, expressed in a number of tendencies in art and thought that are now perceived to be in decline or collapse, is widespread in general literary circles. It is, perhaps, dangerous for social anthropologists to intervene, but they have a genuine interest, if only because of the involvement in these developments of some of the theories popular in social anthropology in the last decade or so. At the same time, there has been a trajectory in social anthropology itself which needs a name and which I am prepared to relate to modernism. This paper was originally conceived for a general intellectual audience, and I have delivered its theme to at least one such. I am preserving the somewhat broad-brush treatment, as I do not expect its argument to be other than provisional. I do, however, address some genuinely puzzling matters.[1]

To begin with, something characteristic of the twentieth century, but which derives from the second half of the nineteenth century, *has* been in decline of late – something that can be summarized as a belief in the once-and-for-all distinction between the present age (called 'modern') and the past. Yet, if that something is to be called modernism, there are as many versions of it as there are speakers and subjects. It resembles one of those indigenous concepts with which we are so often concerned in our fieldwork. In the second part of this paper the essentials of a definition of modernism are laid out in the only way possible – by constructing a general pattern from its various expressions in different fields and disciplines. Readers can turn straight to this if they wish. The term is there exemplified, rather than defined, from certain ways in which social anthropology developed. From this it seems clear that 'modernism', if it is applied to social anthropology, has its own particular meaning, and some important discrepancies occur between its understanding there and in neighbouring fields. Perhaps those between social anthropology and literary criticism are most interesting and striking. A main purpose of this paper is to suggest that structuralist approaches which are called 'post-modernism' (i.e. *not* modernism) in literary circles, are far from 'post-modern' in social anthropology, but are a late stage in modernism itself, albeit an interestingly marked one.[2]

No general or consistent definition of Modernism is usually required or offered by those who engage in literary or artistic debate. It would seem on the face of it, therefore, that it is quite hopeless to relate the uses of a term like this to our own aspirations for precision. There are two points to bear in mind here. The first is that it is a well-known feature of social anthropology that its own general ideas also, in fact, lack precision of definition. Over many years of trying to examine what social anthropology is about, I have been forced to the conclusion that there is no account of the intellectual history of social anthropology in the usual terms ('functionalism', 'structural-functionalism', 'structuralism' and so on) that would command universal support.[3] Yet these terms are consistently used. Social anthropology clearly falls into the artistic spectrum in its habits of self-nomenclature. The second point, and it is an explanation of the first, is that social anthropology is part of the movement of 'modernism' itself, and we are both subject and object of any discussion of it. The announcement of functionalism by Malinowski was, as we shall see, a typically modernist act, which leads us to ask how subjects like social anthropology do partake of general social movements. Furthermore, general movements of this kind are ultimately all we have in the way of a past, in the unthinking memories of our successors. In a study of our own society they are the equivalent of our own myths. So any discussion of this subject is related to the history of social anthropology as we live it daily.

'Modernist' declarations always come to us in the quite specific dress of their own subjects or fields, yet there is (underlying all the specificity) a surprising generality of tone, metaphor and expression. For this reason I do not intend to give a definition of 'modernism' now, but to allow its nature to emerge from its appearance in social anthropology. A few points may, however, be anticipated. One is that modernism was a movement of manifestos. Modernists declared new ages, created of new forms, and in some cases the manifestos were themselves all that the new age consisted of. Other movements had previously proclaimed new ages but usually as a restoration of past virtue: the new ages proclaimed by modernism are totally new, and associated with extremely specific technical ends, as we shall see. It 'knows' that there are historical movements, and it undertakes to label new ones in advance, as it were. Not surprisingly, some of them did not 'happen' – another mark of modernism – and that is the reason why there cannot be any definition of it that is based on common content, only one based on common aspirations. It is a myth not a philosophy. Resting as it did on a denial – better, on a superseding – of the past, it is clearly a reflection of the optimistic phase of the scientific, industrial and social revolutions that followed the Enlightenment. This is not the romanticism of the first phase.[4] It is cool, it is rational, it supersedes history but it is the very peak of history, it is active, it is organized, it is able to solve, it is able to redefine – it is indeed the 'very model of a modern Major-General'. Although we should scrutinize carefully the credentials of any movements defined as 'modern', such was the force of the historical tendency that even the weaker brethren were borne up by it. In the words of President Kennedy (a modernist if ever there was one!), 'when the tide comes in even the beached boats are lifted.'

These remarks have not yet provided a definition, but they have touched on the reason why modernism goes undefined: it has for long been the water in which the ordinary intelligentsia, goldfish-like, has swum – and as everyone knows, 'fish are the last to discover water.' I know no better expression of the modernist condition than these words of Ortega y Gassett (who was also an early critic):

The very name is a disturbing one; this time calls itself 'modern'; that is to say, final, definitive, in whose presence all the rest is mere preterite, humble preparation and aspiration towards this present. Nerveless arrows which miss their mark! (1961: 25).[5]

FUNCTIONALISM AND STRUCTURALISM

Let us start with what lies at the heart of modernism in our subject. Malinowski, an Anglicized Pole whose centenary fell in 1984, was associated with the anthropological movement, method, or outlook we know as 'functionalism'. This, I shall propose, is the form that modernism took at its developmental stage in social anthropology. Malinowski was a person of such personal charisma that he was felt by his contemporaries to have invented functionalism. He encouraged this view. Indeed he said:

Let me confess at once: the magnificent title of the Functional School of Anthropology has been bestowed by myself, in a way on myself, and to a large extent out of my own sense of irresponsibility. The claim that there is, or perhaps that there ought to be, a new school based on a new conception of culture and that this school should be called 'functional', was made first in the article s.v. 'Anthropology' in the 13th edition of The Encyclopaedia Britannica (1926). Among the various tendencies of modern anthropology, I there claimed a special place for 'the Functional Analysis of Culture'. And I briefly defined this method as follows: 'This type of theory aims at the explanation of anthropological facts at all levels of development by their function, by the part which they play within the integral system of culture, by the manner in which they are related to each other within the system, and by the manner in which this system is related to the physical surroundings. It aims at the understanding of the nature of culture, rather than at conjectural reconstructions of its evolution or of past historical events.'

I was fully aware then that I was speaking of a New Movement, which hardly existed, and that in a way I was making myself into the captain, the general staff, and the body of privates of an army which was not yet there. The only thing which I can claim in extenuation of this act of self-appointment was that it was not done without some sense of humour.

'Oh, I am the cook and the captain bold,
And the mate of the Nancy brig:
And the bo'sun tight
And the midship mite
And the crew of the captain's gig ...'

(... and, as many of my colleagues would suggest, for the same reason ...) (1932: xxix–xxx).[6]

At this stage functionalism had obviously many idiosyncrasies which were related to the interests of Malinowski as a person. Many of these were discussed by Leach in 1957 and in various writings since (see Jarvie 1963; Leach, Jarvie and Gellner 1966).[7] It takes some delicacy of analysis to sift out its essential features, as we shall see later. For the moment we note only its most striking one – its phenomenal success. Between approximately 1920 and his death in 1942 Malinowski completely rearranged social anthropology, while his pupils occupied a dominant position from 1945 to at least 1970. High-functionalism is the name used here for the period of Malinowski's own activity. The second, post-war period, has come to be known as structural-functionalism, or the period of consensus. The latter had special features which we shall deal with, and it was finally challenged by other views, some short lived (e.g. transactionalism), and one in particular very powerful. This was structuralism, which itself was also an expression of modernism and which passed through its own trajectory of rise and fall, ending in fragmentation among movements of a quasi-structuralist type – structural Marxism, flirtations with hermeneutics and the ideas of Ricoeur, Derrida, Lacan and the like. Most of these interests declined in the later 1970s and with them modernism, which, in the social anthropological sense, is over (see figure 13.1). The rest of this paper is essentially an amplification of this argument.

Of course, the ideas of the period are not, in some simple way, now abolished from the scene. Intellectual movements crystallize in persons and places, countries and university departments. They become embodied or located. They continue their spread to other persons, or places, or into other intellectual fields. Thus the new archaeology has virtually retraced the steps of structuralist anthropology, and although it is a movement of the 1980s, its sources are of the 1950s, 1960s and 1970s.[8] Structuralist anthropology took its own title and early models from the structural linguistics of a generation before that. Indeed Saussure's *Cours*, a nowadays much misunderstood founding text of linguistic structuralism, came into being at the very moment (1916) that functionalism was being gestated in social anthropology. The out-of-phaseness of such developments in different disciplines is commonplace. Yet their actual contemporaneity produces effects that create still more confusion. Thus, anthropological structuralism was affected by the later transformational linguistics of Chomsky, with which it coexisted. The later Lévi-Strauss has thus some obvious affinities with Chomsky, greater in some respects than those with Saussure. The stress on structures located in the mind, and vocabulary of 'transformation', are obvious examples.[9] Similar 'time-warps' occurred as soon as other disciplines in their turn borrowed from Lévi-Strauss, as we shall see.

For non-anthropologists this is confusing, but for anthropologists an additional confusion occurs as a result of receiving echoes at second or third hand from other subjects of its own terms and concepts. It would frequently be better if each new application had a new name, for the ultimate sources

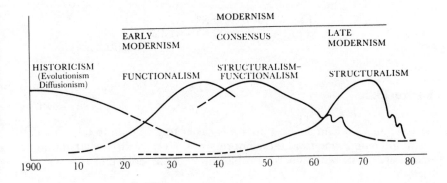

Figure 13.1 Trajectories in British social anthropology

of terms are not in the end irrelevant. Sometimes issues which have been thought through already somewhere else are raised as novelties in one context. They will probably not have been solved, but perhaps clear objections will have emerged that must be taken into account. Some issues may have turned out to be blind alleys. For an example of terminological echoes, consider the following. An article on 'The Post-Structuralist Position of Anthropology' was published in 1978 by Kirsten Hastrup, discussing a paper in which the term had been proposed, which was itself delivered in Oxford by myself in 1973 (see above, chapter 5). Professor Godelier rose at that meeting and announced himself also to be a post-structuralist. The 1973 presenter described the application of the term as part of a technical argument. When Professor McCabe (a literary critic) calls himself a post-structuralist therefore, or when the *Daily Telegraph* attempts to define post-structuralism, we are in a different world.[10]

We have no right to make adverse criticism of this, when we in our turn examine the development of Lévi-Strauss's thought amid the ruins of his often wilful misunderstanding, not only of ethnographic sources, but of a dozen contemporary thinkers; or when Lukes finds the sources for Durkheim's *Elementary Forms of Religious Life* defective, or misconstrued as evidence. Do Durkheim's findings thereby rest on no evidence, or does his 'evidence' no longer matter? To use an idea from the 1973 paper I referred to, we would often be best advised to 'cut the painter' linking us to our stimulating authors, and to let the doomed Titanic steam on its way, while

LIFE

EXPERIENCE → TEXT

TEXT → TEXT

GENRE

Figure 13.2

we row our own course. That advice is easier to give than to take, it would seem: hitching a ride from these impressive vessels is extremely tempting to many, especially when one's own barque is in the doldrums!

GENRE AND LIFE

The development of anthropological ideas is of interest in illuminating this phenomenon. Anthropology at the creative stage consists of the transmuting of a certain kind of experience into a certain kind of text. For a time, only the actual or a similar experience can produce such texts. Later, however, people become skilled in imitating the texts themselves. What was once *life* becomes simply *genre*. Similar processes occur in literature as well as in anthropology – indeed there they are endemic. Thus, although *Jane Eyre*, a great novel which pulsates with its creator's own pugnacious life, remains greater than its shadow, *Rebecca* (or the winner of the Betty Trask Award for romantic novels, or its other ultimate genre successors), many readers can hardly tell the difference, and many will prefer the newer texts. Anthropology passes through this transformation quite commonly. After great innovations even the pupils are great, but soon what once required genius is now performed or 'thought' merely as a matter of professional course. *As experience is made text, life becomes genre.* Within a genre *texts* generate texts. There are therefore two kinds of texts, or texts brought into being in different ways (see figure 13.2).

It is an irony that Lévi-Strauss really did show us how texts create text. He is, we may go so far as to say, the great anthropologist of genre, for The Myth as Text is the very apotheosis of genre. Nevertheless, Myth is, in its oral state, continually restored to life by 'mute inglorious Miltons', and this actual life of myth was inaccessible to much 'cook-book' structuralism that followed Lévi-Strauss's lead. Of course, Lévi-Strauss did fitfully illuminate the other problem, because his texts are after all the brass-rubbings of the ethnographic experience of other ethnographers, of indigenous story-tellers, or of his own; for Lévi-Strauss is still an anthropologist, and *Tristes Tropiques*, for example, is one of the documents of his transmuted experience.

Nevertheless, we know what is meant when it is said that the failure of structuralism was its lack of a practice, or if you like a 'praxis' for social anthropology. It is necessary to add at once that we require something rather more thoroughgoing for a social anthropological practice than for, say, a literary praxis. In so far as he solved, or made trivial, the matter of text generating text, he did produce a praxis for text; and ultimately that is what has sped through literary circles. And why should it not? He himself refers to Dumezil and V. Propp, while the much neglected Czech (or really Slovak) school of folklore analysis had already been influenced by the semiology of Saussure and structural linguistics when Lévi-Strauss was an unknown. Listen to the very titles of Bogatyrev (1931): Prispevek k Strukturalni-etnografii (*Slovenska miscellanea*, Bratislava), or (1935): Funkcno-Strukturalna metoda a ine metody etnografie a folkloristiky (*Slovenske Pohl'ady*). In addition there were other sources, discussed elsewhere.[11] Roland Barthes, for example, was an easier transmitter of structuralism to the thinking masses than was Lévi-Strauss. The canonical bibliography of structuralism (the body of sources Lévi-Strauss and others cited) was also read. Saussure, who is there named as the father of structuralism, is as a result now often termed a structuralist, not at all the same thing. Inevitably those who reject recent movements have turned on Saussure.[12] Piaget termed God a structuralist: so much the worse, perhaps, in due course, for God. The bibliographies were (in any event) read and absorbed. Lévi-Strauss the anthropologist then disappears for practical purposes from literary structuralism.

Although in this way Lévi-Strauss repaid *to* literature what in an important sense he received *from* literature, it is not the case that structuralism as transmitted to literature would have been the same if Lévi-Strauss had never lived. The 'praxis' for text-generation which illuminated criticism received genuine authority, even authenticity, from Lévi-Strauss's treatment of myth. That authority derived from peculiarities of texts that were still only one remove or so from absolute orality, and those 'fitful illuminations' from general anthropology were sufficient to give a kind of generative life to the dead literary texts lying about in library and study. Furthermore, his appropriation of the very term 'structural' for his anthropology, his particular selections from Prague linguistic structuralism for his conception of binary oppositions, his generative terminology, combined with his tremendous *personal* vogue and through it the popularization of all related themes and tendencies, fully establish any claims made on his behalf for responsibility for the literary explosions, however muffled or distant. That vogue supported the simultaneous anthropological discovery of Althusser, Lacan and Derrida. But by the middle 1970s in social anthropology, his home subject, the genuine failure of structuralism had become the chief problem. Its collapse took with it the revisionist Marxism that was associated with it. The rubble buried most of the debate. That was the final collapse of modernism in social anthropology.

MODERNISM

So let us retrace our steps. Can it really be that modernism occupies an almost precisely datable span from 1920 to 1975, as far as social anthropology is concerned? Improbable though it seems, we *can* say that. Anthropological works and anthropological lives are very closely meshed, and are not impossibly numerous, bibliographically or demographically. Malinowski and his generation may have been potential converts to modernism before 1920, and modernism may live on posthumously in plenty of living social anthropologists, but survival is, however, not as widespread as might be imagined. It is hard for social anthropologists to think against the grain of experience, and you can see ideas die among them, rather as if a light has been switched off. Other lights may be working, but the modernist switch *is* off.

And who switched it on? Was it Malinowski? We can say that it was, because other possible actors were very thin on the ground. Although it is often important to look behind the man who receives the credit to the man who really caused it all, there are not many candidates on the ground for the role of *éminence grise* for Malinowski – at least not in social anthropology. In his retrospective *Encyclopaedia Britannica* article (1926a) Malinowski looked back to 1910 as the year of great changes, thereby tactfully dating the break to before his own fieldwork in the Trobriands (although in fact to the year of his own arrival at the London School of Economics). He singled out Seligman, his professor in London, as well as others, naming works published just before, during and after 1910, such as Frazer's *Totemism and Exogamy*, Seligman on the *Melanesians of British New Guinea*, Seligman's monograph with his wife on the Veddas, Van Gennep's *Rites de Passage*, Lévy-Bruhl and Boas on the mentality of primitive man, Rivers on diffusionism and evolutionism, and Thurnwald's various works; while Durkheim, in 1912, brought out *Elementary Forms of Religious Life*.

We now know a good deal more about the influences on Malinowski than we did. Durkheim played his role, no doubt. We have probably underestimated the quiet influence of Seligman in general. His interest in psychoanalysis, for example, has often been noted. Without Malinowski something might have started just the same. But surely the Seminar would not have come into existence – the concentration of anthropological talent in that way, time and place? Many have regretted some aspects of the posthumous effect of Malinowski's ascendancy – myself among them (see above, chapter 1, p. 37) – but a failure of Malinowski to appear on the scene would have redistributed our past in such personal ways that we cannot say *it* would have happened anyway. The *it* in question is, as usual in anthropology, not a school of abstract thought, but a particular way of interpreting experiences. The anthropologists *are* the thought of their discipline in a very direct way, that has an immediate bearing on Malinowski's role in founding functionalism or, what in the present context I will now call early modernist social anthropology. Even today it is very difficult to make comments on the period without biography being brought into the issue by those who knew Malinowski. Leach, Gellner and Jarvie (1966); Kuper (1973); and the early memorialists of the *Man and Culture* volume, valuably illustrate or discuss this feature. Yet in many ways it is all out of proportion, one feels. As Winston Churchill said of the great Midland King Offa: 'in studying [him] we are like geologists who instead of finding a fossil find only the hollow shape in which a creature of unusal strength and size undoubtedly resided' (Churchill 1956: 67). One cannot be happy with that void. Fortunately we can now see that prophetic situations express themselves in exactly that way. What was happening was what I have already called a rearrangement. One can describe the arrangement before the change began and the new arrangement when it was complete, but the rearranging itself stretches language to describe it (see above, chapter 9). The Seminar, we may independently conclude, really was as important as the memorialists all assert. Seminars can be created or imitated from each other, just as texts are. The Malinowski Seminar was (to appropriate our earlier terminology) evidently the Seminar as Life, not the Seminar as Genre.

The feeling of fulfilment lasted twenty years, or probably less. Malinowski went to the United States in 1938, never to return, but the magic space was held steady for long enough for us to see that it was the vessel whereby modernism entered the subject. We shall not be surprised if anthropological Modernism took on a particular experiential shape as a result. I will accept the objection in advance that we do not know that it was 'modernism' that entered, or (despite this paper) that there is something called 'modernism' that could 'enter'. With an admirable provisionality I will speak only *as if* both these things are possible, giving grounds for so proceeding.

The condition that social anthropology passed through was analogous to that of other disciplines, some early, some late, in the last part of the nineteenth century and the first part of the twentieth century. Freud, Keynes, Einstein, Saussure, Picasso, Corbusier, effected obvious changes in psychiatry, economics, physics, linguistics, art and architecture, while in English literature alone there came a row of famous figures – for example, Joyce, Eliot, D. H. Lawrence, the Bloomsburies. There is a *prima facie* case for linking together the phenomena that occurred with the appearance of these and other names. We shall not be surprised that there is overlap, and time-lag – such that for some fields the moment is earlier, for some others later. We shall be strongly tempted (as others have been) to place Marx in the sequence. He would be very early, and he may well have lasted longest.

The first point about modernism is precisely its expropriation of modernity. No rivals were tolerated during its reign. Consider the paradox that as late as 1980, in almost all fields, the term 'modern' was used of events and ideas whose beginning lay in the nineteenth century. Can you imagine 'modern art' being generally used in 1880 of the art of Ingres, or the 'modern novel' of the novels of Fielding? The nineteenth century was a truly modern age; the twentieth century was modern only 'as genre', and so (appropriately) 'modernist'. Modern architecture (coyly called *moderne*) thus came to stalk the land for long after its naive, Jaeger-clad, bicycle-riding, ocean-liner-obsessed founders had vanished. That image is a reminder that functionalism was one of the *moderne* notions – common to the architect Corbusier and to Malinowski. It is hard for us nowadays to recall that 'functional' was then a resonant word – everywhere from engineering to biology to architecture to mathematics. *Isms* too are in themselves marks of the *moderne* – that is the declaring of *isms*. On the wilder shores of the *moderne* – (as in *avant-garde* art) the *isms* notoriously multiply and subdivide. We should already suspect on *a priori* grounds any conscious anthropological *ism* like functionalism of expressing *modernitas*, while Malinowski's own contemporaries quite explicitly saw his role as equivalent to that of the great modernists already listed. In 1938, the now exiled Freud recorded the visit of Malinowski to Belsize Park to present his respects.

A second feature of the modern in the entry period in most areas of thought is that the initial innovation was seen as *technical*. This is very interesting in the light of later developments, but all the moderns have this in common: a *perceived* change of technique, however trivial. They pioneered the use of steel and concrete, or streams of consciousness, or psychoanalysis, or new geometries, or palette-knives, or the dialectic, or the film-documentary, or description, or synchronics, or context of situation, or ethnography, and so into the world of Malinowski's own anthropological contribution to the *moderne*.

Let us now summarize some of these features.

MALINOWSKI'S MODERNISM

The Appropriation of the Modern

This goes without saying, from the tone of Malinowski's writings and that of his successors. 'Modern' social anthropology dates from him, still, sixty years on.

The Declaration of the 'ism'

This modernistic feature has the effect of consciously placing the label before the event. This development was, in modernism, parasitical on philosophies of historical progress, in which styles of the past in thought or taste received labels; the future received its labels in advance. The modern is thus a kind of appropriated future. If it is required to select one central aspect of modernism, this must be the one. The collapse of modernism is inevitably perceived as the collapse of the future.

Functionalism – the Label

I will add here only the point that the term implied the definition of parts by wholes, rather than the reverse. Holism, and Gestalt psychology were current at the time. Linguistics also introduced the idea in a specific way, through Saussure. His successors (contemporary with Malinowski and *his* successors) were of course known as structural linguists. Since we shall need to ask later whether structuralism in anthropology is different from, or part of, modernism, it is important to note that structuralism embodied very clearly, from the beginning, ideas that functionalism (because of its idiosyncrasies) expressed only in strangely muffled ways.

The Technical Advance

1 The method of participant observation was understood as the intervention of the social anthropologist at a point in time and a point in space (or a fixed time in a limited space), in which he or she behaved like an ideal metering device. This process raised the question of what was to be metered. The picture of the space-time process as a kind of flow was quite common among thinking people. The elements that flowed could be concretized as statistical parameters of notionally infinite kinds. The anthropologist cut these parameters in space and time at point S. The model resulting is the cruciform ('Christmas Card') one shown in figure 13.3. Malinowski's observer thus stumbled on the notion of the synchronic system. The idea has strong parallels with the presentation of Saussure, who illustrates the idea of the transect very well. The links with Malinowski are indirect – through the *moderne*. The interest in the synchronic is concretized in the artistic and literary movement through a rejection of a certain

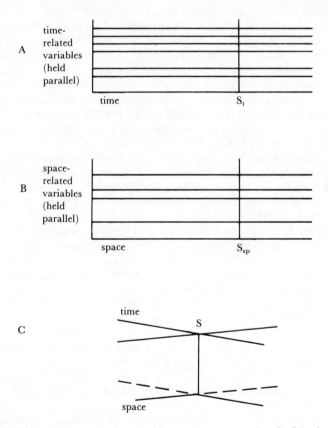

Figure 13.3 The participant anthropologist at point S. Ideal model

kind of history, and the discovery of holistic function in the present. *Joyce's 'Bloomsday' in 1904 is of the same substance, intellectually, as Malinowski's Trobriands.*

2   *The units.* Malinowski did give names to the units in the flow of society: his 'institutions' – hypostatized reifications borrowed from the historicist pre-decessors. His early explanations of them as expressions of 'bodily needs', derives from the evolutionist nature of Malinowski's early thinking. The headings in his note-books were not really the names of concrete 'institutions', but analytical classifications, and the success of the new fieldwork was a result of the examination of the conflict of classifications (actors' and observer's). The synchronic system was thus discovered (if you like) for the wrong reasons, with misplaced concreteness being attributed to the units. These hidden features were made explicit only much later by structuralism and its congeners.

3   *Representativeness ignored.* Functionalism never answered the question why representativeness was not apparently critical to the 'truth' of anthropology. This is the basic paradox of the subject. In Malinowski's time the problem could be avoided by the assumption that the 'distributions' in figure 13.3 were parallel in time and space. This would mean that in a primitive tribe neither a change in space nor a change in time would greatly affect the observing process – an astonishing assumption on the face of it. Yet it embodied quite widespread and tautological assumptions about what is now called the Third World. While every item of classification in the study of the 'First World' was delicately and finely cut, the tropics and other exotic areas were perceived in much broader and clumsier categories. They had 'climate' (stable, large-scale), while we had 'weather' (fine-grained, unpredictable). Spatial variables were seen as relatively massive in scale, so that variation over a territory (sampling in space) was not 'seen' as finely critical. As for representativeness in time, the picture may be quickly blocked in. 'History' had shown that present-day primitives were broadly classifiable with ancient peoples, or peoples reported by the ancients. There was thus the possibility of several thousand years of broad stability. Why not, therefore, tens of thousands, or a hundred thousand years of stability? The gap between today and 100,000 years ago was not perceived as great. This was related to the general 'broadening' of categories where the Third World was concerned. All this stands out clearly in Malinowski's early views of the supposed Trobriand (and 'primitive') ignorance of physiological paternity. At the beginning, there seems to be no doubt that he really thought that there was a survival of 'primaeval' ignorance. Later he back-pedalled vigorously. Now, of course, we may have two million years of hominid 'symbolic' activity, and the timelessness of the primitive has no pseudo-historical support. Meanwhile the whole issue of 'knowledge' and 'ignorance' has been more carefully discussed – indeed in the third edition of *The Sexual Life of Savages*, Malinowski himself already makes many of the relevant points.

4 *Primitivism.* All of the preceding discussion can be contained in the fact that the 'primitive' was, when Malinowski received it, already a notion defined in the West by stability and wholeness. Here the links with the general ideas of the *moderne* are quite direct. The 'Negro Art' phase, and the obsession with the primitive of most of the figures of the modern age is easily documented (consider only Picasso, D. H. Lawrence, Jacob Epstein, even E. M. Forster, and in other ways Freud and the psychoanalysts.) Malinowski's work was just what was required – a modern primitivism for modern people. We may note that the primitive, for the *moderne*, was seen as unhypocritical, in touch with the natural, and at home with the erotic. It is no surprise therefore that, as Leach says (Leach, Jarvie and Gellner 1966), *The Sexual Life of Savages* was the work by which Malinowski became most widely known among the lay adherents of the *moderne*.

5 *Field fact.* It is as well to remind ourselves that anthropology is not primarily concerned to produce intellectual or artistic movements – or so its practitioners assume. Anthropology must be perceived in some sense to work. The idea of a method that would place the study at 'point S' at the centre of the universe would not have been enough if it had not apparently worked. The new functionalist fieldwork was begun when the primitives themselves were politically and physically accessible. Classical fieldwork was done under peculiar conditions that led the synchronic approach to appear to be a perfect fit to the facts. The societies studied were unnaturally peaceful. They were held in a ring, in which conflicts were minimized under colonial rule. If the anthropologists entered, the place was stable. In addition, administrators of the liberal as well as the illiberal kinds were modern-primitivists. They shared with their age the belief that primitives were changeless. Customs were codified, murders and violence were punished, conflicts arbitrated, anthropologists were permitted, and change was shunted off into the towns. The stability lasted for about twenty years. As we have seen, the assumptions about the anthropologist metering life at 'point S', were dependent on the hypothesized transsection cutting through distributions that were parallel. Lo! When anthropologists' studies were made, the distributions *were* parallel! Primitive stability, so long posited, was given concrete form in the colonial territories. Functionalism in its simplest form worked.

6 *Unexpected results.* In sum, Malinowski's technical innovation was successful by a kind of Koestlerian sleep-walking. The idea of parts being informed by the whole really required a theory of opposition and system. The synchronic study of institutions required a theory of classifications. The timelessness of anthropological results derived from a theory of the synchronic yet to be appreciated. Misplaced concreteness reached its limits with the pseudo-timelessness of colonial, or colonialized, societies. In the post-war period the latter point occupied theorists as varied as Leach, Gluckman and Worsley. By then the real world was on the move again.[13]

We see then that the technical advance that functionalism represented, its conscious self-definition, and its appropriation of the future as well as of the past, make it a fairly typical example of the early modernist stream in the thought of the age. Characteristically, in anthropology this stream enters through a particular biographical experience and somewhat idiosyncratic procedures. A real novelty was however introduced, which resulted from the unexpected *kinds* of experience involved. In so far as there is, or will be, a post-*moderne*, it will be from that novelty that it will emerge. Fieldwork was, as it turned out, ontologically timeless: 'the Nuer', not 'the Nuer in 1936'. The discovery of a social time outside time was the paradoxical result of the apparently technical advance – one that ironically laid great stress on 'real time', in long periods of fieldwork.

The post-war period was post-functionalist in the sense that it was an 'unpacking' of the implications of functionalism. The entry of large numbers of new practitioners of social anthropology gave the period a special quality.[14] It came to be called structural-functionalist, but it is the middle period of modernism in social anthropology, called here consensus modernism. Its particular nature derived from the idiosyncrasy of early modernism, which had been incarnated, rather than argued, into existence. Malinowski had stamped it with a charismatic status that was felt by all his pupils. In a way, structural-functionalism was a retrospective re-theorizing, a dropping of the personal history of the founder. It was unfortunate that this took time and involved the famous time-lag.

By the time the 'charisma was routinized', anthropologists were looking back to ideas of the pre-war period in linguistics, science and philosophy. The result was a rapid ingesting of everything the subject had missed in the intervening years – a linking up of anthropological modernism with its more advanced versions in general thought. That is when the new anthropologists came on the scene (see above, chapter 2 and Kuper 1973). It seems clear to me now that their ideas (for example, those of Lévi-Strauss, Douglas or Leach) represented the final recognition that the Malinowskian sychronicities were conceptual. It was recognized at the time, and since, that the non-French new anthropologists were propounding something in some way 'like' the structuralism of Lévi-Strauss, to which all were to some degree attracted.[15] As a result the whole period can be seen to be linked up with the fate of structuralism – the theme with which I began this paper.

We have now confronted the question of whether structuralism was the expected end of the *moderne* or merely its final efflorescence. It is easy to see how there have been conflicting conclusions. By 1960 the post-war consensus (what we may call the conservative rethinking) in social anthropology was eroding rapidly. By 1970 there were no cogent defences for the many omissions of structural-functionalism. The fervour at the student and public level that the new anthropology (what we may call the radical rethinking) produced had all the marks of a genuine change. Yet there were already surprising counter-indications. For example, Malinowski's functionalism had succeeded in wiping out the old historicist anthropology, and had restocked the profession for forty years, entirely within ten or fifteen years of activity. Lévi-Strauss's major work starts in the 1940s, yet structuralism did not take off until the 1960s. It is in a significant sense over by 1975, to be followed by its heir, structural Marxism, within a short time. As for restocking the profession, go to the ASA and *si monumentum requieris circumspice*! High-structuralism, then, came as 'a witness to the light but was not that light.'[16]

In brief, it was because structuralism represented a consumption of anthropological texts, rather than a creation of them, that it can be shown to be an end rather than a beginning. Anthropology not as life, but as genre. Hence the (for some) alarming slither into literary trendiness, that eventually led the original new anthropologists (even at times Lévi-Strauss himself) to begin that train of recantations that, by the end of the 1970s, merged with the queue of recantations from all the other branches of the *moderne*, in their kinds, and in their various garbs. The euphoria of the final period becomes more explicable as a phenomenon when one takes into account its incidence in time. In the intellectual archaeology of the *moderne*, in every field, at a point in the stratification, a line of ash occurs marking the 1960s like the traces of a wild consuming fire, just before the levels peter out. Each is a final effect of the substitution of genre for life in its own particular field. That must help to confirm the general conclusion that structuralism in social anthropology was a part of modernism not a 'postmodernism', and that it will turn out to be so in other fields (such as literary criticism) there can be no doubt. Meanwhile, social anthropology came of scientific age unnoticed by many in neighbouring disciplines, and indeed by many of its junior and senior practitioners, as a rather narrow but understandable concern with the career structure engaged their attention. But its period of 'de-modernization' has revealed that it was not only 'modernism' that entered in 1920. The anthropological method is seen to be concerned with the life of structures, as we have heard from the beginning.

We have been discussing the decline of modernism. That does not mean, let me emphasize with all energy, the decline of social anthropology. The fact is that to be a modernist is now to be backward-looking. Its expropriation of the future has led only to a number of undesirable conditions in the present. Of late, various forms of structuralism (even the misunderstood 'post-structuralism') have been belatedly announced as expressions of 'postmodernism' by various writers. My aim has been to suggest that that cannot be the case for social anthropology, which has some interest in these terms. The epistemological break that structuralism represented compared with functionalism, was for our subject (as we can now see) a subsidiary although important one. More controversially, I am of the opinion that Marxism, even in its various revisionist forms, is for social anthropology also a phase of modernism. I should also make clear to non-anthropologists, especially, that my analysis of the colonial phase of primitivism should not be taken to apply to the present state of social anthropological thought. Modernism, early, middle or late, is a set of ideas and concepts that derive from the folk-thought of the industrial countries in the era of the expanding world. A subject that is concerned with the world as experienced by all its inhabitants in their various cultural modalities will generate its own valid approaches. To that degree, social anthropology is already post-modernist – if it matters. But to demonstrate it would be another lecture. Meanwhile, we recognize the role of Malinowski, the extraordinary man who opened social anthropology to modernism, while providing it ultimately with powerful tools for the criticism of modernism itself – for a return, indeed, from genre to life.

SOME RESPONSES TO QUESTIONS

I have been invited for the published version to expand upon certain ·positions sketched above. This is not a conventional history of social anthropology (for that we should look to the writings of scholars such as Stocking or Urry). I should also like to retain some of its interest for a more general audience. I therefore make a few additional remarks here.

1   As far as Malinowski is concerned, I have since been present at a paper given by J. Jerschina at Krakow on 27 September 1984, entitled 'Polish Modernism and Malinowski's Personality'. For Jerschina, 'Polish Modernism' is a phase that extends from 1885 to 1914, and is associated with the 'Young Poland' movement. Malinowski, who took his doctorate at Krakow in 1906, was associated with thinkers of this group. Such a ready confirmation of the argument of this paper is not unwelcome, but it brings its own problems. For Polish 'modernism' was a 'self-declared' literary grouping which was somewhat 'out-of-phase' with ideas contemporary with it in the West. It retained in particular strong romantic leanings, looking back to Mickiewicz and others; it was (like all Polish movements) much concerned with the national consciousness. It exemplifies at the same time a constant symptom of modernism: a pessimism about the (*really* modern) nineteenth-century civilization that it actually inherited. Nevertheless, a feature of Malinowski's work, which is in a way almost his hallmark – his mode of expression – seems strangely in tune with the 'neo-romantic' shade that Jerschina demonstrates in Polish modernism. The modernism that I discuss is evidently a much broader phenomenon than the limited Polish literary modernism. It is, nevertheless, somewhat paradoxical that Malinowski's characteristic trademark – his style and self-presentation – should probably derive from this 'smaller' modernism, while I would credit him with the feat of introducing social anthropology into modernism at large. This usefully illustrates the way that modernism 'lifted all the boats', and provides a good example of the complex way that ideas and actions fit together (Ardener 1970c).

Malinowski's achievement, I have continually argued, was effected in too short a time for it to have been entirely personal. It was a spark to the tinder. He did not come to London until 1910. He was out of England by 1914. On his return from the Trobriands he stayed in Tenerife until the publication of *Argonauts of the Western Pacific*. When appointed to his London post (after toying with returning to the Jagellonnian University at Krakow) he spent the vacations in the South Tyrol. He was on sabbatical at least once in the early 1930s, and he went to the United States in 1938. We may speculate why the modernization of British social anthropology did not occur elsewhere in the country. Malinowski's very foreignness may have made him ready to attract (in the best sense) 'all and sundry', from all disciplines and from the newer countries of the world, without passing through the traditional British university establishments. The rather narrow intellectual range of structural-functionalism, which some later complained of, may have been a price paid for this.[17]

2   Did structuralism mark the end of modernism, or was it the beginning of something new? In declaring that it was indeed an end, I need to point only to some predisposing features (apart from the general arguments already raised). One is that despite the flexible, and at times inchoate nature of Lévi-Strauss's theories, there has been a clear limit to the degree of development allowed in them by the master and his followers. Few clarifications have been accepted or revisions made. A second is the suspicious rapidity with which structuralism has become naturalized in the study of text, including literary text. I have put it elsewhere in the form: 'structuralism stumbled upon the homology between society and text, but developed no theory to account for it' (see above chapter 11). Third (and connected with the last point), there was no evidence of any difference in fieldwork method that is primarily due to structuralism. If there have been any changes they are not structuralist. They lie in reflexive 'personal anthropologies', or in various fields classed generally as semantic (Crick 1976; Parkin 1982), or the like. The rediscovery of woman owes nothing to it. The improvement in the perception of the place of language perhaps owes more to the 'correctors' of Lévi-Strauss than to structuralism as received. Structuralism did not therefore become an *anthropological* practice.

3   Structuralist-Marxism became a substitute for structuralism for many in the 1970s for a number of reasons, among which the most satisfactory was its apparent provision of the missing 'praxis'. The material world was apparently placed in a causal relationship to the structural phenomena. The problem was that structuralism 'idealized' Marxism, and not that Marxism 'materialized' structuralism. Godelier is thus more interesting when elucidating the origins in geology of Marx's idea of a 'social formation', than he is when arguing the material bases of the social formations themselves. The 'arrows of materiality' were so redefined, 'modes of production' were so re-conceptualized, that we may say that materiality itself became 'text'.

4   The social space is inherently neither materialist nor idealist. Materiality is perceived by certain processes which themselves exhibit quasi-statistical features (see above, chapter 11). The whole is a 'simultaneity'. In

dividing up the simultaneity it is easy for theoreticians mistakenly to separate out an infinity of *conceptual* levels while leaving only one level for materiality. It is the nature of the simultaneity that (figuratively) if a tooth aches in one dimension it will ache in fifteen dimensions. Materiality does not gently fade or attenuate through the levels (so that ultimately only a sensitive princess would feel it like a pea hidden beneath the mattress). The converse is, of course, that *no level of materiality is free from conceptualization.* There are therefore no arrows of causation. Marxism can hardly be radical enough for us, therefore. It is surely enough to recognize its status as a part of modernism. It bears all the stigmata of being the ultimate modernism of modernisms: its appropriation of all futures and all pasts, its technological or scientific aspirations, its definition of other modernisms and its absorption of them to itself, its ultimate irrealism in the literal sense, together with the exaggerated synchronic equilibrium imposed upon the societies in which it is the defining philosophy – all these, combined with the historical period of its development, would suggest that we are in the presence of an archetype of modernism. Politically the statement 'Marxism: the highest stage of capitalism' is thus quite unparadoxical. Its continuous success in inspiring bureaucracies and elites to greater and more rigid technical control makes it the epitome of the transmutation of the life of politics into genre.

5   The 'epistemological break' in social anthropology that occurred with structuralism is genuine enough (see above, chapter 2), but it did not *belong* to structuralism. My analysis at the time of the new anthropology noted most of the problematic features that I refer to in this paper. Perhaps, it would be simpler to express the matter so: high-structuralism and its congeners were *expressions* of the break. Late modernism is thus the disintegration of modernism: that 'consuming fire', to which I refer in the paper itself. The situation after the break is still in process in the wide real world. For reasons I have already touched on, the fact that social anthropology was already transformed by the experience of multiplicity in the world has made it accidentally one of the branches of knowledge most prepared to experience the enormous conceptual changes that are involved.

6   In an earlier lecture (see above, chapter 9) I referred in more detail to the 'stretching' of Western language by the rapid territorial expansion that took place in the age of discovery. It is a characteristic of our present situation that the 'deconstruction' of those 'stretched' (but still Western) concepts should be necessary to accommodate the hitherto unaccommodated cultural representations of the muted majority of the world. So the movements connected with language and relativism were therefore the true motors of the epistemological break in social anthropology. The proper expression of the principles involved has always been a grumbling controversy in social anthropology. The trajectory of that controversy points beyond modernism.

7   The trajectory for modernism in British social anthropology happens to be very clear, but it is part of other trajectories even in anthropology. Thus the line for American cultural anthropology shows fewer breaks, its theoretical horizons are broader; but this is not the place to multiply these diagrams. The representation of anthropology as text has also emerged there in distinguished forms, chiefly through Geertz. The main neglected issue is, of course, the theoretical source of the homology with text. Its neglect has led to the results that we see in the condition of European literary criticism, for which we (in our innocence) are partly responsible.

8   The omission of Radcliffe-Brown and other major figures from my account: this is because Radcliffe-Brown for me represents the course of British social anthropology if Malinowski had decided to accept the Krakow appointment in 1922, and had not politically survived. Put in that way, it is no denigration of Radcliffe-Brown to say that whatever that unrealized future would have been like, it would have lacked certain positive features. We may on the other side hazard a guess that the long structural-functional consensus would not have occurred or would have broken up earlier.

9   A word on Ortega is necessary. He exemplifies the problem of the critic who writes during the period that he criticizes. The saddest feature is the initial optimism of such a critic. Ortega wished to supersede the nineteenth century, which he saw as complacently 'modern'. His critical account of his own age of mass man (1930, 1961) is in fact a penetrating attack on modernism, but he wrongly thought that the age would be over more quickly than could possibly have happened, as if his perception would dissolve it. On the contrary, by 1955, the date of his death, the victory of its ideas was total and at its height. Ortega's initial perception of modernism came through a demographic apprehension: of the sudden appearance of 'masses' of a new kind of people. This image has weakened the proper appreciation of his criticism, for he is describing an intellectual phenomenon, or better, a cultural representation, of tremendous power. The feeling of 'mass' is a by-product, not a cause. In fact, as we know, the individuals in the 'mass' have remained remarkably 'un-modernized'. The perception of peoples as 'mass' is (on the contrary) a key feature of modernism. Ortega's recognition of this is thus ambiguously expressed, because he had no other language than that of modernism in which to express his perception. Analogously, a critic of modernism in the late 1960s might surely have hoped that a newer language was now available. But such critics were themselves overwhelmed by the appropriation of all forms of criticism itself by the hallucinating offspring of late modernism. So once more the time-scale was extended. Yet cases like that of Ortega offer encouragement also. The underlying ambiguities of 1930 now appear to be the main statements, while his own historical period instead of being more apparent, has become irrelevant. It *was* possible to see the invisible, after all. Ironically, Ortega's most apparently 'loony' idea, the unification of

Europe, came to partial fruition in his time, although in totally modernist form.

10   A final word on the apparent autonomy of ideas and their arbitrariness. We have been looking at a set of cultural predispositions which work themselves out at all levels. These predispositions are a class of phenomena that may be given various names ('templates', *p*-structures', are two that have been proposed). They are neither 'infrastructural' nor 'superstructural': their precise realizations are dependent on the contingencies of the time (Ardener, E. 1970c, and above, chapter 5). Their autonomy is therefore an 'optical illusion'. Their arbitrariness of expression is the *result* of their lack of autonomy. Once again we are not in an 'idealist' space.

11   What of the current renewal of the debate on rationality? The rationality of human systems of thought was a topic of discussion in the 1960s associated with Winch, Jarvie, Beattie and many others, in the period of the collapse of structural-functionalism. Yet again it emerged this year, in almost the same terms. Before that, in the dawn of modernism, the intellectualism of Tylor and Frazer had proposed the same issues. In the hiccup between early and middle modernism in social anthropology, Bateson's *Naven* had raised similar questions. We may be tempted to say that this 'skirmish between the lines' (see above, chapter 2, p. 46) recurs at every 'epistemological break' in social anthropological thought. It may more mundanely express the unsolved question of how anthropology can ever be 'logically' possible within the vocabulary provided by the present age.

14
'Remote areas' –
some Theoretical Considerations

I hope that this title will be pleasantly misleading. I have gone behind the theme of this conference, to the idea of places, or peoples, or locations, that anthropologists have considered to be 'fit' for their study. For, if there is anything controversial about the idea of the social anthropologist working at home, or relatively near home, it is because some may fear that the very nature of the subject may be thereby transformed out of all recognition. There is clearly something in the idea that distance lends enhancement, if not enchantment, to the anthropological vision. Yet work in Europe, for example, has clearly yielded results of great general interest. This paper therefore starts from a deliberately obscure and ill-defined term: 'remote'. I choose it from the natural language, and show that in an anthropological sense it can be 'unpacked' in rather striking ways. This paper is related to my basic theoretical papers on the nature of the social space (see above, chapters 5 and 9). I shall refer to the new concept of 'event density' or 'event richness', which (since the space is analysable at all levels in essentially the same way) is the event-homologue of the phenomenon of 'semantic density' described in the concluding parts of my recent paper on social anthropology and reality (see above, chapter 11, part 2). 'Semantic density' is a statistical feature, at the point where definition and measurement intersect and collapse together. We have a number of difficult paths leading away from us, so let us start.[1]

THE PROBLEM OF IDENTITY

It will be no surprise that interest in 'minorities', 'embedded groups', 'plural societies' and the like, has led to problems of definition. The term 'ethnicity' was a useful step on the road, which produced its own difficulties. The resort to 'identity', as a term, was an attempt to restore the self-definitional element that seemed to be inherent in the idea of 'ethnicity', but which was shared by entities other than ethnicities as normally conceived – many kinds of entities have identities. As far as 'minorities' are concerned, majorities are just as important for our comprehension of this problem. We know (at least since Ferguson in 1767) that the definition of entities by mutual (binary) opposition is part of the point.[2] There is always the danger, however, that we may run the risk of so relativizing the distinction that we forget the original problem. The excellent volume called *Belonging* (Cohen 1982) has a title from a fuzzy part of the English lexicon which leaves all options open.

Let me remind you of the statement, that 'among the many things that society *is* or *is like*, it *is* or *is like* identity' (Ardener, E. and Ardener, S. 1965). The social is, in virtue of its categorizing and classifying structures, a space that 'identifies'. It is a chief source of any concept that we may severally have of identity. That there is a multiplicity of identities that coexist from any single perspective is not strictly speaking a problem theoretically. It is one of the proofs – and one of the costs – of the apparent paradox of the continuity between the space and individuals that constitute it. They are defined by the space and are nevertheless the defining consciousnesses of the space.

We hear now a great deal about 'reflexivity'. Before that word loses its concreteness, let us remember that (to state it oversimply) our heads are full of categories generated by the social, which we project back upon the social. Perhaps, in the 'normal course of events' (as we put it), the 'native actor' does not perceive this interaction, for the social space is not for him or her an 'object', except intermittently. For the non-native social anthropologist the act of interacting with an alien social space, even relatively successfully, forms the basis of that 'daily experience of *mis*understanding' (at not only the ethnographic level but the theoretical level) which is the undoubted source of our greater readiness to see the space as object (of study),[3] and thus, like Durkheim, to see 'social facts as things'. To treat the social space as object is almost literally child's play, when it is located in unfamiliar scenes and is already, in any case, predefined as 'other' in relation to our own world. 'Reflexivity' has become a popular, as opposed to a specialist, term in social anthropology as those conditions have changed. The task has not changed, however, save in that the individual/social interaction must be more minutely scrutinized. The currency of the term arises from an increase in theoretical awareness. It will no doubt acquire soft-centred connotations and be abandoned as the situation which produced it becomes commonplace. Nevertheless, it should not be confused with 'subjectivity'.

There was a time when the relativity of cultural categories was raised to a philosophical bogey as 'relativism'. Anthropology then was discovering a mismatch between the categories of the observer and those generated by the purported object – other people. When the differences are more subtle, the gap is narrower between these two; the mismatch is virtually simultaneous. Since mismatch *is* our experience of relativity, then the reduction of 'transmission time' (between the observer and the purported object) and the narrowing of the mismatch (between the categories of the observer and the other), demonstrates that the process that we first called relativization is *not* a form of anti-objectivity, but (as its applicaton to 'familiar' experience more clearly shows) is on the contrary our only mode of objectivization. This is quite an important theoretical proof of what has for social anthropologists been intuitively sensed, and it will be illustrated in the treatment that follows.[4]

REMOTENESS: SOME PHENOMENOLOGY

After these essential preliminaries, I start here from another English term: 'remote'. For the moment it has no theoretical taint (sadly we may change that situation). I wish, by using it, to recapture the feature that started the personal interest of many anthropologists in their traditional areas of study. Elsewhere, I have pointed out that, for Europe, 'remote areas' of the globe have had a different conceptual geography, and have been perceived to exist on a different time-scale from the 'central' areas (see above, chapters 9 and 13). But we are not now opening up a familiar 'centre/periphery' discussion – if only for the reason that most such discussion depends on an acceptance of known centres with known peripheries. On the contrary, the age of discovery showed us that the 'remote' was actually compounded of 'imaginary' as well as 'real' places; yet they were all of equal conceptual reality or unreality before the differences were revealed. 'Brazil', 'California', 'India', 'Africa', 'Libya', 'Ethiopia' – all were to one extent or other imagined (names ransacked from various sources), yet all were located eventually in limited and specific places.[5] Occasionally we are conscious of a loss. Almost the most imaginary of all: the Antipodes (once the outlet of the Celtic Other World, and a home of King Arthur), and Australia (Terra Australis), are now almost the most mundane of all.[6] On the other hand, and conversely, pockets of imaginary places have remained still unrealized within the European centre. When the far Antarctic was made real, Brittany and the Gaels were still 'unrealized', still 'removed' from the canons of Western realities, or indeed *remote* (Latin *removeo*). In the West we are 'space specialists': we easily realize our conceptual spaces as physical spaces – for that is, in many respects, the European theme. 'Remote' areas are, for us, conventionally physically removed, but this obscures the conceptual phenomena associated with 'remoteness', which are real enough for biological anthropologists (for example) to perceive commuter-ridden villages of Otmoor (5–10 miles from Oxford) as 'remote'.

Let me begin from a naive point of view, with a little personal anthropology. The fact has frequently been noted that the discipline of social anthropology itself belongs to a part of the 'academic vocabulary' that is concerned with marginality, regarded from a Western perspective. In that sense, anywhere an anthropologist chooses to go is likely to show the quality I have just called 'remoteness'. There are, however, interesting nuances. I went first to the Ibo of Southern-Eastern Nigeria. It had, however, been expected that I would go to the Plateau area of Central-Northern Nigeria. I had read all the available literature on the many peoples of that zone at the International African Institute in Waterloo Place, guided by the quizzical attentions of Miss Barbara Pym, the then unpublished novelist, who was then embarking on her own peculiar fieldwork.[7] In the event, the Nigerian government vetoed the worker who was going to the Ibo, and I went there instead. I did not personally like the change, for various reasons, and strangely the Ibo never came to seem 'remote' to me. The Plateau certainly *had* seemed so. It was not that the Ibo were lacking in conventionally exotic features. In fact, no people were more 'anthropological' or 'ethnographical' in other ways than the Ibo, but they never fitted the qualities I now examine in retrospect as 'remote'. Of course, once there, parts of Ibo country began themselves to acquire the purely topographical characteristics of 'remoteness' – places more than walking distance, then more than cycling distance, then places in the North and North-West of the area. Nevertheless, I now see that the Ibo were, in the particular sense I am trying to unpack, essentially definers of remoteness in *others*, although with normally unperceived pockets of internal remoteness – in a way, rather like England itself. Indeed, taken as a whole, Southern Nigeria has that quality, compared with certain other African countries. For the moment I am merely trying to pinpoint the quality; what I mean may become clearer when one opposes Nigeria to the Cameroons, which are, in contrast, commonly experienced as 'remote' – not only by me, but by almost everyone who visits the country, and it retains this quality even when after ten or twenty years you are an 'expert' in the area. The more expert, the lonelier you seem to become. To know the Cameroons well is to feel that you are outliving your contemporaries. The Cameroons does not become less 'remote': you become more and more remote yourself. Perhaps this condition is, at a higher level of opposition, one that is characteristic of all anthropologists – as against (say) sociologists. I am feeling towards the statement that although there are always 'real' centres, and 'real' peripheries which move relative to each other, there is an added feature of a more puzzling kind.

There are certainly some topographical elements that are relevant. Mountains conventionally add to the 'remoteness' experience, but so very frequently do plains, forests and rivers – so much so that the inhabitants of 'unremote' places sometimes say that they do not have 'real' mountains, plains, forests or rivers – only something else, hills (say), woods, or streams. Contrariwise, some areas (like Brittany) call their hills 'mountains'. The Scots, resisting the 'remote' vocabulary, perhaps, call their mountains 'hills'. The actual geography is not the overriding feature – it is obviously necessary that 'remoteness' has a position in topographical space, but it is defined within a *topological* space whose features are expressed in a cultural vocabulary. The Bakweri of Cameroon cannot really be said to be objectively remote from the coastal belt of that country. Their more elevated settlements overlook an area of superficial commercial modernization and the sea. Yet they live up the Cameroon Mountain, and the higher seems to be the remoter in this elastic semantic realm.

With the Cameroons we are getting close to the problem I want to discuss. For example, the feature I describe of 'remoteness' (this term you see now is a label for something which is only gradually casting its shadow in language during my exposition) persists when it has lost its geographical correlates – that is, when the 'remote' area has been reached, and when it should now be merely present. Thus people would visit the Cameroons, and (as it were) stagger in to see us as if they had surmounted vast odds; as if the Cameroons had a protective barrier. Yet, from the inside outwards, there was an almost exaggerated contrary sense of the *absence* of any barrier to the world – a peculiar sense of excessive vulnerability, of ease of entry. With every improvement of communication over the decades, the more speedily did people appear to pour in uninvited; and yet the more they seemed to be on the last stages of an expedition to some Everest that terminated in the middle of your floor. That is a law of 'remote' areas – the basic paradox, for that is how you know you are in one. The West still maintains ideals of such places. 'Shangri La' is an image used by French visitors to the former British Cameroons, and by United Nations visitors to both Cameroons. You know you are 'remote' by the intense quality of the gaze of visitors, by a certain steely determination, by a slightly frenetic air, as if their clocks and yours move at different rates. Perhaps that is why the native of such an area sometimes feels strangely invisible – the visitors seem to blunder past, even through him. I think that to formulate this point you have to have stayed for very long successive periods in various spaces, in order to separate out this quality, which I take to be a real one and connected to the experience of time. It is, of course, a conceptual experience. The one-way invisible barrier is a singularity in the social space, which I have mapped already in formal terms in the Munro Lecture (see above, chapter 9).

Yet, as I have mentioned, remoteness does not appear to protect the 'remote areas'. In the Cameroons we penetrated more and more parts which, on the ordinary level of the relativity of conventional geographical remoteness, were remote even in the Cameroons. There were areas so 'remote' anthropologically that there was nothing written on them. Yet, when reached, they seemed totally exposed to the outer world: they were continually in contact with it. Why were they not equally known to 'the world'? Remote areas turn out to be like gangster hide-outs – full of activity, and of half-recognized faces. As the years went by, we had the choice of the blankest part of the Cameroon map: the Fungom area of the Bamenda Plateau, and within that area the Chiefdom of Esu. A thatched house was built on a hill, round which the village-capital nestled. The paradox of living in that blank area summed up the experience of remoteness very well, some of which I shall touch on soon. For the moment I will note that an uncompleted dirt road led to a log over a stream, and a path that wound up that hobbit-like hill. From its top any distant Land-Rover could be heard approaching for miles, its cloud of dust being visible for further miles, until its minuscule occupants alighted and began their ominous ascent, gathering children and helpers as they came.

To the strange arrivals the village was either a scene of 'traditional hospitality of a simple highland folk' or the location of incomprehensible reticences. The very act of having arrived was its own justification. Years later, the new arrivals were a unit of gendarmerie, for this was the remote area of all remote areas for the new Francophone government and, like all areas of this peculiar type, not only perceived to be Shangri La but also the home of purported smugglers and spies. How shall the inhabitants of a 'remote area' evaluate the arbitrary love-hate of its visitors? Are alternating periods of 'unspiledness' and violence their inevitable fate? After the destructions of one generation of strangers how is it that they are asked to play the role of ideal society to the next, before being unthinkingly redeveloped or underdeveloped out of existence by the next? The history of 'remoteness' in Cameroon merges historically into the universal history of political states; my discussion is to show its minimal reflection in 'states of mind'.

The cognoscenti will recognize by now that Western Scotland is an area in which canonical levels of 'remoteness' are to be found. Indeed some may suspect that this has been an elaborate way of introducing the really basic economic and political factors. Such important matters as the Highland Clearances, for example, cannot surely derive from mere conceptualizations? That would be a false opposition, although the improver of the Duchess of Sutherland's estates, the well-known James Loch, was fired with high levels of what looks suspiciously like conceptualization: late-eighteenth-century ideas of betterment, much more powerful than malice. And what conceptualizations fired the undoubted and more easily handled villains of the piece like the factor, Patrick Sellar?[8] Those old ladies carried out of their houses so that the thatch could be burned: beware of being a conceptualization in another person's mind!

The great contribution of Malcolm Chapman's book, *The Gaelic Vision in Scottish Culture* (1978), was to approach this point from its literary expression. A Gael once asked in a poem '*Co sgriobh mi?*' ('Who wrote me?'). When the anthropologist Chapman with the freshness of inexperience innocently replied, 'Oh, didn't you know?: it was Macpherson, Arnold, Renan, the Edinburgh intellectuals...', all hell broke loose. Professor Derick Thomson, in his incarnation as Ruaraidh MacThomais, poet, had himself often asked the same question, but he did not like *that* answer.[9] The reasons are understandable as we shall see, for Chapman, in showing how the very definition of Celticity and Gaeldom was inescapably tainted at source, and how the imposition of it had led to a 'symbolic expropriation' of the Gaelic identity, seemed to ignore the experienced reality of being a Gael. Nevertheless, for the first time, the paradox of Gaeldom was brought out from under the comfortingly drifting layers of binary oppositions: development/underdevelopment, traditional/modern, centre/periphery, that had covered it for years like the soft patter of autumn leaves.

A similar experience occurred for Maryon McDonald (1982) among the Bretons.[10] In her case she showed brilliantly how the Breton militant language movement coexisted uneasily with the native-speakers who were cast as ideal types by their kaftan-wearing admirers. This time it was the militants who filled the newspapers with their violent reactions. I am personally sure the work of Chapman and McDonald will stand as genuine advances. The Gaels and the Bretons have a proper point, however. They want to know, 'who then are we, *really?*' They behave as if they were indeed privileged enough to require to know something that no one can ever know. It is, however, an important feature of the 'remote' social spaces – indeed, as I argue, it is of the peculiar structure of such spaces – that the question imposes itself; and so far it is true that we have given the appearance of tackling only one half of the problem. On one side 'remote areas' are indeed parts of an imaginary world. I had kept for some years an image to print as a dedication to this phase of our studies, and I gave it to Malcolm Chapman to use on his fly-leaf; it is from Lewis Carroll's *Through the Looking-Glass:*

'He's dreaming now,' said Tweedledee: 'and what do you think he's dreaming about? . . . Why, about *you*! And if he left off dreaming about you, where do you suppose you'd be?' 'Where I am now, of course,' said Alice.

'Not you!' Tweedledee retorted contemptuously. 'You'd be nowhere. Why, you're only a sort of thing in his dream!'

'If that there King was to wake,' added Tweedledum, 'You'd go out – bang! – just like a candle!' (1872, cited Chapman 1978).

The expropriation of an image of another is a puzzling thing. I have mentioned the novelist Barbara Pym. Now that she is dead, a strange simulacrum of her is taking shape, which is analogous in its processes to that effect caused by visitors to a remote area. Experts on Barbara Pym now begin to appear who know more about her than she knew herself, or than any single friend knew, while those of us inserted into her novels become symbolized figures, merely narrative elements.[11] There never was, in any purely physical location, that Barbara Pym – it is all 'true' perhaps, but it never existed. The new Pym is a series of storage points in a fuzzy network of information, whose general distribution signals the existence of the ex-Pym, the late Pym, the Pym that passed away. And who has selected those points, and in what space are they located? Similarly, the Gaels, the Cameroonians and others, have had the privileged experience of being made, as collectivities, part of a similar process. They have become, like Pym, at worst a 'text', at best 'art'. The 'remote' social spaces thus merely exhibit, in an exaggerated form, a feature which affects all human beings to some extent. Yet we assert that we are still 'there', in some experienced way, behind the textualization – at least while we are still alive. The social space consists of human persons, so it is right that the Gaels and others should assert: 'however we are perceived or constructed in the worlds of others, nevertheless there *are* real Gaels.'

It is not necessary, therefore, with this readership, to say that the Western Islanders do not see themselves as resembling that artistic or textual remoteness. They are quite ordinary – as ordinary as anybody can be who has the regular experience of wild-eyed romantics tottering through his door. The social space is a material one. A lifetime of being treated as a princess turns you into an ordinary – princess; a lifetime as an untouchable makes you just an unexceptional – untouchable. A lifetime of being in a remote area, turns you into an ordinary . . . ? What?

To answer the question we must consider some paradoxes.

1   *Remote areas are full of strangers.* I know people who hardly experience the idea of 'a stranger'. No suburbanite sees the unknown mass of neighbours as 'strangers'. The city-dweller does not inhabit a world of strangers. To make a city-dweller perceive a stranger he must be marked by such criteria that total rejection is likely to be his reaction. As a result incoming New Zealanders can *really* believe they are Londoners.[12] Try to get away with that, however, in the Hebrides. There every social interaction has its marking preliminaries (*'Cò às a tha thu?'* 'Where are you from?', or the like). People in remote areas have a wide definition of 'strangers', so that, whatever the real numbers of the latter, there will always appear to be a lot of them. This conceptualization interacts, however, with the undoubted tendency for perceived strangers actually to congregate in remote areas. We must be careful in formulating this point. First of all, the stranger remains 'marked' longer, perhaps for ever, so that the residue of strangeness accumulates. We can see already the difficulty of talking of 'real' Highlanders, when biographies are well remembered. But even this is not enough, for the kinds of strangers that congregate in remote areas are quite peculiar and all over Europe one can list them: painters, jewellery-makers, vegetarians, cultists, hunters, prospectors, bird-watchers and *innovators* as we shall see. Some of these categories have been present at all times under different historical guises, including those of monks and invaders.[13]

2   *Remote areas are full of innovators.* Anyone in a remote area feels free to innovate. There is always a new pier being planned, and always some novelty marking or marring the scene. For the Western Islanders there is always the new Highlands and Islands Development Board scheme. The next boom is always on the way: kelp, sheep, deer, sheep again, oil, fishmeal. There is always a new quarry for new road materials. We are always seeing the end of some old order. Meanwhile, beyond the new pier is the old pier, and behind the old pier the even older pier. The Cameroons have had an endless sequence of innovations since 1884, or even since 1858: yet the innovations seem to have a short life.[14] The paradox is that there is always change and intervention in remote areas, while in timeless Leeds stagnation seems to rule.

3   *Remote areas are full of ruins of the past.* The corollary of the above is that the remains of failed innovations, and of dead economic periods, scatter the landscape. There is another paradox here: that remote areas cry out for development, but they are the continuous victims of visions of development. The Cameroons has presented a steady sequence of innovation and ruin. The Highlands and Islands Development Board has been in existence long

enough for its history already to be marked by the monuments of its own failed projects: Breasclete on the Isle of Lewis, Ardveenish on Barra, bidding fair to join the even earlier projects of Lord Leverhulme – before the HIDB period itself passes away as another golden age of innovation, into the past.[15] Remote areas offer images of unbridled pessimism or utopian optimism, of change and decay, in their memorials. The Highlands are, as a whole, a great monument at one level to a Malthusian experiment on a disastrous scale that filled most of the nineteenth century. Within that total landscape with ruins (and few human figures) nest many smaller landscapes with their own lesser ruins.

4 *Remote areas are full of rubbish.* This is a minor corollary of the last. Remote areas are the home of rubbish, because rubbish is not a category there. What appears remarkable is that people elsewhere expect to tidy up the formless universe. Such an aspiration belongs to the worlds that *define* remote areas. These defining worlds do not, of course, perceive their own refuse tips, their own black holes, full of rubbish. In the Hebrides German tourists feel free to criticize your rubbish.[16]

5 *Remote areas are in constant contact with the world.* We must interpret this carefully. Remote areas are obsessed with communications: the one road; the one ferry; the tarring of the road; the improvement of the boat; the airstrip on reclaimed ground or even on the sandy beach. The world always beckons – the Johnsonian road to England, or the coast, or wherever it is, is an attraction to the young, for it leads from your very door to everywhere. It is quite different in this respect from a city street. The road to Cathay does not flow from no. 7 Bloomsbury Mansions. The assiduity with which television is watched in remote areas has a particular quality. A programme on the Mafia is squirrelled away as part of the endless phantasmagoria of life that begins at Oban or Kelvinside. Are we making the contradictory statement that, after all, *remote areas are not remote*? If it seems like that, it is a result of our earlier perception that remote areas, from the inside, feel open and unprotected – the one-way barrier.

6 *Strangers and entrepreneurs* or *remote areas are full of pots.* 'Lianish' is on the very end of the road from the island centre, one of the longest continuous journeys: there are fifteen houses, two bed-and-breakfast ladies, an English potter/cowman/temporary postman, and one child under eleven. The post-bus runs until 4 pm. Only an incomer will work the 'unsociable' evening round. The Englishman takes seriously his 'social service' function, does the drunks' trip to town, and gets home late in the evening. The real postman will be watching the television. A typical incomer, many Gaels will think, without animus. Incomers suffer frequently from remote-area anxiety: the arrival of another new incomer is a sign that the fastness has been penetrated – we may call it the Crusoe effect.

7 *The incomer as entrepreneur,* which we have been gradually approaching, is a cliché of the Hebrides (the phenomenon is widespread, however). On one

island the best private bus is run by an in-married incomer – a woman. The place it stops for tea is at the 'croft' of a man from Bolton, Lancashire, who admirably carries on traditional crofting activities, such as weaving. Almost all the hotels are run or managed by incomers. The Lewis Pakistanis may not all speak the fluent Gaelic that legend says, but the legend marks their assimilation to the averageness of strangeness that characterizes incomers. No amount of Gaelic would turn them into Gaels, but their existence is used to contrast with those incomers who have learnt no Gaelic at all. It is easy to document the entrepreneurs that are recent incomers. But when one looks at the 'island-born' entrepreneurs, there emerge the names of old tacksmen's families, of introduced mainland shepherds and persons of odd biography – internal incomers, former incomers, products of mixed incomer-island marriages.

One may easily concede that bed-and-breakfast ladies will be an exception, that they are from a random selection of hospitable families. Islands differ markedly and on the Long Island it is a matter of report that the Isle of Skye has taken to the hospitality trade to a remarkable extent. In the Outer Hebrides the time, trouble, and expense of catering for guests can hardly be worth the £10 or £12 return that is characteristically charged. Once more the bed-and-breakfast entrepreneur is likely to be upwardly mobile. A surprising number are not Gaelic-speaking. Indeed, the ubiquitous Scandinavian linguist is directed to lists issued by the *Gaelhols* enterprise. Gaels in the general trade are frequently families in which the husband is already the holder of another job.

8   *In remote areas the same set do everything.* Connected to the last point is the interesting observation (which is an actually voiced complaint) that the same people take all the new jobs. Although this seems at first sight strange, the phenomenon is not restricted to the Hebrides. Development money tends to channel through the same entrepreneurs, however tiny their activities by world standards. A kind of micro-economic pluralism is endemic, as a pen-picture will illustrate.

9   *Under Milk Wood of a remote island.*[17] Down to the ferry every evening go the teenagers, earnest with purpose; the grocer fills the cars with petrol (he is in charge of both food and fuel); the taxi-driver hires out the cars, to drive to his two rentable holiday homes; the dustman drives up with the travelling library; the retired English officer's daughter bakes the cakes, and ranges Sloanely to serve them to the airport passengers; the Commander bakes wholemeal bread (for incomers – Gaels prefer Mother's Pride sliced); the retired teacher grows vegetables to be sold in his sister's hostelry (she whose husband in Edinburgh writes for *Acarsaid*, the national journal, edited by The Reverend Archie Hill alias Gillesbuig Mac an Dùin, professional Gael), while the sister's son discusses introducing 'speed boats between the islands' with Donald G., who bought an HIDB craft centre costing the EEC £200,000, for only £40,000, when two managers (incomers) each left to open their own shops; the latter, bearded, twice the size of an

ordinary islander, spends much time on the plane to Glasgow and Corfu; seeing below Mr Mackenzie running his ferries, in turn with taking pay to skipper a subsidized ferry in competition with himself; the postman mows the lawns of his, the *Caolas*, guesthouse at Creagnaculist; Mrs McNeil inscribes her name on the list of *Gaelhols* for language learners; in the loch the Dean of Wyanunk Theological, Ohio, paints the wood of his restored castle with creosote; the Dutch wife of an Australian professor opens her guesthouse and craftshop; A. F., former serviceman and performer in *Man of Aran*, tells oft-told tales to an anthropologist; his charming daughter has 300 Christmas Cards from Americans from whom she half-knowingly extracts the admiration due to the identity-constructing Gael . . .

So we come to the nub.

By now something in the paradox of remote areas can be seen to be systematic. It will be evident that I have used the terms 'remote' and 'remote area' as mere semantic grains upon which to grow a theoretical crystal. I wished to propose an 'empty formative' that would generate the interaction between the anthropologist and his field, the definer and the defined, the classifier and the classified, the imagined and the realized. The condition might have been given any code name, or a letter, or a number, and not illustrated by local colour. Nevertheless, the 'remoteness' paradoxes are well known (although not necessarily in all aspects everywhere the same), and so 'remoteness' may now finish its life in this paper as a technical term. I will therefore provide a theoretical conclusion, inevitably somewhat condensed.

REMOTE AREAS ARE EVENT RICH, OR EVENT DENSE

In the social space, not everything that happens is an event. Much of what passes has for the participants an automaton-like quality. Events are defined within the space by a certain quality which, to avoid a special terminology, we may for the moment call 'significance'. The nature of the event-matrix may be modelled synchronically (see above, chapter 5), or diachronically (see above, chapter 9). Essentially, specifying something in the space introduces a singularity into it, which 'twists off' the specified. The latter is bounded one way – from the perspective of the specifier.

The phenomena outlined above may be expressed in another form, by saying that the information content is high. That is: randomization, the ultimate condition of active systems, is continually resisted. These areas delicately teeter on the edge of perpetual innovation. This feature is both internal and external. Thus 'remoteness' is a specification, and a perception, from elsewhere, from an outside standpoint; but from inside the people have their own perceptions – if you like, a counter-specification of the dominant, or defining space, working in the opposite direction. Thus in the Cameroons the Bakweri were defined by general repute, in their multi-ethnic area, as apathetic (Ardener, E. 1956; Ardener, E., Ardener, S. and Warmington 1960), while the silent villagers saw themselves as involved in a life-and-death struggle with zombies and their masters, which gave deep significance to the slightest act (Ardener 1970c). All the materialities of dominance, economic and conceptual, were present in their traumatic history. These spiritual events are, however, of the utmost seriousness, as serious as the Diwygiad in Wales, or the Disruption in the Kirk which led to the sense of continuous spiritual battle that marks the characteristic religious life of the Presbyterian Hebrides. Their materialities do not lack some possible analogies with those that summoned up the zombies: expropriation, depopulation, landlordism, and definition as dwindling, dying and out of time.

The double specification of remote areas, or double-markedness, produces that note of eccentricity and overdefinition of individuality, if you like an overdetermination – or to exaggerate slightly, a structure of strangers. In the large stable systems of dominant central areas, in contrast, there are equally large regularities, with more automatisms, in which only in periodic 'prophetic situations' do major singularities occur (see above, chapter 9). They are event poor. It is evident that the event quality is not a direct function of numbers or population for, in contrast, it is remote areas as we have defined them that are 'event rich'.

Event richness is like a small-scale, simmering, continuously generated set of singularities, which are not just the artefact of observer bias (as we have seen, observers commonly perceive only a puzzling blankness) – but due to some materiality, that I interpret to be related to the enhanced defining power of indivudals. Event richness is the result of the weakening of, or probably the continuous threat to, the maintenance of a self-generated set of overriding social definitions (including those that control people's own physical world), thus rendering possible the 'disenchainment' of individuals, and that over-determination of individuality, to which I referred. The peculiar driving force of abortive innovation is precisely due to this, and the sense of vulnerability to intrusion experienced in such areas is genuine. The structural time is quite different, and in so far as a 'remote' area is (as it always is) part of a much wider definitional space (shall we say the dominant state) it will be perceived, itself, *in toto*, as a singularity in that space.

If that is so, then event richness can occur within any social space. That is the meaning of our earlier paradox, that we can travel to internal remotenesses that have not yet been actualized, or which still form singularities in our otherwise more informationally random social space. It will be recalled that all individuals are potentially singularities in a social space through their (only intermittently exercised) power of self-definition. Since remote areas are singularities in the total or wider space, all singularities there are reinforced. As more and more internal remotenesses are defined out of our changing societies, it will be no surprise that social anthropologists, addicts of the event rich, will be disappearing into them.

I am afraid that many will think this terminology unnecessarily arcane. They will not have far to seek in the literature for more conventional terms. For them I will, however, phrase it another way. The lesson of 'remote' areas is that this is a condition not related to periphery, but to the fact that certain peripheries are by definition not properly linked to the dominant zone. They are perceptions from the dominant zone, not part of its codified experience. Not all purely geographical peripheries are in this condition, and it is not restricted to peripheries.

Finally, I do not need to stress here that while human beings have theoretically unlimited classifying power, not all classifications have equal experiential density. The feature of a 'remote area' (in our technical sense of a singularity of a particular type) is that those so defined are intermittently conscious of the defining processes of others that might absorb them. That is why they are very crucibles of the creation of identity, why they are of great theoretical interest, and why social anthropology's 'at home' may be very far away indeed.

Postscript 1
The Prophetic Condition
by Kirsten Hastrup

In the Munro Lecture given at Edinburgh in 1975, at which I was present, Edwin Ardener identified the prophetic condition. It is a condition, both for structures and individuals, of being, as it were, between two worlds. While situated in the 'old' world, prophets give voice to a 'new' one. Often the voice of prophecy is not heard; it seems incomprehensible beforehand; afterwards it may seem trivial: when the new world has become commonplace the prophet's voice cannot be distinguished from general speech.

When the new world fails to happen, or when it remains latent for an extensive period, prophets may not be registered at all. When the epistemological gap between the worlds is too great, the structural condition is not in favour of prophecy. Prophets may be discarded along with other anomalies in the social. The privileged prophetic condition obtains at that singular point in time when a discontinuity is beginning to register, but when it is still not capable of expression.

I do not propose to repeat what Edwin Ardener has lucidly expressed elsewhere in this volume, which derives its title, 'The Voice of Prophecy', from the Munro Lecture of 1975. It goes without saying, also, that my thoughts are not patented interpretations of the master's voice. The concept of the prophetic condition, however, serves as an apt starting point for the present thoughts on the work of Edwin Ardener. Quite apart from the obvious qualities of the concept in our dealing with discontinuities in social spaces, the prophetic condition may serve as an allegory for Edwin Ardener's work, and ultimately for the entire anthropological project.

Prophets do not predict the future, in the terms of the present. Rather, they foretell a present reality before it has been accommodated in the collective representations, and in language. Prophets, therefore, have to create a new language which in turn helps define the new reality. This was very much the case of Edwin Ardener, whose vision of a new anthropological reality could be expressed in the current discourse only with difficulty, and whose conceptual universe only gradually could be disclosed as categories were developed. Although there is a remarkable continuity in Edwin Ardener's work, there is also a gradual reshaping of language. What was only dimly perceived in the 1960s could be expressed more simply in the 1980s. The language expanded as new conditions were realized. Once the prophecy is fulfilled a new structural condition obtains, in which the language must of necessity expand still more.

Prophecy links language, space and time. This is why the prophetic condition gives privileged access to the anthropological reality. In the following I shall use these three aspects to label separate entries into this reality, as defined by Edwin Ardener (and as subsequently discovered by this apprentice). Since my aim is not exegetic I shall refer explicitly only to a few of his papers. Given the continuity of his thought, all his papers reflect a singularly integrated view of the world, however, and the range of reference is immaterial. The concepts I single out are chosen for their exemplary qualities and for their short-circuiting of the wide-ranging discussions of 'the real' – to which I shall return in the final section of this paper.

LANGUAGE: SEMANTIC DENSITY

The position of language has long been a major concern in Edwin Ardener's anthropology. Language has a dual relationship to the social, metonymical and metaphorical. In the first sense it is part of the social; it is one feature among others. In the second sense it 'expresses' the social; language represents the world, so to speak. This dual definition of language makes it of singular significance in our determination of the separate realities lived by various peoples.

Language is much more than a linguistic superstructure upon a material reality – language and materiality are not apart, allowing some anthropologists to forget language, and others to forget materiality. Language is closely linked with the material; in the social experience they form a simultaneity. The match between them is virtually tautological, although not in the simple sense of categories shaping thought and experience.

The link between language and materiality, as perceived by Edwin Ardener, is most forcefully expressed in his notion of 'semantic density' (see above, chapter 11, part 2). It concerns the interrelationship between the category system and 'reality' – the statistical and material features of categories, of which certain meanings are socially more significant than others. An example will illustrate this: to an international academic community 'Oxford' has a semantic density around the university; the meaning of the term has a centre of gravity there which make the industrial outskirts and the supermarkets seem peripheral. In one sense, everything in that particular urban area of Southern England is equally 'Oxford'. Within the meaning, however, there is an uneven spread of significance.

All categories may potentially yield similar density patterns; this is not solely a feature of famous locations. Categories always coexist with a statistical feature, which is part of their materiality. Language itself does not reveal this; experience does. This implies that no reality can be exhaustively described by its own categories. In the social experience and in practice categories have unequal densities which lock them into the material world. The categorical and the material form an experiential simultaneity.

Density is related also to frequency, that is to the question of which meanings will be implied more often than others when particular categories are invoked. This is aptly illustrated by identity categories, where peoples are named and defined according to selected criteria, reflecting a semantic density centring around only a minority of the actual population.

Such densities can be identified in anthropological fieldwork. Through experience of an 'other' reality, the fieldworker transcends the language of the obvious and internalizes its material implications. Since densities are not immediately acknowledgeable in language, they cannot be translated. They must be recreated in a separate language, whose creation is the anthropologist's task.

SPACE: EVENT RICHNESS

At a more comprehensive level of analysis the social space as a whole is marked by similar densities. The counterpart of the semantic density of particular categories is the event richness of certain social spaces. Some spaces or some periods seem to generate more events than others. This is not solely a mensurational feature, but also more importantly a feature of registration. For events to be registered as such, they have to be significant. Although events, as happenings, do have objective properties, it is not these properties as such that give them their significance. Significance is projected from a cultural scheme of a different order.

Some social spaces are more event rich than others. This means that more happenings are registered as events, and more behaviours interpreted as actions. Event richness is a feature of 'remote areas' in particular (see above, chapter 14). In 'remote areas' all singularities of the social space are continually reinforced in response to the intruding outer world. The individuals and their actions are defined by the social space, but they are also definers of the space. Consequently, event richness is both a defining feature and a consequence of definition. The material and the definitional merge.

In order to register events and comprehend their significance, one has to have recourse to a larger whole – a world. We may define events as relations, between a happening and a structure of meaning. Worlds, then, are relations between relations and societies are their embodiment. While relations can be inferred from material facts, relations between relations have no direct manifestation. Worlds cannot be seen, they must be experienced. This is comparable to the notion that the meaning of categories cannot be heard. Again, fieldwork is a necessary precondition for knowing the empirical. We will never know the unequal experiential densities of categories and social spaces through hearing and seeing, because the social is no mere text but a lived materiality.

The dual relationship between language and the social has a parallel in the relationship between individuals and their world. There is a continuity between the social space and the individuals that constitute it – a continuity which is also of a dual nature. The individuals are defined by the world of which they are part, but they are simultaneously the definers of the space (see above, chapter 14). Thus, the tautological match is enriched by a feature of unpredictability, individualism and manipulation.

While individuals generally experience and express only what their world singles out for registration, some of them may also step out of it and experiment with either action or expression (see above, chapter 9). Thus the two-faced continuity between individuals and their world is the fundamental precondition for history, containing both continuities and changes; it is also the fundamental precondition for prophecy.

TIME: HISTORICAL DENSITY

History is always in the making. Individual actions either reproduce or transform the structure of the social space. Thus history is always adjective to the world under study. However, the story of the past is a selective account of the actual history. The selection is not accidental – it is the corollary of a structured memory.

Not all events survive in the memory of people. For events to be memorized and to become part of 'history', they have to be or to have been experienced as significant. This apparently self-evident point covers a profound truth: the structuring of history, or the selective memory, is not solely imposed retrospectively. Although the universe created and memorized in history is relative to a series of successive presents, memorability is identified synchronically. Contemporary event registration is the basis for the material left to us as history.

The logic of the relationship between history as reality and history as story, is akin to the relationship between the world and its language, or between the empirical and the definitional aspects of reality. The dimension of space has been replaced by the dimension of time, but even this distinction is more or less an analytical artefact belied by experience. The world and the semantic densities unfold in time, which cannot therefore be separated from the space.

When speaking of long-term history we may still distinguish between synchronic and diachronic perspectives, but in fact even they are mutually defining. In the interest of comprehending the nature of history I shall retain the distinction for the moment, however. The effect of semantic density and of the concurrent event richness, identified in the synchronic dimension, is a generation of a particular historical density in the representation of the diachronic. Historical density, or relative memorability if you wish, is the trace left by previous (re-)constructions of the space. Although the story is always at one remove from history itself, it is no arbitrary reconstruction. The retrospective recasting of events is a continuation of the contemporary process of event registration.

History, then, is a sequence of rememorizations of events originally perceived as such. The structure of the memory, the way in which the past is presented, are very much particular features of the world of which they are a part. The modes of registration and the conventions of representation apply equally to densities in space and time. In that sense, history is as culture-specific as are the meanings of particular categories.

The relativization of history is a mode of objectivization (see above, chapter 14). We cannot deal objectively with history without first acknowledging the profound relativity of memory and story. Histories are stories of the past behaving like memories, but as time passes it is the story itself that is memorized. However, memory relates to a material experience of densities and events which is reflected in the reconstruction that occurs through time. History, therefore, is never, unlike myth, mere story. Like the world itself, history is not reducible to text.

THE ANTHROPOLOGICAL CONDITION

At several points in the preceding discussion I have alluded to the prophetic qualities of anthropology. I will now make this explicit.

Edwin Ardener's vision of the anthropological reality implies a simultaneity of discovery and definition. The anthropologist discovers new worlds while they are defined. In that sense, anthropologists may 'speak' new worlds into being. The gradual or abrupt development of the discursive space of anthropology reflects a changing reality. Usually, anthropologists give voice to contemporary but spatially separate realities. We write other cultures. This is not different from the voice of prophecy, either in principle or in fact – even though prophets are generally thought of as perceiving a temporally separate reality within the same space.

The point is that the prophetic condition is principally defined, not by a linear time referent, but by a multiple referent of time, space and language. The prophet foretells a different time-space; in language he defines a new world. The anthropological condition is an equivalent of this; in narrating and writing the other, the anthropologist is author to a reality.

This principal correspondence between the prophetic and the anthropological condition has a practical implication at the level of anthropological categories. Through our perception of separate worlds, we sense the inadequacy of local categories. In our devising of new categories, different realities may be discovered. In the anthropological discourse, discovery and definition still merge.

Not all anthropologists are equally perceptive, of course. Nor are they all equally creative in the shaping of new language. Only a few are prophets by gift. Edwin Ardener was, in my view, one of these.

Postscript 2
Towards a Rigorously Empirical Anthropology
by Maryon McDonald

Many students of anthropology have found themselves intrigued but confused by the work of Edwin Ardener. No doubt the density and economy of his prose account in part for this. There is more, however, to the apparent opacity of Ardener's ideas. The structure of his work, the metaphors he uses, and the nature of his critique of positivism, are not always those most familiar to, and expected of, post-1960s' anthropology.

The dominant schools of thought in British social anthropology were fairly simple until the 1970s. The common rote, which most students of anthropology acquired, ran through evolutionism and diffusionism, functionalism and structural functionalism, and then structuralism. And then what? Structuralism came and went, the old securities had gone, but somehow little changed. The various versions of post-structuralism or post-modernism which followed provided a happy lifeboat for some, but often within the structures of the same securities from which they imagined themselves to be sailing free. Ardener remained apart from these securities and excitements, seeing them as the stuff of ethnography rather than the means of analysis, and consequently muddled readers and listeners who wished, by means of them, to pin him down.

Most monographs and introductory texts of the 1960s (and many present-day introductory courses in social anthropology) still tend to assert solidly empirical domains such as politics, economics and kinship, and then to add a distinct domain called something like 'beliefs' or 'systems of thought'. Related classifications – social structure and culture, or social relations and ideas, were common, self-evident and acceptable. Such structures were, in part at least, responsible for structuralism's appeal, but they subsumed it. In general terms, structuralism fitted well with many of the moral and political ideals and promises of the 1960s, sitting (as was required) in synonymy with opposition to the Establishment and materialism. Within social anthropology more specifically, structuralism appealed as an invitation to study domains – of values, beliefs, symbolism, myth and

ritual – which functionalism had helped to make expressive, representational and secondary. It was precisely in domains of this kind that the 1960s
found the meaning of life; when structuralism gave priority to these areas,
it appeared open to the charge of idealism, and to lend it credence.

A division of labour developed in anthropology around these dichotomies. This division of labour, which structuralism encouraged, and in
which it was caught, encouraged new specialisms such as symbolic anthropology and cognitive anthropology – specialisms which seemed distinct from
the concerns of the empirical man. Marxian ideas reappeared for a while,
accusing these specialisms of floating well above the ground. Structuralist,
symbolic and cognitive anthropologists seemed, in the meantime, to do
much to confirm the justice of the accusation. Politics, economics, kinship
and social structure were often left untouched; even, perhaps, virtually
scorned as the stuff of empiricist reaction. The empirical and the symbolic,
the real and the ideal, and a host of similar dichotomies, gathered themselves around issues of quantitative and qualitative research, as if around
two naturally separate enterprises. The insights that structuralism could
have brought were lost in an apparent divide between 'rigour', on the one
hand, and '(mere) interpretation' on the other. Much of the anthropology
which is now self-consciously post-structuralist or post-modern has been
trying to pull itself out of this. If structuralism, however, which did, after
all, have the apparently objective (if fictive) underpinning of the 'human
mind', was able so easily to fall into the jaws of the very structures it should
have been examining, then it is perhaps not surprising that many of the
anthropologies that have come since have, within these same structures,
been eaten alive.

Edwin Ardener's work inevitably shares with that of other anthropologists many of the new influences that came into the discipline in the 1960s
and 1970s. An older tradition had to be made sense of somehow, but this
could not be done satisfactorily through accretion, simply tacking the new
ideas on to the old in the bulging category of 'beliefs' or in new specialisms.
Linguistics and linguistic models, theories of meaning, phenomenology,
hermeneutics and much else besides, generally persuaded anthropologists
that positivism was not for them. However, much contemporary anthropology is still celebrating the idea that the discipline is not a natural science.
This is often done within a dated notion of what scientists think and do,
accompanied by embarrassing forays into literary criticism, resulting in
much textualism and poetics, in texts which themselves sometimes show
extremes of selfblindness, or of tortured and self-indulgent reflexivity.
Ardener's critique of positivism was of a completely different order. His
long-standing interest in linguistics gave him a grasp of Saussurean ideas
which other anthropologists, struggling with Saussure through the veil of
structuralism, did not have. He also had a background of many years of
detailed empirical work in the field in Africa, part of which was studiously
quantitative. Moreover, in his case, the context in which re-thinking was
effected was not simply social anthropology, but the human sciences more
generally. All these factors helped to give Ardener's work its own peculiar
stamp, and enabled him to step over the traps that structuralism laid for

the less wary. This meant that his prose was not always attractive to those seeking, in their eschewal of science, the titillation of the arts. When Ardener used the analogies of text and translation (see above, chapter 11) it was to show, through detailed technical examples demanding of the reader, the problems and limitations of such models of the anthropological endeavour, and to send wide ripples of such problems through literature, archeology, ethology and biology. Ardener's critique of positivist anthropologies – of functionalism, say – was not one which criticized them for their neglect of text or poetics, or for their lack of concern for 'meaning' (as if neglecting the soul). Rather, he criticized those who believed themselves to be the champions of empirical rigour for being neither rigorous nor empirical enough (see above, chapter 2). To those still celebrating the joys of 1960s' idealism, this was as incomprehensible as it was to many of the 'old-school' empiricists.

Some of the generalities of Ardener's early critique were filled out in later papers on specific themes. His reflections on population, demography and ethnicity, for example, illustrate in a fairly straightforward way the impossibility of separating qualitative from quantitative concerns. All mensuration is inevitably category-based, as is the apprehension and generation of social reality more generally. Reflections on the old quantitative/qualitative divide are not simply, therefore, reflections on the necessity of knowing the categories through which, as it were, the counting is done. These are reflections which, as they encounter this divide, or any of the other divides mentioned earlier, take us back each time to a classificatory base-line of human cultural life. The cultural worlds which anthropologists study – whether the anthropologists themselves define their focus as economics, politics, kinship, or the more exotic symbolism, myth or ritual – are composed of self-defining worlds of categories in action.

As Ardener makes clear, classification is not always simply contained in, or backed up by, language; if the anthropological endeavour is that of 'translation' between different category systems, then understanding is a question of 'disequation rather than of equation' (see above, p. 183), and this 'disequation' is an inevitable feature of the relative autonomy of these systems as they confront one another. This is in itself apt comment on the excitement, and also the confusion and misunderstanding, which some of Ardener's own work has had the capacity to generate. A focus on classification has been too easily tidied back into the dichotomies I mentioned earlier. However, while some features of reality may feel more material than others, they are none the less conceptual for that. There is no 'more', no 'something else' requiring analytical attachment to the underbelly of classification in order to ground it; no 'real' world of ecology or economics innocent of cultural perception; no analytically distinct area, whether motor or residual, of 'social change'; no gap between classification and social reality. Ardener's work leads us, by a difficult but rewarding route, to the kind of self-aware empiricism that many anthropologists are now seeking. Only in an older language would one feel that the world had been turned on its head because social structure or economics had been pulled, at last, into the domain of 'beliefs'.

Appendix: Edwin Ardener –
a Bibliography

1952 'A Socio-economic Survey of Mba-Ise' (Ibo, Eastern Nigeria), West African Institute of Social and Economic Research, typescript (bound).

1953 'The Origins of Modern Sociological Problems Connected with the Plantation System in the Victoria Division of the Cameroons', West African Institute of Social and Economic Research, conference proceedings, sociological section, March, pp. 89–105.

1953 'A Rural Oil-palm Industry: 1) Ownership and Processing', West Africa, 1909, 26 September, p. 900.

1953 'A Rural Oil-palm Industry: 2) Opposition to Oil Mills', West Africa, 1910, 3 October, pp. 921–3.

1954 'The Kindship Terminology of a Group of Southern Ibo', Africa, 24, April, pp. 85–99.

1954 'Some Ibo Attitudes to Skin Pigmentation', Man, 54 (101), May, pp. 71–3.

1954 'Democracy in the Cameroons', West Africa, 1932, 6 March, p. 203.

1956–9 Various sections in Annual Reports on the Cameroons under United Kingdom Administration (unattributed), HMSO, London.

1956 Coastal Bantu of the Cameroons (The Kpe-Mboko, Duala-Limba and Tangayasa Groups of the British and French Trusteeship Territories of the Cameroons), London, International African Institute (Ethnographic survey of West Africa, 11).

1957 'Sociological investigations of the West African Institute of Social and Economic Research in the Southern Cameroons – Digest of Principal Findings', WAISER, duplicated.

1957 'Cameroons Swing to Tribalism', West Africa, 2090, 4 May, p. 411.

1957 'Numbers in Africa', Man, 226, November, p. 176.

1958 Various sections in Victoria Southern Cameroons 1858–1958 (unattributed), Victoria Centenary Committee, Victoria, Southern Cameroons (now West Cameroon), London, Eyre and Spottiswood).

1958 'Marriage Stability in the Southern Cameroons', Nigerian Institute of Social and Economic Research, conference proceedings, mimeographed.

1958 'The People', in Introducing the Southern Cameroons (unattributed), Federal Information Service, Lagos, pp. 17–21.

1958 'Wovea Islanders', in Nigeria, 59, pp. 309–21.

1958 'The "Kamerun" Idea', West Africa, 2147 p. 533 and 2148. p. 559.

1959 'Lineage and locality among the Mba-Ise Ibo', Africa, 29 (2), pp. 113–34.

1959 'Cameroons Election Aftermath', West Africa, 2185, February, p. 195.

1959 'The Bakweri Elephant Dance', Nigeria, 60, pp. 31–8.

1959 (with D. W. MacRow), 'Cameroon Mountain', Nigeria, 62, pp. 230–45.

1960 'The Linguistic Situation in the Southern Cameroons', Nigerian Institute of Social and Economic Research, mimeographed.

1960 'A Note on Intestate Succession', Nigerian Institute of Social and Economic Research, mimeographed.

1960 (with S. Ardener and W. A. Warmington), *Plantation and Village in the Cameroons*, Oxford, Oxford University Press.

1961 'Duala', in *Encyclopaedia Britannica*.

1961 'Kpe' (Bakweri), in *Encyclopaedia Britannica*.

1961 'Historical Research in the Southern Cameroons', third conference on African history and archaeology, School of Oriental and African Studies, mimeographed, July.

1961 'Crisis of Confidence in the Cameroons', *West Africa*, 2306, 12 August.

1961 'Cautious Optimism in West Cameroon;, *West Africa*, 2313, 30 September, p. 1071.

1961 'Social and Demographic Problems of the Southern Cameroons Plantation Area, in Southall, A. (ed.) 1961, *Social Change in Modern Africa*, Oxford, Oxford University Press.

1962 'The Political History of Cameroon', *The World Today*, 18 (8), pp.341–50

1962 *Divorce and Fertility – An African Study*, Oxford, Oxford University Press.

1963 'Imperialism and the British Middle Class', *West Africa*, 2391, March, p. 357.

1965 Contributions to *La Population du Cameroun Occidental* (unattributed), Société d'Etudes pour le Développement Economique et Social, Paris.

1965 *Historical Notes on the Scheduled Monuments of West Cameroon*, West Cameroon, Government publication. Translated into German 1969 as *Anmerkungen zur Geschichte de geschuetzten Denkmaeler West Kameruns*, Buea; Government publication.

1965 (with S. Ardener) 'A Directory Study of Social Anthropologists', *British Journal of Sociology*, 16 (4), pp. 295–314.

1965 Review of 'The Revolution in Anthropology', Jarvie, I. C. 1963, *Man*, 65, p. 57.

1966 Comment on 'Frazer and Malinowski: the Founding Fathers', Leach, E. R. and Jarvie, I., *Current Anthropology*, 7 (5), December, p. 570.

1966 Contributions to the English version of *La Population du Cameroun Occidental* (unattributed), Société d'Etudes pour le Développement Economique et Social, Paris.

1967 Comment on 'Competence and Incompetence in the Context of Independence', Colson, E. *Current Anthropology*, 8 (1–2), February–April, pp. 101–3.

1967 'The Nature of the Reunification of Cameroon', in Hazelwood, A. (ed.) *African Integration and Disintegration*, Oxford, Oxford University Press.

1967 'The Notion of the Elite', *African Affairs*, February.

1968 'Documentary and Linguistic Evidence for the Rise of the Trading Polities between Rio del Rey and Cameroon 1500–1650', in Lewis I. M. (ed.) 1968, *History and Social Anthropology* (ASA monographs 7), London, Tavistock.

1970 *Kingdom on Mount Cameroon: Documents for the History of Buea, 1844–1898* (forthcoming).

1970 Review of *Custom and Politics in Urban Africa: A Study of Hausa Migrants in Yoruba Towns*, Cohen, Abner, *Oxford Magazine*, 7, Hilary, pp. 199–200.

1970 'Witchcraft, Economics, and the Continuity of Belief', in Douglas, M. (ed.) *Witchcraft Confessions and Accusations*, London, Tavistock, pp. 141–160.

1970 'Galileo and the Topological Space', *Journal of the Anthropological Society of Oxford*, 1 (3), pp. 125–30.

1971 'The New Anthropology and its Critics' (Malinowski Lecture, 1970, with appendix), *Man*, 6 (3) pp. 449–67.

1971 (ed.) *Social Anthropology and Language* (ASA Monographs 10), London, Tavistock.

1971 Introduction to *Social Anthropology and Language*, Ardener, E. (ed.) 1971, pp. ix–cii.

1971 'Social Anthropology and the Historicity of Historical Linguistics', in Ardener, E. (ed.) 1971, pp. 209–41

1972 'Language, Ethnicity and Population', *Journal of the Anthropological Society of Oxford*, 3 (3) pp. 125–32; reprinted in Beattie, J. H. M. and Lienhardt, R. G. (eds) 1975.

1972 'Belief and the Problem of Women', in La Fontaine, J. (ed.) 1972, *The Interpretation of Ritual*, London, Tavistock; also in Ardener, S. (ed.) 1975, *Perceiving Women*, London, Dent.

1972 Introduction and commentary to reprint of *Specimens of Dialects: Short Vocabularies of Languages: And Notes of Countries and Customs in Africa*, Clarke, J. 1848 Farnham, Gregg International.

1973 'Behaviour: a Social Anthropological Criticism', *Journal of the Anthropological Society of Oxford*, 4 (3) pp. 152–4

1974 'Social Anthropology and Population' (Wolfson Lecture, 1973, 'Population and "Tribal Communities"'), in Parry, H. B. 1974, *Population and its Problems*, Oxford Clarendon Press, pp. 25–50.

1975 'The Cosmological Irishman', *New Society*, 14 August.

1975 'Language, Ethnicity and Population' (see 1972), in Beattie, J. H. M. and Lienhardt, R. G. (eds) 1975, *Studies in Social Anthropology: Essays in Memory of E. E. Evans-Pritchard*, Oxford, Clarendon Press, pp. 343–53.

1975 'The Problem of Women Revisited' in *Perceiving Women*, London, Dent; USA, Wiley, pp. 19–27 (also contains 'Belief and the Problem of Women', pp. 1–17, first published 1972, in La Fontaine, J. (ed.)

1975 'The Voice of Prophecy: Further Problems in the Analysis of Events', (Munro Lecture) (forthcoming).

1976 '"Social Fitness" and the Idea of "Survival"', *Journal of the Anthropological Society of Oxford*, 7 (2), pp. 99–102.

1977 'Comprehending Others', paper given to the Wenner-Gren Symposium, part 2 published as 'Social Anthropology, Language and Reality', in Parkin, D. (ed.), 1982, and in Harris, R. (ed.) 1982, part 1 published as 'Ethology and Language', in Harré, R. and Reynolds, V. (eds) 1984.

1977 Introduction to *Social Anthropology and Language* Ardener, E. (ed.) 1971 was issued in three parts in Spanish translation, in the series *Biblioteca de Linguistica y Semiologia* (Paidos: Buenos Aires), 6–8, 6, *Antropologia Social y Lenguaje*, 7, *Multilinguismo y Categoria Social*, 8, *Antropologia Social y Modelos de Lenguaje*.

1978 'Some Outstanding Problems in the Analysis of Events' (ASA conference paper, 1973), in Schwimmer, E. (ed.) 1978, *Yearbook of Symbolic Anthropology*, London, Hurst, pp. 103–120; reprinted in Foster, M. and Brandes, S. (eds) 1980, *Symbol as Sense*, New York, Academic Press.

1979 'Social Anthropology', in *A New Dictionary of Sociology* Duncan Mitchell G. (ed.), London, Routledge and Kegan Paul.

1980 'Ten Years of JASO', in *Journal of the Anthropological Society of Oxford*, 11 (2), pp. 124–31.

1981 'The Problem of Dominance', *Journal of the Anthropological Society of Oxford*, 12 (2), pp. 116–21; reprinted in Dube, L., Leacock, E. and Ardener, S. (eds) 1986, *Visibility and Power: Essays on Women in Society and Development*, Oxford, Oxford University Press.

1982 'Preliminary Chronological Notes for the South of Cameroon – Rapport de Synthèse', *Contribution de la Recherche Ethnologique à l'Histoire des Civilisations du Cameroun*, 2, pp. 563–77, ed. Claude Tardits, Centre National de la Recherche Scientifique, Paris, 1982.

1982 'Social Anthropology, Language and Reality', in Parkin, D. (ed.) 1982, *Semantic Anthropology*, New York Academic Press; reprinted in Harris, R. (ed.) *Approaches to Language*, Oxford, Pergamon Press.

1983 'The ASA and its Critics', *Royal Anthropological Institute Newsletter*, 56.

1984 'Ethology and Language', in Harré, R. and Reynolds, V. (eds) *The Meaning of Primate Signals*, Cambridge, Cambridge University Press; Paris, Editions de la Maison des Sciences de l'Homme.

1985 'Social Anthropology and the Decline of Modernism', in Overing, J. (ed.) *Reason and Morality* (ASA Monographs 24), London, Tavistock.

1986 'Barbara Pym and the Social Anthropologists', *Sunday Telegraph*, 6 July.

1987 '"Remote Areas"; some Theoretical Considerations', in Jackson, A. (ed.) *Anthropology at Home*, London, Tavistock.

1987 'Edward Sapir (1884–1939)', *Journal of the Anthropological Society of Oxford*, 18.

1987 Japanese translations of 'Belief and the Problem of Women' and 'The Problem of Women

Revisited', respectively pp. 33–58, and 121–34, of *Women, Nature and Culture*, Tokyo, Shobun-sha.

In press and forthcoming:

'Evidences of Creation', ASA conference paper, in Tonkin, E. McDonald, M. and Chapman, M. (eds) 1989, *History and Ethnicity*, London, Tavistock.

Facing Mount Cameroon: Studies in the History of the Cameroon Coast 1500–1970, edited and introduced by Ardener, S.

Note on 'Cameroon Chain-Gang', relating to Mary Kingsley's visit to Cameroon, to be published by the Royal Anthropological Institute.

'Ritual and the Social Space', conference paper delivered in the University of Cracow (September 1985), and reconstructed from notes by Chapman, M. and Hastrup, K.; forthcoming in Polish translation by Mach, Z.

'Identity and Identification', conference paper delivered in Oxford and Cracow (January 1987), and reconstructed from notes by Chapman, M.; forthcoming in Polish translation by Mach, Z.

Notes

Note to introduction

1 A variety of appreciations followed Ardener's death. The following is not a complete survey, but see: *The Journal of the Anthropological Society of Oxford* (1987, XVIII: 2), for pieces by Anthony Boyce, Malcolm Chapman, David Parkin, Zdzislaw Mach and Andrzej Paluch; *St John's College Notes* 1987, for pieces by Freddy Beeston and Anthony Boyce; *Anthropology Today*, (1987, III: 4), for a piece by Malcolm Chapman and Maryon McDonald; *West Africa*, (3660, 5/10/88), for a piece by Martin Njeuma. There were also unattributed obituaries in *The Times* (9/7/87), *The Oxford Times* (12/7/87), *The Oxford Mail* (10/7/87), *The Jericho Echo*, and *Jericho News*.

Notes to chapter 1

1 (*Editorial note*) The papers contained in the volume *Social Anthropology and Language*, to which chapter 1 of this book was an introduction, were:

H. Henson, 'Early British Anthropologists and Language', pp. 3–32
R. H. Robins, 'Malinowski, Firth, and the 'Context of Situation', pp. 33–46
D. Hymes, 'Sociolinguistics and the Ethnography of Speaking ', pp. 47–94
J. B. Pride, 'Customs and Cases of Verbal Behaviour', pp. 95–120
W. H. Whiteley, 'A Note on Multilingualism', pp. 121–8
E. Tonkin, 'Some Coastal Pidgins of West Africa', pp. 129–56
N. Denison, 'Some Observations on Language Variety and Plurilingualism', pp. 157–84
D. Crystal, 'Prosodic and Paralinguistic Correlates of Social Categories', pp. 185–208
E. W. Ardener, 'Social Anthropology and the Historicity of Historical Linguistics', pp. 209–42
G. E. Milner, 'The Quartered Shield: Outline of a Semantic Taxonomy', pp. 243–70
C. Humphrey, 'Some Ideas of Saussure applied to Buryat Magical Drawings', pp. 271–90

2 (*Editorial note*) *Supplementary text, taken from original, p. lxviii–lxix*:
It was through the German-born Max Müller at Oxford that the comparative linguists had their chief effect. Müller developed his views in the more speculative phase of linguistic studies of the age of Bopp and Schleicher, before the rise of the Neogramma-

rians. He remains, however, the only theorist with anything remotely like a modern approach to myth. Tylor's interest in deaf-and-dumb and sign languages prefigures some of the proposed semiology of Saussure, but he held firmly to an evolutionist view that early linguistic signs were 'motivated'. The use of 'native' categories like *mana*, *totem*, and *taboo* did not at this earlier period (nor, indeed much later) lead on to a consideration of the relation of category to language. Nevertheless, the collection of 'comparative' material under these heads did lead to important advances in the hands of other theorists (*totemism*: Lévi-Strauss 1962a; *taboo*: Freud 1913; Steiner 1956; Firth R., 1966: 109–13; *mana*: Mauss 1950: 101–15; Firth, R., 1940; Milner 1966).

3 If not never, then hardly ever. The correspondence involving Bohannan (1956, 1958a, 1958b) with Beals (1957) and Taylor (1958), for example, is curiously muffled on the subject. Bohannan seems to argue that linguistics does not help in the learning of languages. This brief interchange comes from a milieu that was nevertheless exceptional in retaining an interest in language (see above, p. 36).

4 See also Hjelmslev 1943: 49; trans. 1963: 53; Malmberg 1964: 128; Capell 1966: 39 (where it is not correctly demarcated). Hjelmslev also alludes to other systems: differentiation of siblings by sex and age as between Magyar, French and Malay (see Hjelmslev 1957: 104); differentiation of 'tree-wood-forest' between French, German and Danish (1957: 106; 1943: 50; trans. 1963: 54). See also Ullman (1951).

5 Newton (December 1675) thought the seven colours would correspond to the seven intervals in our octave:

> For some years past, the prismatic colours being in a well darkened room cast perpendicularly upon a paper about two and twenty foot distant from the prism, I desired a friend to draw with a pencil lines across the image, or pillar of colours, where every one of the seven aforenamed colours was most full and brisk, and also where he judged the truest confines of them to be, whilst I held the paper so, that the said image might fall within a certain compass marked on it. And this I did, partly because my own eyes are not very critical in distinguishing colours, partly because another to whom I had not communicated my thoughts about this matter, could have nothing but his eyes to determine his fancy in making those marks (correspondence in I. B. Cohen 1958: 192; Turnbull 1959: 376–7).

Berchenshaw wrote of Newton's system (10 February 1676):

> That the natural genuine, and true reason of the excellency and fullness of the harmony of three, four, five, six and seven parts, may clearly be discerned by the system of seven parts (Cohen ibid.: 226).

6 *GPC* (1968), s.v. *glas*, divides the colour referents into (1) blue, azure, sky-blue, greenish-blue, sea-green; (2) green, grass-coloured, bluish-green, light-blue, pale-blue or pale-green, greyish-blue, slate-coloured, livid, pallid, pale, grey. A further puzzle could not be elucidated without the structural diagram in figure 1.2: *glas*, finally, can sometimes have the same referent as *llwyd*, 'grey', 'holy of clerics', which is explicable because of their neighbouring positions at the point where the Welsh axes of hue and brightness join.

7 E. Ardener (1954). It was Miss M. M. Green (a linguist and anthropologist) who first mentioned the characteristics of *ocha* to me. In the functionalist terms of the day I expressed the *ocha/ojii* antinomy in terms of 'attitudes'. A simplified orthography has been used here. The 'African Alphabet' renderings, where they differ from those in the text, are as follows: ɔcha, ɔbara ɔbara, uhyɛ uhyɛ, ahehea ndə, akwəkwɔ ndə. The theory of a historical order in the succession of types of colour classification comes from Berlin and Kay (1969). In their view, systems may contain (1) 'black' and 'white' only; (2) 'black' plus 'white' plus 'red'; (3) 'black' plus 'white' plus 'red' plus 'yellow' or 'green' (4) 'black' plus 'white' plus 'red' plus 'yellow' and 'green'; (5) 'black' plus 'white' plus 'red' plus 'yellow' plus 'green' plus 'blue' (6) 'black' plus 'white', plus 'red' plus 'yellow' plus 'green' plus 'blue' plus 'brown'; and so on. Thus Hanunóo would be in phase 3, Ibo and Early Welsh in phase 4.

8   The translation presents some difficulties, but 'the crepuscular light' is attested in other Celtic sources: 'terram pulcherrimam obscuram tamen et aperto solari lumine non illustratam' (Loomis 1956: 165).

9   These cases support Kroeber (1909) and what I take to be the present position of Needham (see Needham 1971).

10   Von Humboldt (1836/1967) is the intellectual ancestor of the field theory, although his 'mother tongue mysticism' is not always attractive. It dates in its modern form from 1910 with R. Meyer's analysis of military terminology. Weisberger, Trier, Porzig, Jolles and Ipsen (who first used the term 'field') are the chief names (full references in Ullmann 1951: 152–70; see also Ullmann 1963: 250).

11   (*Editorial note*) *The following example has been removed from the main text here (original, p. xxix)*: The Banyang and Bangwa are two neighbouring peoples of West Cameroon. Among the former the linguistic term *ngo* refers to both 'gun' and 'fire'. Among the latter the word ŋwo, borrowed from the former, means 'gun' while emɔ means 'fire'. The implication that the Bangwa first received firearms from the Banyang direction is useful, since it was at least possible, on general grounds, that they received them from peoples on the other side. So far, then, linguistic data have suggested a historical implication. However, the Banyang themselves received the gun from the Efik via the Ejagham. In each case the artifact was exchanged without the Efik word. Yet Efik (and Ejagham) also label 'gun' and 'fire' by one term (Efik *ikaŋ*, Ejagham *ngon*). The Banyang accepted *both* the gun *and* (through translation) its identification with fire. This identification did not, as we see, survive the onward transmission to the Bangwa. The problem we now face is the explanation of the different kinds of linguistic contact between Efik (and Ejagham) and Banyang, and Banyang and Bangwa. We note, however, that physical contact between Banyang and Bangwa is interrupted by a high escarpment. The further analysis of these differences and similarities would lie in both linguistics and social anthropology, and in social anthropology for its own sake – not simply for the assistance (if any) this may yield to linguists.

12   (*Editorial note*) *The following text has been removed from the main text here, and slightly amended (original, pp. xxxi–xxxii)*:

The process of the reconstruction of Saussure's lectures is itself of keen anthropological interest:

All those who had the privilege of participating in his richly rewarding instruction regretted that no book had resulted from it. After his death, we hoped to find in his manuscripts, obligingly made available to us by Mme de Saussure, a faithful or at least an adequate outline of his inspiring lectures. At first we thought that we might simply collate F. de Saussure's personal notes and the notes of his students. We were grossly misled. We found nothing – or almost nothing – that resembled his students' note-books. As soon as they had served their purpose, F. de Saussure destroyed the rough drafts of the outlines used for his lectures. In the drawers of his secretary [read 'secrétaire' or 'writing-desk'!] we found only older outlines which, although certainly not worthless, could not be integrated into the material of the three courses (Saussure 1916, 1922 edn: 7–8; trans. 1964: xiii).

So it was that the notebooks of seven students were pooled, and the courses reconstructed.

The problem of re-creating F. de Saussure's thought was all the more difficult because the re-creation had to be wholly objective. At each point we had to get to the crux of each particular thought by trying to see its definitive form in the light of the whole system. We had first to weed out variations and irregularities characteristic of oral delivery, then to fit the thought into its natural framework and present each part of it in the order intended by the author even when his intention, not always apparent, had to be surmised (1922: 9; trans. 1964: xv).

Thus was compiled and published the *Cours de linguistique générale*, and with it was founded the Geneva school of linguistics which Bally and Sechehaye carried on in succession to the master until 1945, dying in 1946 and 1947 respectively. Since then all the sources have been published and critically analysed (Gödel 1957; Engler 1967, 1968). It is somehow appropriate that the Cours and Saussure should coexist like signifier and signified in one of his own linguistic signs!

13 I give the page references both of the Cours (1922 pagination) and of the translation (1964 edition), but generally quote the latter, despite its detailed inadequacies, so that the flow of the English text may not be broken up by frequent passages in French. Nevertheless, I have amended the translation in various places where noted, since sometimes it is seriously misleading, and at least once unintentionally comic.

14 'Social anthropology in Britain (to speak only of that country where it has acquired most renown in recent decades) had been inspired by certain general ideas, subtly derived from the early French sociologists, which have had a singular theoretical influence, and much of the progress is to be attributed to them.

They are analytical notions such as "transition", "polarity" (opposition), "exchange", "solidarity", "total", "structure", "classification". Now these are not theories but highly general concepts; they are vague, they state nothing. At first sight there is nothing to be done with them, and certainly they cannot be taught as elementary postulates in introductory courses of social anthropology. Indeed, their significance is only apprehended after arduous application to the task of understanding social phenomena; the less one knows about human society and collective representations the less they appear to mean. Yet they have proved to possess a great and perennial analytical value, such that it may be claimed that it is they which are essentially the "theoretical capital" of social anthropology' (Needham 1963: xlii–xliii).

15 Thus, Von Wartburg (1969: 194).

16 Collinder (1968: 183) says that Schuchardt expressed the notion of *la coupe verticale* and *la coupe horizontale* of language in 1874. For Collinder:

Das Panorama, das im Cours de linguistique générale aufgerollt wird, ist kein getreues Bild der wirklichen Sprachwelt. Dieses *système où tout se tient* ist nicht einer urwüchsigen Landschaft ähnlich; es gleicht viehmehr einem altmodischen zugestutzten französischen Schlosspark (p. 210).

We see here the wrong-headed but common complaint that a formal model does not generate 'reality'.

17 With reference to Wittgenstein's *Philosophical Investigations* (1953), Ullmann says:

There is an unmistakable affinity between some of his ideas and contemporary linguistic thought – an affinity all the more remarkable as Wittgenstein does not appear to have been familiar with books on linguistics (1959: 303).

We may note this also in Waismann (1968).

18 For example: Bogatyrev 1931 (which I have been unable to consult) and 1935.

19 I am aware that a 'panchronistic linguistics' has been several times previously announced (Ullmann 1951: 258–99). It is no coincidence that it should have had an important part in a vision of semantics. Nevertheless, in discussing the diachrony/synchrony distinction of Saussure, we must recognize that this exists at the level of models of formal systems (see Ardener, E. 1971c). Similarly, the 'panchrony' of Saussure must be realizable at the model level: so far only the transformationalists have credibly demonstrated, if only partially, the possibility of such a model. It is interesting that 'panchrony' was generally ignored in exegesis of Saussure by structural linguists, from whom his message was a charter for synchrony, and for whom even diachrony was of lesser import (e.g. see Wells 1947, in Joos 1957).

20 The term *semiotic* goes back to Locke, as 'the doctrine of signs'. Its use was developed by C. S. Pierce. Morris, Carnap and Hjelmslev helped its modern vogue. Margaret Mead coined the term *semiotics* for the study of 'patterned communication in all modalities'

during a discussion at the Indiana Conference of 1962, which is reported in Sebeok, Hayes and Bateson (1964, see pp. 1–7, 275–6). *Semiotics* thus lies close to Saussure's *sémiologie* (closer indeed than does Barthes's *sémiologie*). It may be useful to retain *semiology* to describe the study of *semiotics*, used as the plural of *semiotic*. In its turn, a *semiotic* is a sign system. The coexistence in society of large numbers of *semiotics* means that any useful description must be made through models of systems, abstractions, ideal systems.

21 McLuhan (1970: 39) speaks of chairs 'outering' the human body, leading then to tables, and a restructuring of the human environment. His 'pop' usages sometimes curiously, but inadequately, reflect modern 'structuralist' trends.

22 The brief discussion of the phoneme included here is obviously selective, and might be omitted were it not that the term as discussed by Lévi-Strauss still has a mysterious aspect for some of his readers. Their questions are not necessarily directly answered by turning to standard works on linguistics. I include the section, aware of its European bias. This may be balanced by consulting Fries (1963) on the Bloomfieldians. He notes that 'the strong stress upon the procedures and techniques of analysis . . . did not stem directly from Bloomfield' (p. 22). In general, see Mohrmann, Norman and Sommerfelt (1963); Mohrmann, Sommerfelt and Whatmough (1963); and Hockett (1968: 9–37).

23 (*Author's note, supplemented by text from original, p. lxix–lxx*):
Shaw says of Sweet's polemic Oxford reputation:

> With Higgins's physique and temperament Sweet might have set the Thames on fire. As it was, he impressed himself professionally on Europe to an extent that made his comparative personal obscurity, and the failure of Oxford to do justice to his eminence, a puzzle to foreign specialists in his subject . . . although I well know how hard it is for a man of genius with a seriously underrated subject to maintain serene and kindly relations with the men who underrate it and who keep all the best places for less important subjects which they profess without originality and sometimes without much capacity for them, still, if he overwhelms them with wrath and disdain, he cannot expect them to heap honours on him (*Pygmalion*, preface, 1941 edn: 8–9) (see also Jakobson 1966).

Just as German comparative philology was not a good exemplar for anthropologists of the day, British phonetics was not in a position to be very helpful. Sweet, who was at that time at Oxford, had to fight (as did many of his successors) for a place for a version of linguistics other than that enshrined in the humanities syllabus. His polemical reputation may have convinced our grandfathers that the synchronic problem of language was essentially a technical matter of transcription. Nevertheless, the early anthropologists, with few exceptions, were hardly aware even of the 'phonetic' problems. It may well be that the native genius for the exotic expressed through deep linguistic study was almost totally absorbed in the study of the classics, on the one hand, and in imperial duties, on the other. There is every reason indeed to look back past the early pre-emptors of the name 'anthropology' to Sir William Jones, sometime President of the Asiatic Society. His famous *Discourse* of 1789, delivered in Calcutta, which by common consent first clearly asserted the relationship of Sanskrit to the Classsical languages and Gothic and Celtic, is otherwise more of an ethnographical disquisition than a linguistic one (Jones, 1799; now in Lehmann 1967: 10–20). Like Sweet he was a polemical figure:

> In the parliamentary election of 1780, as a candidate for the University of Oxford, his detestation of the American War and of the slave trade were too strongly expressed to be agreeable to the voters, and he was forced to withdraw from the contest. In the same year he failed to secure election as Professor of Arabic in the University for similar reasons (Firth, J. R. 1957a: 161).

> Certain precursors of Koelle (1854) in Africa might be mentioned for their ethnographic as well as their linguistic contributions. Latham has been mentioned by Hymes (1964: 3), to whom may be added Clarke (1848).

24 Jarvie (1963) no doubt was justifiably reacting against this. The present writer reviewed Jarvie's book in a critical vein (Ardener, E. 1965b) because it seemed unaware of the

important developments outside the Malinowski tradition, to which I refer. My own concern is with the excessively long time that recognition of the obvious changes in the climate of thought in the subject, and in the skills required, has taken to percolate through. We are virtually forced to fall back on *ad hominem* explanations, in a small subject like social anthropology. Malinowski's impatience with contrary opinion was accepted as fair exchange for scientific advance. His failure to recruit and keep many students of a sceptical bent from the mainstream of the European tradition must surely account for his neutral intellectual legacy. The death of Nadel (in Australia) was a loss. Whatever Radcliffe-Brown's faults, the existence of his works enabled the dissidents from Malinowskian anti-intellectualism to find a temporary alternative stimulus, if only through attack (e.g. Evans-Pritchard and Leach). For some reason, women anthropologists in the Malinowski tradition also maintained a lively presence, and continue to do so.

25   *(Editorial note) The text from the beginning of this paragraph to the end of the section (p. 40), has been transposed from its original position, pp. lxx–lxxiv of the original.*

26   I accept Tambiah's point (1968: 203) that Malinowski's views were at times closer to those of Evans-Pritchard than we might expect.

27   *(Editorial Note) The following text has been taken from the original at this point*:

Similarity of terminology can, however, bring confusion. The Chomskyan system is characterized by precision of expression, where Lévi-Strauss is programmatic. Detailed point-by-point comparisons are not to be recommended. Thus, the antinomy between 'deep' and 'surface' structure occurs in Lévi-Strauss, as in Chomsky ('Ainsi l'analyse structurale se heurte à une situation paradoxale, bien connue du linguiste: plus nette est la structure apparente, plus difficile devient-il de saisir la structure profonde . . .' – 1958). The 'deep structure' of Chomsky, as applied, for example, to sentences with ambiguous surface structures, is revealed through clearly stated sequences of transformations within one model, say that of English (see Hymes, D. 1971: 53). The 'competence' of the transformationalists can, of course, be seen as a kind of generalized 'deep structure', or a generalization of the base rules for the set of all deep structures of a language. The semantic component of the language is tied to the deep structures. Lévi-Strauss's deep structures in the analysis of myth, on the contrary, are derived from units already ascribed a conventional meaning. The transformations of inversion, sign reversal, and the like, operate to demonstrate, through the differences or contradictions in surface meaning between related myths, the nature of the myth-logic itself (1964, 1966b, 1968).

Compared with Lévi-Strauss, Chomsky is (paradoxically for a proclaimed 'rationalist') more 'empiricist' in style. There is generally recognized to be a difference in tone and aims between the Chomsky of before *Aspects of the Theory of Syntax* (1965) and the subsequent Chomsky. *Pre-Aspects* Chomsky still shows signs of his explicit concern with exact models: as his system was received at the time, it appeared as a rebuttal of simple, 'left-to-right' generated models of language, of a 'finite-state' type. Such models derived ultimately from the original work of Shannon in communication theory (1948), and with Chomsky the main wave of direct application of that theory to language subsides. The finite-state model is expressed in 'box-and-arrow' form as in computer studies: so are the alternative, more powerful models of *Syntactic Structures* (1957) and of *Current Issues* (1964). *Post-Aspects* Chomsky has turned from prime and only concern with the output of his model – the corpus of utterances – to a more difficult problem, which in a sense was left over from the destruction of the finite-state model with its implied statistical probabilities. This was: how does a child acquire the model of competence (the generative grammar) for his language?

'From this point of view, one can describe the child's activities as a kind of theory construction. Presented with highly restricted data, he constructs a theory of the language of which this data is a sample (and, in fact, a highly degenerate sample, in the sense that much of it must be excluded as irrelevant and incorrect – thus the child learns rules of grammar that identify much of what he has heard as ill-formed, inaccurate and inappropriate). The child's ultimate knowledge of language obviously extends far beyond the data presented to him. In other words, the theory he has in some way developed has a predictive scope of which the data on which it is based constitute a negligible part' (1969: 63).

Chomsky maintains, therefore, that the organism has 'as an innate property' a structure that will account for this mode of acquisition – put frivolously by McNeill (in Lyons and Wales 1966: 116): 'Metaphorically speaking, a child is now born with a copy of *Aspects of the Theory of Syntax* tucked away somewhere inside.' Chomsky has turned to Descartes, Leibnitz, and the rationalist philosophers of innate ideas for a philosophical charter for his approach; these thinkers being opposed to Locke and the empiricists, whose most extreme descendants are taken to be the psychological behaviourists. The philosophical basis of Chomskyan mentalism is a subject of disputation. In effect he gives an ontological status to what behaviourists see as a 'capacity' or a 'capability' for language. It would be out of place here to attempt a detailed discussion (see, for example, Cohen 1966: 47–56; Hook 1969; Lyons and Wales 1966; Lyons 1970). It is sufficient to note for our purposes that the Chomskyan system began with a transformational generative grammar, with the characteristics of a well-defined system. It has now at least two other systems hooked on to it: a language acquisition model genetically located in the organism, and a phonological model that commands the chains of phonemes. The mental status of the competence model itself has occasioned disagreement. Is it 'present' as an analogue of a full write-out of a transformational analysis, or is it expressed in some other form – in the way that, for example, the cogs of a clock only indirectly enact what we know about the movements of the sun and earth from the Newtonian Laws of motion? (L. J. Cohen, in Lyons and Wales 1966: 164)

28 (*Editorial note*) *The following has been taken from the main text here (original, pp. lxv–lxvii):*

We can transpose these remarks in terms of Hockett's (1968) critical review of Chomsky's theory. He sets up a summary formulation of Chomsky's system (at 1965) in nineteen points, which were largely endorsed by Chomsky himself. The case is then argued with considerable skill and documentation through the volume that *no physical system, and in particular language, is well defined*. His attack is upon the original programme, therefore, for its *arbitrariness*. But it is by now self-evident that a model of a formal system (which is well defined) says nothing of the 'well definition' of the natural order. Truly generative models *are* models: they are, of course, less than the phenomena they help to explain. Nevertheless, Hockett's criticisms confirm in a different way our awareness of the ambiguity of the Chomskyist movement. We have said that what seems to have begun in 1957 as a conscious application of model-building to post-war structural linguistics – its 'generative' and 'transformational' terminology is quite clear on this point – has now outgrown its early phases. The well-known capacity of Chomsky for fresh and creative development has disguised the fact that his total system is no longer itself well defined.

Hockett's critique thus paradoxically falls on two contradictory grounds: If Chomsky's model of a system were formal and thus well defined, it would not be counter to the system to say that language as a natural phenomenon is not well defined; and, in so far as Chomsky's system is *not* well defined, Hockett has no criticism. In fact, Hockett's discomfort probably derives from an intuition of the contradiction between the formalism of the transformationalist terminology and the lively and speculative accretions of the transformationalist world-view. In my paper (1971c) I suggest that the neogrammarian model of comparative philology was totally generative. Its basic 'inextensibility' should illuminate both the power of truly generative models and the dangers of forgetting their functions. The dissatisfaction of Chomsky with his earlier aim, and the extension of the search to meaning and beyond, have been highly productive, but no total formal system has yet been set up for this. Chomsky is both Bopp in level of achievement of his programme, and Brugmann in his search for precision. It is this desire for a totally formalistic presence that falsely sets him apart from Lévi-Strauss, who disguises his own formalism in literary metaphor.

These are presumptuous remarks coming from a social anthropologist. The reason why I feel impelled to make them is precisely because the generous aims of the transformationalists and those of the new social anthropology are, within their disciplines, rather similar. It is interesting that their thinking covers some of the same ground. It seems sometimes that the transformationalist approach would benefit from a more careful consideration of non-behaviourist social anthropology, which would in turn no doubt gain much from the encounter. The kinds of criticism made of the latter by the survivors of Malinowski (who occur in all age-groups) resemble those made by the American post-Bloomfieldians of the transformationalists. The older social anthropology finds the newer variety 'incredible', precisely for its apparent indifference to a particular positivist view of the natural order. The neo-anthropologists are also asked to provide the equivalent of 'discovery procedures', and they too seem to regard the aim as only of subsidiary interest, although in fact large amounts of 'empirical' data have been analysed (I refer specifically to their work in kinship and symbolism). They too began with the establishment of elegant and simple models of formal systems. They too have grown out of these earlier aims in the direction of theories of wide-ranging scope. They too are prepared to consider the existence of universals, beyond the scope of ethnographic solipsism.

29 The only critique of stylistic interest comes indeed from the American Marvin Harris (1969), a 'plague-on-all-your-houses' cultural materialist. He speaks with reluctant if ironical admiration of 'professional idealists, as distinct from eclectic American amateurs who have rubbed shoulders with logical positivism and behaviourism too long to know how to really get off the ground' (p. 505).

30 See also below, note 32, and chapter 2. I use the nonce-term 'neo-anthropology' to cover post-functionalist movements of a creative type, not all of which would accept the term 'structuralist'. Some of them clearly have a good deal in common in subject-matter with the so-called 'new ethnography' of the United States (Sturtevant 1964). Leach, a senior exponent, still ambiguously claims to be a 'functionalist'. The neo-anthropologists are recognizably different in interests and style from the majority of the British profession in characteristic ways, but since they do not necessarily agree even with each other (and may refuse to be linked together) they lack the earmarks of a school. In this respect they have remained isolated and divided *vis-à-vis* the relatively united 'Palaeo' group.

31 Barnes (1963), Freedman (1963), Goody (1966), Maquet (1964), Worsley (1966) made valuable points. Leach may have inadvertently set off the fashion (1961), but his language was not properly understood. As long ago as 1954 (pp. 92–3) Leach wrote, in reviewing Pocock's translation of Durkheim (1951), of a 'general revival of interest in ideas and ideals for their own sake, in contrast, for example, to the extreme empiricism of Malinowski'. In the 1960s hardly an issue of the main international professional journals failed to contain some discussion of the views of Needham and his pupils. Hardly a literary journal lacked some exegesis of Lévi-Strauss. Douglas (1966) did much to draw the attention of social anthropologists in general to some of the important themes. The activity of Evans-Pritchard's colleagues and pupils (other than Needham) has been mentioned. Yet the significance of none of this was truly taken note of until the end of the decade by the representative professors of the subject. For a *justified* pessimism, see now Needham (1970).

32 (*Editorial note*) *At this stage in the original text, the section entitled 'The Present Volume' began. The last few paragraphs of this section, which have an 'end of piece' feel to them, have been given the title 'Inarticulate Rationalities', and kept as a conclusion to the present chapter. Of the remainder of 'The Present Volume' section, some, where it seemed appropriate, has been incorporated either into the main text or into its notes. What follows in this note is a further piece from 'The Present Volume' which, while it is specifically concerned with papers not presented here, also contains characteristic ideas and asides which are of some importance, concerning socio-linguistics, transactionalism, linguistic typologies, pidgins and creoles, diatypes and so forth:*

Professor Hymes shows, in his comprehensive review (Hymes 1971), what is meant in sheer scope and method when we refer to American anthropological linguistics. His essentially undoctrinaire writings provide a mine of varied material, to which all interested in 'socio-linguistics' from a wide range of disciplines are indebted. His book of readings alone (1964) is in itself, because of his commentaries and scholarship, an original work. There is, nevertheless, a special consistency of view that emerges in his contribution below, as in other writings (1962; Gumperz and Hymes, 1964), which derives from his firm hold upon the 'ethnography of speaking'. The idea is effectively a realization of the social anthropology of *la parole*. Hymes's encyclopaedic approach may superficially appear to be irreconcilable with those deriving from the continental linguistic schools, for which this introduction has argued equally consistently. This impression would be mistaken. Hymes directs our attention to the plane at which language is generated in society – in this respect he is close to what many working linguists and anthropologists ideally demand of a 'socio-linguist'. Any analysis of material acquired from this standpoint has, however, to be organized through models, and through less conscious organizing systems, set up by speakers and actors, by social anthropologists and linguists and socio-linguists – or by ethnographers of speaking.

The fecundity of Professor Hymes's insights comes from the fact that so many structural statements made from different logical premisses must meet at the 'plane of articulation'. Whether it be Chomsky's 'performance: competence', or Bernstein's 'restricted: elaborated codes', they are all open to revision, illustration, confirmation, or comment at this meeting-place. The plane of the ethnography of speaking may thus be placed diagrammatically at right angles to their plane, in the same conceptual relationship as *syntagm* to *paradigm*. As there is a choice of 'paradigms', so there is a choice of 'syntagms', although this is commonly less clearly realized (for the use of the terms *paradigm/syntagm*, see above chapter 2; also Ardener E. 1971b, p. lxxxviii, note 26). Professor Hymes exercises this choice with great freedom. There is hardly a branch of linguistics and social anthropology in which the ethnographer of speaking may not appear. Thus Colson and Gluckman write on gossip, but where is the gossip delineated? 'Ethnographic accounts are rife with terms that in fact denote ways of speaking, though they are not always recognized to be such' (Hymes 1971: 77). Hymes's basic approach is formally consistent, despite the variety of paradigmatic systems it cross-cuts, which makes his paper in itself an introduction to socio-linguistic writings. Had post-war functionalism developed Malinowski's own linguistic insights, it might well have extended ethnographically in the plane of Hymes's interest. 'Context of situation' itself belongs to that syntagmatic plane.

On these grounds Professor Pride's rejection of the view that contexts of situation are *necessarily* 'below the level of a general abstract theory' (Pride 1971: 96) seems particularly convincing. As a socio-linguist coming from the direction of linguistics, he places himself at the plane of linguistic transactions: thus linking it with Barth's model of social anthropological analysis. The interest of Barth's model is that it too falls in the syntagmatic plane, with a clear definition of the elements of the model: the notional 'transactions'. In social anthropology it is sometimes complained of as 'rigid', 'partial', 'mechanistic' – all, as we shall agree by now, the honourable stigmata of a model of a formal system. If fully articulated it could probably be shown to be truly 'generative' in the formal rather than the metaphorical sense. Gluckman's interchange with Paine on gossip (Paine 1967, 1968; Gluckman 1968), where Paine takes a 'transactional' view, is based in part on a failure to see that syntagmatic models are not in the same plane as paradigmatic models (Gluckman's 'transactions between individual persons cannot explain institutional structures', 1968: 30, is thus a truism).

In social anthropology, 'transactional' imagery may be described as a part of the 'highest stage of functionalism'. That is: a functionalism become aware (or about to become aware) that the field of behaviour or action, even when arbitrarily isolated from the ideological programme that determines its meaning, must itself be structured by the observer before it can be 'observed'. The interest to the socio-linguist of this approach pinpoints certain differences in the histories of anthropological and linguistic enquiry. Functionalist anthropology was (in loosely Saussurean terms) concerned with the social as *parole*. The most recent developments have led social anthropology to be concerned with the social as *langue*. During the same period, linguistics has been mainly concerned with *langue* (the diachronic and synchronic versions, as well as the 'structural' and 'transformational' views, differed until very recently only in emphasis in this particular respect). It is natural that now socio-linguists, in seeking to study language as *parole*, should either use functionalist approaches or find those of functionalist social anthropology converging on the same area.

The relative lack of formalism in the old functionalist world-view will undoubtedly be amended by this, but there is still an uncertainty in the newer developments. 'Theory', to the functionalist, has long meant the confusion of statements based on models of a syntagmatic type (to which the stress on observation binds him) with paradigmatic statements. The confusion became the worse confounded because the truly paradigmatic statements of writers like Evans-Pritchard were interpreted as *syntagmatic* ones. I have already referred to the notion of 'opposition' in *The Nuer* (paradigmatic) being reinterpreted as 'conflict' (syntagmatic). Douglas (1970a: xiv–xxii) now shows how *Witchcraft, Oracles and Magic*, which was about 'cognitive structure' (paradigmatic), was reinterpreted as about 'social control' (syntagmatic). I have developed some of these points elsewhere (see above, chapter 2). It is necessary to touch on them lightly here however, in order to suggest that there are two approaches to socio-linguistics which parallel those of functionalist and post-functionalist ('neo-anthropological') social anthropology. They may be expressed diagrammatically as follows:

| Paradigmatic | Social Anthropology A ('structuralist' of Lévi-Strauss; 'neo-anthropological' of Needham, Leach, Douglas) | Socio-linguistics A |
| Syntagmatic | Social Anthropology B ('functionalist', 'neo-functionalist': transactions, networks, etc.) | Socio-linguistics B |

Socio-linguistics as generally described is essentially a Socio-linguistics B. It is that of Malinowski, of Hymes in his most characteristic phases, and of Pride at his most analytical, as well as of Whiteley, Denison and others. Socio-linguistics A is essentially the approach developed above: which some may possibly consider only an epistemological raid from Social Anthropology A, for the writers who have set it out from the linguistic side are not normally thought of as *socio*-linguists. The names that would be cited (Saussure, Jakobson, Hjelmslev, the later Firth, the German semanticists, Sapir, Whorf and their American exemplifiers) are leading names in general linguistics. Furthermore, the transformationalist approach (for some the very antithesis of a socio-linguistics) has its nearest anthropological congener in Social Anthropology A. At the 1969 ASA Conference much debate was generated between A-type and B-type social anthropologists, as well as between A-type social anthropologists and B-type linguists and socio-linguists. Some B-type social anthropologists rejected linguistics of any type. In such circumstances of confusion it is wisest not to give hostages to new labels, and certainly not to new 'disciplines', built on any outmoded nineteenth-century style: with their nation-state apparatus of buildings, professorships and degree structures. It looks likely that Socio-linguistics B will for some time to come appear to be the major bearer of the label 'socio-linguistics', while Socio-linguistics A will be apprehended as a kind of social anthropology, a kind of linguistics, or a kind of philosophy, according to the point of view of the practitioner.

The existence of multilingual situations has long provided a field for the comparison of models of language and of society. The loosening of rigid terminological distinctions between 'language', 'dialect', 'register', 'code', and the like has greatly extended the range of relevance of such studies. We now see that the problems presented by the coexistence of several varieties of 'one language' are not different in kind from those presented by the coexistence of 'different languages' in a multilingual speech community. 'Multilingual' situations provide a genuine field for empirical work in which both syntagmatic and paradigmatic approaches may be brought to bear. So far most of the work that has been carried out has been of a syntagmatic type, but there is no lack of hints for 'paradigmatists'.

Dr Tonkin has attempted 'a social history' of the succession of pidgins, ending in Pidgin English, on the Guinea coast (see Tonkin 1971). This is a 'diachrony' of the *social* situation not of the *linguistic* situation – for which there is only scattered phonological or other documentation. Yet such studies bring into doubt certain supposedly 'linguistic' typologies, by revealing the sociological assumptions that lie behind them. In particular, the distinction creole/pidgin disappears. The supposed difference lay essentially in the presence (in creoles) or absence (in pidgins) of monolinguals in the language type, and of transmission between generations. More deeply, perhaps, it derived from conflicting analytical reluctances: on the one hand, from a reluctance to award the full status of 'a language' to what might be thought to be 'invented', or 'limited', jargons; and, on the other, from a reluctance to deny it to forms of speech which had become mother tongues to some, if not all, of their speakers.

Pidgins have been a stumbling-block to all the great schools of linguistics. Both pre-Saussurean and post-Saussurean linguistics have usefully operated with models in which the basis of the diachronic or synchronic system was the single language. We have seen that the treatment of languages as if they were well-formed systems has led to great advances. An unsatisfactory treatment of pidgins was part of the price paid for those advances, for most of the efficient models of language have 'snipped out' pidgin phenomena, with the very shears that demarcated their field of operation (see Ardener, E. 1971c: 222). We may note, further, that West African Pidgin English has in reality always been a part of a multilingual or plurilingual context in combination with English or with one or more African languages. Where it has become supposedly 'creolized' it has become in fact diglossic – primarily with forms of standard English. 'Available evidence suggests that most of Africa has been multilingual for a long time, even if the domains of such behaviour were characteristically restricted, e.g. to trade or hostility' (Whiteley 1971: 22). Dr Denison's detailed analysis of the linguistic diatypes of Sauris – a 'trilingual' community in the Carnian Alps, in which a variety of German coexists with Friulian and Italian – is thus concerned with a situation that is also common in Africa, and throws light on other possibilities in the past of Europe (see Denison 1971).

One may perhaps note in socio-linguistic thought so far a certain prejudgement in the attribution of a 'social status' to certain varieties of language. We should not lose sight of the fact that much work in this field is still in the classifying phase. To simplify a little: at the first stage it may well appear intuitively (or from statements and observations) that certain diatypes have 'high' or 'low' status. From there we may proceed with C. A. Ferguson (1959) and Fishman (1968b) to 'H' and 'L' divisions of diatypes. We may then appear to discover that H diatypes are being used in L social contexts, or the like. Theory here is now at the dangerous phase: the original source of the differentiation (which was an *ad hoc* assessment of the status of contexts of use) begins to pass out of recognition, and we are all set for many comfortable years of exemplification of 'H-ness' and 'L-ness', until the basis of the typology is again revised.

As Dr Denison rightly points out, the Sauris situation, in any event, appears to require an 'M' diatype (for 'middle'). The various diatypes are in effect in opposition to each other. We first need a model of the structure of these oppositions in the whole linguistic context. We require, likewise, a model of the structural oppositions within the society at large. We may attempt to map these two models (or sets of models) upon each other; it may be, as we hope, that there will be some transformational links between them. Thus we avoid prejudging the basis of the mapping; for the term 'status' itself ceases to have any particular privileges in such an analysis. Furthermore, the possibility of negative and inverse transformations (perceived as 'contradictions' or 'exceptions') becomes a normal expectation and can be examined as such. The language of paradox and of incipient nominalism (*some H settings have L diatypes*) gives way to the language of structure – here derived from social anthropology, despite its resemblance to that of transformational linguistics. Denison's material illustrates this well with the oppositions Italian/Friulian, Italian/German, Friulian/German, Friulian of Sauris/Friulian of Udine, German of Sauris/standard German, on the linguistic side, together with the no doubt more delicate ones that he is able to observe. On the social anthropological side one can already detect some crude relevant oppositions – Udine/Sauris, rural/urban, home/school, adult/child, architect/foreman, foreman/workman and so on. The rich material in Denison 1968 (e.g. pp. 584–5), would suggest many more.

One might suspect a temporal structure also, cyclical perhaps, in which the tourist season (more Italian spoken?) may be opposed to the rest of the year. It is also possible that the young, who speak more Italian, will not retain this tendency when their social prospects are firmly assured. This point is worth making because of the question of prediction. Is Sauris German dying out (Denison 1968: 589)? To take an example: it has been said through most of our lives that congregations in Soviet churches consist of persons over the age of fifty, and thus that organized religion is 'dying out'. It is clear, however, that the fifty-year-olds of today were adolescents in the 1930s. The congregations seem to have acquired a pattern of recruitment by age. The *possibility* of such a structure over time means that the opposition *youth/age* may outlive the present occupants of the 'age-slots' concerned. All of these comments are highly speculative, and take the excellently documented case merely as a convenient example. A full social anthropological study would start from hints such as these, and even *if not expressed in this terminology* would proceed to the further finer distinctions that a field-study would yield. The division H and L would be subsumed in such an analysis, while the middle term M could be dispensed with. The results might not turn out to look very different but we should have avoided an *ad hoc* terminology (an avoidance that is, indeed, part of the spirit of Ferguson's original analysis – see Hymes 1964: 431) (see Ardener, E. 1971b: xxxviii, note 27, for further comparison).

These remarks are relevant to some social anthropologists who find it difficult to visualize how a structural analysis in the newer sense can be the subject of 'empirical' study (I am referring, of course, to a social anthropological study without overt linguistic aims.) The Sauris-type situation could never, however, be easily handled by a social anthropologist without Dr Denison's linguistic skill. It would be possible to imagine a social anthropological study, nevertheless, which produced models of Sauris society that would assist the linguist. The 'diatypes' are, we may guess, symbolically realized at more levels than one.

33 To contrast a statistical study with a symbolic study of the same ethnographic phenomena: see Ardener, E.1962 (marital instability) and 1972b, above, chapter 4 (symbolism and women); and Ardener, E., Ardener, S. and Warmington, W. (economics), and Ardener, E. 1970c (belief).

Note to chapter 2

1 Saussure himself actually used the term 'série associative' for the paradigmatic relations (1922: 170–84).

Notes to chapter 3

1 To distinguish them from the distant Batanga of the South Cameroon coast.
2 Under the name of Romby – Ardener, E. 1968, 1972c.
3 For a full–scale treatment of this problem see chapter 7.

Notes to chapter 4

1 This paper was read at Dr Kaberrry's seminar in University College London in late 1968. In presenting it for Dr Audrey Richards's festschrift, I acknowledged my debt to her for the main part of my early anthropological training. Her astringent humour and basic open-mindedness are qualities that I have respected ever since. I also thanked Dr Jean La Fontaine for her appreciative remarks on the paper, and for entering into the spirit of the analysis in her comments as editor (see La Fontaine, ed. 1972).

2 This version was given in 1929 by Charles Steane, a Bakweri scholar, to B. G. Stone (MS 1929).

3 *Moto, eto,* and *ewaki* are the ordinary words for 'person', 'rat', and 'ape'. *Mojili or Mojele* is to the coastal Bakweri a spirit. For inland Bakweri his name is a euphemism for 'ape'. It is likely that the term belongs to the animal world, but is borrowed from the fishing peoples. Possibly it is the manatee.

4 When the term is used *in isolation* the spelling *liengu* will be used (not, that is, the 'Africa' alphabet spelling *liɛngu*, nor the occasional spelling with orthographic subscript *liengu*). The belief appears to be of coastal origin. There it is concerned with men, fishing and the dangers of the deep. This paper is concerned with the *liengu* belief as utilized by the Bakweri. Elements of content are differently combined even between the coast and the mountain. Ittmann's rich material (1957) is to be used with caution because it combines several different systems. The pidgin English translation for water-spirit is 'mammy-water'. The 'mammy-water' myth has wide currency in West Africa in urban contexts. The ambiguity of the position of women in African towns makes this secondary elaboration of the belief very appropriate.

5 See also Ardener, E. (1956).

6 Various forms cited by myself (1956) and Ittmann (1957) are closer to 'fattening room' seclusion rites of the Cross River area in form and content. Their assimilation to the *liengu* belief is explicable because the latter belief most clearly organizes the women's world-view for the Bakweri.

7 Here is a subtle case of identical content yielding different meaning. The Duala mer-people hate European objects, but the *maengu* are often male. There they symbolize men's domination of the deep; they particularly detest paper (conceived of as the bible).

8 For the *liengu* language, see Ardener (1956) and Ittmann (1957). It is a code calqued upon Bakweri with vocabulary from various sources.

9 Dr La Fontaine commented on this paper that men plus wild = death, destruction; women plus wild = agriculture, fertility. She, a woman, thus expresses that faith in the female civilizing mission shared by so many reflective members of her sex!

10 For some unresolved puzzles of a new woman fieldworker see Bovin (1966). For a resolution through literature see Bowen (1954).

Notes to chapter 8

1 The paradox is that studies of the cultural relativity of ideas of 'women' should seem to increase rather than reduce the tendency to see this as a 'women's' subject.

2 I think the date was 1966.

3 For those familiar with this terminology, the following diagram will suffice:

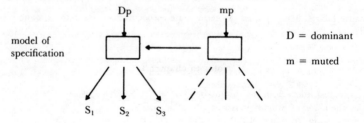

model of specification

Dp   mp

D = dominant

m = muted

S_1 S_2 S_3

The 'reality' configurations (*s*-structures) are generated from *p*-structures. Dominant p-structures generate s-structures relatively directly. Subdominant *p*-structures generate only indirectly – through the mode of specification of the dominant structure.

4   Since the 'wild' is always 'symbolic' it is not surprising that women do sometimes see *themselves* as part of it (cf. Ortner 1973). Her approach, by a greatly different route, complements mine.

5   I should like to add here that I find myself in general agreement with much of Mathieu's own position. In misreading mine she has really done my paper too great an honour: she has judged it by the standards of length of a monograph. To push through an argument in a short paper one begins with certain common-sense categories in order to dissolve them. The terms are redefined between the beginning and the end. I accept then that there are 'generalizations'. But I do not think that the many examples of ethnographers to whom the women *have* 'spoken' (among whom I am after all one!) touch the central point that within social anthropology 'no one could come back from an ethnographic study... having talked only *to* women and about men, without professional comment and some self-doubt. The reverse can and does happen constantly.' I have not replied to all points, not because they are without interest or are too compelling, but because the central charge of biologism is so improbable that it distorts all her presentation. As a final exemplification of it I quote from her last words: 'Vouloir rendre la parole aux classes inarticulées en allant rechercher "aux niveaux les plus profonds" du symbolisme ce que, tels des schizophrènes, ils tenteraient d'exprimer, présente le même danger en ethnologie que l'explication constitutionnaliste de la schizophrénie en psychíatrie...'. It is astonishing that here the Laingian approaches to the 'meaning' of schizophrenia, with which my approach is most comparable, are interpreted as 'constitutionalist' psychiatry.

Notes to chapter 9

1   Particularly in chapters 5, 7 and 8. There are further details in chapters 2, 3 and 6.

2   'That the founder of a new literature and the founder of a new state should both be saturated in the legends of Cú Chulainn was something peculiar enough to suggest that both of them were being used by some force outside themselves. It is true that both were fortunate in their periods. Yeats because his coincided with a general disillusionment regarding the values of Victorian life and literature, Pearse because the time was ripe for a whole series of national independence movements.' (O'Connor 1967: 7).

3   *Feadag* and *Gobag* also mean 'whistling' and 'biting' of winds, as in the saying 'Feadagan e tuilleadh gu Féill Pàdruig – whistling and biting winds on to St Patrick's day'. But we also find A'*Ghobag* explained as the day before *Féill Brìde*, Candlemas day (2 February) which itself gives its name to February month in some areas, including Ireland (Nicholson 1881: 414; Dwelly 1920: 511).

4   This period has parallels in the Welsh *y marwfis* ('the dead month') and *y mis du* ('the black month'), with parallels too in Welsh scholarly attempts to fix once and for all whether they referred to 'January' or 'December' or even 'October' (Parry 1939: 40–2; Richards 1950: 204–5). There are exact Gaelic equivalents and *Am mios dubh* ('the black month') is ascribed by the undaunted Nicholson to November, and *Am mios marbh* ('the dead month') to December/January.

5   *Faol* 'wolf' is assumed here to be the etymology lying behind Carmichael's adjective 'ravenous'. The other words in brackets are the literal meanings of the 'month' names – and the interpretations resemble Nicholson's.

6   The rather *ad hoc* names for the summer months are similarly related to the fact that *Samhradh* was reserved for canonical 'summer'. The terms for 'spring' (*An t-Earrach*) and 'autumn' (*Am Foghar*: 'harvest') look rather out of place, the one being already pre-empted by the *Am Màrt* or *An Céitean* periods, and the latter by the vague *An t-Sultainn*, and by the important *An t-Samhainn*, 'Hallowtide'.

7   January, February, March, April, July and December are named after the Latin months or Christian feasts. The three old ritual epochs give their names to May (*An Bhealtaine*)

August (*mí na Lúnasa*), and November (*mí na Samhna*). June was named 'mid-summer' (*an Meitheamh*) and the vague September and October named 'mid-Autumn' (*Meán Fhómhair*) and 'end of autumn' (*Deireadh Fómhair*).

8 Quoted in Ornstein 1975, which is a useful discussion of some of the 'psychological' aspects of time.

9 The world that Lowes began to explore was that of Coleridge's mind, but Lowes's essentially modern contribution was to locate that mind in its textual and historical sources, without reducing that mind *to* its sources. Elsewhere we recognize the problem of the anthropologist in the study of events, when he says: 'above all . . . , it may not be forgotten that we are disengaging the strands of an extremely complex web. It is, however, one of the limitations of our finite minds that we are compelled to consider *in succession things which in reality are simultaneous*' (1927: 55).

10 Mr Joseph Deacon's remarkable autobiography is now published (Deacon 1974). It took twelve months to dictate.

11 The simple definition space works of course as a static diagram. For definition of conjugality, for example, let us define conjugality by criterion ω (say 'sexuality') specified by non-sexual parameters, for example: α', 'duration of relationship' and α" 'jural rights'. If we reduce the α to vanishing point, then the defining parameters become sexual (ω' and ω") and the previous parameters are collapsed in the new space. There is no reason why this transformation in a definition space should have reality homologues, but it happens that the resulting transformation in this case may resemble definitions of prostitution or the like.

Parameter collapse – marriage stability

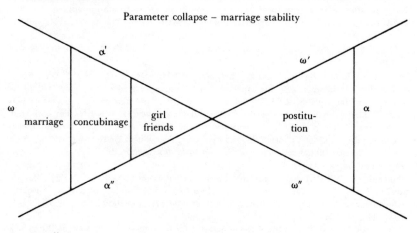

ω = sexuality
α = other defining features

Note to chapter 10

1 See Barltrop 1975: 48–50. This interesting case ran as follows. In 1914 a member of the Peckham branch, Mr Wren, violated the SPGB's 'Hostility Clause' by signing a petition to a Liberal MP. On orders from Executive Committee (EC) the Branch expelled Wren by fourteen to seven. The minority of seven were then expelled (by a poll of all party members) by 103 to twenty–seven. The twenty–seven were then pursued. Ten members voted against the final expulsion and EC demanded that these also should be expelled, but branch secretaries and members were becoming elusive and the matter petered out in 1917. Barltrop asks (p. 190) 'what is there to be said for persistent membership of a small party whose electoral returns are absurdly small, whose influence is restricted; and which will not change its mind? Above everything else the SPGB remains the only custodian of the vision of socialism.'

Notes to chapter 11

1 For an account of the traditionally weak relations of British social anthropology to formal linguistics, and the particular nuances of its concern with language, see chapter 1 and Henson 1974. For a detailed discussion of the search for meaning in social anthropology, see Crick 1976. Bibliographies embodying my intellectual sources will be found in my other publications (see now also Hastrup 1978). The West African examples derive, unless stated, from my own field work.

2 It will be obvious that this section is not addressing the wider questions of whether language-like symbolizations can occur among non-human primates, whether primate communication occurs, and whether these things can be studied. It is not argued that the usages I discuss are typical of primatological research, nor in any case do I use them for any but illustrative purposes.

3 For the development of the term 'behaviour' in scientific usage see chapter 6. The term always meant 'socially-ordered activity'. Its appearance in scientific use in the 1850s represented a demonstration that nature was orderly. 'Behaviour' was subsequently also used to denote an activity for which the demonstration of orderliness was only an aspiration – thus the paradox of 'random behaviour', and the desocialization of the term.

4 See Ellen and Reason (1979) for recent contributions, and bibliographical references. Durkheim and Mauss (1963) was a founding study.

5 The Ibo live in South-Eastern Nigeria, the erstwhile Biafra, and number some 7 million. The language is conventionally rendered *Igbo*. This spelling is not used here. The *gb* phoneme is not a labiovelar but an imploded bilabial. The spelling Ibo, although strictly non-phonetic, thus leads to a less misleading English pronunciation than *Igbo*, which is often mispronouced *Ig-bo*. Ibo is also the normal Nigerian-English spelling. The spelling of examples is simplified here; it is not the official spelling, in which certain vowels are distinguished by subscript dots, nor is it an IPA rendering. In the examples, *nye* has an open *e*, the vowels of *mkpisi* are both *i* with subscript dot (a close *e*), *okhu* has undotted *o* (approximately as in *not*) and a dotted *u* (roughly as in *put*), *ukwu* has dotted *u* in both syllables. Tones are not marked here. *Aka* and *ukwu* both have two high tones. See also Green and Igwe (1963).

6 When English butchers classify the carcasses of (dead) animals a series of separate usages appears, including a distinction between front and rear limbs. Thus:

Beef	shin	leg
Mutton	shoulder	leg
Pork	hand	leg

The shift of human categories is very notable in butchery terms. The 'hand' of pork is not strictly like an *aka* of dog, because the 'hand' of pork excludes the 'pig's feet' or 'trotters' which are attached to it.

7 The body has different categories for different classes of classifier. 'The "polite" body has many fewer subdivisions than the "sexual" body. The "medical" body may have more divisions than either and can be ambiguously polite or sexual' (see chapter 1, p. 14). Victorian polite 'throat' included much of the female trunk, and 'limb' replaced 'leg'. Traces of such phenomena can still be discovered in the history of body labelling.

8 Callan (1970: 43) argues that the categories 'greeting', 'rank', 'hierarchy', 'dominance' and the like are applied to animals by what she calls the 'Aha!' reaction: 'what one tends to get is a double thrill of recognition . . . – "aha! here's an animal being territorial (or dominant)", "aha! human beings are territorial (or dominant) as well" . . . Concealed premiss: that we know and can recognize territoriality or dominance in animals without having drawn on our own workaday model of society in the first place.'

9 This presentation is not the occasion to take the matter further, but a hint of the dynamism of the processes concerned may be further exemplified. *Nwa nna* (see above) is contrasted with *nwa nne* ('mother's child' or 'full-sibling'). This is also used for 'patrilineal relative' when closeness of relationship is emphasized. These usages are totally context dependent, but in a regular manner (see Ardener, E. 1954a and 1959b). We have then two unit categories each with its own frequency gradient, transferred as a pair to represent relative 'nearness' and 'distance' of patrilineality. At this new 'meta'-level of categorization, the old frequency gradients are now symbolic only. Put oversimply the close associations of *nwa nna* with 'half-sibling' and of *nwa nne* with 'full-sibling' are reduced to degrees of patrilineality defined by other criteria, in different contexts. Here again we catch a category peeling away from materiality with no indication in the linguistic terminology to warn us.

10 Cf. G. Steiner (1975: 316): 'the codified strangeness of most translations from the Persian, the Chinese, or the Japanese *haiku*'.

11 Anthropology's use of 'native' terms (*totem, taboo, mana*) is related to this discussion. Henson (1974: 25–30) has a good account. See also F. Steiner's *Taboo* (1956) where totemism 'demarcated . . . a solid block of otherness'.

12 N. MacAlpine (1832), E. Dwelly (1920) and J. Munro (no date) all contain lists of the names. There are some variants (MacAlpine's Iomhar = Evander) but the lexicographers do not have any doubts that 'translations' exist. Gilleasbuig means 'Servant of the Bishop'. *Gille* and *Maol* ('tonsured servant', literally 'bald') were interchangeable in religious dedication names, of which this was one. The element *bald* (from old English *beald*, 'simple/bold') in Archibald (from old English Eorcenbeald) may have influenced the 'translation'. Perhaps the 'arch' of Archibald suggested 'Archbishop', kindling associations with the 'easbuig' (Gaelic for 'bishop') of Gilleasbuig. Ruaraidh is not related to Roderick or Derek. Tearlach is the Anglo-Irish Turlough. Tormoid was a name of the Campbells. The English equivalent Norman may refer to the Norse element the name exhibits. The women's names present more puzzles than can be discussed here.

13 I choose Danish because a conventional translation works rather easily – thus, Hobbiton = Hobbitrup, Baggins = Saekker. Although Westron often becomes Danish in this manner, however, the Danish translator does not reshape the nomenclature of Rohan into Old Norse (my thanks to J. Ovesen for the text).

14 Thus *mam* for Northern English dialects may be derived fom a different Middle English source, reinforced or influenced from Welsh or other Celtic usage. *Mom* is from *momma* which may be a restressed [mɔma:]. *Mum* may be similarly derived. Effects of initial and final labial nasals may be involved. Any such results still show complexities. The *OED* is not helpful.

15 Or, as he translates: 'to complain of having no cudgel during a duel which arises in the forest is preposterous.' Do we feel that his register is a little inappropriate?

16 Cf. G. Steiner (1975: 407): 'to demonstrate the excellence, the exhaustiveness of an act of interpretation and/or translation is to offer an alternative or an addennum.'

Notes to chapter 12

1 See Hudson, D. *Munby, Man of Two Worlds: The Life and Diaries of Arthur J. Munby 1828–1910*, London, Murray, 1972, for a biography of A. J. Munby, who was psychologically obsessed by working women. Nevertheless, his accounts of their way of life are of great value, and very revealing.

2 See above chapters 4 and 8; also Ardener, S. 1975a, 1975b and 1978. The argument of this paper has special relevance to the theory of 'muting' and the way groups are defined.

3 For work on life-trajectories, see Ardener, S. 1978: 40–3.

Notes to chapter 13

1 My thanks to, amongst others over the years, Jonathan Webber and Herminio Martins who invited me to speak on the theme of modernism at a seminar in early 1983. For 'intellectuals' many 'structuralist' themes, and ideas like 'deconstruction', are being treated as 'post-modern' novelties. From social anthropology we can see that this is a misconception. They are, of course, in a sense novelties outside social anthropology, but I shall be saying in the end that the whole structuralist movement is the fiery decline of modernism itself. This paper is then on a small theme related to larger matters. Much of what I have said is an illustration of approaches in other papers.

2 My Malinowski Lecture (see chapter 2) should be compared with the present exposition. There the 'new anthropology' was shown to have suffered a failure of nerve, but it was hoped that structuralism would develop out of its early phase. This did not happen.

3 See Kuper 1973; Harris 1969. The varied uses of the term 'structuralism' form the most confusing element.

4 Romanticism reflected the revolutions themselves. The image was of the devil unchained (Blake, Byron, Brontë) in the form of the unpredictable individual of almost cosmic scope and creative power. In those days it was not unfashionable to seek to attribute the industrial and social explosion to someone, rather than to a process. The romantic hero, like the entrepreneur, is the individual embodying process. Modernism made *process* the hero. The only personal heroes recognized by modernism were the founders of the modernist movement. These founders became virtually immune from personal criticism, while the romantic heroes were ruthlessly exposed as smaller than life, with 'feet of clay'. Yet, because the social and cultural development was slower in various countries, the romantic expression coexisted chronologically with modernism in different places. Despite the implacability of the dominant successor, it has shown power to survive it.

5 I may have improved the grammaticality of J. Kennedy. My citation of Ortega does not mean that he was a modernist. Modernism redefined the past, and provided only one acceptable language for critics of the past. Ortega attempted to find a language 'between the lines'. (See further, 'Some responses to questions'.)

6 The special foreword to the third edition of *The Sexual Life of Savages* (1932) was the source of these remarks. A typescript of the 1926 contribution to the *Encyclopaedia Britannica* is lodged in the Library of the Institute of Social Anthropology, Oxford. There are many corrections in his own hand.

7 This discussion at times seemed to suggest that it was incorrect to criticize Malinowski only by his writings, (e.g. Leach Jarvie and Gellner et al. 1966: 565).

8 My warm thanks to Dr Hodder, of Cambridge, Dr D. Miller of London University, Dr Henrietta Moore and many others of the New Archaeologists, who allowed me to be present at their early symposia. I hope they do not disagree seriously with these words, and that they will recall that I had urged them to place their excellent sources figuratively in the hold, as 'Not wanted on the voyage', and to develop the New Archaeology from its own problems. As far as I know, that is what they are doing.

9 For some of these 'transformational' characteristics, see Ardener 1971b: lxi–lxviii. Transformational generative grammar (Chomsky 1957, 1965 and elsewhere) was the linguistic version of late modernism, and had the same or greater impact. It could not be called structuralism because linguists already called their own period of 'functionalism' (synchronic, descriptive) structuralism! The linguistic movements were always less blurred, and more theoretically explicit than the anthropological ones. Nevertheless, it is always confusing when neighbouring disciplines borrow 'last year's clothing' from each other.

10 The same situation prevails in social anthropology now as it did then. The argument was that the language of 'structure' was exhausted. The post-structural position was one which lacked any other specification than that it was non-structuralist. It was argued that a new trajectory must already be in existence. Our bad experience of the premature expropriation of the term does not change the argument. It accounts, however, for why

one does not wish to name any post-modernist possibilities in social anthropology, lest another 'nerveless [terminological] arrow miss its mark'!

11 There is no space to go over Central Europe's place in the terminological spectrum. We have here 'functional-structural' preceding 'structural', before Malinowski was even dead. Were they 'mere' labels? At one level, yes, but ultimately nothing more expresses the unity of modernist terminology than the appearance of these combinations all over our time-period.

12 To 'blame' Chomsky on Saussure as some now do, can raise eyebrows. Yet in linguistics the progression from 1916 has a certain unity.

13 By 'misplaced concreteness' I mean that the 'synchronic space' is timeless, not located in real space and time. Our residual primitivism makes it possible for us to speak as if ethnographies represent 'really' synchronic unities.

14 One study (Ardener, E. and Ardener, S. 1965) shows that the tiny demography of the social anthropological profession in 1961 had nevertheless been greatly enlarged by the graduation classes of 1949–52.

15 It is possible in the mid-1980s for a graduate to ask in all innocence, 'who were the New Anthropologists?'. This suggests that many of their views are now quietly assimilated.

16 Imagine at any other time after 1920 being asked 'where is the *avant garde*?' and being unable to point to some recognizable person or tendency. Yet since 1975 or so, we would have to reply, 'They were with us when we set out but we have not seen any lately.' this vacuum occurs all over the humane disciplines (We may ignore the embarrassing party going on in criticism around the corpses of structuralism and its congeners). The notion of an *avant garde* is of course the very product of modernists. They claimed to live in the expropriated future. The disappearance of the *avant garde* is one of the evidences of the end of modernism, for without that future, where will it reside?

17 As a profession we have a propensity to lose touch with the common language of our time. This, which is one source of our strength, is also the source of our failure to influence general thought, save at very rare intervals.

Notes to chapter 14

1 This is a paper of some degree of abstraction. It is not an account of the Western Isles, but it should not, despite the terminology, be other than obvious to Gaels. It takes a great deal of explanation, they will be aware, to state the facts to those outwith.

2 Adam Ferguson wrote, in *An Essay in the History of Civil Society* (1767: 31): 'the titles of *fellow citizen* and *countryman* unopposed to those of *alien* and *foreigner*, to which they refer, would fall into disuse, and lose their meaning.' This had a great influence on Evans-Pritchard (see Pocock 1961: 78; and chapter 1, p. 36). Despite this, an ESRC correspondent referred to it as a recent and untried theory.

3 See above, chapter 1, p. 7. Thus: 'even the most exemplary technical approach to language would not in fact have solved the basic problem of communication. The anthropological "experience" derives from the apprehension of a critical lack of fit of (at least) two entire world-views, one to the other.'

4 There is endless useless confusion between relativity and relativization on the one hand, and a chimera called (usually by non-anthropologists) 'cultural relativism' on the other. Like many contemporaries (cf. Gellner 1983; Edwards 1985) I am not a '*cultural relativist*'. The very act of the comparison of cultures implies the existence of appropriate canons of comparison. By those canons judgements can be made. The relativity of social worlds is a mere fact, beyond all judgements: they are constructed differently, not equally. It is, of course, inappropriate to charge a culture with inferiority because it has few hue terms, or does not separate arm from hand terminologically. Judgements may, however, be made

about the 'adequacy' of a terminological system. It is sufficient evidence to support this assertion to point out that judgements of inadequacy are daily made, even *within* a culture. Thus doctors devised anatomical terms, and artists construct colour charts. It is no great step further to assert, if we want to: 'cultures are extremely unequal in their cognitive power' (Gellner 1968: 401). The sentence remains, of course, a sentence in our own language.

5 'Brazil' was a red dye-wood; later an imaginary Atlantic island was so named in maps; even after it was localized in South America, a non-existent 'Brazil Rock' remained on British Admiralty charts until the second half of the nineteenth century. California was taken from a story of 1510, published in Madrid; it was near the Indies and the terrestrial paradise. India: variously placed, particularly in Indonesia and the Antilles. Libya: once Africa. Africa: once Tunisia. Ethiopia: once any African land occupied by people with 'burnt faces'.

6 See Loomis (1956: 61–76) for the Arthurian Antipodes, and once more the terrestrial paradise.

7 Barbara Pym included known anthropologists and African linguists in several of her novels, in particular *Less than Angels* (1955), or as composite characters ('Everard Bone' and the like).

8 The Highland Clearances were already under way at the time of Samuel Johnson's visit to the inner isles in 1776. The sagacious doctor greatly blamed the landlords for encouraging emigrations. In some sense they are still going on. The period for which the term is notorious, some time between 1790 and 1860, was marked as such precisely because of its *ideological* nature. The Duchess of Sutherland's commissioner, James Loch, wrote: 'it was one of the vast changes which the progress of the times demand and will have, and I shall feel ever grateful that I have had so much to do with (these) measures' (cited Richards 1982: 185). At ground level the Morayshire agricultural entrepreneur, Patrick Sellar, with his colleague William Young, provided a practical sense of purpose to the implementation of the fashionable ideas after 1809. 'It was during these removals' (in Strathnaver) 'that Patrick Sellar was alleged to have set fire to houses and barns, and caused the deaths of several people, including a nonagenarian woman called Chisholm. He was brought to trial and acquitted in 1816' (Richards 1982: 312).

Derick Thomson writes, in his well-known poem, 'Srath Nabhair':

> Agus sud a'bhliadhna cuideachd
> a shlaod iad a'chailleach do'n t-sitig,
> a shealltain cho eòlach 's a bha iad air an Fhìrinn
> oir bha nid aig eunlaith an adhair
> (agus cròthan aig na caoraich)
> ged nach robh àit aice-se anns an cuireadh i a ceann fòidhpe.

In his own translation: 'And that too was the year/they hauled the old woman out onto the dung-heap,/to demonstrate how knowledgeable they were in scripture,/for the birds of the air had nests/(and the sheep had folds)/though she had no place in which to lay down her head' (Macaulay 1976: 153).

9 The line is from Iain Mac a' Ghobhainn:

> 'Có sgrìobh mi? Có tha dèanamh bàrdachd
> shanas-reice de mo chnàmhan?
> Togaidh mi mo dhòrn gorm riutha:
> 'Gàidheal calma le a chànan.

'Who wrote me? Who is making a poetry/of advertisements from my bones?/I will raise my blue fist to them:/"A stout Highlander with his language"' (Macaulay 1976: 179).

Derick Thomson writes:

Cha do dh'aithnich mi 'm bréid Beurla,
an lìomh Gallda bha dol air an fhiodh,
cha do leugh mi na facail air a' phràis,
cha do thuig mi gu robh mo chinneadh a' dol bàs.

'I did not recognize the English braid,/The Lowland varnish being applied to the wood,/I did not read the words on the brass,/I did not understand that my race was dying' (Macaulay 1976:157).

The Glasgow and Edinburgh reviewers of Chapman's book were unnecessarily outraged, but see the careful consideration, in two long articles by James Shaw Grant, in the *Stornoway Gazette* (1978), and the appreciative review by Parman in Man.

10 The tendency for publicists to react ambiguously to those using the threatened language in a non-private way is comprehensible.

11 See Holt and Pym (1984), and its reviews.

12 It is not thought odd that the London regional television programme should have the Scots presenter interviewing local representatives with Northern accents. The suddenness of city explosions, when they occur, suggests that there are some pockets of remoteness within these blank spaces!

13 Adamnan's *Life of St Columba* is a medieval classic of remote area studies.

14 The Baptist settlement of 1858 had an 'improving' philosophy; the German annexation of 1884 led to the establishment of plantations.

15 HIDB friends will not be offended; they read worse every day in the press. Ardveenish may yet take off. Lord Leverhulme's ambitions for Lewis and Harris were a benign form of paternalism.

16 Round a crofthouse in Lewis were the following items, according to the writer Derek Cooper (one of the most sensitive reporters of the Hebrides): '5 cwt van (*circa* 1950s); Ford tractor minus one wheel; fragment of pre-Great War reaper; upright piano; 37 blue plastic fishboxes; 7 green lemonade crates; 2 chimney pots; a sizeable pyramid of sand; a pile of cement blocks; 7 lobster creels; assorted timber; 2 bales of barbed wire (rusted); broken garden seat; Hercules bicycle frame; piece of unidentifiable machinery (loom?); a sofa' (Cooper 1985: 192).

17 This is a carefully fictionalized picture, and several islands are combined. Tamara Kohn has pointed out that Hebrideans nevertheless are used to pulling apart composite pictures and painstakingly reassembling them. In any case, there are no prizes!

References

Adler, I. 1958 *The New Mathematics*, New York, Day.

Althusser, L. 1969 *For Marx*, London, Allen Lane.

Ardener, E. 1954a 'The Kinship Terminology of a Group of Southern Ibo', *Africa*, 24, pp. 85–99.

—— 1954b 'Some Ibo Attitudes to Skin Pigmentation', *Man*, 54, pp. 71–3.

—— 1956 Coastal Bantu of the Cameroons, London, International African Institute.

—— 1957 'Numbers in Africa', *Man*, 226.

—— 1958 'The "Kamerun" Idea', *West Africa*, 2147 and 2148.

—— 1959a 'The Bakweri Elephant Dance', *Nigeria*, 60, pp. 31–8.

—— 1959b 'Lineage and Locality among the Mba-Ise Ibo', *Africa*, 29 (2), pp. 113–34.

—— 1961 'Social and Demographic Problems of the Southern Cameroons Plantation Area', in Southall, A. (ed.) 1961.

—— 1962a *Divorce and Fertility – An African Study*, Oxford, Oxford University Press.

—— 1962b 'The Political History of Cameroon', *The World Today*, 18 (8), pp. 341–350.

—— 1965a *Historical Notes on the Scheduled Monuments of West Cameroon*, West Cameroon, government publication.

—— 1965b Review of Jarvie, I. C. 1963, *Man*, 65, p. 57.

—— 1967a 'The Nature of the Reunification of Cameroon', in Hazelwood, A. (ed.) 1967.

—— 1967b 'The Notion of the Elite', *African Affairs*.

—— 1968 'Documentary and Linguistic Evidence for the Rise of the Trading Polities between Rio del Rey and Cameroon 1500–1650', in Lewis, I. M. (ed.) 1968.

—— 1970a *Kingdom on Mount Cameroon: Documents for the History of Buea, 1844–1898* (forthcoming).

—— 1970b 'Galileo and the Topological Space', *Journal of the Anthropological Society of Oxford*, 1 (3), pp. 125–30.

—— 1970c 'Witchcraft, Economics, and the Continuity of Belief', in Douglas, M. (ed.) 1970, pp. 141–60.

—— 1971a (ed.) *Social Anthropology and Language* (ASA Monographs 10), London, Tavistock.

—— 1971b Introduction to *Social Anthropology and Language*, Ardener, E. (ed.) 1971, pp. ix–cii.

—— 1971c 'Social Anthropology and the Historicity of Historical Linguistics', in Ardener, E. (ed.) 1971, pp. 209–41.

—— 1971d 'The New Anthropology and its Critics', (Malinowski Lecture 1970, with appendix), *Man*, 6 (3), pp. 449–67.

—— 1972a 'Language, Ethnicity and Population', *Journal of the Anthropological Society of Oxford*, 3 (3), pp. 125–32; reprinted in Beattie, J. H. M. and Lienhardt, R. G. (eds) 1975.

—— 1972b 'Belief and the Problem of Women', in La Fontaine, J. (ed.) 1972 (also in Ardener, S. (ed.) 1975).

—— 1972c Introduction and commentary to reprint of J. Clarke, *Specimens of Dialects*, Clarke, J. 1848, Farnham, Gregg International.

—— 1973 'Behaviour: a Social Anthropological Criticism', *Journal of the Anthropological Society of Oxford*, 4 (3), pp. 152–4.

—— 1974 'Social Anthropology and Population' (Wolfson Lecture, 1973, 'Population and "Tribal Communities"'), in Parry, H. B. 1974, pp. 25–50.

—— 1975a 'The Problem of Women Revisited', in Ardener, S. (ed.) 1975, pp. 19–27.

—— 1975b 'The Voice of Prophecy: Further Problems in the Analysis of Events', (Munro Lecture) (forthcoming).

—— 1976 '"Social fitness" and the idea of "Survival"', *Journal of the Anthropological Society of Oxford*, 7 (2), pp. 99–102.

—— 1977 'Comprehending Others', paper given to the Wenner-Gren Symposium, published in part as 'Social Anthropology, Language and Reality', in Parkin, D. (ed.) 1982, and in Harris, R. (ed.) 1982.

—— 1978 'Some Outstanding Problems in the Analysis of Events' (ASA conference paper, 1973), in Schwimmer, E. (ed.) 1978, reprinted in Foster, M. and Brandes, S. (eds) 1980.

—— 1979 'Social Anthropology', in *A New Dictionary of Sociology*, Duncan Mitchell G. (ed.), London, Routledge and Kegan Paul.

—— 1980 'Ten Years of JASO', *Journal of the Anthropological Society of Oxford*, 11 (2), pp. 124–31.

—— 1981 'The Problem of Dominance', *Journal of the Anthropological Society of Oxford*, 12 (2); reprinted in Duke, L., Leacock, E. and Ardener, S. (eds) 1986.

—— 1982 'Social Anthropology, Language and Reality', in Parkin, D. (ed.) 1982 and in Harris, R. (ed.) 1982.

—— 1984 'Ethology and Language', in Harré, R. and Reynolds, V. (eds) 1984, pp. 111–15 (first delivered as part of Ardener, E. 1977).

—— 1985 'Social Anthropology and the Decline of Modernism', in Overing, J. (ed.) 1985.

—— 1987a '"Remote Areas" – some Theoretical Considerations', in Jackson, A. (ed.) 1987.

—— 1987b 'Edward Sapir 1884–1939', *Journal of the Anthropological Society of Oxford*, 18 (1), pp. 1–12.

—— 1987c 'Evidences of Creation', ASA conference paper, forthcoming in Tonkin, E., McDonald, M. and Chapman, M. (eds) *History and Ethnicity*, London, Tavistock.

Ardener, E. and Ardener, S. 1965 'A Directory Study of Social Anthropologists', *British Journal of Sociology*, 16 (4), pp. 295–314.

Ardener, E., Ardener, S., and Warmington, W. A. 1960 *Plantation and Village in the Cameroons*, Oxford, Oxford University Press.

Ardener, S. 1958 'Banana Co-operatives in the Southern Cameroons', *Nigerian Institute of Social and Economic Research: Conference Proceedings*, pp. 10–25, Ibadan.

—— 1968 'Eye-witnesses to the Annexation of Cameroon, 1883–1887', Buea; Government publication.

—— 1975a (ed.) *Perceiving Women*, London, Dent.

—— 1975b Introduction to Ardener, S. (ed.) 1975a.

—— 1978 (ed.) *Defining Females*, London, Croom Helm.

Armstrong, R. A. 1825 *A Gaelic Dictionary*, London, J. Duncan.

Banaji, J. 1970 'Anthropology in Crisis', *New Left Review*, 64, pp. 71–85.

Banton, M. (ed.) 1966 *Anthropological Approaches to the Study of Religion* (ASA Monographs 3), London, Tavistock.

Barltrop, R. 1975 *The Monument – The Story of the Socialist Party of Great Britain*, London, Pluto Press.

Barnes, J. A. 1949 'Measures of Divorce Frequency in Simple Societies', *Journal of the Royal Anthropological Institute*, 79, pp. 37–62.

—— 1963 'Some Ethical Problems in Modern Fieldwork', *British Journal of Sociology*, 14 (2), pp. 118–34.

Barnes, R. H. 1984 *Two Crows Denies It: A History of Controversy in Omaha Sociology*, Nebraska, University of Nebraska Press.

Barnett, C. 1972 *The Collapse of British Power*, London, Eyre Methuen.

Barth, F. 1966 *Models of Social Organisation*, occasional paper, 23, London, Royal Anthropological Institute.

—— 1969 *Ethnic Groups and Boundaries*, London, Allen and Unwin.

Barthes, R. 1964 *Eléments de Sémiologie*, Paris, Le Seuil.

—— 1967 *Elements of Semiology*, trans. of Barthes 1964, London, Cape.

Bates, R. H. 1970 'Approaches to the Study of Ethnicity', *Cahiers d'Etudes Africaines*, 10; pt. 40, pp. 546–61.

Bateson, G. 1936 *Naven*, Cambridge, Cambridge University Press.

Bazell, C. E., Catford, J. C., Halliday, M. A. K. and Robins, R. H. (eds) 1966 *In Memory of J. R. Firth*, London, Longman.

Beals, R. L. 1957 'Native Terms and Anthropological Methods', *American Anthropologist*, 59, pp. 716–17.

Beattie, J. H. M. 1957 'Nyoro Personal Names', *Uganda Journal*, 21, pp. 99–106.

—— 1960 'On the Nyoro Concept of Mahano', *African Studies*, 19, pp. 145–50.

—— 1964a *Other Cultures*, London, Cohen and West.

—— 1964b 'Kinship and Social Anthropology', *Man*, 64, pp. 101–3.

—— 1968 'Aspects of Nyoro Symbolism', *Africa*, 38 (4), pp. 413–42.

—— 1970 'On Understanding Ritual', in Wilson, B. (ed.) 1970.

—— 1971 'Has Social Anthropology a Future?', *Journal of the Anthropological Society of Oxford*, 2 (3), pp. 111–20.

Beattie, J. H. M. and Lienhardt, R. G. (eds) 1975 *Essays in Social Anthropology – Essays in Memory of E. E. Evans-Pritchard by his Former Colleagues*, Oxford, Clarendon Press.

Beck, B. E. F. 1969 'Colour and Heat in South Indian Ritual', *Man* (n.s.) 4 (4), pp. 553–72.

Beidelman, T. O. 1964 'Pig (Guluwe): an Essay on Ngulu Sexual Symbolism and Ceremony', *Southwestern Journal of Anthropology*, 20, pp. 359–92.

Benedict, B. 1972 'Social Regulation of Fertility', in Harrison, G. A. and Boyce, A. J. (eds) 1972.

Benvéniste, E. 1939 'La Nature du Signe Linguistique', *Acta Linguistica*, 1, pp. 23–9, reprinted in Benvéniste 1966, pp. 49–55.

—— 1966 *Problèmes de Linguistique Générale*, Paris, Gallimard.

Bergsland, K. and Vogt, H. 1962 'On the Validity of Glottochronology', *Current Anthropology*, 3, pp. 115–58.

Berlin, B. and Kay, P. 1969 *Basic Colour Terms, their Universality and Evolution*, Los Angeles, University of California Press.

Bernstein, B. 1958 'Some Sociological Determinants of Perception: an Inquiry into Subcultural Differences', *British Journal of Sociology*, 9, pp. 159–74, reprinted in Fishman (ed.) 1968.

—— 1960 'Language and Social Class', *British Journal of Sociology*, 11, pp. 271–6.

—— 1961 'Aspects of Language and Learning in the Genesis of the Social Process', *Journal of Child Psychology and Psychiatry* 1, pp. 313–24, reprinted in Hymes (ed.) 1964.

—— 1964 'Elaborated and Restricted Codes: their Social Origins and some Consequences', in Gumperz and Hymes (eds) 1964, pp. 55–69; and in Smith (ed.) 1966, pp. 427–41.

—— 1965 'A Socio-linguistic Approach to Social Learning', in J. Gould (ed.) 1965, pp. 144–68.

Berry, J. 1966 Introduction to second edition of Malinowski, 1935, vol. 2, pp. vii–xvii, London, Allen and Unwin.

Blacking, J. 1963 Review of Pocock 1961, *African Studies*, 22 (4), pp. 194–5.

Blanc, R. 1960 *Manuel de Recherche Démographique en Pays Sous-développés*, CCTA, Paris.

Bloch, M. 1977 'The Past and Present in Present' (Malinowski Lecture, 1977), *Man* (n.s.) 12, pp. 278–92.

Bloomfield, L. 1922 'Review of Edward Sapir's Language' in Koerner K. (ed.) 1984.

—— 1933 *Language*, New York, Holt, Rinehart and Winston.

Boas, F. 1913 *The Mind of Primitive Man*, Lowell Institute Lectures 1910–11, New York.

Bogatyrev, P. 1931 'Prispevek k Strukturalni Etnografii', *Slovenska Miscellanea*, Bratislava.

—— 1935 'Funkcno-strukturalna Metoda a ine Metody Etnografie a Folkloristiky', *Slovenske Pohl'ady*, 51, pp. 550–8.

Bohannan, L. 1952 'A Genealogical Charter', *Africa*, 22, pp. 301–15.

Bohannan, P. 1956 'On the Use of Native Language Categories in Ethnology', *American Anthropologist*, 58, p. 557.

—— 1958a 'On Anthropologists' Use of Language', *American Anthropologist*, 60, pp. 161–2.

—— 1958b Rejoinder to Taylor 1958, *American Anthropologist*, 60, pp. 941–2.

Borges, J. L. 1971 'Tlön, Uqbar, Orbis Tertius' in Borges, J. L. *Ficciones*, Madrid, Allianza Emece.

Bovin, M. 1966 'The Significance of the Sex of the Field Worker for Insights into the Male and Female Worlds', *Ethnos*, 31 (supp.), pp. 24–7.

Bowen, E. S. 1954 *Return to Laughter*, London, Gollancz.

Braithwaite, R. B. 1960 *Scientific Explanation*, Cambridge, Cambridge University Press.

Brown, R. W. and Lenneberg, E. H. 1954 'A Study in Language and Cognition', *Journal of Abnormal and Social Psychology*, 49, pp. 454–62, reprinted in Saporta (ed.) 1961.

Brugmann, K. 1885 *Zum Heutigen Stand der Sprachwissenschaft*, Strasburg, Carl J. Trubner.

—— 1902–4 *Kurze Vergleichende Grammatik der Indogermanischen Sprachen*, Strassburg, Carl J. Trubner.

Brugmann, K. and Delbruck, B. 1886–1900 *Grundriss der Vergleichenden Grammatik der Indogermanischen Sprachen*, Strassburg, Carl J. Trubner.

Buea (ms) 1926 *Assessment and Intelligence Reports on Ngie, Ngwaw, Mogamaw and Ngemba*, Cameroon archives, Buea.

Burling, R. 1964 'Cognition and Componential Analysis: God's Truth or Hocus Pocus', *American Anthropologist*, 66, pp. 20–8.

—— 1969 'Linguistics and Ethnographic Description', *American Anthropologist*, 71 (5), pp. 817–27.

Buyssens, E. 1943 *Les Langues et le Discours: Essais de Linguistique Fonctionelle dans le Cadre de la Sémiologie*, Brussels, Lebegue.

Callan, H. 1970 *Ethology and Society – Towards an Anthropological View*, Oxford, Clarendon Press.

Campbell, Lord Archibald 1889 *Waifs and Strays of Celtic Tradition*, vols 1–5.

Campbell, J. F. 1872 *Leabhar na Féinne: Heroic Gaelic Ballads collected in Scotland chiefly from 1512 to 1871*, London, Eyre and Spottiswoode (photo-reprint 1972, Shannon, Irish University Press).

Campbell, J. G., 1900 *Superstitions of the Highlands and Islands of Scotland*, Glasgow, MacLehose and Son.

Capell, A. 1966 *Studies in Sociolinguistics*, The Hague, Mouton.

Carmichael, A. 1900 *Carmina Gadelica*, Edinburgh, Oliver and Boyd.

Carnap, R. 1937 *The Logical Syntax of Language*, London, Kegan Paul, Trench, Trubner.

Carroll, J. B. (ed.) 1964 *Language, Thought and Reality; Selected Writings of Benjamin Lee Whorf*, Cambridge, Mass., MIT Press.

Casagrande, J. B. 1963 'Language Universals and Anthropology', in Greenberg (ed.) 1963, pp. 279–98.

Cassirer, E. 1933 'La langue et la construction du monde des objets', *Journal de Psychologie*, (numéro exceptionnel) 30 (1), pp. 18–44.

—— 1953 *Philosophy of Symbolic Forms*, vol. 1, New Haven, Yale University Press.

—— 1954 *An Essay on Man*, New York, Doubleday.

Chadwick, H. M. 1945 *The Nationalities of Europe*, Cambridge, Cambridge University Press.

Chagnon, N. A. 1972 'Tribal Social Organization and Genetic Microdifferentiation' in Harrison, G. and Boyce, A. (eds) 1972.

Chalmers, N. 1977 'The Heterogeneity of Play', paper for the Wenner-Gren Symposium, July.

Chapman, M. 1977 'What Science is Saying about the Celts', *Journal of the Anthropological Society of Oxford*, 8 (2), pp. 84–94.

—— 1978 *The Gaelic Vision in Scottish Culture*, London, Croom Helm.

—— 1982 '"Semantics" and the "Celt"', in Parkin, D. (ed.) 1982.

—— (with M. McDonald) 1987 'E. W. Ardener – Obituary Notice', *Anthropology Today*, 3 (6), pp. 21–3.

Chapman, M., McDonald, M. and Tonkin, E. (eds) 1989 *History and Ethnicity* (ASA Monographs 27), London, Routledge.

Chilver, E. M. 1966 'Zintgraff's Explorations in Bamenda, Adamawa and the Benue Lands, 1889–1892,' Buea, Government publication.

Chilver, E. M. and Kaberry, P.M. 1968 *Traditional Bamenda*, Buea, Government publication.

Chomsky, N. 1957 *Syntactic Structures*, The Hague, Mouton.

—— 1964 *Current Issues in Linguistic Theory*, The Hague, Mouton.

—— 1965 *Aspects of the Theory of Syntax*, Cambridge, Mass., MIT Press.

—— 1966a *Topics in the Theory of Generative Grammar*, The Hague, Mouton.

—— 1966b *Cartesian Linguistics*, New York, Harper and Row.

—— 1968 *Language and Mind*, New York, Harcourt.

—— 1969 'Language and Philosophy', in Hook, S. (ed.) 1969.

Chomsky, N. and Halle, M. 1965 'Some Controversial Questions in Phonological Theory', *Journal of Linguistics*, 1, pp. 97–138.

Chowning, A. 1970 'Taboo', *Man*, (n.s.) 5, pp. 309–10.

Churchill, W. S. 1956 *A History of the English-Speaking Peoples*, vol. 1, London, Cassell.

Clarke, J. 1848 *Specimens of Dialects: Short Vocabularies of Languages; and Notes of Countries and Customs in Africa*, Berwick-on-Tweed.

Cohen, Abner 1969 *Custom and Politics in Urban Africa*, London, Routledge and Kegan Paul.

Cohen, Anthony (ed.) 1982 *Belonging*, Manchester, Manchester University Press.

Cohen, I. B. (ed.) 1958 *Isaac Newton's Papers and Letters on Natural Philosophy and Related Documents*, Cambridge, Cambridge University Press.

Cohen, L. J. 1966 *The Diversity of Meaning*, second revised edition, London, Methuen (first edition 1962).

Cohen, M. 1948 *Linguistique et Matérialisme Dialectique*, Paris, Perches; also in *Cinquante Années de Recherches Linguistiques, Ethnographiques, Sociologiques, Critiques et Pedagogiques* 1955, pp. 38–52, Paris, Klincksieck.

Colby, B. 1966 'Ethnographic Semantics: a Preliminary Survey', *Current Anthropology*, 7 (1), pp. 3–32.

Collinder, B. 1968 *Kritische Bemerkungen zum Saussure'schen Cours de Linguistique Générale*, Uppsala, Acta Societatis Linguisticae Upsaliensis, Almqvist and Wiksell.

Conklin, H. C. 1955 'Hanunóo Color Categories', *Southwestern Journal of Anthropology*, 11, pp. 339–44, reprinted in Hymes, D. (ed.) 1964.

Cooper, D. (1985) *The Road to Mingulay – a View of the Western Isles*, London, Routledge and Kegan Paul.

Cowgill, W. 1963 'Universals in Indo-European Diachronic Morphology', in Greenberg (ed.) 1963.

Cox, J. C. 1910 *The Parish Registers of England*, Parish Register Society, Public Records Office, London.

Crabb, D. W. 1965 *Ekoid Bantu Languages of Ogoja*, Cambridge, Cambridge University Press.

Crick, M. 1973 'Some Reflections on the ASA Decennial Conference', *Journal of the Anthropological Society of Oxford*, 4 (3), pp. 176–9.

—— 1976 *Explorations in Language and Meaning: Towards a Semantic Anthropology*, London, Dent.

Crossland, R. 1951 'A Reconsideration of the Hittite Evidence for the Existence of 'Laryngeals' in Primitive Indo-European', *Transactions of the Philological Society*, pp. 88–130.

Crystal, D. 1971 'Prosodic and Paralinguistic Correlates of Social Categories', in Ardener, E. (ed.), 1971a.

Deacon, J. J. 1974 *Tongue Tied*, London, National Society for Mentally Handicapped Children.

De Bono, E. 1969 *The Mechanism of Mind*, Harmondsworth, Penguin.

Delancey, P. and Schraeder, M. 1986 *Cameroon – World Bibliographical Series Vol. 63*, Oxford, Clio Press.

Denison, N. 1968 'Sauris: A Trilingual Community in Diatypic Perspective', *Man*, (n.s.) 3 (4), pp. 578–92.

—— 1971 'Some Observations on Language Variety and Plurilingualism', in Ardener, E. (ed.) 1971a.

Deutsches Kolonialblatt (DKB), Berlin (series).

Devereux, G. 1955 *A Study of Abortion in Primitive Societies*, New York, Julian Press.

Dominic, H. 1901 *Kamerun: Sechs Kriegs– und Friedensjahre in Deutschen Tropen*, Berlin.

Doroszewski, W. 1933 'Quelques Remarques sur les Rapports de la Sociologie et de la Linguistique: Durkheim et F. de Saussure', *Journal de Psychologie*, (numéro exceptionnel) 30 (1), pp. 82–91.

Douglas, M. 1966a *Purity and Danger*, London, Routledge and Kegan Paul.

—— 1966b 'Population Control in Primitive Groups', *British Journal of Sociology*, 17 (3), pp. 263–73.

—— 1968 'The Social Control of Cognition: Some Factors in Joke Perception', *Man* (n.s.) 3, pp. 361–76.

—— 1970a *Natural Symbols*, London, Cresset.

—— (ed.) 1970b *Witchcraft Confessions and Accusations* (ASA Monographs 9), London, Tavistock.

Dresch, P. 1975 'Marxist Analyses and Social Anthropology', *Journal of the Anthropological Society of Oxford*, 6 (3), pp. 213–17.

—— 1976 'Economy and Ideology: an Obstacle to Materialist Analysis', *Journal of the Anthropological Society of Oxford*, 7 (2), pp. 55–77.

Duke, L., Leacock, E. and Ardener, S. (eds) 1986 *Visibility and Power – Essays on Women in Society and Development*, Oxford, Oxford University Press.

Dumond, D. E. 1965 'Population Growth and Cultural Change', *Southwestern Journal of Anthropology*, 21, pp. 302–24.

Dumont, L. and Pocock, F. F. 1957–66 contributions to Indian Sociology Series, The Hague, Mouton.

Dumont, L. 1975 Preface to the French edition of *The Nuer*, in Beattie J. H. M. and Lienhardt, R. G. (eds) 1975.

Durkheim, E. 1912 *Les Formes Elémentaires de la Vie Religieuse*, Paris.

—— 1951 *Sociology and Philosophy*, translated by D. F. Pocock from French edition of 1898, London, Cohen and West.

Durkheim, E. and Mauss, M. 1963 *Primitive Classification*, translated with an introduction by R. Needham, London, Cohen and West.

Dwelly, E. 1920 *The Illustrated Gaelic-English Dictionary: Containing Every Gaelic Word and Meaning Given in All Previous Published Dictionaries, and a Great Number Never in Print Before*, 2nd (standard) edition (reissued by Glasgow, Gairm).

Edwards, J. (1985) *Language, Society and Identity*, Oxford, Basil Blackwell.

Ellen, R. F. and Reason, D. 1979 *Classifications in their Social Context*, New York, Academic Press.

Ellis, J. 1966 *Towards a General Comparative Linguistics*, The Hague, Mouton.

Engler, R. 1967 *Edition Critique* of Saussure 1916, Wiesbaden, Harrassowitz.

—— 1968 *Lexique de la Terminologie Saussurienne*, Utrecht/Antwerp, Spectrum.

Epale, S. J. 1985 *Plantations and Development in Western Cameroon, 1885–1975: or, 'A study in Agrarian Capitalism'*, New York, Vantage Press.

Epstein, A. L. 1958 *Politics in an Urban African Community*, Manchester, Manchester University Press.

—— (ed.) 1967 *The Craft of Social Anthropology*, London, Tavistock.

Evans-Pritchard, E. E. 1934 'Imagery in Ngok Cattle Names', *Bulletin of the School of Oriental*

and African Studies, 7 (3), pp. 623–8.
—— 1937 *Witchcraft, Oracles and Magic among the Azande*, Oxford, Clarendon Press.
—— 1940 *The Nuer*, Oxford, Clarendon Press.
—— 1948 'Nuer Modes of Address', *Uganda Journal*, 12 (2), pp. 166–71, also in Hymes (ed.) 1964.
—— 1950 'Social Anthropology, Past and Present' (Marett Lecture), *Man*, 50, pp. 118–24.
—— 1954a 'Zande Texts', *Man*, 54, p. 164.
—— 1954b 'A Zande Slang Language', *Man*, 54, pp. 185–6.
—— 1955 'Zande Historical Texts I', *Sudan Notes and Records*, 36, pp. 123–45.
—— 1956a 'Zande Historical Texts II', *Sudan Notes and Records*, 37, pp. 20–47.
—— 1956b '*Sanza*, A Characteristic Feature of Zande Language and Thought', *Bulletin of the School of Oriental and African Languages*, 18, pp. 161–80.
—— 1956c *Nuer Religion*, Oxford, Clarendon Press.
—— 1957 'Zande Historical Texts III', *Sudan Notes and Records*, 38, pp. 74–99.
—— 1960 Preface to Hertz 1960.
—— 1961a *Anthropology and History*, Manchester, Manchester University Press.
—— 1961b 'A Note on Bird Cries and Other Sounds in Zande', *Man*, 61, pp.19–20.
—— 1962a 'Three Zande Texts', *Man*, 62, pp. 149–52.
—— 1962b 'Some Zande Texts, pt. 1', *Kush*, 10, pp. 289–314.
—— 1962c 'Ideophones in Zande', *Sudan Notes and Records*, 63, pp. 143–6.
—— 1962d *Essays in Social Anthropology*, London, Faber and Faber.
—— 1962e 'The Divine Kingship of the Shilluk of the Nilotic Sudan', in Evans-Pritchard 1962d.
—— 1963a 'Some Zande Texts, pt. 2', *Kush*, 11, pp. 273–307.
—— 1963b 'Meaning in Zande Proverbs', *Man*, 63, pp.4-7.
—— 1963c 'Sixty-one Zande Proverbs', *Man*, 63, pp. 109–12.
—— 1964 The Oxford Library of African Literature series (co-editor with W. Whiteley and R. G. Lienhardt), Oxford, Clarendon Press.
—— 1965a *The Position of Women and Other Essays in Social Anthropology*, London, Faber and Faber.
—— 1965b 'The Position of Women in Primitive Societies and in Our Own', in Evans-Pritchard, E. E. 1965a.
—— 1965c 'The Comparative Method', in Evans-Pritchard, E. E. 1965a.
—— 1965d *Theories of Primitive Religion*, Oxford, Clarendon Press.
—— 1970 'Social Anthropology at Oxford', *Journal of the Anthropological Society of Oxford*, 1 (3), pp. 103–9.
—— 1973a 'Some Reminiscences and Reflections on Fieldwork', *Journal of the Anthropological Society of Oxford*, 4 (1), pp. 1–12.
—— 1973b 'The Intellectualist (English) Interpretation of Magic', *Journal of the Anthropological Society of Oxford*, 4 (3), pp. 123–42.
Ferguson, A. 1767 *An Essay in the History of Civil Society*, London.
Ferguson, C. A. 1959 'Diglossia', *Word*, 15, pp. 325–40, also in Hymes (ed.) 1964.
Field, M. J. 1960 *Search for Security*, London, Faber and Faber.
Field, M. 1969 'The Prime Minister's Lodge, Buea', Buea, Government publication.
Finnegan, R. 1969a 'Attitudes to the Study of Oral Literature', *Man*, (n.s.) 4 (1), pp. 59–69.
—— 1969b 'How to do Things with Words', *Man*, (n.s.) 4 (4), pp. 537–52.
—— 1970 *Oral Literature in Africa*, Oxford, Clarendon Press.
Firth, J. R. 1934 'Linguistics and the Functional Point of View', *English Studies*, 16 (1), pp. 18–24.
—— 1957a *Papers in Linguistics, 1934–1951*, Oxford, Oxford University Press.
—— 1957b 'Ethnographic Analysis and Language with Reference to Malinowski's Views', in Firth, R. (ed.) 1957 and Palmer (ed.) 1968.
—— 1957c 'A Synopsis of Linguistic Theory 1930–1955', in *Studies in Linguistic Analysis*,

Oxford, Basil Blackwell, pp. 1–32.

Firth, R. 1940 'The Analysis of *Mana*: an Empirical Approach', *Journal of Polynesian Society*, 49, pp. 483–510.

—— 1951 'Contemporary British Social Anthropology', *American Anthropologist*, 53 (4), pp. 474–89.

—— (ed.) 1957 *Man and Culture, an Evaluation of the Work of Malinowski*, London, Routledge and Kegan Paul.

—— 1966 'The Meaning of Pali in Tikopia', in Bazell et al. (eds) 1966, pp. 96–115.

Firth, Rosemary 1971 'Anthropology within and without the Ivory Towers', *Journal of the Anthropological Society of Oxford*, 2 (2), pp. 74–82.

Fishman, J. A. (ed.) 1968a *Readings in the Sociology of Language*, The Hague, Mouton.

—— 1968b 'Sociolinguistic Perspectives on the Study of Bilingualism', *Linguistics*, 39, pp. 21–49.

Fortes, M. 1945 *The Dynamics of Clanship among the Tallensi*, Oxford, Oxford University Press.

—— 1949 *The Web of Kinship among the Tallensi*, Oxford, Oxford University Press.

—— 1970 *Time and Social Structure*, London, Athlone Press.

Fortes, M. and Dieterlen, G. (eds) 1965 *African Systems of Thought*, Oxford, Oxford University Press.

Foster, M. and Brandes, S. (eds) 1980 *Symbol as Sense*, New York, Academic Press.

Fox, R. and Tiger, L. 1972 *The Imperial Animal*, London, Secker and Warburg.

Frake, C. O. 1961 'The Diagnosis of Disease among the Subanun of Mindanao', *American Anthropologist*, 63, pp. 113–32.

Frazer, J. G. 1910 *Totemism and Exogamy* (4 vols), London, Macmillan.

Freedman, M. 1963 'A Chinese Phase in Social Anthropology', *British Journal of Sociology*, 14 (1), pp. 1–19.

Freeman, D. 1962 Review of Leach, E. R. *Rethinking Anthropology* in *Man*, 62.

Freud, S. 1913 *Totem and Taboo*, translated and published 1950, London, Routledge and Kegan Paul. Standard edition, vol. 13, London, Hogarth.

Fries, C. C. 1963 'The Bloomfield "School"', in Mohrmann, Sommerfelt and Whatmough (eds) 1963, pp. 196–224.

Garvin, P. L. (ed.) 1957 *Report of the Seventh Annual Round Table Meeting on Linguistics and Language Study*, Washington, Georgetown University Press.

Gellner, E. 1968 'The New Idealism: Cause and Meaning in the Social Sciences', in Lakatos, I. and Musgrave, A. (eds) 1968.

—— 1983 *Nations and Nationalism*, Oxford, Basil Blackwell.

'Gertrude' 1978 'A Postface to a few Prefaces', (translated by McDonald, M.) *Journal of the Anthropological Society of Oxford*, 9 (2), pp. 133–42.

Gibbon, E. 1787 *The Decline and Fall of the Roman Empire*, vol. 3 (reprinted 1954), London, Dent.

Gladwin, T. and Sturtevant, W. C. (eds) 1962 *Anthropology and Human Behaviour*, Washington, Anthropological Society of Washington.

Glass, D. V. and Eversley, D. E. C. 1965 *Population in History*, London, Arnold.

Gleason, H. A. 1955a *An Introduction to Descriptive Linguistics*, New York, Holt, Rinehart and Winston.

—— 1955b *Workbook in Descriptive Linguistics*, New York, Holt, Rinehart and Winston.

Gluckman, M. (ed.) 1964 *Closed Systems and Open Minds*, Edinburgh, Oliver and Boyd.

—— 1968 'Psychological, Sociological and Anthropological Explanations of Witchcraft and Gossip: a Clarification', *Man*, (n.s.) 3, pp. 20–4.

Gödel, R. 1957 *Les Sources Manuscrites du Cours de Linguistique Générale de F. de Saussure*, Paris, Droz.

—— (ed.) 1969 *A Geneva School Reader in Linguistics*, Bloomington, Indiana University Press.

Golding, W. 1955 *The Inheritors*, London, Faber and Faber.

Goodenough, W. H. 1956 'Componential Analysis and the Study of Meaning', *Language*, 32, pp. 195–216.

—— 1957 'Cultural Anthropology and Linguistics', in Garvin, P. L. (ed.) 1957.

Goody, J. 1958 *The Development Cycle in Domestic Groups*, Cambridge, Cambridge University Press.

—— 1966 'The Prospects for Social Anthropology', *New Society*, 13 October, pp. 574–6.

Gosse, E. 1907 *Father and Son*, London, Heinemann (reprinted Harmondsworth, Penguin 1949).

Gould, J. (ed.) 1965 *Penguin Survey of the Social Sciences 1965*, Harmondsworth, Penguin.

GPC, 1964 *Geriadur Prifysgol Cymru*, pt. XVIII, Cardiff, Gwasg Prifysgol Cymru.

GPC, 1968 *Geriadur Prifysgol Cymru*, pt. XXII, Cardiff, Gwasg Prifysgol Cymru.

Grant, I. F. 1961 *Highland Folk Ways*, London, Routledge and Kegan Paul.

Graunt, J. 1662 *Natural and Political Observations upon the Bills of Mortality*, London, reprinted 1964, *Journal of the Institute of Actuaries*, 90, pt. 1 (no. 384), pp. 4–61.

Green, M. M. and Igwe, G. E. 1963 *A Descriptive Grammar of Igbo*, Oxford, Oxford University Press.

Greenberg, J. H. 1948 'Linguistics and Ethnology', *Southwestern Journal of Anthropology*, 4, pp. 140–7.

—— 1955 *Studies in African Linguistic Classification*, New Haven, Compass.

—— (ed.) 1963a *Universals of Language*, Cambridge, Mass., MIT Press.

—— 1963b *The Languages of Africa*, The Hague, Mouton.

—— 1966 'Synchronic and Diachronic Universals in Phonology', *Language*, 42, pp. 508–17.

Gumperz, J. J. and Hymes, D. (eds) 1964 *The Ethnography of Communication*, Menasha, Wis., American Anthropological Association.

Guthrie, M. 1948 *The Classification of the Bantu Languages*, London, International African Institute.

—— 1953 *The Bantu Languages of Western Equatorial Africa*, London, International African Institute.

—— 1962 'Some Developments in the Pre-history of the Bantu Languages', *Journal of African History*, 3, pp. 273–82.

Haas, M. R. 1969 *The Prehistory of Languages*, The Hague, Mouton.

Hammel, E. A. (ed.) 1965 *Formal Semantic Analysis*, American Anthropologist, special publication 67 (5), pt. 2.

Hamp, E. P. 1958 'Consonant Allophones in Proto-Keltic', in *Lochlann*, 1, Oslo, Oslo University Press pp. 209–17.

Hardman, C. 1973 'Can there be an Anthropology of Children?', *Journal of the Anthropological Society of Oxford*, 4, pp. 85–99.

Harré, R. and Reynolds, V. (eds) 1984 *The Meaning of Primate Signals*, Cambridge, Cambridge University Press.

Harré, R. and Secord, P. 1972 *The Explanation of Social Behaviour*, Oxford, Basil Blackwell.

Harris, M. 1969 *The Rise of Anthropological Theory*, London, Routledge and Kegan Paul.

Harris, R. (ed.) 1982 *Approaches to Language*, Oxford, Pergamon Press.

Harris, Z. S. 1951 *Methods in Structural Linguistics*, Chicago, Chicago University Press.

Harrison, G. A. and Boyce, A. J. (eds) 1972 *The Structure of Human Populations*, Oxford, Clarendon Press.

Hart, H. L. A. 1961 *The Concept of Law*, Oxford, Clarendon Press.

Hastrup, K. 1978 'The Post-structuralist Position of Social Anthropology', in Schwimmer, E. (ed.) 1978.

—— 1982 'Establishing an Ethnicity: the Emergence of the "Icelanders" in the early Middle Ages', in Parkin, D. (ed.) 1982.

—— 1985 *Culture and History in Medieval Iceland*, Oxford, Oxford University Press.

Hastrup, K., Ovesen, J. and Ramlov, K. 1975 *Den Ny Antropologi*, Copenhagen, Borgen/Basus.

Hauschild, R. 1964 *Die Indogermanische Volker und Sprachen Klienasiens*, Berlin, Akademie-Verlag.

Hawthorn, G. 1970 *The Sociology of Fertility*, London, Macmillan.

Hayes, E. N. and T. (eds) 1970 *Claude Lévi-Strauss: The Anthropologist as Hero*, Cambridge, Mass., MIT Press.

Hazelwood, A. (ed.) 1967 *African Integration and Disintegration*, Oxford, Oxford University Press and RIIA.

Heelas, P. 1970 'Meaning for Whom?', *Journal of the Anthropological Society of Oxford*, 1 (1), pp. 1–10.

Henson, H. 1971 'Early British Anthropologists and Language', in Ardener, E. (ed.) 1971a.

—— 1974 *British Social Anthropologists and Language: a History of Separate Development*, Oxford, Clarendon Press.

Hertz, R. 1960 (first published 1909) *Death and the Right Hand*, translated by R. and C. Needham, London, Cohen and West.

—— 1973 'The Pre-Eminence of the Right Hand: A Study in Religious Polarity', translated and reprinted in Needham, R. (ed.) 1973.

Highland Society of Scotland, 1828 *Dictionarum Scoto-Celticum: A Dictionary of the Gaelic Language* (2 vols), Edinburgh, Blackwood.

Hjelmslev, L. 1943 *Omkring Sprogteoriens Grundlaeggelse*, Copenhagen, Munksgaard.

—— 1957 'Pour une Sémantique Structurale', in Hjelmslev (ed.) 1959, pp. 96–112.

—— (ed.) 1959 *Essais Linguistiques*, Copenhagen, Nordisk Sprogog Kulturforlag.

—— 1963 *Prolegomena to a Theory of Language* (translation by F. J. Whitfield of Hjelmslev, 1943; first edition, 1961) Menasha, Wis., University of Wisconsin.

Hocart, A. M. 1937 'Kinship Systems', *Anthropos* 22, pp. 345–51; reprinted in Hocart, 1970.

—— 1970 *The Life-giving Myth*, edited by R. Needham (2nd edition), London, Methuen.

Hockett, C. F. 1954 'Chinese versus English: an Exploration of the Whorfian Hypothesis', in Hoijer, H. (ed.) 1954.

—— 1958 *A Course in Modern Linguistics*, London, Macmillan.

—— 1968 *The State of the Art*, The Hague, Mouton.

Hoenigswald, H. M. 1960 *Language Change and Language Reconstruction*, Chicago, Chicago University Press.

Hoijer, H. (ed.) 1954 *Language and Culture*, Chicago, Chicago University Press (second edition 1971).

Hollingsworth, T. H. 1969 *Historical Demography*, London, Hodder and Stoughton.

Holt, H. and Pym, H. 1984 *A Very Private Eye – the Diaries, Letters and Notebooks of Barbara Pym*, London, Macmillan.

Homans, G. and Schneider, D. M. 1955 *Marriage, Authority and Final Causes*, New York, Free Press.

Hook, S. (ed.) 1969 *Language and Philosophy*, New York, New York University Press.

Householder, F. W. 1952 review of Jones, D., *The Phoneme*, *International Journal of American Linguistics*, 18, pp. 99–105.

—— 1957 'Rough Justice in Linguistics', in Garvin (ed.) 1957, pp. 153–65.

—— 1970 review of Hockett, 1968 *Journal of Linguistics*, 6 (1), pp. 129–34.

Hudson, D. 1972 *Munby, Man of Two Worlds: The Life and Diaries of Arthur J. Munby 1828 – 1910*, London, Murray.

Humboldt, W. von 1836 *Über die Verschiedenheit des menschlichen Sprachbaues und ihren Einfluss auf die geistige Entwicklung des Menschengeschlechts*, Berlin, Königliche Akademie der Wissenschaften. Photo-reprint, Bonn, Dummlers Verlag, 1967.

—— 1969 *De l'Origine des Formes Grammaticales suivi de Lettre à M. Abel Rémusal*, Bordeaux, Ducros.

Humphrey, C. 1971 'Some Ideas of Saussure applied to Buryat Magical Drawings', in Ardener, E. (ed.) 1971a.

Hurault, J. 1969 'Eleveurs et Cultivateurs des Hauts Plateaux du Cameroun: la Population du Lamidat de Banyo', *Population*, 5, pp. 963–94.

Huxley, F. 1966 *The Invisibles*, London, Hart-Davis.

Hymes, D. 1960 'Lexicostatistics so far', *Current Anthropology*, 1 (1), pp. 3–44.

—— 1962 'The Ethnography of Speaking', in Gladwin, T. and Sturtevant, W. C. (eds) 1962.

—— (ed.) 1964 *Language in Culture and Society*, New York, Harper and Row.

—— 1971 'Sociolinguistics and the Ethnography of Speaking', in Ardener, E. (ed.) 1971a.

IPA 1949 *The Principles of the International Phonetic Association*, London, International Phonetic Association.

Ittmann, J. 1953 *Volkskundliche und religiose Begriffe im nordlichen Waldland von Kamerun*, Afrika u. Übersee, Beiheft 26, Berlin.

—— 1957 'Der Kultische Geheimbund djengu an der Kameruner Kuste', *Anthropos*, 52, pp. 135–76.

Jackson, A. 1987 *Anthropology at Home* (ASA monographs 25), London, Tavistock.

Jackson, K. H. 1953 *Language and History in Early Britain*, Edinburgh, Edinburgh University Press.

Jacquard, A. 1968 'Evolution des Populations d'Effectif Limité, *Population*, 2, pp. 279–300.

Jakobson, R. 1960 'Why "Mama" and "Papa"?', in Kaplan, B. and Wapner, S. (eds) 1960.

—— 1966 'Henry Sweet's Path towards Phonemics', in Bazell et al. 1966, pp. 242–54.

—— 1968 *Child Language, Aphasia and Phonological Universals*, The Hague, Mouton.

Jakobson, R. and Halle, M. 1956 *Fundamentals of Language*, The Hague, Mouton.

Jarvie, I. C. 1963 *The Revolution in Anthropology*, London, Routledge and Kegan Paul.

Jenkins, T. 1975 'Althusser's Philosophy', *Journal of the Anthropological Society of Oxford*, 6 (1), pp. 1–17.

—— 1977 'The Death of Marx: a Media Event', *Journal of the Anthropological Society of Oxford*, 8 (3), pp. 116–24.

Jerschina, J. 1983 'Polish Modernism and Malinowski's Personality', unpublished symposium paper, Krakow, 27 September.

Johnson, S. and Boswell, J. (1775/1785) *Journey to the Western Islands and A Tour to the Hebrides* (edited by R. W. Chapman, 1930, and subsequent editions), Oxford, Oxford University Press.

Jones, D. 1962 *The Phoneme: Its Nature and Use*, revised edition, Cambridge, Heffer.

—— 1964 *The History and Meaning of the Term 'Phoneme'*, London, International Phonetic Association.

Jones, G. and Jones, T. J. 1949 *The Mabinogion*, London, Dent.

Jones, Sir W. 1799 'The Third Anniversary Discourse on the Hindus', *The Works of Sir William Jones* 6 vols, London, Robinson and Evans; reprinted in Lehmann (ed.), 1967.

Joos, M. (ed.) 1957 *Readings in Linguistics I; The Development of Descriptive Linguistics in America 1925–1956* (reprinted 1967), Chicago, Chicago University Press.

Kaberry, P. M. 1939 *Aboriginal Woman: Sacred and Profane*, London, Routledge and Kegan Paul (reprinted Gregg International, 1970).

—— 1952 *Women of the Grassfields*, London, HMSO (reprinted Gregg International, 1970).

—— 1974 'A Glimpse of Malinowski in Retrospect', *Journal of the Anthropological Society of Oxford*, 5 (2), pp. 104–8.

Kaplan, B. and Wapner, S. (eds) 1960 *Perspectives in Psychological Theory*, New York, International Universities Press.

Kardiner, A. and Preble, E. 1961 *They Studied Man*, London, Secker and Warburg.

Kilmister, C. W. 1967 *Language, Logic and Mathematics*, London, English Universities Press.

King, R. 1969 *Historical Linguistics and Generative Grammar*, Englewood Cliffs, Prentice Hall.

Koelle, S. W. 1854 *Polyglotta Africana*, London, Church Missionary Society.

Koerner, K. 1984 *Edward Sapir: Appraisals of his Life and Work*, Amsterdam and Philadelphia, John Benjamins.

Kondo, S., Kawai, M. and Ehara, A. (eds) 1975 *Contemporary Primatology*, Basel, Karger.

Krahe, H. 1962–3 *Indogermanische Sprachwissenschaft*, vol. 1, 1962, vol. 2, 1963, Berlin, De Gruyter.

Krapf-Askari, E. 1969 *Yoruba Towns and Cities*, Oxford, Clarendon Press.

Kroeber, A. L. 1909 'Classificatory Systems of Relationship', *Journal of the Royal Anthropological Institute*, 39, pp. 74–84.

Kuper, A. 1973 *Anthropologists and Anthropology: The British School 1922–72*, London, Allen Lane.

La Fontaine, J. (ed.) 1972 *The Interpretation of Ritual*, London, Tavistock.

Lainé-Kerjean, C. 1942/3 'Le Calendrier Celtique', *Zeitschrift fur Celtische Philologie*, 23, pp. 249–84.

Lakatos, I. and Musgrave, A. (eds) *Problems in the Philosophy of Science*, Amsterdam, North Holland.

Langendoen, D. T. 1968 *The London School of Linguistics: A Study of the Linguistic Theories of B. Malinowski and J. R. Firth*, Cambridge, Mass., MIT press.

Leach, E. R. 1954a review of Durkheim, 1951, *Man*, 54, pp. 92–3.

—— 1954b *Political Systems of Highland Burma*, London, Bell.

—— 1957 'The Epistemological Background to Malinowski's Empiricism', in Firth, R. (ed.) 1957.

—— 1958 'Concerning Trobriand Clans and the Kinship Category *Tabu*', In J. Goody (ed.) 1958.

—— 1961a *Rethinking Anthropology*, London, Athlone Press.

—— 1961b 'Two Essays Concerning the Symbolic Representation of Time', in Leach, E. R. 1961a.

—— 1962 'Classification in Social Anthropology', *Aslib Proceedings*, 14 (8), pp. 239–42.

—— 1964 'Anthropological Aspects of Language: Animal Categories and Verbal Abuse', in Lenneberg, E. H. (ed.) 1964.

—— 1969 *Genesis as Myth and Other Essays*, London, Cape.

—— 1970 *Lévi-Strauss*, London, Fontana/Collins.

—— 1971a 'More about Mama and Papa', in R. Needham (ed.) 1971.

—— 1971b Review of M. Douglas, *Natural Symbols*, *New York Review of Books*.

Leach, E. R., Jarvie, I. C., Gellner, E., et al 1966 'Frazer and Malinowski: on the Founding Fathers', *Current Anthropology*, 7 (5), pp. 560–76 (earlier, in part, in *Encounter*, October, 1965).

Lees, R. B. 1953 'The Basis of Glottochronology', *Language*, 29, pp. 113–27.

Lefèbvre, H. 1966 *Le Langage et la Société*, Paris, Gallimard.

Lehmann, W.P. (ed. and trans.) 1967 *A Reader in Nineteenth Century Historical Indo-European Linguistics*, Bloomington, Indiana University Press.

Lehmann, W. P. and Malkiel, Y. (eds) 1968 *Directions for Historical Linguistics*, Austin, University of Texas Press.

Leitner, G. W. 1874 discussion in *Journal of the Royal Anthropological Institute*, 4, pp. 212–14.

Lenneberg, E. H. (ed.) 1964 *New Directions in the Study of Language*, Cambridge, Mass., MIT Press.

Lenneberg, E. H. and Roberts, J. M. 1956 *The Language of Experience*, Baltimore, Waverly Press, Indiana University Publications in Anthropology and Linguistics 13; reprinted in Saporta (ed.) 1961.

Leopold, J. 1973 'Tylor's Solar Sixpence', *Journal of the Anthropological Society of Oxford*, 4 (1), pp. 13–16.

Leroy, M. 1967 *The Main Trends in Modern Linguistics*, Oxford, Basil Blackwell.

Leroy, R. 1922 'Syndrome of Lilliputian Hallucinations', *Journal of Nervous and Mental Disease*, 56, p. 325.

Leroy-Gourhan, Z. 1964 *Le Geste et La Parole*, Paris, Albin Michel

Le Vine, V. and Nye, R. 1974 *Historical Dictionary of Cameroon (African Historical Dictionaries, no. 1)*, Metuchen, New Jersey, The Scarecrow Press.

Lévi-Strauss, C. 1949 *Les Structures élémentaires de la Parenté*, Paris, Presses Universitaires de France (2nd edition 1967).

—— 1953 'Social Structure', *Anthropology Today* (ed. Kroeber), Chicago, Wenner Gren Foundation (see also *Structural Anthropology*, 1963)

—— 1955 *Tristes Tropiques*, Paris, Plon.

—— 1958 *Anthropologie Structurale*, Paris, Plon.

—— 1962a *Le Totemisme Aujourd'hui*, Paris, Presses Universitaires de France.

—— 1962b *La Pensée Sauvage*, Paris, Plon.

—— 1963a *Structural Anthropology* (translation of Lévi-Strauss, 1958), New York, Basic Books.

—— 1963b *Totemism* (translation of Lévi-Strauss, 1962a, by R. Needham), Boston, Beacon Press.

—— 1964 *Mythologiques 1: Le Cru et le Cuit*, Paris, Plon.

—— 1966a *The Savage Mind* (translation of Lévi-Strauss, 1962b), London, Weidenfeld and Nicolson.

—— 1966b *Mythologiques 2: Du Miel aux Cendres*, Paris, Plon.

—— 1966c Introduction to third edition of Mauss, 1950, Paris, Presses Universitaires de France.

—— 1967a *The Scope of Anthropology* (translation of *Leçon Inaugurale Faite Le Mardi 5 Janvier 1960*), London, Cape.

—— 1967b *Les Structures Elémentaires de la Parenté* (2nd edition) Paris, Presses Universitaires de France.

—— 1968 *Mythologiqes 3: L'Origine des Manières de Table*, Paris, Plon.

—— 1969 *The Elementary Structures of Kinship*, translated and edited by R. Needham (translated from revised edition (1967) of Lévi-Strauss, 1949), Boston, Beacon Press.

—— 1970 *The Raw and the Cooked* (translation of Lévi-Strauss, 1964), London, Cape.

Lévy-Bruhl, L. 1910 *Les Fonctions Mentales dans les Sociétés Inférieures*, Paris.

Lewin, K. 1935 *A Dynamic Theory of Personality*, New York, McGraw-Hill.

—— 1936 *Principles of Topological Psychology*, New York, McGraw-Hill.

—— 1952 *Field Theory in Social Science*, London, Tavistock.

Lewis, H. 1943 *Yr Elfen Ladin yn yr Iaith Gymraeg*, Cardiff, Gwasg Prifysgol Cymru.

Lewis, I. M. (ed.) 1968 *History and Social Anthropology*, London, Tavistock.

—— 1971 *Ecstatic Religion*, Harmondsworth, Penguin.

Lienhardt, R. G. 1961 *Divinity and Experience*, Oxford, Clarendon Press.

Loomis, R. S. 1956 *Wales and the Arthurian Legend*, Cardiff, University of Wales Press.

Lorimer, F., et al. 1954 *Culture and Human Fertility*, UNESCO, Paris.

Lounsbury, F. G. 1956 'A Semantic Analysis of the Pawnee Kinship Usage', *Language*, 32, pp. 158–94.

—— 1965 'Another View of Trobriand Kinship Categories', in Hammel, E. A. (ed.) 1965.

—— 1969 'Language and Culture', in Hook (ed.) 1969.

Lowes, J. L. 1927 *The Road to Xanadu: A Study in the Ways of the Imagination*, London, Constable.

Lyons, J. 1968 *Introduction to Theoretical Linguistics*, Cambridge, Cambridge University Press.

—— 1970 *Chomsky*, London, Fontana/Collins.

Lyons, J. and Wales, R. J. (eds) 1966 *Psycholinguistic Papers*, Edinburgh, Edinburgh University Press.

MacAlpine, N. 1832 *Pronouncing Gaelic-English Dictionary*, reissued 1973, Glasgow, Gairm.

Macaulay, D. (ed.) 1976 *Nua-Bhàrdachd Ghàidhlig (Modern Scottish Gaelic Poems)*, Edinburgh, Southside.

McCall, G. 1970 '£.s.d. Varna', *Journal of the Anthropological Society of Oxford*, 1 (3), pp. 131–6.

McDonald, M. E. 1978 'Language "At Home" to Educated Radicalism', *Journal of the Anthropological Society of Oxford*, 9 (1), pp. 13–34.

—— 1982 'Social Aspects of Language and Education in Brittany', Oxford, unpublished D. Phil thesis (forthcoming, 1989, London, Tavistock).

Macdonald, S., Holden, P. and Ardener, S. (eds) 1987 *Images of Women in Peace and War*, London, Macmillan.

Macintosh, D. 1819 *Collection of Gaelic Proverbs and Familiar Phrases*, Edinburgh, Stewart.

McLuhan, M. 1970 *Counterblast*, London, Rapp and Whiting.

Maguire, M. 1974 'Criminology and Social Anthropology', *Journal of the Anthropological Society of Oxford*, 5 (2), pp. 109–17.

Mair, L. 1972 'Recent Writings on Witchcraft', *Journal of the Anthropological Society of Oxford*, 3 (1), pp. 33–41.

270   References

Malinowski, B. 1926a 'Anthropology', *Encyclopaedia Britannica*, 13th edition s.v.
—— 1926b 'Anthropology', typescript of 1926a presented to E. E. Evans-Pritchard, Tylor Library, Oxford.
—— 1932 special foreword to *The Sexual Life of Savages*, 3rd edition, London, Routledge and Kegan Paul.
—— 1935 *Coral Gardens and their Magic*, vol. 2, 2nd edition 1966, with an introduction by Berry, J., London, Allen and Unwin.
—— 1944 *A Scientific Theory of Culture*, University of North Carolina Press.
Malmberg, B. 1964 *New Trends in Linguistics*, Stockholm, Lund.
Mandelbaum, D.G. (ed.) 1949 *Selected Writings of Edward Sapir*, Los Angeles, University of California Press.
—— 1956 *Edward Sapir: Culture, Language and Personality*, Los Angeles, University of California Press.
Maquet, J. J. 1964 'Objectivity in Anthropology, *Current Anthropology*, 5 (1), pp. 47–55.
Mathieu, N.-C. 1973 'Homme-Culture et Femme-Nature?', *L'Homme*, July–Sept., pp. 101–13.
Mauss, M. 1950 *Sociologie et Anthropologie*, 3rd edition, 1966, Paris, Presses Universitaires de France.
—— 1954 *The Gift*, translated by I. Cunnison, with an introduction by E. E. Evans-Pritchard (corrected edition, 1969), London, Cohen and West.
Maxwell, J. C. 1871 *The Theory of Heat*, 3rd edition, 1872, London.
Maybury-Lewis, D. 1965 'Prescriptive Marriage Systems', *Southwestern Journal of Anthropology*, 21, pp. 207–30.
—— 1967 *Akwe-Shavante Society*, Oxford, Clarendon Press.
Meek, C. K. 1931 *Tribal Studies in Northern Nigeria*, London, Kegan Paul, Trench, Trubner.
Meillet, A. 1933 'Sur le Bilinguisme', *Journal de Psychologie*, 30, pp. 167–71.
—— 1937 *Introduction à l'Etude comparative des Langues indo-européennes*, reprinted 1964, Alabama, Alabama University Press.
—— 1950 *Les Dialectes indo-européens*, Paris, Champion.
Meyer, R. 1910 'Bedeutungssysteme', *Kuhns Zeitschrift fur Vergleichende Sprachforschung*, 43, pp. 352–68.
Milner, G. B. 1954 Review of J. Perrot, *La Linguistique*, Man, 54, p. 172.
—— 1966 'Hypostatization', in Bazell et al. 1966, pp. 321–34.
—— 1969 'Siamese Twins, Birds and the Double Helix', *Man*, (n.s.) 4, pp. 5–23.
—— 1971 'The Quartered Shield: Outline of a Semantic Taxonomy', in Ardener, E. (ed.) 1971.
Missionary Herald, Baptist Missionary Society series, London.
Mitchell, J. C. 1966 'Theoretical Orientations in African Urban Studies', in *The Social Anthropology of Complex Societies* Banton, M. (ed.), London, Tavistock.
—— 1967 'On Quantification in Social Anthropology', in Epstein, A. (ed.) 1967.
Mohrmann, C., Norman, F. and Sommerfelt, A. 1963 *Trends in Modern Linguistics*, Utrecht/Antwerp, Spectrum.
Mohrmann, C., Sommerfelt, A. and Whatmough, J. (eds) 1963 *Trends in European and American Linguistics 1930–1960*, Utrecht/Antwerp, Spectrum.
Moore, O. K. and Olmsted, D. L. 1952 'Language and Professor Lévi-Strauss', *American Anthropologist*, 54 (1), pp. 116–19.
Morris, C. 1946 *Signs, Language and Behavior*, Englewood Cliffs, Prentice Hall.
Munro, J. (no date) *Gaelic Vocabulary and Phrase Book*, reissued Glasgow, Gairm.
Murdock, G. P. 1951 'British Social Anthropology', *American Anthropologist*, 53 (4), pp. 465–73.
—— 1957 *Africa: Its Peoples and Culture History*, New York, McGraw-Hill.
—— 1965a *Culture and Society*, Pittsburgh, University of Pittsburgh Press.
—— 1965b 'Cross-language Parallels in Parental Kin Terms', in Murdock, G. P. 1965a.
Nadel, S. F. 1957 *The Theory of Social Structure*, Cohen and West, London.
Needham, R. 1954 'The System of Teknonyms and Death-names of the Penan', *Southwestern Journal of Anthropology*, 10, pp. 416–31.

—— 1958 'A Structural Analysis of Purum Society', *American Anthropologist*, 60, pp. 75–101.

—— 1960a 'Descent Systems and Ideal Language', *Philosophy of Science*, 27, pp. 96–101.

—— 1960b 'The Left Hand of the Mugwe: an Analytical Note on the Structure of Meru Symbolism', *Africa*, 30, pp. 20–33.

—— 1962 *Structure and Sentiment*, Chicago, Chicago University Press.

—— 1963 Introduction to Durkheim and Mauss 1963, London, Routledge and Kegan Paul.

—— 1967 'Right and Left in Nyoro Symbolic Classification', *Africa*, 37 (4), pp. 425–52.

—— 1970 'The Future of Social Anthropology: Disintegration or Metamorphosis?', in *Anniversary Contributions to Anthropology: Twelve Essays*, Leiden, Brill.

—— (ed.) 1971 *Rethinking Kinship and Marriage* (ASA Monographs 11), London, Tavistock.

—— (ed.) 1973 *Right and Left: Essays on Dual Symbolic Classification*, Chicago, University of Chicago Press.

Nicholson, A. 1881 *A Collection of Gaelic Proverbs and Familiar Phrases, based on Mackintosh's Collection*, Edinburgh, Stewart.

Njeuma, M. 1987 'Pioneer in Cameroon Studies – E. W. Ardener', obituary notice, *West Africa*, 5 October, (3660), pp. 1963–5.

Nutini, H. G. 1965 'Some Considerations on the Nature of Social Structure and Model Building: a Critique of Claude Lévi-Strauss and Edmund Leach', *American Anthropologist*, 67, pp. 707–31; also in Hayes E. N. and T. (eds) 1970, pp. 70–107.

O'Connor, F. 1967 *The Backward Look, A Survey of Irish Literature*, London, Macmillan.

Ojo, G. 1966 *Yoruba Culture: a Geographical Analysis*, London, University of London Press.

O'Rahilly, T. 1972 *Irish Dialects Past and Present*, Dublin, Institute for Advanced Studies (1st edition 1932).

Ornstein, R. 1975 'Temporal Dimensions of Consciousness', *New Scientist*, 27 March, pp. 772–3.

Ortega y Gasset, J. 1921 *El Tema de Nuestra Tiempo*, Madrid.

—— 1961 *The Revolt of the Masses*, London, Allen and Unwin.

Ortner, S. B. 1973 'Is Female to Male as Nature is to Culture?', *Feminist Studies*, 1 (2); also in Rosaldo M. Z. and Lamphere, M. (eds) 1974.

Osthoff, H. and Brugmann, K. 1878 introduction to *Morphologische Untersuchungen auf dem Gebiete der Indogermanischen Sprachen*, 1, pp. iii–xx, Leipzig, Hirzel.

Overing, J. (ed.) 1985 *Reason and Morality* (ASA Monographs 24), London, Tavistock.

Ovesen, J. 1978 'Maurice Godelier and the Study of Ideology', *Journal of the Anthropological Society of Oxford*, 9 (1), pp. 1–12.

Paine, R. 1967 'What is Gossip About? An Alternative Hypothesis', in *Man*, (n.s.) 2, pp. 278–85.

—— 1968 'Gossip Transaction', *Man*, (n.s.) 3, pp. 305–8.

Palmer, F. R. (ed.) 1968 *Selected Papers of J. R. Firth 1952–1959*, London, Longman.

Palmer, L. R. 1954 *The Latin Language*, London, Faber and Faber.

Parkin, D. (ed.) 1982 *Semantic Anthropology* (ASA Monographs 22), London, Academic Press.

Parry, H. B. (ed.) 1974 *Population and its Problems*, Oxford, Clarendon Press.

Parry, T. 1939 'Y marwfis, y mis du', *Bulletin of the Board of Celtic Studies*, 9 (1), pp. 40–2.

Paul, H. 1880 *Prinzipien der Sprachgeschichte*, Tübingen, Niemeyer (8th edition, 1968).

Pedersen, H. 1931 *Linguistic Science in the Nineteenth Century*, translated by J. Spargo, Cambridge, Mass., Harvard University Press; reissued Bloomington, Indiana University Press, 1962.

Piaget, J. 1971 *Structuralism*, London, Routledge and Kegan Paul.

Pike, K. L. 1954, 1955, 1960 *Language in Relation to a Unified Theory of the Structure of Human Behaviour*, 3 vols, Glendale Summer Institute of Linguistics.

—— 1956 'Towards a Theory of the Structure of Human Behaviour', reprinted in Hymes, D. (ed.) 1964.

Pocock, D. F. 1961 *Social Anthropology*, London, Sheed and Ward.

—— 1973 'The Idea of a Personal Anthropology', ASA conference paper (unpublished).

—— 1974 'Nuer Religion: a Supplementary View', *Journal of the Anthropological Society of Oxford*, 5 (2), pp. 69–79.

Popper, K. R. 1957 *The Poverty of Historicism* (originally published 1944–5; paperback 1961), RKP, London.

Pride, J. B. 1971 'Customs and Cases of Verbal Behaviour', in Ardener, E. (ed.) 1971a.

Pym, B. 1955 *Less than Angels*, London, Macmillan.

Radcliffe-Brown, A. R. 1957 *A Natural Science of Society*, Glencoe, Free Press.

—— 1977 'Two Letters from Radcliffe-Brown to Evans-Pritchard', 8 (1), pp. 49–50.

Rees, A. and Rees, B. 1961 *Celtic Heritage*, London, Thames and Hudson.

Reyher, R. H. 1952 *The Fon and his Hundred Wives*, New York, Doubleday.

Reynolds, V. 1975 'Problems of Non-comparability of Behaviour Catalogues in Single Species of Primates', in S. Kondo et al. (eds) 1975, pp. 280–6.

Richards, A. I. 1956 *Chisungu: A Girls' Initiation Ceremony among the Bemba of Northern Rhodesia*, London, Faber and Faber.

Richards, E. 1982 *A History of the Highland Clearances – Agrarian Transformation and the Evictions 1746 – 1886*, London, Croom Helm.

Richards, M. 1950 'Y mis du', *Bulletin of the Board of Celtic Studies*, 13 (4), pp. 204–5.

Richardson, I. 1956–7 *Linguistic Survey of the NW Bantu Borderland*, 2 vols, London, International African Institute.

Rivers, W. H. R. 1911 address to the Portsmouth meeting of the British Association.

Robins, R. H. 1967 *A Short History of Linguistics*, London, Longman.

—— 1971 'Malinowski, Firth, and the "Context of Situation"', in Ardener, E. (ed.) 1971a.

Rosaldo, M. Z. and Lamphere, M. (eds) 1974 *Woman, Culture and Society*, Stanford, Stanford University Press.

Ross, A. 1958 *On Law and Justice*, London, Stevens.

Ross, A. S. C. 1958 *Etymology with Special Reference to English*, London, Deutsch.

Ruel, M. 1969 *Leopards and Leaders: Constitutional Politics among a Cross River People*, London, Tavistock.

Sapir, E. 1916 *Time Perspective in Aboriginal American Culture: a Study in Method*, Ottawa, Canada Geological Survey.

—— 1921 *Language: an Introduction to the Study of Speech*, New York, Harcourt.

Saporta, S. (ed.) 1961 *Psycholinguistics*, New York, Holt, Rinehart and Winston.

Saussure, F. de 1878 *Mémoire sur le Système Primitif des Voyelles dans les Langues Indo-Européennes*, Geneva, now translated in Lehmann (ed.) 1967.

—— 1916 (2nd edition 1922) *Cours de Linguistique Générale*, Paris/Geneva, Payot.

—— 1964 *Course in General Linguistics*, translated from Saussure 1916 by W. Baskin, New York, Philosophical Library, 1959; London, Peter Owen, 1960 (reprinted 1964).

Savitsky, N. and Tarachow, S. 1941 'Lilliputian Hallucinations during Convalescence of Scarlet Fever', *Journal of Nervous and Mental Disease*, 93, pp. 310–12.

Schwimmer, E. (ed.) 1978 *Yearbook of Symbolic Anthropology*, London, Hurst.

Sebeok, T. A., Hayes, A. S. and Bateson, M. C. 1964 *Approaches to Semiotics*, The Hague, Mouton.

Sechehaye, A. 1933 'La pensée et la langue ou: comment concevoir le rapport organique de l'individuel et du social dans le langage?', *Journal de Psychologie*, (numéro exceptionnel) 30 (1), pp. 57–81.

—— 1940 'Les trois linguistiques saussuriennes', *Vox Romanica* V, pp. 1–48, Zurich; reprinted in Gödel (ed.) 1969.

Seligman, C. G. 1910 *The Melanesians of British New Guinea*, Cambridge, Cambridge University Press.

Seligman, C. G. and Seligman, B. Z. 1911 *The Vedas*, Cambridge, Cambridge University Press.

Shannon, C. E. 1948 'A Mathematical Theory of Communication', *Bell System Technical Journal*, 27, pp. 379–423; also in Shannon and Weaver, 1949.

Shannon, C. E. and Weaver, W. 1949 *The Mathematical Theory of Communication*, Urbana, University of Illinois.

Shaw, G. B. 1916 *Pygmalion*, Harmondsworth, Penguin, 1941.

Simonis, Y. 1968 *Claude Lévi-Strauss, ou la 'Passion de l'Inceste'*, Paris, Montaigne.

Smith, A. G. (ed.) 1966 *Communication and Culture*, New York, Holt, Rinehart and Winston.

Southall, A. (ed.) 1961 *Social Change in Modern Africa*, Oxford, Oxford University Press.

Spencer, P. 1965 *The Samburu*, London, Routledge and Kegan Paul.

—— 1973 *Nomads in Alliance: Symbiosis and Growth among the Rendille and Samburu of Kenya*, Oxford, Oxford University Press.

Sperber, D. 1975 *Rethinking Symbolism*, Cambridge, Cambridge University Press.

Spier, L., Hallowell, A. and Newman, S. (eds) 1941 *Language, Culture and Personality: Essays in Memory of Edward Sapir*, Menasha Wis., Sapir Memorial Publications Fund.

Srinivas, M. N. 1977 'The Changing Position of Indian Women', *Man*, (n.s.) 12 (2), pp. 221–38.

Steiner, F. 1956 *Taboo*, London, Cohen and West (also 1967, Pelican).

Steiner, G. 1975 *After Babel: Aspects of Language and Translation*, Oxford, Oxford University Press.

Stone, B. G. 1929 'Notes on the Buea District' (manuscript), Victoria Divisional Office, Cameroon.

Sturtevant, E. 1942 *The Indo-Hittite Laryngeals*, Baltimore, Linguistic Society of America.

Sturtevant, W. 1964 'Studies in Ethnoscience', *American Anthropologist*, 66 (2), pp. 99–131.

Swadesh, M. 1950 'Salish Internal Relationships', *International Journal of American Linguistics*, 16, pp. 157–67.

Talbot, P. A. 1912 *In the Shadow of the Bush*, London, Heinemann.

—— 1926 *The Peoples of Southern Nigeria*, Oxford, Oxford University Press.

Tambiah, S. J. 1968 'The Magical Power of Words', *Man*, (n.s.) 3 (2), pp. 175–208.

Taylor, D. 1958 'On Anthropologists' Use of Linguistics', *American Anthropologist*, 60, p. 940.

Teitelbaum, M. S. 1972 'Factors Associated with the Sex Ratio in Human Populations', in Harrison, G. and Boyce, A. (eds) 1972.

Thomas, K. V. 1971 *Religion and the Decline of Magic*, London: Weidenfeld and Nicolson.

Thomas, N. W. 1910 *Anthropological Report on the Edo-speaking Peoples of Nigeria*, pt. 1, London, Harrison.

—— 1914 *Specimens of Languages from Southern Nigeria*, London, Harrison.

Thompson, D'Arcy, W. 1966 *On Growth and Form*, Cambridge, Cambridge University Press.

Thurneysen, R. 1899 'Der Kalender von Coligny', *Zeitschrift für Celtische Philologie*, 2, pp. 523–44.

Thurnwald, R. 1912 *Forschungen auf den Salomon-Insel und dem Bismarck-Archipel*, Berlin.

Tolkien, J. R. R. 1954 *The Return of the King, The Lord of the Rings*, vol. 3 London, Allen and Unwin (Danish edition, 1974, *Ringenes Herre*, Copenhagen, Gyldendals Bogklub).

Tonkin, J. E. A. 1971a 'The Use of Ethnography', *Journal of the Anthropological Society of Oxford*, 2 (3), pp. 134–6.

—— 1971b 'Some Coastal Pidgins of West Africa', in Ardener, E. (ed.) 1971a.

Trier, J. 1931 *Der Deutsche Wortschatz im Sinnbezirk des Verstandes*, Heidelberg, Carl Winter.

Trubetzkoy, N. 1933 'La Phonologie Actuelle', *Journal de Psychologie*, (numéro exceptionnel) 30 (1), pp. 227–46.

—— 1968 *Introduction to the Principles of Phonological Descriptions*, The Hague, Nijhoff.

Turlot, F., Durupt, M. J. and Holin, F. 1969 *La Population Du Cameroun Occidental*, Société d'Etudes pour le Développement Economique et Sociale, Paris.

Turnbull, C. M. 1972 'Demography of Small-scale Societies', in Harrison, G. and Boyce, A. (eds) 1972.

Turnbull, H. W. 1959 *The Correspondence of Isaac Newton*, vol. 1, Cambridge, Cambridge University Press.

Turner, V. W. 1964 'Symbols in Ndembu Ritual', in Gluckman, M. (ed.) 1964.

—— 1965 'Ritual Symbolism, Morality and Social Structure among the Ndembu', in Fortes, M. and Dieterlen, G. (eds) 1965.

—— 1966 'Colour Classification in Ndembu Ritual', in Banton, M. (ed.) 1966.

—— 1967 *The Forest of Symbols: Aspects of Ndembu Ritual*, Ithaca, Cornell University Press.

—— 1969 *The Ritual Process*, London, Routledge and Kegan Paul.

Ullman, S. 1951 *The Principles of Semantics*, Glasgow, Jackson.

—— 1959 *The Principles of Semantics*, 2nd edition, with additions, Oxford, Basil Blackwell.

—— 1963 'Semantic Universals', in Greenberg (ed.) 1963.

Van Gennep, A. 1909 *Les Rites de Passage*, Paris.

Vendler, Z. 1967 *Linguistics in Philosophy*, Ithaca, Cornell University Press.

Vendryes, J. 1921 'Le Caractère Social du Langage et la Doctrine de F. de Saussure', *Journal de Psychologie*, 18, pp. 617–24; also in Vendryes, 1952, pp. 18–25.

—— 1933 'Sur les Tâches de la Linguistique Statique', *Journal de Psychologie*, 30, pp. 172–84.

—— 1952 *Choix d'Etudes Linguistiques et Celtiques*, Paris, Klincksieck.

Ventris, M. and Chadwick, J. 1956 *Documents in Mycenaean Greek*, Cambridge, Cambridge University Press.

Voegelin, C. F. and Harris, Z. S. 1945 'Linguistics in Ethnology', *Southwestern Journal of Anthropology*, 1 (4), pp. 455–65.

Voegelin, C. F. and Harris, Z. S. 1947 'The Scope of Linguistics', *American Anthropologist*, 49 (4), pp. 588-600.

Waismann, F. 1968 *The Principles of Linguistic Philosophy* Harré, R. (ed.) London, Macmillan.

Wallerstein, E. 1960 'Ethnicity and National Integration in West Africa', *Cahiers d'Etudes Africaines*, 1 (3), pp. 129–39.

Wartburg, W. von 1943 *Einführung in Problematik und Methodik der Sprachwissenschaft*, Tübingen, Max Niemeyer.

—— 1969 *Problems and Methods in Linguistics* (translation of Wartburg, W. von 1943), Oxford, Basil Blackwell.

Weinreich, U., Labov, W. and Herzog, M.I. 1968 'Empirical Foundations for a Theory of Language Change', in Lehmann and Malkiel (eds) 1968.

Wells, J. 1906 *The Oxford Degree Ceremony*, Oxford, Clarendon Press.

Wells, R. S. 1947 'De Saussure's System of Linguistics', *Word*, 3 (1), pp. 1–31; reprinted in Joos (ed.) 1957.

Whiteley, W. 1966 'Social Anthropology, Meaning and Linguistics', *Man*, (n.s.) 1 (2), pp. 139–57.

—— 1971a *Language Use and Social Change*, Oxford, Oxford University Press.

—— 1971b 'A Note on Multilingualism', in Ardener, E. (ed.) 1971a.

Whorf, B. L. 1952 *Collected Papers on Metalinguistics*, Washington, Department of State, Foreign Service Institute.

—— 1964 (1956, 1st edition) *Language, Thought and Reality*, edited by J. Carroll, Cambridge, Mass., MIT Press.

Wiener, N. 1948 *Cybernetics* (2nd edition 1961), Cambridge, Mass., MIT Press.

Wilson, B. (ed.) 1970 *Rationality*, Oxford, Basil Blackwell.

Winch, P. 1958 *The Idea of a Social Science and its Relation to Philosophy*, London, Routledge and Kegan Paul.

Withycombe, E. G. 1969 *The Oxford Dictionary of English Christian Names*, Oxford, Clarendon Press.

Wittgenstein, L. 1963 *Philosophical Investigations*, Oxford, Basil Blackwell (first English edition, 1953).

Woolf, V. 1928 *A Room of One's Own*, London, Hogarth.

Worsley, P. 1966 'The End of Anthropology?', paper for 6th World Congress of Sociology (mimeographed).

Wright, E. M. 1913 *Rustic Speech and Folklore*, Oxford, Oxford University Press.

Y Cymro 1970 March 25.

Yeats, W. B. 1950 *The Collected Poems of W. B. Yeats* (2nd edition), London, Macmillan.

Index

Apology: the following index must be regarded primarily as a citation and author index. As a subject index, it is subsiduary to the titles of the papers themselves, which provide broad-ranging cross-reference that has not been replicated below: for example, 'social anthropology' and 'population' have not been cross-referenced in relation to chapter 7, nor 'social anthropology' and 'language' in relation to chapter 1. The entire volume might be regarded as a multi-dimensional cross-reference between social anthropology and linguistics, society and language, and persistent cross-reference of this kind must therefore be assumed. To attempt to capture this indexically would only be to recreate, in a less-accessible form, the volume itself. Many words used by Ardener are both ubiquitous and central to his work, and at the same time transformed by his treatment, which makes them unsuitable index headings – symbol, belief, and structure (for example). Furthermore, many aspects of Ardener's thought are realized in dualities and oppositions (which are often simultaneously dissolved), in a conceptual space of many dimensions; again, an index can only aspire to provide hints of this. Lastly, Ardener was always anxious to keep his conceptual structures moving, and was quick to abandon a phrase or idea that seemed to risk becoming merely formulaic or conventional. The continuity and development of his own work is, therefore, not necessarily terminologically expressed within itself. His work demands to be read and pondered, not consulted.